THE THEATRE OF SEÁN O'CASEY

James Moran is Associate Professor in the School of English Studies at the University of Nottingham, UK. His research is primarily concerned with modern Anglophone literature, with a particular interest in the theatre of twentieth-century Ireland. He is the author of *Staging the Easter Rising* (2005) and *Irish Birmingham: A History* (2010).

THE THEATRE OF SEÁN O'CASEY

James Moran

Series Editors: Patrick Lonergan and Erin Hurley

Bloomsbury Methuen Drama

Bloomsbury Methuen Drama
An imprint of Bloomsbury Publishing Plc

50 Bedford Square	1385 Broadway
London	New York
WC1B 3DP	NY 10018
UK	USA

www.bloomsbury.com

Bloomsbury is a registered trade mark of Bloomsbury Publishing Plc

First published 2013

© James Moran, 2013

British Library Cataloguing-in-Publication Data
A catalogue record for this book is available from the British Library.

HB:	978-1-4081-7534-7
PB:	978-1-4081-7535-4
ePDF:	978-1-4081-6595-9
ePub:	978-1-4081-6596-6

Typeset by Newgen Imaging Systems Pvt Ltd, Chennai, India
Printed and bound in India

Costello   Name the greatest Irishman.

Ruairi   Er . . . Michael Collins? No? William Butler Yeats. No. Johnny Giles? Er . . . fuck. What was the name of that other fucking play writer fellah?[1]

---

[1] Richard Bean, *The Big Fellah*. London, Oberon, 2010, p. 47.

CONTENTS

Contents

PART 2 NEW PERSPECTIVES

ACKNOWLEDGEMENTS

The research for this book would have been impossible without the generous advice and assistance of a number of friends and colleagues. I am particularly grateful to Neal Alexander, Thomas Conway, Jan Culik, Mairéad Delaney, Janette Dillon, Stephan Dörschel, Mark Dudgeon, Margaret Eaton, Clare Finburgh, Isaac Gewirtz, Garry Hynes, Jiří Krejčík, Patrick Lonergan, Rory Lorton, Cynthia Marsh, Tony Meech, Victor Merriman, Angela Moran, Paul Murphy, Julia Nemirovskaya, the late Breon O'Casey, Shivaun O'Casey and Wolfgang Trautwein. I would also like to thank my own students at Nottingham for remaining indulgent as I have tested the various ideas in this book, and the expert staff at the Archiv der Akademie der Künste, British Film Institute, British Library, Cambridge University Library, English National Opera Archive, Irish Film Institute, National Library of Ireland, New York Public Library and Princeton University Library. My thanks go to Dot Emm for launching me upon this whole enterprise; to Alana and Michael Moran for consistent support; and to Robert, Janice and Catherine Lough, without whose warm hospitality I would have been down and out in London and Dublin. Most of all, I owe thanks to Tom and Joe for being such daarlin' boys; to their grandparents for unpaid babysitting; and to Maria for keeping the whole show on the road.

The following institutions and individuals have kindly given permission to quote from unpublished or copyright materials: the British Library Board; MacNaughton Lord Representation acting on behalf of the Estate of Seán O'Casey; Faber and Faber Ltd; Princeton University Library; the National Library of Ireland; the Henry W. and Albert A. Berg Collection of English and American Literature, the New York Public Library Astor, Lenox and Tilden Foundations; the *Irish Independent*; the *Irish Times*; the *Guardian*; Merryn Williams;

the Society of Authors on behalf of the Bernard Shaw Estate; and Blake Friedmann Literary, TV and Film Agency for the permission to reproduce a section of GHOST LIGHT by Joseph O'Connor. First published in Great Britain by Harvill Secker. Copyright © 2010 Joseph O'Connor.

ABBREVIATIONS

ABC   American Broadcasting Company
ANC   African National Congress
BBC   British Broadcasting Corporation
GDR   German Democratic Republic
GPO   General Post Office, Dublin
IRA   Irish Republican Army
IRB   Irish Republican Brotherhood
NBC   National Broadcasting Company
NLI   National Library of Ireland
NYPL   New York Public Library
RAF   Royal Air Force
RTÉ   Raidió Teilifís Éireann

PRERUMBLE

Seán O'Casey is one of Ireland's best-known playwrights. At the country's national theatre, his works have been performed more than those of any other writer. His three most famous plays, *The Shadow of a Gunman*, *Juno and the Paycock* and *The Plough and the Stars*, remain in print almost 100 years after he wrote them, and are the subject of study in school and university classrooms across the English-speaking world. Elsewhere, his writings are frequently revived in countries including the Czech Republic and Germany, where adaptations of his one-act farces have continued to hold the stage well into the twenty-first century.

Yet O'Casey's legacy is a mixed one. During his lifetime, his work caused riots and became a target for censors. After his early successes, O'Casey abandoned his homeland for England, from where he attacked Irish habits and attitudes, quarrelled with influential critics and supporters, and embarked upon a series of experimental plays that have never found a regular place in the theatrical repertoire. Although his Dublin dramas are frequently revived, his later works are rarely seen on the Anglophone stage, and since the mid-1990s his London publisher has kept in print less than half the scripts once included in the writer's 'complete plays'.[1]

Accordingly, O'Casey tends to have a polarizing effect on his audiences and readers. George Orwell, for example, believed that O'Casey expressed an upsetting contempt for England, and so accused the playwright of peddling 'the worst extremes of jingoism and racialism'.[2] By contrast, Eugene O'Neill commented 'I wish to God I could write like that!', and Marilyn Monroe declared her personal desire to meet 'Shawn'.[3] Even O'Casey's admirers tend to have contradictory feelings about his oeuvre, with Seamus Heaney, for instance, distinguishing between the 'surefooted language' of the playwright's early 'masterpieces' and 'the shakier conventions of his later, more experimental work'.[4]

Throughout O'Casey's works, we find an evident compassion for the poor, a determination to bring injustice to public attention, and an irritation with the forces of repression and inequality. In his greatest plays, O'Casey is able to combine such ideas with sharp comedy, engaging plotting and verbal pyrotechnics. However, in his weaker moments, O'Casey is also guilty of overly sentimental, repetitive and polemical writing. He is, as his character Mr Gallogher puts it in *Juno and the Paycock*, 'a parrotox', and perhaps we might remember the comic ambiguity of that line, which inspires O'Casey's characters to think of how 'a parrot talks'.[5] Ultimately, this image may be a good way of understanding O'Casey: a writer who, like the avian narrator of John Skelton's famous poem 'Speke, Parrot', aims to puncture the hypocrisies of the time through a voice that combines Biblical allusion, popular songs and a rhythmical language, in a way that is often maddening but which frequently proves witty and profound.

In the first part of this book, I therefore outline O'Casey's biography as well as the storylines and historical-literary contexts of the full-length plays that O'Casey wrote from across his entire life, in the belief that these scripts are serious attempts at dramatic writing, and that examining only the most popular pieces would give an incomplete idea of the writer's overall career and legacy. I also include a discussion of O'Casey's prose autobiographies, largely because, as we shall see, these have enjoyed their own success in adapted form on stage and screen, and have informed many audiences for the plays, so deserve a place in a book claiming to speak about O'Casey's theatre. Finally, I analyse the way that O'Casey's reputation has shifted and changed since the premiere of his first work, pointing to some of the differing critical approaches and assumptions that have produced widely varying evaluations of the writer.

In the second part of the book, three leading experts on Irish theatre, Garry Hynes, Victor Merriman and Paul Murphy, offer a set of new perspectives on key aspects of the playwright's work. These figures consider in turn how O'Casey's dramas relate to the requirements of the modern director, to postcolonialism and to social class; and all three experts point to the meaning and significance that O'Casey might continue to have for readers and spectators in our current age. Ultimately, O'Casey is revealed to have created a body of work that consistently innovates and seeks to comment upon the political conditions of the era in which the author was writing, and, while some of these efforts may not be as fully achieved as others, the playwright's voice continues to resonate in an assortment of later twentieth- and twenty-first-century contexts.

PART 1

O'CASEY'S LIFE, WORK AND LEGACY

CHAPTER 1
BIOGRAPHY, 1880–1964

Early Life

In 1996, the Irish–American writer Frank McCourt published the novel-cum-memoir *Angela's Ashes* about a harrowing childhood in Ireland during the 1930s. The book became an international bestseller, shifting more than four-million copies in hardback during the author's lifetime.[1] McCourt later declared:

> There is no happily ever after in Sean O'Casey [. . .] He's the first Irish writer I ever read who writes about rags, dirt, hunger, babies dying. The other writers go on about farms and fairies and the mist that do be on the bog and it's a relief to discover one with bad eyes and a suffering mother.[2]

This description specifies a thematic debt to O'Casey, whose autobiographies detail urban childhood poverty, the death of siblings and a mother who largely raises her family single-handedly, as well as the playwright's struggles with a chronic eye-disease caused by poverty. McCourt would rework and revitalize each of these ideas, inspire many imitators and so, inadvertently, make O'Casey into the granddaddy of the 'mis-lit' paperback that, by the turn of the millennium, could be found clogging supermarket shelves and bestseller lists alike.

Earlier in the 1990s, the Dublin writer Roddy Doyle enjoyed a similar literary payday when he became the fastest-selling winner of the Booker prize with the novel *Paddy Clarke Ha Ha Ha*, a *tour de force* that also describes the privations of Irish childhood. Again, Doyle pointed out that O'Casey had provided a source of inspiration for a modern writer wishing to speak of Dublin's working class, with *Paddy Clarke* affecting the distinctive stylistic ticks of the playwright's earlier autobiographies.[3] In this way, O'Casey set the template for those Celtic-Tiger penmen whose descriptions of childhood impoverishment and trauma proved so lucrative in the dawning age of Amazon.com.

Indeed, O'Casey's youth in the slums remains one of the most widely recounted things about him. For example, in 2005 the state broadcasters in Ireland and the United Kingdom televised a documentary made by Seán O'Casey's daughter, Shivaun. The film is skilfully constructed, contains some fascinating archive footage and received nominations for a number of awards.[4] The narration follows the assertions made in Seán O'Casey's autobiographical writings, describing, for example, how he was the last of 13 children, of whom 8 died in infancy. Footage of the elderly playwright shows him reminiscing that at the age of 12 or 13 he 'didn't really know how to read or write', and viewers learn that he had to leave his homeland in 1926 because of being 'literally persecuted in Ireland'.

Such ideas remain among the best known about O'Casey, but have all been widely contested by biographers who hold that such statements bear little resemblance to the factual details of the playwright's life. Indeed, Shivaun O'Casey's documentary is careful to emphasize that the film presents only a 'story about Seán told mainly through his own words'. After all, the writer first known as John Casey carefully shaped the character of 'Seán O'Casey', with that familiar hibernicized forename and amphibrachic surname, through many thousands of words of autobiography, letters, newspaper articles and plays.

In reality, John Casey, the future Seán O'Casey, had been born into a Protestant family in the predominantly Catholic area of Dublin's Northside on 30 March 1880. This setting proved far from salubrious, but the family's location undoubtedly involved an element of choice. O'Casey's father worked as a clerk for the Irish Church Missions, an evangelical society that aimed to convert Catholics. Strategically, then, the family had opted to live in close proximity to a very large group of unsaved souls living in stark material deprivation.[5]

The mature writer retained strong memories of being raised in the midst of such poverty, and his autobiographies state:

It had often been recorded by the Press, by those who could guess shrewdly, that Sean was a slum dramatist, a gutter-snipe who could jingle a few words together out of what he had seen and heard. The terms were suitable and accurate, for he was both, and, all his life, he would hold the wisdom and courage that these conditions had given him.[6]

However, O'Casey's biographer Christopher Murray has pointed out that, despite the impoverishment of Dublin, the family itself belonged securely to the lower middle class. O'Casey's father earned a yearly wage of 70 pounds, an income just below that of a skilled tradesman, and O'Casey probably had seven older siblings, of whom two died in infancy. Moreover, O'Casey's birthplace at 85 Upper Dorset Street, an address that he deliberately obfuscates in his autobiographies, could scarcely be considered a slum. His father probably acted as the landlord of this three-storey Georgian house in a busy commercial area.[7] Martin Margulies emphasizes that the young O'Casey possessed a reasonably good school record, passing exams in reading and writing and even receiving an illuminated scroll at the age of seven for demonstrating 'proficiency in Holy Scripture and Church Formularies'.[8] Nevertheless, the notion that O'Casey had been born into the most extreme poverty has proved an enduring simplification. On his death, the *Irish Times* commemorated the 'Slum Child Who Became [a] World Famed Dramatist'.[9]

Such ideas about O'Casey's childhood lasted throughout the twentieth century, at least in part because O'Casey achieved fame at a time when the reading public had been primed to think about the appalling living conditions that existed in the Irish capital. In 1913, the Dublin Housing Inquiry interviewed 76 witnesses for 17 days and uncovered evidence of a truly horrifying situation.[10] Indeed, the results of this investigation proved so disturbing that they appeared in lurid detail across the Irish and international press during the spring of 1914, including publications such as the *Glasgow Herald* and *The Times* of London. The *New York Times* described 28,000 Dubliners living in houses that were scarcely suited for human beings, in a situation that looked like Dante's 'Inferno'.[11] The widespread reporting of this Gehenna helped pave the way for O'Casey's international career as a dramatist, and presented him with an opportunity to speak for this constituency. Indeed, in his first professionally produced script, which he wrote eight years after the press furore, O'Casey included the figure of one of Dublin's slum landlords, who complains to a tenant about 'your writin' letters to the papers about me an' my house' (I, 102). After all, the poverty of Dublin's tenements now had a kind of brand recognition across Britain and the United States, and O'Casey's audiences understandably inferred that he had emerged from the kind of Stygian misery that the newspapers had trumpeted so widely in the preceding years.

O'Casey's only direct experience of living in a tenement was a short time in 1920–1, when he shared a room with his friend Michael Mullen at 35 Mountjoy Square, a formative period in creating the dramatist's first successful play, *The Shadow of a Gunman*.[12] Indeed, one surviving extract of early handwriting by O'Casey is a scrawled six-word moment of inspiration in one of his notebooks: 'Michael Mullen as a character in a play'.[13] Yet, although O'Casey may have enjoyed a more comfortable upbringing than many Dubliners, his youth looks far from sybaritic by modern Western standards. For a start, O'Casey could not avoid the maladies endemic to a poverty-stricken city. One of the reasons why there may be dispute about details such as the number of his siblings is that he conveyed the information he had been told by his own mother, herself traumatized by trying to raise a family in the midst of widespread croup, stillbirth and disease. Indeed, when O'Casey was nine years old, one of the most original poets of the age, the then unknown Englishman Gerard Manley Hopkins, had died nearby from typhoid. O'Casey himself suffered terribly with trachoma, an infectious eye-disease, which in turn affected his school attendance, and perhaps encouraged him to convey a distrust of formal schooling in his later writing. We might remember that, in *Juno and the Paycock*, the affected character who ruins and abandons the family, Charles Bentham, works as a teacher.

For another thing, O'Casey's family was soon deprived of the relative prosperity enjoyed during Seán's early years, and the would-be writer, just like the young James Joyce and G. B. Shaw, faced the helter-skelter of downward mobility. When O'Casey reached the age of six his father died, so the family lost its main source of income and had to survive in the working-class East Wall district for a decade.[14] Little wonder that the playwright's later work famously focuses on how domestic life in Dublin might be terminally interrupted and insecure.

During his youth, O'Casey saw the lice and ringworm of the poor all about him, he lived in a family with parlous and declining finances and must have worried about the prospect of how bad things might get. Thus, as Nicholas Grene has argued, O'Casey cannot simply be labelled an excursionist in the tenements any more than the dramatist can straightforwardly be called a slum child.[15] Nevertheless, the fact that O'Casey started from a lower-middle-class background, together with his religious affiliation, should have prevented him from ending up as a manual labourer. His older sister Bella had trained as a schoolteacher, and helped him to read despite his bloodshot and congealed eyes. Meanwhile another sibling, Isaac, became entranced by the stage, and the brothers watched melodrama at the Queen's Theatre in Dublin, as well as acting out Shakespeare and Boucicault plays together at home, thus fostering the writer's long-term enthusiasm for drama.[16] During O'Casey's lifetime, many people mistakenly believed that he had little or no experience of the playhouse until he emerged, fully formed, from the tenements in adulthood. The co-director and co-founder of the Abbey Theatre, Lady Gregory, helped to launch his career by announcing that 'In the first years of his life, owing to bad eyesight, he was not able to learn to read, but when he was sixteen years of age he taught himself. His studies gradually progressed, and, after studying other volumes, he read Shakespeare, from which time his dramatic education began'.[17] In reality, however, O'Casey had begun to learn about theatre during his childhood, and towards the end of his career, he himself reacted strongly against the notion of a 'natural' playwright who could simply produce groundbreaking scripts without training. In 1953 he wrote in the *New York Times*, describing the years of arduous work needed in order to become an artist.[18]

Nevertheless, O'Casey first began to earn his living in a realm that was scarcely one of creativity and artistic endeavour, taking a job at the age of fourteen with a firm selling hardware and china. At interview, his boss asked only one question: 'You are a Protestant, young man, are you not?'[19] O'Casey could happily answer in the affirmative, but despite being eased into this world of white-collar work, O'Casey repeatedly found himself at odds with his supervisors and unable to hold down a job. He later reflected on being temperamentally unsuited to the realm of regular employment, 'He had come to hate the shop and hate the men who owned it. Why, he couldn't say rightly' (*Auto* I, 248). After being sacked by his first employer, he lasted for a week as a vanboy at Eason's booksellers, and then worked from 1903–11 for the Great Northern Railway, handling a spade, carrying a hod and erecting scaffolding. Eventually O'Casey quarrelled with his superintendents, and thereafter toiled as a casual labourer instead.[20]

Nationalism

O'Casey's life so far had seen him move from being the lower-middle-class son of a Protestant missionary, to a member of Dublin's labouring class, which was predominantly Catholic, and O'Casey embraced some of the political viewpoints associated with his new situation. As a young man he joined Gaelic League, for whose handwritten journal he wrote his first stories.[21] He also Gaelicized his name to Seán Ó Cathasaigh, learnt how to speak Irish, took up hurling and became a founder member of St Laurence O'Toole's pipe band, alongside the prominent Fenian and future leader of the Easter Rising, Tom Clarke. Indeed, despite O'Casey's later fulminations against Catholicism, Ernest Blythe (who would act as government minister and director of the Abbey) recalled that the 20-something O'Casey 'told me one time that he said the rosary every night. From all that he said on religious questions, I thought it wouldn't be long before he turned Catholic'.[22] In 1926 O'Casey was told he would 'die a Catholic' by one acquaintance, to which O'Casey replied, perhaps only partly in jest, 'I'm half living a Catholic already'.[23] The playwright later toyed with the idea of writing a script about a character 'turning Protestant; turning Catholic; turning Protestant', and continued to read the Catholic *Universe* newspaper and the Lenten pastoral letters of the Roman bishops for many years, if only for amusement.[24] In the end, however, O'Casey gave up the observance of any kind of Christian faith during his twenties, and, although he remained deeply concerned with religious ideas, he looked elsewhere for a personal sense of fulfilment and purpose.

In about 1905 O'Casey joined the IRB, a secret, oath-bound group dedicated to the revolutionary overthrow of British rule in Ireland.[25] Patrick Pearse, a fellow member of the Brotherhood, would spearhead the armed uprising against Britain in 1916, but before the rebellion he spent his time running a progressive Dublin school where teachers conducted their lessons in the Irish language. Pearse clearly shared some of O'Casey's interests during this period. For example, O'Casey's first published work was a 1907 article about education policy, pointing out that children are 'de-Irished and stupefied by a system which a paternal Government calls education', with schools teaching pupils 'to admire and revere the things of Europe, Asia, Africa, America, Australia, and especially England; while their own country is to them bare of all useful and inspiring memories – her history unknown, her language unspoken, her music unheard, her achievements despised, and her character unloved'.[26] This argument found its echo in Pearse's later pedagogical writings, where the teacher and future insurrectionist explains:

> It is because the English education system in Ireland has deliberately eliminated the national factor that it has so terrifically succeeded [. . .] Three-quarters of a century ago there still remained in Ireland a stubborn Irish thing [. . .] a national language. After three-quarters of a century's education that thing is nearly lost. A new education system in Ireland has to do more than restore a national culture. It has to restore manhood to a race that has been deprived of it. Along with its inspiration it must, therefore, bring a certain hardening. It must lead Ireland back to her sagas.[27]

Such convictions impressed O'Casey, who supported the school that Patrick Pearse established. When Pearse staged an Irish pageant in 1913, O'Casey advertised it in the *Irish Worker*, albeit in an odd, and maybe teasing, way that connected the celibate teacher to masturbation: 'Workers for Ireland, let us help now to fertilize the seed sown by

Padraig Mac Piarais [. . .] Slaves, and worse than slaves, are we if it should be that this man's hope and this man's effort are as water spilled upon the ground'.[28]

Indeed, for many years, Pearse's educational doctrines did fertilize O'Casey's own thinking. When the playwright lived in England he would move to Devon specifically so that his offspring could attend a private school where, in a strikingly un-English way, the children's own interests and ideas determined parts of the administration and curriculum. Despite that institute's progressive approach, O'Casey clashed with the head-teacher there, and pointed the schoolmaster back to 'this great man, Pearse' as an example of a model educationalist.[29]

However, despite this fondness for Pearse and the IRB, during the pre-eminent moments of the country's struggle for independence O'Casey displayed a disregard for nationalism, and an increasing commitment to the socialist cause. In 1911, a year of Labour discontent, the Great Northern Railway identified O'Casey as a potential rabble-rouser, and so sacked him, leaving him with an abiding attraction to left-wing politics, particularly through his friendship with Ireland's best-known Labour leader, Jim Larkin. As D. H. Lawrence put it, 'Bolshevists somehow seem to be born on the railway'.[30] In 1913 Larkin led a strike to support two sacked tram-workers, and the action spread across Dublin as employers sought to break the influence of Larkin's union. During this period, O'Casey played a prominent part in providing humanitarian assistance, acting as secretary to the Women and Children's Relief Fund, and providing food for the hungry. On 31 August 1913 he witnessed the brutality of 'Bloody Sunday', when Larkin's supporters clashed with police in Dublin, leaving hundreds injured, and afterwards O'Casey played a significant role in establishing the Irish Citizen Army, a militia that would supposedly fight on behalf of the workers in any future conflict. O'Casey drafted the army's constitution of March 1914, opening with the declaration, 'That the first and last principle of the Irish Citizen Army is the avowal that the ownership of Ireland, moral and material, is vested of right in the people of Ireland'.[31] Two years later these words would be appropriated by Patrick Pearse, who, during the Easter Rising, famously read the proclamation of the Irish Republic, stating, 'We declare the right of the people of Ireland to the ownership of Ireland, and to the unfettered control of Irish destinies, to be sovereign and indefeasible'. As O'Casey himself later ruminated, 'it was our fight in 1913 that lit the first fire that predicated [*sic*] Easter Week'.[32]

However, in the build-up to 1916, he grew increasingly cool towards nationalism, and in particular towards Pearse, who, to O'Casey's dismay, chose to ride the trams during the lockout, something that the playwright saw as a betrayal of the striking transport workers. In 1914, O'Casey wrote:

> Pearse is worse than all. When the workers were waging a life and death struggle to preserve some of the 'liberties' which ought to be common to all Irishmen, this leader of democratic opinion consistently used the trams on every possible occasion, though the controller of the Dublin tramway system was the man who declared the workers could submit or starve.[33]

O'Casey also resigned from the Irish Citizen Army after, in 1914, he questioned the role occupied within the organization by the aristocratic Countess Markievicz. In 1916, then, when the Countess and the Irish Citizen Army joined with Patrick Pearse's Irish Volunteers to fight for Ireland's independence, an isolated O'Casey remained at home, nursing his grievances as well as his sick mother.

O'Casey had known many of the rebels, had helped to establish one of the main groups that fought in the uprising, and had, indirectly, helped to draft the proclamation of independence. Retrospectively, various commentators have reimagined O'Casey as being at the heart of the battle. His close involvement is implied in the US film *Young Cassidy*, as well as by his German publisher (whose website declares 'At the Easter Rising in 1916 he was arrested and narrowly escaped execution'), and by the Korean playwright Yu Chi-jin, who describes O'Casey's capture by the British and imprisonment in a flour mill.[34] But in reality, O'Casey refused to join in the revolutionary battle of 1916, believing it wrongheaded to confront Britain when the capitalist employer-class provided the real enemy. He later published his own history of the Irish Citizen Army, as well as writing the play *The Plough and the Stars* to lampoon Patrick Pearse's insurrection, and in both works an undoubted element of survivor guilt can be discerned.[35] He later described his awkwardness in post-revolutionary Ireland: 'If one said anything about economics, art, religion, etc., one was asked, "Were you out in Easter Week?" And if you hadnt carried a gun then, you were silenced at once'.[36]

Dublin Playwright

Dublin's famous Abbey Theatre had been founded by the poet W. B. Yeats when O'Casey was just 24. But, for a number of years, O'Casey avoided this venue. He later claimed that the cost of tickets had been prohibitive, although perhaps his political sympathies also drew him away from here: Gaelic Leaguers tended to be suspicious of an establishment run by members of the Protestant Ascendancy.[37] Instead O'Casey became involved in theatricals at Liberty Hall, the venue that provided Jim Larkin's headquarters and the training ground for the Irish Citizen Army. Nevertheless, the Easter Rising caused O'Casey to reappraise his previous affiliations, with one of his notebooks containing a short poem:

> Will I keep my old Cumán [hurley stick]
> and Club Jersey, or will I hand
> over the Cumán to one who may
> need it, & wear the jersey to work
> till it is ragged and useless?
> Old comrades go your
> lonely way
> I've other work to do,
> new things to say.[38]

After Easter Week, 1916, the 36-year-old abandoned his puck-about with nationalists, and mumming with the socialists, and began to write his own plays. At first, following the insurrection, he developed his singing and storytelling skills at the drama group that developed within the St Laurence O'Toole Club, even taking the main part in the club's production of Thomas Moylan's *Naboclish* in 1917. His enthusiasm for such activity was undoubtedly fired by his love for Máire Keating, a schoolteacher who helped with the productions, and with whom O'Casey enjoyed a relationship between 1917 and 1920.[39] But O'Casey grew distanced from this group when, in 1918, its members refused to produce a text he had written called *The Frost in the Flower*, satirizing one of the founders of the club, Frank Cahill.[40] Instead, O'Casey increasingly focused on the Abbey Theatre, to which he initially submitted his play *Profit and Loss* in 1916, although the script returned within only four days, presumably giving some indication of quality.[41] Undaunted, he sent a further four efforts to the theatre: *The Harvest Festival*, *The Frost in the Flower*, *The Seamless Coat of Kathleen* and *The Crimson in the Tricolour*. The Abbey rejected each one, and today only *The Harvest Festival* survives.[42] Nevertheless, O'Casey proved tenacious, and the payment of 15 pounds, or roughly ten weeks' wages, for his prose history *The Story of the Irish Citizen Army* convinced him of his writerly vocation.[43] Finally the Abbey accepted his sixth attempt, originally entitled *On the Run,* and in April 1923 the theatre unveiled O'Casey's effort under a new title: *The Shadow of a Gunman.*

The theatre programmed its first O'Casey play for three evening performances and a matinee, the standard run for a new work.[44] But *The Shadow of a Gunman* exceeded management expectations by immediately enjoying great commercial and critical success. Of course, by the time of his breakthrough the playwright had reached the age of 43, and thus looked rather mature when compared to the other writers repeatedly quoted in his play. O'Casey was now only nine years younger than Shakespeare was at death, and had already lived for almost a decade and a half more than Shelley. Nevertheless, as if to make up for lost time, during the next three years O'Casey wrote and staged two even more accomplished plays in the same style as *The Shadow of a Gunman. Juno and the Paycock* appeared on the Abbey stage in 1924 and *The Plough and the Stars* in 1926, with both works quickly becoming, in the words of Adrian Frazier, 'not just popular, but recognized to be great in the sense that Shakespeare's plays are great: literary, human, profound, tragi-comic and pleasurable'.[45]

The first three plays tend to be grouped together and labelled the 'Dublin trilogy', although the collective term is somewhat misleading. These works do not share characters or plots, and are non-sequential. What the three scripts do have in common, however, is a setting and theme. The dramas all take place in Dublin's tenements during the recent Irish revolution, 1916–23, and express sympathy for the urban poor, antipathy towards British rule, as well as a strong dislike for the violence that Irish patriotism might inspire. Such was the success of these shows that by the time the Abbey premiered the third part of the trilogy, would-be audience members queued around the block, with spectators roaring in approval and leading a standing ovation for the author.[46]

Today, however, what people tend to remember about that third Dublin play is that it triggered a riot, conducted by a group of republican women on the fourth night of the initial run. This play, *The Plough and the Stars*, is set during the Easter Rising of 1916 and allowed O'Casey to express his exasperation with the rebellion and its participants. He particularly singled out Patrick Pearse for mockery, and, for many, O'Casey's play felt like a grotesque distortion of historical events, slandering those men who had given their lives so that Ireland might be free.[47]

Nevertheless, O'Casey's first three Dublin dramas would enjoy a long life on the Irish stage, and today their reputation contrasts significantly with that of the later plays. There are a number of reasons for this, and Chapter 6 will explore some of the complexities of O'Casey's reception. But one of the simplest explanations revolves around the basic plotting of the dramas. As dramatists from Brecht to Beckett have identified, theatre audiences primarily tend to seek entertainment, and O'Casey never forgot, in the early Dublin plays, to divert his spectators by using devices that would create and maintain feelings of suspense. *Juno and the Paycock*, for instance, often leaves onlookers in fits of giggles for much of the first half, but only a very strange audience, or a very odd production, will generate belly-laughs at the final curtain. The characters are full of contradictory instincts, and the urge to discover the fate of those onstage propels the plot forward, particularly for first-time viewers. Unexpected arrivals and pronouncements cause a sea-change in the course of events, leaving spectators to ask: Will Seumas Shields and Donal Davoren escape the British? Can Nora Clitheroe retain Jack? Will Charles Bentham reappear?

Furthermore, as we shall see in Chapter 2, O'Casey managed to combine a surprising, and counter-intuitive, range of influences when writing his early plays, making the dramas feel fresh and insightful, and distinguishing his work from the earlier style of the Abbey Theatre. Of course, after O'Casey had written this trilogy, he continued to read voraciously and to draw upon other, equally diverse, sets of influences, leaving some O'Casey enthusiasts to feel bewildered about why the later works have failed, in the Anglophone theatre world at least, to generate the critical and commercial excitement of the early pieces.[48] Perhaps some hint about the difference in reputation is provided by the dramatist David Mamet, who defines two contrasting types of theatrical writing. For Mamet, one sort of drama presents the enjoyment of the 'hunt', where audiences enjoy a carefully constructed set of revelations, equivalent to a storyteller declaring 'And you'll never guess what happened next . . .' By contrast, other scripts present an idea, upon which an audience can ruminate, and thus allow a writer to set down the equivalent of a lecture or a sermon.[49]

In the three Dublin plays, O'Casey comes closest to Mamet's 'hunt'. The characters negotiate an environment that is informed by the writer's own ambiguous political and personal affiliations, and O'Casey refuses to present a demonstrably good option for the characters. To take up arms in the cause of Irish nationalism is only to follow a path to murderous destruction. But acquiescing to the Brits shows toleration of brutality and bloodshed. How about taking the ostrich option and staying at home? Again no, the tenement life described is scarcely one of domestic contentment. Here exists poverty, family disintegration and the threat of murder arriving from the street outside. This is the terrain that the characters of the Dublin trilogy must navigate, as they search for the least-worst path through life.

By contrast, O'Casey's later scripts tilt more towards what Mamet calls the 'lecture' rather than the 'hunt', often encouraging audiences to reflect upon issues of social justice but perhaps not necessarily to feel the same investment in particular situations or dilemmas. As the fourth and fifth chapters of this book will show, O'Casey wrote a series of pro-communist dramas that scarcely allow space for an audience to endorse fascism, and then a number of anti-Vatican plays in which no sane spectator could sympathize with the priestly opponents of youth and vitality.

However, O'Casey's later plays are scarcely monolithic, and the present volume discusses the major works from his long writing career in order to show the considerable variety and range of his writing. Analysis of O'Casey's work beyond the Dublin trilogy reveals a playwright with a brave commitment to formal innovation, and a laudable determination to avoid replicating his own earlier style. Today, a great deal of the drama produced on Broadway, the West End and of course in Hollywood consists of commercially driven sequels, franchises and imitations. But such an approach held little interest for O'Casey after 1926. If *The Plough and the Stars* was any good, he wished to let the piece stand rather than wasting time on *The Plough and the Stars II*.

London Playwright

Following the riot of 1926, O'Casey cocked a snook at Dublin by abandoning Ireland for London. Years earlier, O'Casey had written a satirical poem about an English journalist who found that 'Ireland is a very curious place', and who eventually decided: 'faith I'll pack my luggage on my back an' for England now I'll sail'.[50] But by 1926, O'Casey found himself packing up and sailing for that same destination. He travelled to collect a prestigious literary award in London, to the dismay of one of his Citizen Army co-founders, Jack White, who complained that O'Casey 'took a literary prize from the hands of Asquith, Prime Minister of the Government that shot Conolly [*sic*], his old chief [. . .] but men have their function at their time and place and according to their lights, O'Cathasaigh to write in ink, Conolly in blood'.[51] Still, in England O'Casey became a newspaper celebrity, and befriended G. B. Shaw. O'Casey also paid a press agency to send cuttings that mentioned him, and even married a little-known but strikingly beautiful Dublin-born actress, Eileen Carey, with celebratory images of their wedding circulating on newsreels in British cinemas.[52] London now looked more attractive than Dublin, and O'Casey decided to settle in England, where he would remain for the rest of his life.

During this time he recorded his feelings about Dublin and London in a notebook. He detailed a meeting with the vice-president of the Irish government, Kevin O'Higgins:

Kevin O Higgins: Like London?

Yes.

KOH: Better than Dublin?

Yes.

K. O Higgins: Strange – why?

Because in Dublin you can never get away from Ireland; but in London you can always get away from England.[53]

Two weeks later, back in the Irish capital, Kevin O'Higgins would be gunned down by anti-Treaty forces on his way to Mass. O'Casey, on hearing of the murder, must have realized that his conception of Dublin as a place where 'you can never get away from Ireland' had been proven true in the most gruesome possible manner. He scarcely felt tempted to return.

However, if O'Casey had rejected Dublin, a seemingly tit-for-tat insult came with the Abbey Theatre's verdict on O'Casey's next play, *The Silver Tassie*. This play could have provided a fresh start for O'Casey: his first work written in England, submitted to coincide with the birth of his son Breon, and using a more expressionist style as well as a new subject matter, the First World War. Dublin anticipated another success. In April 1928 the Irish press excitedly reported that 'friends of Mr. O'Casey who have been privileged to read his new play have passed high opinions on its merits, and its production is being eagerly awaited'.[54] However, during that same month, W. B. Yeats, who found both the literature of the First World War and the expressionist style deeply problematic, ordained that his playhouse would reject the play. O'Casey knew that the popularity of his Dublin trilogy was guaranteeing the economic survival of the Abbey Theatre, with a run of one of his plays worth almost 50 per cent more than a production by one of his rivals. Between 1925 and 1932, the Abbey's average weekly ticket sales stood at £236, but for those weeks in which the playhouse included O'Casey on the bill, that figure rose to £341.[55] O'Casey now felt so distressed by the management's apparent ingratitude over *The Silver Tassie* that he suffered something like a nervous breakdown. He believed that Ireland had unfairly turned against him again, just as it had done over the *Plough* riots, even if, in reality, the *Plough* was proving particularly popular with audiences, and, away from Yeats's idiosyncrasies, the Dublin Drama League and Dublin's Gate Theatre both offered to produce *The Silver Tassie*.[56]

Nevertheless, O'Casey became fixated on Yeats's rejection, and, never one to play by Queensberry rules, decided to publish all the related correspondence in the *Observer* and the *Irish Times*, bringing public attention to the literary spat. Yeats felt so shocked by this indiscretion that he took to his bed for two days.[57] G. B. Shaw, however, supported O'Casey, cementing their friendship by praising *The Silver Tassie* as 'a hell of a play!', and accompanying O'Casey to the opening night in London, where the director Charles Cochran premiered the work.[58] Shaw was not the only celebrity to fete O'Casey in the English capital: Alfred Hitchcock produced a motion-picture version of *Juno and the Paycock*, and then began to work with O'Casey on a highly stylized film about Hyde Park.[59]

Hitchcock soon tired of this latter plan and abandoned the collaboration. But O'Casey continued to mull over the Hyde-Park idea, using it as the basis for his next play, *Within the Gates*. His surviving notebooks show how O'Casey visited Hyde Park and noted down snippets of conversations that he overheard there:

Woman: There is no such thing as an atheist in the world.

Man: I'm an atheist.[60]

O'Casey wove such ideas into the play *Within the Gates*, a work that, like *The Silver Tassie*, is haunted by the effect of world war. Throughout any performance of *Within the Gates*, a memorial to the fallen remains a permanent fixture onstage, questioning whether everyday life can continue in the wake of the mechanized slaughter of the Western Front. However, after the box-office gold of his Dublin trilogy, the short-lived world premieres of *The Silver Tassie* and *Within the Gates* felt disappointing, and both plays have since been generally neglected by the theatre. From today's perspective, we can see that O'Casey's duo of Great-War dramas anticipate the music-hall style of Theatre Workshop's *Oh What a Lovely War*, with crazy shifts of time and tone, refusal of easy religious consolations, and contrasts between the sacrifice of the front and the comforts of the civilian, as well as large casts that would make productions unprofitable. But to many who first saw O'Casey's two post-Dublin scripts, the works looked unimpressive, particularly as O'Casey had the misfortune to open *The Silver Tassie* in the same London playhouse that had premiered R. C. Sherriff's smash-hit First-World-War drama *Journey's End*, starring Laurence Olivier, only ten months previously. For those expecting something akin to Sherriff's acclaimed work, which gave a realistic depiction of the trenches, involved half the number of actors, and focused on personal narratives, O'Casey's sprawling, expressionist montage must have appeared bewildering. Indeed, in his personal collection of press cuttings, O'Casey kept the *Daily Sketch*'s hostile review of *The Silver Tassie*, and he highlighted the section that argued 'There is nothing of the human sympathy which drives home the poignancy of "Journey's End"'.[61] O'Casey himself described Sherriff's play as 'backboneless and ribless', and later admitted that 'of course, I was jealous'.[62]

The leading English critic of the day, James Agate, after seeing *Journey's End*, had devoted his entire weekly radio broadcast to the work, and the play had then enjoyed a run of 600 performances.[63] But after Agate saw O'Casey's *Within the Gates* he described the work as 'pretentious rubbish' in *The Sunday Times*, and so earned O'Casey's long-term animosity.[64] The initial run of *Within the Gates* lasted for only 28 performances, and O'Casey responded to this failure by writing a collection of articles called *The Flying Wasp* in which he hurtfully denounced Agate as well as the writer Agate most admired, Noël Coward.

The bitterness of this attack, and its crude hints about Coward's homosexuality, show O'Casey at his worst, being both personally venomous and lacking in tactical nous.[65] Indeed, O'Casey's surviving letters reveal a persistent homophobia as one of his least pleasant character traits. Soon after moving to London O'Casey mocked the literary 'Nancy Boys' whose 'refined sentimentalities' might be 'hurt' by O'Casey's blunt language.[66] His views then grew more forthright after he experienced a difficult decade between 1935 and 1945, when, apart from revivals at the Abbey and one Dublin premiere, his plays received no professional productions.[67] Perhaps he felt that his dramas, so insistently inhabited by shapely and good-looking young women, suffered at the hands of gay actors, directors and critics, and in 1945 he commented, 'I shouldn't call dislike of "conceited amateurs, arrogant homosexuals, & impertinent dilettantes" a prejudice. I hate them'.[68] O'Casey repeatedly made slighting references to anyone he labelled a 'cissy', one of the 'frillies' or a 'girly wirley'; asserting that 'I simply cant stand them, or anything like them'.[69] He pronounced that 'These things, to me, are the products of Bourgeois "civilization", and can only be banished when the present way of artificial life is ended'.[70] Most repellently of all, when the director Ronald Kerr committed suicide, O'Casey commented:

> The fellow that gave a terrible production to "Oakleaves [*sic*] & Lavender", accused of an assault on a boy, & unable to face the charge, has left the world by way of a gas-oven. The Theatre here seems to be redolent with Cissies. [James] Agate, I'm told, when he suddenly collapsed, was at a party of them, dressed up as a Fairy Queen. It seems almost incredible to me; but then the kink in them is probably resented by the kink in me, for today I am just as enamoured by the trim figure & pretty face of a lass as I was when I was twenty-one.[71]

Here we have another of the paradoxes of O'Casey. He strongly believed that all men are created equal, and remained genuinely outraged by political and social injustices across the globe, yet felt no compunction about joking over the death of a member of a criminalized gay minority. To an extent, this homophobia simply reflects one of the most common prejudices of his time, shared by influential literary figures such as Richard Aldington and, ironically, Lord Alfred Douglas, but it is impossible to avoid feeling that O'Casey's political sympathies should have made him alert to the predicament of another oppressed group. O'Casey harboured a keen sense of his own outsider status, yet singularly failed to recognize and empathize with the analogous experience of the homosexual male.

Of course, O'Casey's homophobia was far from the only self-defeating aspect of his personality. If O'Casey had cultivated some of England's leading theatre producers and reviewers rather than responding to the failure of *Within the Gates* by producing *The Flying Wasp*, a volume subtitled 'a laughing look-over of what has been said about the things of the theatre by the English dramatic critics', then perhaps his later works would have found a home on the London stage. The critic James Agate tried to make amends by naming *Juno and the Paycock* the best play from the previous quarter century, declaring *The Plough and the Stars* the runner-up, and even asserting that O'Casey's subsequent play *The Star Turns Red* should be considered 'a masterpiece'.[72] But the damage had been done, and O'Casey's ability to maintain such grudges against those he felt had wronged him would become one of the defining features of his later career.

In 1934 O'Casey announced in the *New Statesman* that the deadening British theatre and its negative-minded managers tended to ignore and obliterate potentially great dramatic talents such as that of the young D. H. Lawrence.[73] Yet O'Casey also travelled for the first and only time in his life to the United States, where he appreciated the chance to see *Within the Gates* produced on Broadway, and where the play notched up more than a hundred performances. O'Casey retained a lifelong love of New York as a result. Here O'Casey also befriended and charmed the influential US critics George Jean Nathan and Brooks Atkinson, who would both play a key role in promoting O'Casey's reputation across the Atlantic. The dramatist later reflected on this 'happy and exciting' time, declaring that 'America has always been a friend to the Irish people'.[74] Less positively, however, a group of clergymen interrupted the planned tour of *Within the Gates*, successfully campaigning to ban performances in Boston, where Hitchcock's film of *Juno* had already been vetoed in 1931 because of its alleged endorsement of drunkenness. Toronto soon followed Boston's example and the tour disintegrated.[75] At the same time, the Irish state's conservative brand of Catholicism made its influence felt in the shape of the Censorship Board, which banned O'Casey's *Windfalls*, a collection of stories, poems and short plays.[76] For the man who had once devoutly prayed the rosary, the Catholic Church now emerged as a major antagonist.

Nevertheless, in one move of reconciliation, Yeats asked for permission to stage an O'Casey work from outside the famous trilogy, and *The Silver Tassie* opened at the Abbey in 1935, although O'Casey found some Dubliners spoiling to continue the fight started by *The Plough and the Stars*. One member of the Abbey board resigned in protest at the 1935 production, and right-wing Catholics appeared in Irish newspapers to condemn the 'offensiveness' of O'Casey's writing, promising riots if the *Tassie* ever appeared at the Abbey again.[77]

Cream of Devonshire

Eileen O'Casey gave birth to a second son, Niall, in 1935, and a daughter, Shivaun, in 1939. After Niall's birth, G. B. Shaw, under some influence from Eileen, recommended to Seán that the best place to educate the children would be the progressive Dartington Hall school in Devon.[78] The staff mooted the abortive idea of O'Casey becoming the college's affiliated playwright, to work with Anton Chekhov's nephew, Michael, who already ran the theatre at Dartington.[79] O'Casey declined this intriguing offer, but his Pearse-like notion of education meant that he nonetheless wanted his children to attend the institution, and in order for them to do so without boarding the family moved to Devon in 1938, 'a delightful county' where O'Casey lived until his death, discerning a deep Celtic influence in the area, and insisting that the region had once been known as 'East Ireland'.[80]

Shortly after relocating to Devon, he finished his play *The Star Turns Red*, which, although containing some interesting stylized effects, has attracted few admirers. O'Casey wanted to justify the ways of Stalin and the USSR, which the dramatist now saw as the best hope for humanity. Of course, other writers and commentators also wished for the best from the Soviet system during these years. But whereas Alan Sillitoe, for example, would visit the country to see the situation for himself, consequently revising his initial optimism and denouncing Russian human-rights abuses, O'Casey talked about the situation from the detached seclusion of Devon.[81] Indeed, as G. B. Shaw's example showed, even if O'Casey had visited the USSR, it was possible for a true believer to remain blind to the horrors of Stalin's regime. In 1926 O'Casey had been willing to satirize his own communism as well as nationalism in *The Plough and the Stars*, but at the end of the 1930s, in the era of Franco, Mussolini and Hitler, the dramatist attempted something more propagandistic, if considerably more sophisticated than agitprop. Still, *The Star Turns Red* scarcely suited theatre managers who kept an eye on box-office receipts, and this drama proved the first of his plays, although by no means the last, to enjoy a premiere by an amateur rather than a professional company.[82]

In 1939 O'Casey turned away from the playhouse to publish the first instalment of his autobiography, a Stakhanovite endeavour that, by 1954, would consist of some half-a-million words, printed in six volumes. These books enjoyed strong sales during the mid-twentieth century, and enjoyed critical and commercial success when performed on Broadway in the late 1950s.[83] Indeed, at the height of the popularity of the autobiographies, O'Casey made an LP recording of certain sections, while Hollywood adapted parts of the work into the film *Young Cassidy*.[84]

Critics have sometimes felt frustrated that O'Casey's autobiographical volumes are 'worthless' as a factual source.[85] But the author makes quite clear in his autobiographies that he wishes to avoid creating a historian's narrative, and one of his notebooks contains a candid summary of what he had attempted: 'I thought I would weave fact with fancy, & so I write the abstract & brief chronicles of a Dublin lad of the tenements in a way never done before; setting down, too, Dublin's aspect, her gaiety & gloom'.[86] In any case, he had long been suspicious of the notion of 'truth' in autobiographical pronouncements, telling Joseph Holloway in the 1920s about the problem of speaking to newspaper interviewers:

journalists might misrepresent you or cause you to dissimulate, things 'might slip from one also that would be best left unprinted. It is hard to be interview-haunted. It robs life of any pleasure'.[87] Similarly, in the 1950s, O'Casey declared that interviews with the press 'are very trying, and I am all against them. GBS advised me NEVER to grant one; rather ask for written questions to be sent, and answered in a quiet and serious way, saving any danger of an interviewer giving a wrong impression of an answer'.[88] So when O'Casey composed his autobiographies, in order to sidestep the notion that the volumes might be evaluated for historical accuracy, he wrote of himself in the third person and included a series of passages that are self-evidently fictional, mythological or allegorical.

More problematically, although O'Casey's prose is lively and at times poetic, the way in which the books have been published tends to make the project feel overwhelming. He intended his autobiographies to appear as six discrete publications, but after the last had been printed, O'Casey's publisher, Macmillan, created a two-volume edition (first published in New York in 1954 as *Mirror in My House*, and then in London as *Autobiographies* between 1963 and 1992). Today, the only English-language edition currently in print is the three-volume version based on Macmillan's compilation and produced since 2011 in the 'Faber Finds' series, lacking the attractive frontispieces of the first publications, and so missing something of the pleasure of reading the original, standalone books. Indeed, even Frank McCourt, who in 1999 admitted to admiring and emulating O'Casey's autobiographies, and whose brother Malachy played a prominent role in New York's centenary celebrations of O'Casey's birth, gave a subsequent series of talks that described the work in unflattering terms. The older McCourt summarized O'Casey's autobiographical writing as 'poetic and flamboyant. I can hardly read it. It annoys me', and repeated that 'I don't care much for the writing anymore – it's very florid and ornate'.[89] Despite such criticisms, when the reader encounters the discrete volumes of O'Casey's autobiographies, the writing is far less repetitive and can often be extremely affecting. The books are also complemented by the quietly winning autobiographies written by his wife in the 1970s, in which Eileen O'Casey, although careful to speak well of her husband, admits to a series of her own personal mistakes and limitations.[90]

O'Casey spent the years of the Second World War championing the USSR, engaging in domestic duties around the house, and socializing with the US soldiers billeted in nearby parts of Devon.[91] He also wrote one of his most commercially successful plays, *Purple Dust*, a comedy about two upper-crust Englishmen who have fled their wartime homeland for Ireland, and *Red Roses for Me*, a highly autobiographical play that has won a great deal of critical praise.[92] *Red Roses* describes a Dublin militant who dies on behalf of the workers during a dispute with a railway company, evidently inspired by O'Casey's own arguments with his one-time employers at the Great Northern Railway. The play opened at Dublin's Olympia Theatre in 1943, the first premiere of an O'Casey play in the city for 17 years, and enjoyed a reasonably favourable reception, although, sadly for O'Casey, Seán O'Faoláin published a well-known review in *The Bell*, declaring that O'Casey's exile from Ireland had introduced 'some fog' between playwright and subject matter.[93] *Purple Dust* first appeared at an amateur theatre in Newcastle-upon-Tyne during 1943, but reappeared in New York 13 years later, where the play won critical acclaim and long-term success at the box office. Nevertheless, the *Irish Times* declared that 'If the play had been written by an Englishman, it would possibly be dismissed as "stage-Irish"'.[94]

O'Casey took such criticism to heart, but in some respects this rhetoric reflected the reality of a wider situation. By the mid-twentieth century, many Irish migrants had travelled to England, from where they could often be viewed with suspicion from home for potentially acquiring disturbingly foreign habits and attitudes. O'Casey showed little concern to flatter those back in Ireland and so found himself attacked for being 'Clotted, perhaps, with the rich cream of Devonshire', from where he 'denounces us all to his wide audiences in England and America'.[95]

Despite such sniping, O'Casey continued to work at a prolific rate throughout his sixties and seventies, with his daily writing regime commencing at about seven or eight in the evening, and then continuing until three or four in the morning.[96] In the 1940s and

1950s he composed the plays *Oak Leaves and Lavender*, about an Irish butler in an aristocratic English house; *Cock-A-Doodle Dandy*, in which a giant cockerel, symbolizing sex and fertility, invades a puritanical and priest-ridden Irish town; and *The Bishop's Bonfire*, in which an Irish community nervously awaits the arrival of the local bishop. None of these are tremendously well known today. *Oak Leaves* first appeared in Sweden in 1946, *Cock-A-Doodle* was premiered by the nonprofessional People's Theatre in Newcastle-upon-Tyne in 1949, and although *The Bishop's Bonfire* attracted Tyrone Guthrie to direct the first version at Dublin's Gaiety Theatre in 1955, many of O'Casey's countrymen disapproved of the work. O'Casey had increasingly focused his ire on what he called the 'Vatican Church', angering many in Ireland at the time, although providing an attack on clerical hypocrisy and abuse in a way that now looks remarkably prescient.

After *Cock-A-Doodle Dandy* and *The Bishop's Bonfire*, O'Casey wrote another of his broadly anti-Vatican plays, *The Drums of Father Ned*, which he planned to premiere at the second Dublin theatre festival during 1958. The scripting and staging of this drama provided an important therapeutic process for O'Casey, as he composed the piece while mourning the loss of his son, Niall, who at Christmas 1956 had returned to the family home from university in London, complaining of feeling unwell. A local doctor diagnosed Niall with cancer, and the death followed just three weeks later.[97] The following year, Seán tried to cope with his grief by scripting *The Drums of Father Ned*, a comedy that describes Father Ned calling young people to enjoy the singing, dancing, vibrant pulse of life. However, Dublin's Catholic Archbishop, John Charles McQuaid, refused to allow the celebration of Mass at the start of the cultural festival when he heard that works by O'Casey and Joyce would be incorporated into the event. McQuaid was no philistine, as attested by his financial support for the poet Patrick Kavanagh, but did endorse a deeply conservative and dogmatic version of Catholicism that could scarcely accommodate O'Casey. The festival's organizers consequently contacted the playwright, asking for permission to make changes to his text, but O'Casey reacted with choler. From his point of view, the bigots within the barque of Peter had spurned and insulted the very play he had written in order to help him recover from his son's death, so put a moratorium on the play in Dublin, something that lingers in the minds of those organizing the city's theatre festival which is still held annually.

Although Samuel Beckett and O'Casey remained congenitally shy men, during the mid-twentieth century they both conquered their dislike of telephone conversions in order to talk to one another, and when Beckett heard the news from Dublin he also withdrew work in support of O'Casey, leading to the collapse of the festival that year.[98] The premiere of *Father Ned* eventually appeared, under the direction of the O'Casey scholar Robert Hogan, at the Little Theatre in Lafayette, Indiana, in 1959. Indeed, O'Casey felt that his homeland had continually rejected him since 1926, and so decided to ban professional productions of all of his plays in the country, a self-censorship that would largely continue until the writer's death.[99] During this prohibition, he also satirized Ireland in the one-act piece *Figuro in the Night* and his final full-length play, the anticlimactic *Behind the Green Curtains*, both of which received their premieres during 1962 in the university playhouses of the United States.[100]

For all of the harsh words written by and about him, O'Casey remained newsworthy in Ireland until the end of his life, even if he had become something of a nonentity in Devon. He lived for over a quarter of a century in the English county, where he saw the eccentric characters, historic buildings and local rivalries that helped inspire his late writings, most of which are set in similarly small towns rather than the capital cities he had once described. Yet today Devon does little to remember the writer. Only in late 2012 was a commemorative plaque unveiled on his home at St Marychurch, and although there is another marker in Devon outside his house at 'Tingrith', that second plaque is obscured by a busy main road and often by wheelie bins. By contrast, visitors to Dublin can see how O'Casey has helped to define the city by crossing the 'Seán O'Casey' bridge over the Liffey, visiting the striking 'Seán O'Casey Community Centre' in East Wall, or drinking in 'Seán O'Casey's Bar' opposite the Abbey.[101]

On Friday 18 September 1964, the 84-year-old writer suffered from nose bleeds and from pains in his side. An ambulance arrived, and his wife held his hand on the way to a local nursing home. On arrival, members of staff put O'Casey into bed, and Eileen begged them to ensure that her husband would suffer from no more pain. She need not have worried; Seán O'Casey had already died of coronary thrombosis in the ambulance.[102] For a man whose life had been so engaged with high-profile arguments, riots and overall 'chassis', he eventually died in such a peaceful manner that nobody had actually noticed the moment of his passing.

CHAPTER 2
DUBLIN, 1880–1926

The Shadow of a Gunman (Staged 1923)

This play is set during the fighting of the Anglo–Irish War, with British soldiers fighting against the guerrilla forces of the IRA. Against this backdrop, two men share a room in a poverty-stricken Dublin tenement: Seumus Shields, who is lazy and superstitiously religious, and Donal Davoren, who has recently joined Shields as a lodger and who harbours ambitions of being a poet. The other residents of the tenement mistakenly believe that the newly arrived Davoren is an IRA gunman on the run, and Davoren is flattered by their suspicion, particularly as the rumours win him the attention of the attractive Minnie Powell. However, one of the flatmates' acquaintances is a real IRA gunman, although this is unknown to the duo, and he has abandoned a bag of Mills bombs in their room before being killed in an ambush. Davoren and Shields only realize what has been left with them shortly before British soldiers begin a raid on the building. Minnie protects Davoren and Shields by bravely taking the explosives to her own room, but is caught and dragged away while the two men cower and hide, and the play concludes with the news that Minnie has been shot.

Juno and the Paycock (Staged 1924)

The action occurs during the Irish Civil War, when Irishmen are fighting one another over whether or not to accept the 1921 treaty with Britain (a treaty allowing Ireland to have self-governing, dominion status within Britain's empire, but requiring allegiance to the British monarch). In this setting, the audience is presented with another impoverished tenement room, this time inhabited by the Boyle family. The head of this household is the workshy Captain Boyle, who spends his time drinking and carousing with his sycophantic friend Joxer Daly. Boyle's wife, the long-suffering Juno, attempts to provide for her family, but is hindered by her husband's fecklessness and the fact that her son Johnny has been disabled in the recent fighting. The family's fortunes appear to improve when Bentham, who is a teacher as well as a lawyer's apprentice, discloses that the Boyles have inherited the estate of a dead cousin, and the family embarks upon a spending spree. However, Bentham has filled out the legal documentation incorrectly, and after leaving the Boyles with nothing but a pregnant daughter he flees to England. Meanwhile Johnny is revealed to have betrayed a former republican comrade, and so is taken away to his execution. The play concludes with Juno and her daughter escaping to establish a new life away from the men, and with Captain Boyle and Joxer alone onstage, engaging in drunken and incoherent nationalist blather.

The Plough and the Stars (Staged 1926)

The final play of the trilogy is set before and during the Easter Rising of 1916, with armed Irish nationalists seizing control of a number of prominent sites in Dublin. Again, the main onstage action takes place in a tenement, in which the recently wedded Nora and Jack Clitheroe are discovering the mundane realities of married life. Jack is weary of his wife's affections and inspired instead by the notion of fighting for Ireland. Despite Nora's attempts to protect him, he is promoted to officer in the Irish Citizen Army and dashes off to fight the British. In the second act, he and others are further excited by a nationalist leader's bloodthirsty rhetoric, which is ironically undercut by the boozy pratfalls and prostitution of a Dublin pub. The bleak, later section of the play is set during the last phase of the failed uprising, when a pregnant Nora tries to haul Jack back into the safety of the tenement, and when he pushes her away and causes her to miscarry. Another young child in the tenement dies of consumption, Jack himself is killed, and Nora goes mad with grief. At the end of the play, a Protestant neighbour, Bessie Burgess, attempts to care for Nora, and is in turn shot while dragging Nora away from an exposed position by a window. Finally a group of British soldiers invade the building and sing 'Keep the Home Fires Burning' as Dublin blazes in flames outside.

Former Nationalist

Between 1916 and 1923, Ireland witnessed a period of conflict that profoundly reshaped the country's relationship with Britain and continues to affect Irish politics to this day. O'Casey's Dublin trilogy deals with three pivotal moments during this time, the first of which, the Easter Rising of 1916, saw a small group of rebels launch a short-lived rebellion in Dublin that proclaimed the country an independent republic. The second moment is the Anglo–Irish War of 1919–21, during which IRA members took inspiration from the events of 1916 to wage a guerrilla campaign against Crown forces, compelling the British to negotiate a peace treaty. The concluding period is that of the Irish Civil War of 1922–3, when former republican colleagues turned on each other in a bitter dispute over the settlement with Britain, with 'die hards' such as O'Casey's Johnny Boyle rejecting the terms accepted by the 'Free Staters'. Somewhat confusingly, O'Casey's Dublin trilogy deals with these moments in reverse order, so that the first instalment, *The Shadow of a Gunman,* deals with events that had been the most recent, those of the Civil War, while the last part of the trilogy deals with 1916.

Before these revolutionary events began, Ireland existed as part of the United Kingdom, in a political union with Britain, and governed from Westminster. But by 1923, the South of Ireland had gained self-governing status as the Irish Free State, whereas the six counties in the northeast of the island stayed outside this new formation and continued to be administered as part of the United Kingdom. Meanwhile, during that period, O'Casey himself grew increasingly alienated from the independence movement, turning towards socialism as an alternative route to emancipation. In his later plays, O'Casey would repeatedly present the Dublin lockout of 1913 as a far more significant moment in the nation's history than any of the conflicts commemorated in the nationalist calendar. The Dublin trilogy therefore unravels O'Casey's earlier enthusiasms in a way that some audience members found impossible to forgive.

However, the playwright never really made a clean break with nationalism. It has long been a commonplace of O'Casey criticism to assert, in the words of Vivian Mercier, that the author 'had lost faith in nationalism even before 1916' and that the Dublin trilogy 'began to strike a series of hammer blows at the romantic image of three different phases of the revolutionary movement'.[1] Yet O'Casey's divorce from the cause was neither as wholehearted nor as absolute as this kind of analysis indicates.

Although O'Casey had quarrelled with the Irish Citizen Army before the Dublin Rising, and so sat out the insurrection, he wrote a number of works to extol the rebels in the aftermath of Easter Week. In 1917, for example, O'Casey published a prose pamphlet, *The Story of Thomas Ashe*, about one of the heroes of the revolt who had subsequently died on hunger strike in a British jail.[2] O'Casey describes Ashe's cachexia as having a catalysing effect upon other patriots, and portrays the martyr as someone whose heart throbbed 'strongly and so fervently for Ireland and down-trodden man'. This piece gives an emotive description of Ashe's final moments, before concluding, 'Thou hast said, farewell, to Ireland, Thomas Ashe, but Ireland will not part with thy soul. What can we think of the Power [Britain] that robbed us of the life of this dear dead man[?]'.[3]

The following year, in 1918, O'Casey published the poem, 'England's Conscription Appeal to Ireland's Dead'. This verse imagines the British army confronting a range of Irish heroes, from Wolfe Tone to the 'Brave, noble Spirits' who recently fought in the Easter Rising.[4] Here O'Casey attempted to forge a link between the 1916 rebels and the previous patriots who had died for Ireland, with such a rhetorical strategy feeling familiar in Ireland. After all, the proclamation of the republic had itself begun by describing 'the dead generations from which she [Ireland] receives her old tradition of nationhood'.

In another poem of 1918, 'The Bonnie Bunch of Roses, O!', O'Casey imagines the Irish insurrectionists of more than a century earlier, Robert Emmet and Wolfe Tone, resisting England alongside the leader of 1916, James Connolly. 'The Bonnie Bunch of Roses' is a title that refers to England, Scotland and Ireland, and had been used in earlier folk songs to describe the common resistance offered by these islands to France during the Napoleonic wars.[5] But in O'Casey's version, this 'Bonny Bunch of Roses' is evoked in an ironic way, as the writer castigates England for the ills visited upon the neighbouring realms, and puts Connolly on a pedestal alongside the greatest of Ireland's martyrs.

So in the years immediately after the Easter Rising, O'Casey continued to publish material praising the attack on British rule and mocking the Empire's increasingly desperate attempts to clutch onto that oldest of colonies. But in the 1920s, Ireland lurched into a Civil War, which, as historian Fearghal McGarry points out, 'was an inevitable consequence of the legacy of the Rising'.[6] After all, the rebels who had sacrificed everything in 1916 now played Banquo's ghost during political discussion, with their refusal to compromise setting an adamantine example for those who followed. The martyrs had died in order to proclaim a 32-county republic in 1916, the most extreme version of nationalism advocated in Ireland at that time, and during the Civil War many IRA members believed that agreeing a treaty that settled for anything else constituted a gross betrayal of those dead men. The bitter internecine bloodshed of the Civil War caused O'Casey to question the uncompromising zeal of both the current combatants and, retrospectively, their immediate antecedents, with his trilogy consequently targeting a range of nationalists from the 1916–23 period. As Seumus Shields puts it in *The Shadow of a Gunman*, 'I draw the line when I hear the gunmen blowin' about dyin' for the people, when it's the people that are dyin' for the gunmen!' (I, 132).

In O'Casey's next play, *Juno and the Paycock*, the audience is confronted by an Irish patriot who, like Thomas Ashe, is pictured as enfeebled and facing death. However, unlike O'Casey's description of Ashe, there is little redemptive message in the demise of Johnny Boyle.

Johnny has been terribly maimed, twice, for Ireland, having been hit in the hip by a British bullet during 1916 and then losing his arm in an explosion when fighting the Free Staters during the Civil War. But such self-sacrifice cuts little ice with the republicans who now blame him for fatal treachery. Despite all of his devotion to the cause, then, Johnny is ultimately dragged from the stage as a disgraced informer. We see no glory, but only the funerals, mourning and fear that accompany nationalism, with Johnny's mother begging for 'a little less respect for the dead, an' a little more regard for the livin' (I, 58).

By the time that O'Casey scripted *The Plough and the Stars* he felt happy to portray the desire to die for Ireland as a fundamentally selfish, self-absorbed and borderline-deranged activity. Here Jack Clitheroe physically assaults his pregnant wife in order to join the Easter Rising, and after his death the boast that 'Mrs Clitheroe's grief will be a joy' is undermined by the vision of Nora driven to insanity by grief and loss (I, 244).

The Dublin trilogy thus revisits and refutes the playwright's earlier attachment to specific nationalist figures. For example, in O'Casey's poetry of 1918, one of the martyred leaders of the Easter Rising, James Connolly, is presented as prophetic and heroically anti-British, praised as someone whose 'teachings true in Ireland soon/ Shall flourish like the flowers in June'.[7] O'Casey modified this view in 1919, when he published a prose history called *The Story of the Irish Citizen Army*, in which Connolly emerges not only as a 'broad and noble soul', but also as a leader who sold out the cause of Labour at Easter 1916. *The Story of the Irish Citizen Army* argues that Connolly had followed ideas 'which were, in many instances, directly contrary to his life-long teaching of Socialism', claiming the siren call of Irish nationalism ultimately proved 'in his ears a louder cry than the appeal of the Internationale'.[8] O'Casey's Dublin trilogy gives a still harsher critique of Connolly, with *The Plough and the Stars* castigating the leader as the figure who directly coaxes men to their death, away from the love and comfort of home life. At one point, Nora rages at her husband: 'Is General Connolly an' th' Citizen Army goin' to be your only care?' (I, 189).

Poetaster

It is not only Irish patriots who find themselves disparaged, however, in O'Casey's early dramas. Indeed, before any nationalist appears, the very first scene of *The Shadow of a Gunman* presents a satirical portrait of the play's author himself. Donal Davoren sits at a typewriter in the centre of the stage, from where he utters the opening lines of the trilogy, a stanza of love poetry that contains the sexual image of lovers spending 'ravish'd hours' together (I, 94). Davoren not only recalls the luxuriating Duke Orsino but also parallels the real-life O'Casey, who in around 1918 had written a range of replikit love lyrics for Máire Keating, with the verse that Davoren speaks lifted straight from O'Casey's own poem 'Sunshadows'.[9]

Yet Davoren is repeatedly exposed as pretentious and chicken-hearted, far removed from the persona he would like to project. For instance, he repeatedly quotes a line from Shelley's *Prometheus Unbound*, 'Ah me! alas, pain, pain ever, forever!' (I, 96), but does so in situations that scarcely do justice to the poet's original context. In Shelley's work this line is spoken by Prometheus, who has attempted an act of cosmic significance in stealing fire from Zeus, and whose subsequent punishment is the torment of being 'Nailed to this wall of eagle-baffling mountain'.[10] By contrast, in O'Casey's play, Davoren quotes the line in humdrum situations, such as when a landlord demands the rent, and when intrusive conversation stymies the poet's creativity.[11]

Furthermore, although Davoren fancies himself as a *littérateur*, one of the running jokes of *The Shadow of a Gunman* is that the other tenement dwellers evidently know more about poetry than he does, even if they wear their learning considerably more lightly. His flatmate recognizes quotations from Shelley and Shakespeare, and at one point Davoren tries to impress Minnie with a clever allusion, but bungles the reference by confusing the poetry of William Douglas with that of Robbie Burns (I, 109).[12] Minnie quotes a line by Douglas straight back at Davoren, and gets the reference entirely correct, but Davoren's own citation is addled, adding Robbie Burns to the list of those whose identities are mistaken in the play. Overall, then, Davoren never convincingly establishes himself as a literary figure. He remains the shadow of a poet as well as the shadow of a gunman.

Davoren's counterpart in the second play of the trilogy is Jerry Devine, another poetaster, whose verse is only heard after Jerry has acted in a conspicuously ignoble way towards his former sweetheart. Jerry has told Mary Boyle 'I love you', and 'No matther what happens, you'll always be the same to me' (I, 80, 19), but when he discovers her pregnant by another man he abandons her in an instant, asking 'have you fallen as low as that?' (I, 81). In response, she recites some of his poetry word-for-word, asking 'Do you remember, Jerry, the verses you read when you gave the lecture in the Socialist Rooms some time ago, on Humanity's Strife with Nature?' (I, 81). From a realistic perspective the scene is unlikely: how can Mary possibly remember Jerry's rhyme so precisely after having heard it only once? But, as we shall see, O'Casey often had little interest in devising lifelike scenarios, preferring here to create a somewhat unreal episode in order to highlight a deeper truth about the insincere posing and absurd pretentions of Dublin's literary wannabes.

Jerry Devine offers a critique of O'Casey just as Donal Davoren does in the earlier play, with Jerry obsessing over the author's favoured Labour cause, and writing poems that again sound suspiciously like O'Casey's earlier efforts.[13] Such satire was unfair to the dramatist, who in real life proved far more loyal and humane than Jerry. Indeed, Christopher Murray recounts that when O'Casey's wife became pregnant for a time as the result of an extra-marital affair, the playwright reassured her that 'Mostly it's my fault'.[14] Yet O'Casey took aim squarely at himself in the trilogy, repeatedly puncturing his own grandiloquence. For example, he had filled his notebooks with classically inspired poems, entitled 'A Walk with Eros' or 'A Stroll with Venus and her Boy'.[15] Accordingly, in *Juno and the Paycock*, another fictional surrogate attempts to do something similar, with Charles Bentham visiting the Boyle family and commenting:

Bentham: Juno! What an interesting name! It reminds one of Homer's glorious story of ancient gods and heroes.

Boyle: Yis, doesn't it? You see, Juno was born an' christened in June; I met her in June; we were married in June, an' Johnny was born in June, so wan day I says to her, 'You should ha' been called Juno', an' the name stuck to her ever since. (I, 31–2)

Even if we find Boyle's response naive, Bentham scarcely makes himself likeable with such lofty comments. Here we find the portrait of a self-regarding prig, who singularly fails to understand or empathize with the world of the tenement around him, and if we laugh along with this joke we are placed in the awkward position of wondering whether we too share something of Bentham's condescension. A similar impulse is found elsewhere in O'Casey's Dublin trilogy, perhaps most notably in the stage direction that describes Minnie Powell as being unable to 'converse very long on the one subject', just 'like all of her class' (I, 107). Hence the scripts ask whether readers and spectators can ever really enter into imaginative empathy with the residents of the slums, or whether we retain the snobbish separatism of Bentham, whose ironic name points out that he is really concerned only with the greatest happiness of himself.

The Dublin trilogy thus reveals its author as an equal-opportunities insulter, and the final instalment again scoffs at the kind of reading and writing that the real-life O'Casey had been doing. When besotted by Máire Keating, he had jotted the following love poem:

> 'Mid buzz of bees and song of bird
> Veil'd in a sky of blue,
> [. . .] As you sit close to me, my love,
> And I sit close to you.[16]

This poem owes much to the popular verse, 'When You and I Were Young, Maggie', which had been set to music in the 1860s.[17] In *The Plough and the Stars*, Clitheroe sings this song to his wife, although he changes the name from 'Maggie' to 'Nora':

> Th' trees, birds and bees sang a song, Nora,
> Of happier transports to be,
> When I first said I lov'd only you, Nora,
> An' you said you lov'd only me! (I, 187)

Indeed, the prompt book now held at the Abbey Theatre reveals that O'Casey had originally planned to include his own love poetry directly at this point in the play. In that manuscript, that song 'Nora' is glued on top of, and thus obscures, a different and notably syrupy verse.[18] Closer inspection of those earlier words reveals them to be part of an O'Casey poem that he eventually entitled 'The Garland' for publication in 1934, but which he had again composed when love-struck by Máire Keating.[19] In the final part of the Dublin trilogy, then, just as in the earlier instalments, O'Casey set about putting his own phrases into the mouth of character who scarcely provokes feelings of sympathy. After all, following this poetic declaration of love, Jack Clitheroe rejects his wife with such vehemence that he causes her to miscarry.

The Plough and the Stars also satirizes O'Casey's left-wing reading habits. He describes elsewhere how, in the build-up to the Easter Rising, he had spent his time absorbed by the *Communist Manifesto* (*Auto* II, 224), which, according to Robert Lowery, O'Casey admired 'as much for its literary merits as for its political content'.[20] But *The Plough and the Stars* mocks those who would seek refuge in such works during a time of Irish revolution. In the play we find The Covey (whose name comes from the unflattering Dublinese for 'fellow', or 'cove') who tells those that he meets, whether British Tommy or Irish prostitute, that they should read 'Jenersky's *Thesis on the Origin, Development, an' Consolidation of the Evolutionary Idea of the Proletariat*' (I, 197, 249). Of course, anyone who tries to find a copy of Jenersky in the library will be frustrated. The book is O'Casey's invention, but is certainly based on Marx, with an earlier draft of the script featuring The Covey's prototype asking, 'what does Karl Marx say in the 220th Chapter o[f] Das Kapital on the Mechanism of Exchange?'[21] The Covey's faith that reading left-wing theoretical work can solve the problems of those around him, who are facing immediate poverty, illness and violence, makes him appear comically aloof, and offers a condemnation of the kind of socialism that personally attracted O'Casey.

Unjustly, in later years a number of commentators have associated O'Casey with a po-faced unwillingness to question himself. Critics have tended to find that O'Casey 'defends himself against any critic in prose of astonishing copiousness and vigour', or, less kindly, that O'Casey produces only 'vitriol and vinegar'.[22] Such a view of O'Casey is predicated upon his mid-century writings, with their wearisome and self-regarding attacks on figures such as the poet George Russell or the novelist George Orwell. But the Dublin trilogy reveals O'Casey's willingness to deride his own enthusiasms, to display a flexibility of mind, and indeed to demonstrate a certain playfulness in challenging his allegiances and changing his affiliations. O'Casey certainly ridiculed the political views of others, but also proved willing to take a long, hard look in the fairground mirror of his own satire.

Music Hall

Of course, O'Casey's Dublin trilogy would scarcely have enjoyed critical success in Dublin if he had simply lampooned nationalism or provided a coded self-portrait. Instead, O'Casey's drama felt fresh and innovative because O'Casey fused together a number of different theatrical forms, creating a hybrid that looked distinct from the earlier offerings of the Abbey stage.

Strikingly, O'Casey emulated the energies of Dublin's music hall. During his youth, performers such as Fergusson and Mack, 'the Greatest of all Irish-American Knockabout Comedians', had enjoyed great popular success in the city.[23] This particular duo, for instance, appeared at the city's Star Music Hall in July 1884, when O'Casey had been four years old, and they repeatedly found a warm welcome in Dublin's theatres until 1921, just two years before O'Casey's work first appeared at the Abbey Theatre.[24] Fergusson and Mack delivered routines characterized by 'outlandish patter and knockabout and tumbling business' in pantomimes and burlesques, and in shows with titles such as 'The Dimple Sisters' or 'The Battle of May-Go'.[25] But this mode of comedy, replete with pratfalls and semi-improvised dialogue, could scarcely have been recorded in any full way, and so today we have largely forgotten the skill and popularity that such double-acts demonstrated for decades on the Dublin stage. However, some of this style of clowning is occasionally preserved in manuscript form, and, although shorn of the accompanying extra-textual comedy, such transcribed dialogue does give a flavour of such performances.

In the following extract, for example, Fergusson and Mack are playing the parts of 'McCarthy and Mulligan', two friends recovering from a heavy drinking binge, with McCarthy suffering from a particularly severe hangover:

Mc: Mull, will you do me a favour

Mull: Anything in my power, name it

Mc: Turn the water tap on me

Mull: Well, you & water have been strangers for many a day, here try some of this

Mc: What is that

Mull: This is mineral water, that I have imported for my special use from Bulgaria

Mc: Where is Bulgaria

Mull: I don't know, but I am informed by good authority, that it is on the coast of Switzerland, or the borders of Siberia, or somewhere there about. How long ago is it since you were here before

Mc: I think it's about 9 years ago, last Thursday

Mull: Or Friday

Mc: Saturday or Sunday

Mull: Mc if you remember rightly, your last visit here, I had me daughter

Mc: I think you had, I think you had, I think you had

Mull: I have two more now

Mc: Happy new year, happy new year, happy new year, you are quite a family man.[26]

This section of script helps to illuminate a type of playing that enjoyed popularity in Dublin during O'Casey's youth, with such comic performances prefiguring the double acts of Davoren and Shields, and Joxer and Captain Boyle. For anyone familiar with the wisecracking of Dublin's variety hall, there could be little surprise in the cross-talk of O'Casey's characters, in whose words, just as in the passage above, we find repetitions of key phrases ('a daaarlin' thing' (I, 10)); twisting and inversions of logic ('I'll have a right laugh at you when both of us are dead' (I, 97)); and quasi-philosophical questions about the world ('what is the stars?' (I, 26)). O'Casey's Dublin plays also include slapstick moments when, for instance, the characters begin brawling, chasing, or hiding objects from one another, in theatrical tableaux that owe much to the sensibility of the music hall.

However, O'Casey adds a set of disturbing and darker dimensions to this pre-existing variety framework. As Fintan O'Toole argues, the best interpretations of O'Casey's Dublin characters tend to be those such as John Kavanagh's version of Joxer Daly at the Gate Theatre in 1986, where Kavanagh showed that all the comic antics were driven by 'the rat-like hunger of a half-starved man'.[27] In the cinema, Charlie Chaplin's genius had been to combine the physical antics of the music hall with the power of the filmmaker's close-up to cause empathy towards the main character, particularly through the pathos of the tramp's often hungry, wronged and dispossessed face. In the playhouse, O'Casey achieved something similarly revelatory by wedding music-hall comedy to the recognizable poverty and political violence of Dublin. Hence we find in his trilogy a transformed version of the hangover japes of the variety artistes. Fergusson and Mack's extant script is a collection of sketches that concludes with 'pleasant' singing and dancing, but O'Casey's Dublin works consistently deny such an upbeat resolution.[28] *The Shadow of a Gunman* associates alcohol with the barbarism of an occupying army; *The Plough and the Stars* connects drinking with the misguided frenzy of martyrdom; and at the very end of *Juno and the Paycock*, a drunken conversation is performed incoherently in the aftermath of murder, financial ruin and the implosion of the Boyle family. In this last example, although the comic double-act remains onstage at the end, the duo has descended into an introverted, disjointed rambling that anticipates Samuel Beckett rather than reprising the sing-along joviality of the variety hall.

Shakespeare

In the *Observer* in 1929, Sean O'Casey reflected: 'Shakespeare was my education. When I was a boy in Dublin thirty years ago, the Benson Company came to the city, and I spent all my small wages and went without food in order to see all the plays that were performed. I could hardly read or write at the time'.[29] With this comment, O'Casey describes the work of Frank Benson's touring theatre group, usually remembered in Ireland for being fleetingly and unsuccessfully involved with the Irish Literary Theatre in 1901, but which actually enjoyed many years of highly praised productions in Dublin.

O'Casey claimed to have felt particularly inspired by watching the Benson version of *Julius Caesar*:

> [. . .] the first Shakespeare play to present itself to me. Afterwards
> I and my brother used to play the quarrel scene between Brutus
> and Cassius; or I would give the speech of Brutus in the Forum,
> my brother acting the crowd, or he would give Anthony's speech
> while I acted the crowd. During the week of Shakespeare's plays,
> I saw five of them, and found no difficulty in loving them all.[30]

O'Casey scarcely found himself alone in enjoying the Benson Company's production. Dublin audiences adored this *Julius Caesar*, and the forum scene proved a particular highlight, providing spectators with the famously conflicting oratory of Brutus and Mark Antony. The company's actor–manager, Frank Benson, played the latter part himself in Dublin, and received such fervent applause that he felt compelled to return to the stage at the end of the scene. In 1893 this part of the play created in the auditorium a feeling of 'unbounded enthusiasm such as has not often been witnessed', and when Benson came back the following year, he was once more 'recalled again and again' by the transfixed audience at the end of this particular sequence.[31]

Benson's technique in playing Mark Antony was to interpret the part initially as careless and carefree, but to show how the soldier's outlook changes entirely when, in a moment that today would look comically exaggerated, Antony gazes on the body of Caesar, after which Benson became a startlingly different and more histrionic, avenging figure. The 'Friends, Romans, Countrymen' speech gave Benson the chance to show this range, with the actor playing up the satire of the opening, and then rousing the plebeians into fury, with 'a rare touch of genius; it was a triumph of elocution and declamation'.[32]

In a letter of 1964 O'Casey's later described himself acting out Shakespearean scenes with his older brother after seeing Benson's troupe, and this comment is endorsed by his 1942 autobiographical writing. In both instances, O'Casey remembers the forum scene as being one of the key moments that he and his brother rehearsed, with the autobiographies describing how the duo had formed a drama society, and charged audiences 'to see Archie [O'Casey's brother] playing the Duke of Gloucester to Johnny's [O'Casey's] Henry the Sixth; or to see Johnny playing Brutus in the Forum scene, followed by Archie as Mark Antony' (*Auto* I, 298).

Accordingly, in future years, O'Casey would write plays that showed the strong influence of Shakespeare's writing, not only in the verbal cadences and conscious allusions in the texts, but in the very stagecraft itself. In a central part of the forum scene that had brought the house down in Dublin, Mark Antony declares:

> But here's a parchment with the seal of Caesar;
> I found it in his closet; 'tis his will.
> Let but the commons hear this testament,
> Which, pardon me, I do not mean to read.[33]

The surrounding plebeians then repeatedly implore Mark Antony for 'The will, the will! [. . .] Read the will!', and he eventually demands that first they must encircle the corpse of Caesar who wrote it. He then stirs the crowd with such heartbreaking memories of the dead man that they all completely forget why they are surrounding the body. Somewhat comically, Antony has to remind them, 'You have forgot the will I told you of', at which point the crowd again shout that they want to hear the will, and he reveals at last that Caesar has left a generous bequest 'To every Roman citizen'.[34]

In *Juno and the Paycock*, O'Casey recycles Shakespeare's plotting. Juno Boyle tells her husband that Bentham has arrived with 'great news [. . .] news that'll give you the chance o' your life' (I, 28–9). However, like the forgetful plebeians of *Julius Caesar*, the Captain is distracted away from this discussion. First he has to take off his trousers, then search for his braces. There follows a discussion of the sacrifices that Johnny Boyle has made for Ireland, and the wounds that he has received on that account, just as Mark Antony regales his listeners with tales of Caesar's injuries in the cause of Rome. Bentham even remarks that he is reminded of 'ancient gods and heroes', before he finally reads out 'a copy of the will that I have here with me', telling the Boyles that they have inherited a fortune (I, 31–2).

In Shakespeare's play, before Mark Antony has spoken, the crowd comments that 'This Caesar was a tyrant [. . .] We are blest that Rome is rid of him'.[35] Yet after Mark Antony has read the will, the mood of the plebeians changes entirely, and they vow 'We'll burn his body in the holy place,/ And with the brands fire the traitors' houses'.[36] When O'Casey scripted *Juno and the Paycock* he reused this part of Shakespeare's play, placing the sentiments of the mob into the mouth of Captain Boyle. At the moment that Boyle hears about the death of his cousin, the Captain condemns the deceased relative as a 'prognosticator an' procrastinator!', but after the will has been read out, leaving a large bequest to the family, Boyle declares that the family will go into mourning at once (I, 32–3).

In addition, the forum scene in *Julius Caesar* is dominated by the central image of the fallen Caesar, who has been repeatedly stabbed and now displays 'wounds,/ Weeping as fast as they stream forth thy blood'.[37] Accordingly, in *Juno and the Paycock* Johnny is haunted by a similar vision, imagining the dead Robbie Tancred with 'the wouns bleedin' in his breast' (I, 46). This image of Caesar's corpse finds its echo elsewhere in the Dublin trilogy: in *The Shadow of a Gunman* O'Casey presents the description of a dead Minnie Powell with 'the blood pourin' out' (I, 156); while in *The Plough and the Stars* Nora has seen a mangled body 'in th' middle o' th' sthreet' (I, 221). The Benson company's forum scene concluded with the sight of flames rising around the bloody body of Caesar, and in *The Plough and the Stars* we learn that Jack Clitheroe ultimately meets the same fate. Thus, Shakespeare became central to O'Casey's dramatic vision, with Frank Benson having opened O'Casey's eyes to theatrical possibilities that would be explored in the Dublin trilogy.

Boucicault

O'Casey also found inspiration in the popular melodramas staged in Dublin during his youth. In the 1920s, this element felt novel to Abbey audiences, not least because W. B. Yeats hated such works and had deliberately established the playhouse to provide the antidote to such 'buffoonery and easy sentiment'.[38] Nevertheless, on the boards of Yeats's theatre, O'Casey now emulated the dramaturgical style of the earlier Dublin-born playwright, Dion Boucicault, whose Irish-themed play, *The Colleen Bawn* ('the fair-haired girl'), had proved the theatrical smash-hit of the late 1800s.[39]

Disingenuously, O'Casey later distanced himself from this source, claiming of his plays, 'you'll see that there isnt sight or sound of Boucicault in any of them'.[40] But in reality the Dublin dramas are suffused with admiration for the earlier playwright, and the plot of *Juno and the Paycock* draws heavily upon *The Colleen Bawn*.[41] Boucicault's play revolves around a landed family that has fallen on hard times, with marriage proposed as the solution. The son of the household must wed his cousin, the richest heiress in Kerry, although he is already secretly married to a fair-haired girl (the 'colleen bawn' of the title). A malformed and obsequious servant called Danny Mann decides to help the family by murdering the existing, secret wife, although in the event he is killed instead and all ends happily.

Juno and the Paycock replays some of these stock ideas from Boucicault. Here again an impecunious family faces crisis, and marriage looks likely to help provide an escape route. Just as in Boucicault, the plan backfires because of a problem with the proposed marriage, while Johnny Boyle meanwhile adopts the Danny-Mann role, which involves being connected with murderous treachery, suffering a physical deformity that indicates moral turpitude, and ultimately being shot.

Of course, at the end of Boucicault's play, according to the saccharine strictures of melodrama, all ends well. The colleen bawn survives the attempt to kill her, she is reconciled with her newly uxorious husband, and the characters simply cease to worry about debt. However, O'Casey re-imagines the plot in a far bleaker way. At the end of *Juno and the Paycock*, Johnny is dragged to his death, Juno leaves her husband, and Mary is abandoned by the unborn child's father. Furthermore, the family belongings are repossessed, and those who have wronged the Boyles remain unpunished. O'Casey's writing may have been inspired by the older melodrama, but concludes in a very different place. Indeed, at the end of *Juno and the Paycock*, one of the only things that Joxer and Boyle can do is express regret that they are not characters in an older version of the tale, with Joxer asking Boyle, 'D'jever rade Willie . . . Reilly . . . an' his own . . . Colleen . . . Bawn? It's a darlin' story, a daarlin' story!' (I, 89).[42]

In the 1890s the young O'Casey watched another Boucicault hit, *The Shaughraun* ('the Vagabond'), at the Queen's Theatre.[43] As with Shakespeare, O'Casey and his brother again acted out scenes from Boucicault's show, and even performed the play in public, at the Mechanics' Theatre in around 1899.[44] This work gave O'Casey an introduction to political theatre, showing how a commercially successful drama might deal with recent civil events, and could, despite the rawness of those occurrences, include various comic elements. Boucicault's play had first appeared in London in 1875, little more than seven years after the Fenian attacks in Manchester and London that are described in the text.[45] Yet Boucicault's play revolves around a heroic Fenian who is on the run, hunted by the British and hindered by a malevolent police informer. When O'Casey began his trilogy, he decided to write with the same political immediacy, setting *The Shadow of a Gunman* in May 1920, the height of the Anglo–Irish War. The play first appeared on the stage of the Abbey Theatre in April 1923, as the final bullets of the Civil War still echoed in the streets, and so the theatre programme included a note to reassure spectators: 'During the second act the sounds customary during a raid by the Auxiliaries are heard'.[46]

One of the central scenes of both Boucicault's *The Colleen Bawn* and *The Shaughraun* is a raid by British soldiers upon an Irish home, and again O'Casey transplanted this into his own Dublin plays. In *The Shaughraun* the British army arrives in order to search for a Fenian, confronting inhabitants who are nervously aware that this very rebel is hiding in the kitchen. Similarly, in *The Shadow of a Gunman*, a group of soldiers arrive to find someone 'that's going to overthrow the British Empire' (I, 148), and the tenement denizens have good reason to fear: most of those in the block believe that they are sheltering an IRA gunman, with the two who know the truth about Davoren's identity also concealing an incriminating bag of IRA explosives. The situation is repeated in a still more terrifying way when the British arrive in the Dublin tenement of *The Plough and the Stars*, as the residents have only just learned the full and grisly details of Jack Clitheroe's death, which involve Jack being shot twice, suffering haemorrhage and hypoxia, before being crushed under falling masonry and – for good measure – cremated. The slum-dwellers are uncomfortably aware that they now unwillingly shelter another rebel fighter, and that any hint of his identity may herald a similarly merciless fate for them.

Of course, O'Casey was no cut-and-paste man, and his versions of British incursions diverge from those presented by Boucicault. One of O'Casey's foremost innovations was his decision to include the army raids of earlier melodrama, but to use the tenements of Dublin as the domestic space into which the soldiers intrude. These buildings had originally been constructed by the Anglo–Irish community of the eighteenth century, wealthy Protestants who largely quit the Irish capital after the Act of Union in 1800. But in the following years, Dublin suffered from a long-lasting property crash. According to Kevin Kearns, Georgian houses purchased for £8,000 in 1791 were sold for £500 in the hungry 1840s.[47] Slum landlords came to manage the formerly aristocratic houses, which grew 'colonized' by the urban poor, and therefore provided O'Casey's early plays with an atmosphere of protracted and irreversible impoverishment. The rooms that had been designed for light and space by their architects were, by the time of the Dublin trilogy, packed tightly with residents, with O'Casey showing how intimate family life might therefore be made impossible by the consistent interruptions of neighbours, friends and enemies. When the Cockney soldiers arrive, then, they carry the ghosts of the past with them, conducting an invasive English 're-colonization' of the down-at-heel Georgian buildings.

Furthermore, Boucicault had designed his own work for commercial success in London, and so the members of the British army who invade the Irish properties in his plays are polite and chivalrous. Indeed, the redcoat captain of *The Shaughraun* carries a flame for the rebel's sister and so remains particularly remorseful about violating her home. O'Casey's soldiers, by contrast, bring little other than chaos and death, and scarcely present a benign picture of empire.

As a result, in *The Shadow of a Gunman* and *The Plough and the Stars* there is no natural sympathy between those living in the building and those overrunning it, even where we might expect such an affinity to exist. For instance, in *The Shadow of a Gunman*, Mrs Grigson is a Dublin Protestant who displays a picture of William of Orange over her mantelpiece and who leaves her bible open on the page stating 'Honour the King'. Nevertheless, the British troops incorrectly identify the picture as Robert Emmet, throw the bible on the floor, and filch her husband's alcohol. A still worse fate befalls the equivalent character in *The Plough and the Stars*. Bessie Burgess takes pride in singing 'God Save the King', and boasts of her only son, who has enlisted in the British Army and is being sent home from the front after shattering his arm during the fighting. Nevertheless, a British corporal still mistakes her for a 'Shinner' [supporter of Sinn Féin], and she ends the play being shot dead by a British bullet (I, 260).

Indeed, by the time that O'Casey wrote this final section of his Dublin trilogy, he had shown a broader inversion of clan and family commitments. The revolutionary bloodshed has so stunted Dublin's life that the actual children of the building are now either dead or miscarried, and instead the grown-up characters regress to infancy. The British corporal calls one of the Irish characters 'mother' and another 'daddy' (I, 250, 253), and immediately before Bessie Burgess dies she nurses the ailing Nora with all the delirious tiredness of a mother caring for a new-born baby, only to turn on Nora with ferocity after suffering that fatal injury (I, 253). In this way, by scripting Bessie's death as a swerve away from the maternal, O'Casey leaves the audience to consider the predicament of her actual son: this injured Tommy will soon arrive home from the Western Front to find that his own mother has been killed by one of his supposed comrades. Thus, in the trilogy, Johnny Boyle is not the only character betrayed by his own one-time allies. Bessie Burgess's son provides the unionist mirror image, having lost his arm by enlisting for the trenches just as Johnny has lost his arm by joining the republicans. Overall, then, there is a 'plague on both your houses' quality to O'Casey's Dublin plays. Notably, at the end of *The Shadow of a Gunman*, the action concludes with the news of Minnie's death, but it is impossible to know who exactly has killed her. For all of her cries of 'Up the Republic' (I, 152), O'Casey leaves us with a crucial ambiguity. Who exactly shot her? Did her British enemies pull the trigger, or was she peppered by one of her own side during the reported nationalist ambush on her captors?

Dalton and Connolly

Alongside the Shakespearean, music-hall and melodramatic elements outlined above, O'Casey also included in his trilogy a number of ideas from Dublin's earlier naturalistic dramas. One of the things seldom observed about *The Plough and the Stars* is that it repeats much of the cynicism of an earlier play by Maurice Dalton, *Sable and Gold*, which presents a thoroughly unheroic version of the Easter rebels, and which the Abbey staged in 1918, only two years after the Rising. *Sable and Gold* revolves around a character called Gregory, who travels from Cork to fight at the GPO, but sneaks away from the slaughter in a cowardly fashion, and cannot admit this truth to his mother, who rejoices in his participation and apparent bravery. O'Casey certainly knew of the Abbey's earlier work, and his unpublished notebooks reveal that during the brouhaha over *The Plough and the Stars* he prepared to defend himself in public by citing 'Gregory in "Sable & Gold"'.[48] After the riots, the fact that this earlier play, with all of its disparagement of the rebels, had been staged unproblematically in Dublin must have struck O'Casey as both curious and unjust.[49]

However, in reality, O'Casey's work is more incendiary than that of Dalton. *The Plough and the Stars* criticizes the real-life James Connolly by name, and constitutes a specific reaction against a play that Connolly had written and first staged in March 1916. Connolly's play had been called *Under Which Flag?*, with that titular question asking what kind of banner Irish men and women ought to support: that is, whether to join Britain's wartime battle for the freedom of small nations, or whether, instead, to take the chance of striking out for an independent Ireland. Of course, at the end of Connolly's play the audience learns that the latter answer is the correct one, a simplistic moral that infuriated O'Casey when he saw the piece.[50] The title of *The Plough and the Stars* therefore provides a rebuke to Connolly's question, by referring to the flag of the Labour movement. Perhaps, O'Casey suggests, Irishmen could rally behind these colours. Nevertheless, by the end of O'Casey's script, even this emblem proves inadequate. In the Dublin trilogy, fighting for any cause is portrayed as empty and dehumanizing, with political idealism insistently drawing men away from life and from love.

Patrick Pearse

Although *The Plough and the Stars* attacks Connolly, O'Casey trains his fire on another of the leaders of 1916 in a more sustained way. Patrick Pearse became president of the provisional government during the rebellion, he suffered execution at the hands of the British after the surrender, and subsequently became Ireland's best-known martyr. By the 1920s, Irishmen had grown accustomed to impersonating Pearse in a respectful and prayerful way, as Clair Wills observes, 'commemoration had taken on a self-referential life of its own. In provincial ceremonies up and down the country, children and young men stood on wooden platforms and in front of statues to read the Proclamation'.[51] At such events, Pearse would often be invoked by a local man reading the proclamation of the Irish republic, which the martyr had declaimed outside the GPO at Easter 1916.

O'Casey, of course, dissented from such hagiography and decided to take a different tack. He picked out some well-known examples of Pearse's most bloodthirsty writing, and inserted them into *The Plough and the Stars*, where they appear in the mouth of an anonymous and faceless speaker who rants at a crowd from an offstage position.[52] Worse still, O'Casey's orator evokes Pearse at the same time as being upstaged by disorderly drunkards and a prostitute, who inhabit the main stage and thus allow O'Casey to equate nationalist enthusiasm with the bawdy, the bibulous and the brutal.

This central part of *The Plough and the Stars* developed out of a stand-alone sketch called *The Cooing of Doves*, which Yeats had rejected in 1923 and which remained seemingly lost until 2005. The shorter piece, which is now held at Princeton University Library, includes embryonic versions of the phrases and characters that would fill the Pearse section of *The Plough and the Stars*, and is similarly set in a pub while a political meeting takes place outside. But in the first version, Pearse is conspicuously absent. Indeed, an appearance from this martyr would have been incongruous here, as the action of *The Cooing of Doves* occurs during 1923, seven years after Pearse's death, with O'Casey originally reserving his scorn for the pro- and anti-treaty nationalists who contested that year's general election.[53] For sure, *The Cooing of Doves* does bring some earlier patriots into the orbit of its cynicism. Kevin Barry, Wolfe Tone and Robert Emmet are all named, while the prostitute's moniker of 'Dinah Connel' suggests the nineteenth-century 'emancipator' Daniel O'Connell, just as her later incarnation as Rosie Redmond recalls the nationalist leader John Redmond. Yet, in the first iteration of this scene, the rebels of 1916 go completely unmentioned, and only when O'Casey rewrote *The Cooing of Doves* as part of *The Plough and the Stars* did he decide to include Patrick Pearse.

Nonetheless, O'Casey fretted about this addition. After all, O'Casey had long admired Pearse's pedagogical ideas, writing in 1913, 'Our hopes are your hopes; your work shall be our work; we stand or fall together'.[54] One member of the original cast remembered the playwright having a disturbing premonition about the production:

before the opening night O'Casey worried that 'there are people who knew Pearse who might object'.[55]

This actor, Gabriel Fallon, told O'Casey to avoid tampering with the script, but O'Casey ignored this advice and made a number of additions that significantly revised the Pearse character. In O'Casey's original typescript of *The Plough and the Stars*, now found in the National Library in Dublin, on every occasion that the orator speaks, O'Casey drafted a large number of embellishments and painstakingly glued them onto his text.[56] Of course, Pearse had never written or spoken these newly added words, but that was entirely the point. O'Casey created a watered-down version of the orator, whose bombast would contain only a proportion of recognizably Pearsean words in the midst of a broader, fictional tirade. Similarly, in a later holograph notebook now held in the New York Public Library, O'Casey again redrafted the demagogue's speeches, for example changing Pearse's line, 'When war comes to Ireland she must welcome it as she would welcome the Angel of God!' (I, 203), to the calmer, and less recognizable, 'When war comes to Ireland, we must not shrink from it, for we shall be fighting for the independence of our country'.[57] O'Casey's revisions thus defamiliarized the Pearse figure, and potentially paved the way for a less controversial show.

However, such alterations never survived into performance, and there is no trace of them in the 1926 Abbey promptbook nor in any printed version of the text.[58] O'Casey probably realized that his revisions weakened the play, and hoped instead that, in performance, the orator might receive sympathetic treatment from the actor playing the part. O'Casey later told one correspondent that the orator should be considered the brother of Lincoln or Washington, someone who is 'not vain; he is dangerous[ly] sincere [. . .] I knew this "Orator" well – Padraig Pearse, and there were none more charming, gentle, or brave than he'.[59]

This paradoxical desire to tear into Pearse, but then to fret about the effect of that attack, can be found elsewhere in O'Casey's Dublin trilogy. In *Juno and the Paycock* the cowardly Captain Boyle declares, 'Today, Joxer, there's goin' to be issued a proclamation be me, establishin' an independent Republic, an' Juno'll have to take an oath of allegiance' (I, 27). With this reference to the proclamation of the republic, Boyle imagines himself stepping into the shoes of Pearse at the GPO, just as the drunken captain will end the play by vaingloriously boasting of having fought in Easter Week. But Boyle's proclamation is revealed as little more than a comic sham only a moment after he mentions it. When Juno appears, far from taking any oath of allegiance, she berates her workshy spouse. In this context, the spoiled will begins to look increasingly like a parody of those other ruined documents, the proclamation of the republic and the Anglo–Irish treaty, which, in O'Casey's view, had bequeathed such a bitter and disappointing legacy to Ireland. However, as with the depictions of Pearse in the *Plough*, O'Casey apparently felt some anxiety about making such a travesty of 1916, and in his notebooks began sketching out an unused alternative version of that *Juno* scene.[60]

As such revisions indicate, in spite of everything, O'Casey continued to admire the men of 1916, and retained a particular fondness for Pearse. Although O'Casey is often considered a historical 'revisionist', in reality he had a complicated and fluid relationship with nationalism, and when he decided to participate in a public debate about the *Plough* in 1926, he devoted special attention to answering the charge of maltreating Pearse. O'Casey drafted an explanation to say that he never had any intention, 'stated or implied to hold up to ridicule the passion the enthusiasm, & the idealism of Pearse. His sympathies with the poor & the toil-ruined working men & women may, possibly, have been deeper & greater than mine'.[61]

The Plough and the Stars certainly does ridicule Pearse, but the playwright appears to have almost immediately regretted this, and repeatedly offered a *mea culpa* in later work, writing, for example, a 1942 article that describes the martyr as a 'great heart', a 'great humanist', and a 'sad loss to Ireland'.[62] In the same vein, O'Casey's autobiographical writings present such a flattering depiction of Pearse that the northern unionist St John Ervine wrote a review in the *Spectator* lamenting the portrayal.[63] In response, O'Casey pointed out that Pearse 'was a very handsome man, and always carried himself with grace and dignity'.[64] When St John Ervine again demurred, O'Casey wrote another encomium, praising the leader of the Rising in hyperbolic terms as 'a pioneer in Education', 'a born man of the theatre in its widest sense', and a prophetic 'foreseer'.[65]

O'Casey undoubtedly vacillated, but, during this historical period, loyalties on all sides remained in flux. For instance, at the Abbey, Arthur Shields midwifed the first production of *The Plough and the Stars* by acting as assistant producer as well as by playing Lieutenant Langon. Yet in real life Shields had fought in 1916 on the rebel side, willing to face death for the same cause that his theatrical work now subjected to a testing critique.

Of course, *The Plough and the Stars* does not present an unmitigated attack on the rebels of Easter Week. Indeed, in one of the most powerful moments of the play, Fluther Good highlights the appallingly unequal odds faced by the republicans.[66] When a British sergeant asks why the Irishmen refuse to fight fairly, Fluther explodes: 'Fight fair! A few hundhred scrawls o' chaps with a couple a' guns an' Rosary beads, again' a hundhred thousand thrained men with horse, fut, an' artillery . . . an' he wants us to fight fair! (*To Sergeant*) D'ye want us to come out in our skins an' throw stones?' (I, 255). Such a section of script scarcely endorses the view that O'Casey's play entirely eviscerates the rebels and their cause. Indeed, when John Ford directed the film of *The Plough and the Stars* in 1937, he used this part of the text in order to give a fulsome endorsement of the rebel viewpoint. In Ford's version, Jack Clitheroe survives the fighting, and then speaks the line immediately after an interpolated scene that depicts James Connolly as a Christ-like figure who forgives the British firing squad: evidently all those characters called JC made such a religious interpretation too tempting to resist. O'Casey himself disliked what Ford had done, yet the filmmaker's decision to foreground that statement about stones merely highlighted one of the latent sympathies of the original text. After all, in later correspondence, O'Casey himself repeated Fluther's words along with a somewhat wishful counterfactual question: 'a few hundred badly-armed lads held back the British power for a week. How much longer would they have held out if they had had a well-armed force say of 10,000, backed by a united people?'[67]

Furthermore, when O'Casey wrote *The Plough and the Stars* he cut out and kept a newspaper clipping from the summer of 1924, when the high court in London handled a libel action concerning the Amritsar massacre in India. O'Casey retained the evidence given by a British general who claimed that 'Officers were justified in bombing and machine-gunning any crowds they saw in order to re-establish law and order', and that 'flogging was proper punishment'. When this commander had been asked if he would apply the same discipline in an English city, he replied 'one would not treat London as a negro village. This punishment would be suitable for Indians but not for Englishmen'.[68] O'Casey avidly followed these reports as he prepared his play about the Easter Rising, undoubtedly realizing that many of the Empire's masterminds held similar beliefs about Ireland. Ironically, although the British response to the Dublin insurrection was designed to keep Ireland within the United Kingdom, the shelling and executions served only to emphasize the anomalous status of Ireland, as the army would scarcely have contemplated the same treatment for urban disorder in London, Leeds or Liverpool.

In later years, O'Casey indicated that he remained wedded to the cause of Irish republicanism, and felt heartened by the example set in Easter Week. In Wales, more than two decades after the Dublin rebellion, he felt thrilled to find a 1916-style nationalist movement, allowing him to advocate exactly the course of action that he had condemned in Dublin, namely 'to persuade the Welsh people I meet that Wales should, must break away from England, & establish her own independence. National Freedom must, unfortunately, come before Communism'.[69] Similarly, in 1940 he spent time writing letters to British ministers, instructing them to 'hold your hand and spare the lives' of two men sentenced to death for the IRA bombing of Coventry; while in 1947 he engaged in a press campaign to free thirty-nine IRA prisoners from England, enjoining the jailors to 'Open the prison gates!'.[70] In the late 1950s he wrote, 'there is nothing wrong or foolish about being proud of Easter Week: the sorrowful thing is that those who followed have betrayed the ideals of the men who fought for Ireland then'.[71]

Riots

The Plough and the Stars opened on Monday 8 February 1926, and despite the initially positive reception, audience disquiet increased during the week, until on Thursday a full-scale riot broke out, featuring a co-ordinated appearance from the real-life widows and bereaved women of 1916. Patrick Pearse's own mother arrived at the theatre, watching the protestors who booed and hissed, who belted out nationalist songs and slogans, and who set about destroying lamps and stage curtains. One spectator even smacked two of the female cast members in the face, before being clobbered by the actor playing Fluther. Meanwhile, W. B. Yeats rose to the front with either deplorable self-regard or commendable *sang-froid*, to declare, 'You have disgraced yourselves again', and to proclaim the evening O'Casey's 'apotheosis'.[72] Of course, few people could hear or understand Yeats, and even O'Casey had to consult a dictionary in order to decipher the speech. Yeats ended up delivering most of his words *con sordino*, and someone else tried to put an end to the misery by lobbing a shoe at his head.

Undeterred, the Abbey management decided that the play should complete its run, and pressed on with three more performances that week. The second act provoked a renewed bout of barracking, but the chaos of Thursday night was not repeated. Plain-clothes policemen packed the theatre, and audience members were encouraged to puff on cigars throughout the performance to counteract the effects of stink bombs. Three gunmen also attempted to kidnap members of the cast, compelling the Abbey management, for some time, to lock the actors inside the theatre.[73]

Yet not all of those who protested against the final part of O'Casey's Dublin trilogy could be classed as the writer's violent antagonists. Although O'Casey thought the 'outburst of opposition was probably spontaneous', in reality the events had been carefully pre-arranged by the nationalist Frank Ryan. The meeting notes for *Cumann na mBan* (the 'Irishwomen's Council'), whose members dominated the protests, record that: 'The Secretary said she had got in touch with Frank Ryan who told her he would require ten girls to help him in a job he intended doing in the Abbey Theatre'.[74] Paradoxically, Ryan had been, and would be again, a close friend of O'Casey, and according to one of the rioters, Ryan 'thought a lot of O'Casey's plays'. Needless to say, for Ryan, arranging the disruption had little to do with personal amity or literary taste, and everything to do with consolidating his position within the post-Civil-War IRA.[75]

Similarly, when Owen Sheehy Skeffington later recalled the way that his mother had led the protest inside the theatre he declared:

> She didn't deny at all that what he said in the play was true, but she said, it's not the whole truth and these things are too close to us now, to have a play put on which is so one-sided. My own feeling at that time, and I argued it with her because I was, by that time, seventeen, was that O'Casey was not trying to show the rebellion, he was trying to show the impact of a revolution upon the submerged tenth, upon the person who is so oppressed by poverty and exploitation.[76]

Sixteen years after the riot, Owen Sheehy Skeffington wrote to O'Casey to declare the *Plough* 'a really great play. The fact that it is often misunderstood in several different ways does not detract from its greatness'.[77] Yet in 1926, Owen's mother Hanna had played a central role in disrupting that first production, complaining about the script in the pages of the *Irish Independent*, and launching a broadside against O'Casey at a public discussion to which the playwright had been invited, inevitably, by Frank Ryan.[78]

O'Casey had now had enough. After all, he deeply admired Hanna Sheehy Skeffington's late husband, Francis, who had died during the Easter Rising. Francis was no gunman, but an ardent pacifist who had been trying to prevent looting in the streets. During the chaos, the British army had detained him, taken him to Portobello Barracks, and shot him dead, along with two other men. An appalled O'Casey declared Francis 'the first martyr to Irish Socialism' and 'The living antithesis of the Easter Insurrection: a spirit of peace'.[79] But now even the wife of this non-combatant martyr had set about excoriating O'Casey. The writer's eyes troubled him as they had done in his youth, and when confronted by Hanna Sheehy Skeffington at the public meeting he almost collapsed.[80] He had planned to launch a sally, full of clever literary allusions, on a number of her positions, and the draft of his speech included the comment:

> Mrs Skeffington & good many – some anyhow, of her comrades seem to me to have an obsession to appear as immaculate saints in the eyes of the English people. The thing essential with her & others seems to be the determination that to the all-important British People Empire the Irish People should appear as Rosy-red men & Lily-white women enjoying costumes of idealism in a glowing garden of green.[81]

In the event, however, O'Casey could barely speak, and that criticism, of playing to a foreign audience, became associated with him rather than with his opponents. This was no country for men like O'Casey. As he later put it:

> The Easter Rising had pulled down a dark curtain of eternal separation between him and his best friends; and the few that had remained alive and delightful, now lay deep, with their convivial virtues, under the smoking rubble of the Civil War. It was getting very dark in Ireland, so his flight to London would be a leap in the light. (*Auto* II, 508)

The melee over the *Plough* created for O'Casey the reputation of being the commander-in-chief of Irish iconoclasm, hell-bent on tearing down the country's most cherished ideas and symbols. After all, in the Dublin trilogy O'Casey had set high patriotic principles against the lowbrow slapstick of the music hall; had co-opted melodramatic techniques without the attendant drive to sentimentalism and reconciliation; and had presented a morbific version of Irish nationalism. By the time of the Abbey protests, O'Casey had even made a Prince Hal of Patrick Pearse, setting the martyr's words alongside the bawdy frivolities and verbal high-jinks of the alehouse. This performance came only a few weeks before the tenth anniversary of the Rising, in a theatre that stood amidst the 1916 battleground, given by an acting company in receipt of a subsidy from the Irish Free State.[82] A hostile reaction was not entirely unpredictable.

Yet O'Casey scarcely perceived himself as the binary opposite of the rebels, and felt wounded that figures such as Hanna Sheehy Skeffington viewed him as an enemy. The final part of the Dublin trilogy left him divided from many people who might have been his natural allies, and denounced by nationalists in the press and on the public platform, even though he would continue insisting in 1945 that 'in thought I am still a Fenian'.[83] Ultimately, then, less than one month after the opening night of *The Plough and the Stars*, O'Casey decided to follow the well-trodden route of the Irish writer, taking the path out of Ireland, and then situating himself in England for the rest of his life.

CHAPTER 3
REJECTION, 1926–39 AND BEYOND

The Silver Tassie (Published 1928)

The play is set during the First World War, and the first act begins in familiar O'Casey territory: the domestic apartments of Dublin. The lusty Harry Heegan enters, borne aloft by cheering admirers who adore him for having led his soccer team to win a cup, the 'silver tassie' of the title. His girlfriend Jessie kisses and cheers him, but Heegan is on leave from the fighting and must return to the front, with his mother eager to send him back safely. The second act opens in the trenches, and presents a highly stylized portrayal of warfare, in which participants chant and repeat rhymes in front of a symbolic set. The action then moves to a hospital ward, where we see a frustrated, impotent and paralysed Harry in a wheelchair. He is visited by family and friends, but although Jessie's arrival is reportedly imminent, she fails to appear and instead the act concludes with another character bringing in the flowers that Jessie intended to give. In the final scene, set in the dance hall of Harry's football club, the one-time hero wheels himself in anger around the healthy bodies of his contemporaries. When he sees Jessie embracing his friend Barney, Harry curses them, attacks Barney, and smashes the cup that had been won at the start of the play.

Within the Gates (Published 1933)

Within the Gates revolves around a young and beautiful woman called Jannice. Her real father is a bishop, who fathered Jannice when a young theology student, and hid his paternity by placing her into a Catholic institution run by hellfire-obsessed nuns. Her atheist stepfather released her, but Jannice then faced a violent mother and a job with a sexually abusive shop-manager, and ended up working as a prostitute. Now Jannice is unwell, suffering from a heart complaint. She meets her real father, the bishop, and although neither of them at first recognizes the other, she appeals for his help. He silently realizes her identity, but his solutions involve Jannice either living with her mother, or going back into a Catholic institution. Jannice prefers instead to take refuge in the arms of a young man called 'the dreamer', who offers her a world of joy, laughter and sensual pleasure. In a final dance with 'the dreamer', Jannice collapses. The bishop fails to reveal that he is her father, but does accompany her in her dying moments, and in her final act she asks him to guide her hand in making the sign of the cross.

Autobiographies (Published 1939–54)

O'Casey began writing his autobiographies after the Abbey Theatre had rejected *The Silver Tassie*, and the six volumes repeatedly return to this incident as well as broadly telling of the way that the writer abandoned Dublin in order to become a major international literary figure based in England. The first volume sets out O'Casey's birth and childhood in late nineteenth-century Ireland, describing the death of his father and taking us up to the point where O'Casey 'learned poethry and had kissed a girl' (*Auto* I, 175). The second volume begins with the death of Parnell, and, as Ireland deals with the aftermath of the failure to gain Home Rule, O'Casey gains an interest in national history, as well as in theatre and sex. In the third instalment he loses his Christian faith and instead gains a belief in socialism, although sympathizing with those who participate in the Easter Rising, which concludes the book. In the fourth volume the Irish Free State is established, but O'Casey feels distanced from this new, pious and censorious country, and decides to leave for England. The fifth part begins with O'Casey's arrival in London, where he faces the Abbey's rejection of *The Silver Tassie*, as well as other travails of the professional writer, but where such struggles are offset by meeting his wife and starting a family. The final volume is set against the backdrop of the Second World War, and concludes with the thought that despite the Allied victory, worse conflicts may be predicted for the future. Nevertheless, the writer reflects that he is still able to raise a toast to 'Life, to all it had been, to what it was, to what it would be. Hurrah!' (*Auto* III, 417).

Rejection

After the riots over *The Plough and the Stars* O'Casey set to work on another play about the violence of the revolutionary period. In his earlier works he had tackled the Easter Rising, the Anglo–Irish War and the Irish Civil War. Now he turned his attention to Ireland's experience of the First World War, in a play that would surely prove another box-office triumph. After all, as the Abbey director Lennox Robinson put it, *Juno and the Paycock* and *The Shadow of a Gunman* had saved the Abbey Theatre 'from bankruptcy'.[1] Lauren Arrington calculates that the week before the Abbey premiered *Juno and the Paycock*, a production of works by Edward McNulty and George Shiels brought in £173, whereas O'Casey's play earned £254 in its first week, £246 in its second week and nearly £650 when revived for two weeks in the following month.[2]

The *Manchester Guardian* observed, 'One would imagine that when he offered his new play "The Silver Tassie" to the Abbey Theatre of Dublin its directors would drain the bowl without stopping to taste it', and O'Casey had indeed received words of encouragement from the playhouse as he completed and submitted the work.[3] Lady Gregory wrote, 'I long to see it – I'm sure the wine you have filled it with is of the best vintage', and Lennox Robinson hailed the arrival of the manuscript with the declaration, 'Your play arrived this morning. Three cheers!'[4] After this, however, things scarcely went to plan.

The Abbey directors had been subjecting O'Casey to stringent editorial control for the past 12 years, often accompanied by withering comments about his efforts. Thus O'Casey had learned that his writing was 'seldom dramatic', 'puzzling' or 'too definite a piece of propaganda for us to do'.[5] The following table (Table 3.1) shows how the Abbey treated O'Casey's submissions.

Table 3.1 O'Casey's submissions to the Abbey Theatre

Date that O'Casey submitted his play	Name of O'Casey play	Was it accepted?
2 March 1916	*Profit and Loss*	No: Script returned to O'Casey on 6 March 1916
29 October 1919	*The Harvest Festival*	No: Script returned to O'Casey on 24 January 1920
10 November 1919	*The Frost in the Flower*	No: Script returned to O'Casey on 26 January 1920
6 January 1921	*The Crimson in the Tricolour*	No: O'Casey spoke in person with Gregory about the play on 10 November 1921. She later revealed that she wanted to produce the piece 'but Yeats was down on it'.[6]
10 April 1922	*The Seamless Coat of Kathleen*	No: Script returned to O'Casey on 17 April 1922
28 November 1922	*The Shadow of a Gunman* (Submitted under the title 'On the Run')	Yes: Play produced on 12 April 1923
23 August 1923	*The Cooing of Doves*	No: Script returned to O'Casey on 24 September 1923
30 August 1923	*Cathleen Listens In* (Title originally recorded in logbook as 'Kathleen Listens In')	Yes: Play produced on 1 October 1923
28 December 1923	*Juno and the Paycock*	Yes: Play produced on 3 March 1924
8 August 1924	*Nannie's Night Out* (Submitted under the title 'Irish Nannie Passes')	Yes: Play produced on 29 September 1924
12 August 1925	*The Plough and the Stars*	Yes: Play produced on 8 February 1926
21 March 1928	*The Silver Tassie*	No: Script returned to O'Casey on 10 May 1928[7]

To say the least, this success rate is underwhelming. When O'Casey delivered *The Silver Tassie*, fewer than half of his submissions had been accepted by the theatre, and even after he had achieved a critical triumph with *The Shadow of a Gunman*, the directorate had still declined his next work. Again, when he submitted *The Plough and the Stars* in 1925, the play failed to gain unanimous approval: the theatre's usual producer, Michael J. Dolan, wrote to Gregory to complain that O'Casey's language was 'beyond the beyonds', and the Abbey minute book for 22 September 1925 shows that the board decided only three to one in favour of the play, with the government representative voting against production.[8]

In response to such criticisms, O'Casey could be sulky. He told the theatre's managers that the 'contemptuous dismissal' of *The Frost in the Flower* made him feel 'like Lucifer', that the rejection of *The Crimson in the Tricolour* had been 'a bitter disappointment', and later reflected that when Yeats and Gregory made editorial suggestions, 'I knew too little to withstand them'.[9] Consequently, we may suspect that in *Juno and the Paycock* the portrait of the arrogant Charles Bentham, with his pretentious literary references and his willingness to discuss esoteric theosophical beliefs, owes something to O'Casey's experience of being treated *de haut en bas* by Yeats.[10] However, up until 1928, O'Casey always found himself swiftly reconciled with the Abbey. Indeed, he even expressed thanks for the playhouse's critical rigour. In 1923, despite his initial disappointment, he later told Lady Gregory 'how grateful he was to me because when we had to refuse the Labour one, *The Crimson in the Tri-colour*'.[11] For the Abbey, then, *The Silver Tassie* simply needed subjection to the same fastidious editorial attention as all of O'Casey's earlier submissions, with the directors giving little thought to O'Casey's sensitivities and his developing reputation, but instead sharpening the blue pencil.

However, O'Casey believed, with some justification, that by 1928 he deserved to be treated differently. His works had provided a financial lifeline for the Abbey during the lean years, and he may reasonably have supposed that, even if his writing had fallen below par, the work might nevertheless be welcomed here. In any case, *The Silver Tassie* is far from being a bad play, and from a modern perspective can

average of £387. By contrast, plays by Yeats had been revived there on only six occasions, with these weeks earning an average of only £204. Indeed, in the ensuing months, even when the theatre produced Yeats's short works as part of a programme that included otherwise successful pieces, Yeats's dramas tended to drag the figures down. For example, when Yeats's *The Countess Cathleen* was staged as part of a double bill with O'Casey's *The Shadow of a Gunman* in February 1930, the week earned only £177, and when Yeats's *The Words Upon the Window Pane* appeared alongside *Shadow* in June 1931 the week brought in just £147. Yet *Shadow* was usually one of the theatre's best-earning pieces, and customers paid an average of £306 between 1927 and 1931 during the other weeks when the playhouse staged O'Casey's play. Indeed, in between the two poorly attended productions when Yeats's work was added to the programme, *The Shadow of a Gunman* appeared as part of an alternative double bill with T. C. Murray's play *The Pipe in the Fields* and earned £324 during that week.[15] The starkly contrasting fortunes that Yeats and O'Casey enjoyed in that same theatre space raises the question of how far the rejection may have been connected to sour grapes, and a desire to show that, even if O'Casey had achieved popular and commercial success, the younger writer still needed the Nobel laureate's help in order to create plays that would be considered great when judged by a more meaningful set of aesthetic criteria.

Meanwhile O'Casey had become a celebrity in Britain, where recent headlines had fussed over news such as 'O'Casey in a Hat' and 'Sean O'Casey Weds in a Pullover'.[16] A well-known writer like this could potentially have unveiled his work in any number of locations. Indeed, the wealthy and well-connected British director Barry Jackson, who premiered ambitious work such as Shaw's *Back to Methuselah*, made overtures to O'Casey in July 1926.[17] Apparently, O'Casey had therefore promised 'first glimpse' at the *Tassie* to Jackson (*Auto* III, 23), but O'Casey thought an Abbey production remained assured in any case, and attached tricky preconditions when he submitted the manuscript to Jackson, prompting the English director to decline, and to declare, 'I am looking forward to the day when some kind person offers to risk ten thousand pounds on my work so that I can "condish" too – only I shall ask for the Albert Hall & Charlie Chaplin'.[18] O'Casey took his revenge by satirizing Jackson in the autobiographies, but must have known that a good opportunity had gone begging. If O'Casey had doubted that an Abbey production was in the bag, he may have handled Jackson and the theatrical egos of London more carefully.

War Stories

Quite aside from the personal rivalries that existed at the Abbey, Yeats had deep misgivings about the whole issue of literary writers tackling the world war. When he edited the 1936 *Oxford Book of Modern Verse* he consciously omitted the war poets, famously explaining that 'passive suffering is not a theme for poetry'.[19] If much of mankind had grown obsessed by military conflict, Yeats instead declared coolly, 'I give it as little thought as I can'.[20]

O'Casey, by contrast, gave the war a great deal of thought, and felt exasperated by Yeats's attitude. In response to the rejection, O'Casey published an open letter to Yeats, asking, 'How do you know that I am not interested in the Great War? Perhaps because I never mentioned it to you. Your statement is to me an impudently ignorant one to make'. O'Casey continued:

> You say 'you never stood on its battlefields'. Do you really mean that no one should or could write about or speak about a war because one has not stood on the battlefields? Were you serious when you dictated that – really serious now? Was Shakespeare at Actium or Phillipi; was G. B. Shaw in the boats with the French or in the forts with the British when St. Joan and Dunois made the attack that relieved Orleans? And someone, I think, wrote a poem about Tir nan nog who never took a header into the Land of Youth.[21]

O'Casey may never have seen action at the front, but he knew a great deal about its victims, later claiming that he 'lost most of his comrades – not in the streets of Dublin – during the Easter Rising, but in Suvla Bay in the battle for the Dardanelles'.[22] In addition, during

1915 he needed surgery on tubercular glands that had swollen up in his neck, and found himself admitted to St Vincent's Hospital, which had been commandeered as a field hospital, with O'Casey therefore witnessing at first hand the sufferings of the gassed, the shell-shocked and the maimed.[23]

Indeed, the fate of certain soldiers lived long in O'Casey's memory. Shortly after O'Casey arrived at the hospital, his surgeon, Richard Tobin, lost an only son who had been fighting with the Royal Dublin Fusiliers. In O'Casey's autobiographies, we find a sad portrait of this father, 'trying to conjure up the ghost of his son from the songs and stories of the wounded men' (*Auto* II, 231). The patients would, in all likelihood, have discussed the extensive newspaper reports of the younger Tobin's final battle, as well as the initial announcement of his death, soberly detailing his membership of 'the 7th Royal Dublin Fusiliers, the "Pals" Battalion'. If O'Casey had seen such notices, he would have noticed how they characteristically included details of the sporting prowess of the deceased, and the same part of the newspaper that announced the fate of young Tobin contained information about other soldiers: one man who 'enlisted with the Irish Rugby footballers', another 'well known in football circles', and another 'very useful member of the cricket and hockey elevens'.[24]

The doctor's dead son, Paddy Tobin, had been a member of Lansdowne FC, a Dublin rugby club, and had appeared regularly in earlier Irish newspapers on account of these achievements.[25] By 1913, this sportsman had matriculated at Trinity College Dublin, and in the following year had established himself as part of the university first team, playing alongside others who would die at the Dardanelles during the same assault.[26] Paddy Tobin's enthusiasm for rugby was well-known at his father's hospital, which in 1914 had fielded a team that included the student.[27] These and other stories doubtless circulated on the wards that O'Casey inhabited during 1915, preparing the way for Harry Heegan's tragic narrative.[28]

When O'Casey came to write *The Silver Tassie*, he decided to dramatize the dichotomy implied in these war reports, between the young and healthy bodies of the athletic men before the war, and the destruction of the front. Of course, other writers also made such links at this time. In *Ulysses*, James Joyce portrays a group of schoolboys who come from, as Robert Spoo puts it, 'well-to-do families with English or Scottish names like Cochrane, Talbot, and Armstrong – [who] will be officer material in ten years'.[29] Hence Joyce's description of a hockey match in 1904 prefigures the horror of trench warfare and bayonet fighting, with the schoolboys engaging in 'the frozen deathspew of the slain, a shout of spear spikes baited with men's bloodied guts'.[30]

But if Joyce hints at the horror of the trenches, O'Casey confronts audiences with a more extensive meditation on the consequences of war. By act three of *The Silver Tassie*, the cup-winning footballer is confined to a hospital ward, with the lower half of his body irredeemably paralysed. The play's final act contains ironic echoes of the first, triumphant appearance of Harry, but now the slogans and the sporting achievements are viewed through the prism of destruction and loss, with the club's motto positioned onstage alongside a list of war dead. Terence Brown therefore suggests that *The Silver Tassie* took inspiration from a poem of Wilfred Owen's published in 1919, 'Disabled', a piece describing a former footballer who had been 'After the matches, carried shoulder-high', but whose legs were amputated during the war and now sits in a wheelchair while the 'women's eyes/ Passed from him to the strong men that were whole'.[31] Certainly *The Silver Tassie* shows a football hero being carried shoulder-high at the start of the play, but who ends up confined to a wheelchair, impotent and dismally aware that his one-time girlfriend yearns for other men.

Anti-Christ

When O'Casey wrote *The Silver Tassie* he also recycled ideas from a naturalistic Abbey play, set in wartime London, called *Anti-Christ*. This drama, by the Dubliner Frank Hugh O'Donnell, premiered in March 1925 and describes a demobilized captain of an infantry regiment who before the war had been a dandy and a ladies' man, but who lost his eyesight in an explosion at the front. Another soldier in the play is a former violinist, for whom all sense of beauty has vanished after he bayoneted a German. Robert Hogan describes the drama as a 'seminal' influence on *The Silver Tassie*, and O'Casey's own comments on O'Donnell's work betray some familiar anxiety about influence.[32] When O'Casey saw the premiere of *Anti-Christ* he told Lady Gregory that he 'didn't care a lot for the play', although he did manage to sit through the play for a second time that August.[33]

The most significant reimagining of *Anti-Christ* comes in the final scene of *The Silver Tassie*, when Harry Heegan interrupts the music, dancing and courtship of a party to remind the participants of his own shattered body. Here O'Casey directly emulates the final scene of O'Donnell's play, in which a dance is in progress, featuring young men and women who are 'all young, all in love'.[34] Into this setting stumbles a character who tells the assembly that the blind captain, John Boles, has been committed to a lunatic asylum, and when the partygoers greet this news with indifference, the messenger launches a verbal attack on them:

> What does anyone care? All hopping and flapdoodling. To-morrow when people read the papers they'll just say to one another at street corners 'So Boles was mad poor devil. It's well they got him in time'. Then they'll all go back to their small jobs again, all falling mechanically into their groves – the blind doddering idiots. And Boles can keep shouting and hoping – blind – blind – do you hear – for you and all of you [. . .] (*He laughs hysterically as if he discovers some great truth. He goes to the door and hisses back at them*) Men died for you. You lot of fools, mad men. (*He screams with laughter and goes*).[35]

The Silver Tassie replicates this scene, but literalizes the violence, as Harry interrupts the ballroom dance, castigates his former girlfriend as 'whore', and threatens her, Othello-style, 'If I had my hands on your white neck I'd leave marks there that crowds of kisses from your Barney wouldn't wipe away' (II, 99). Harry then brawls with Barney and flings the silver tassie to the floor.

Expressionism

O'Casey had found it difficult to write *The Silver Tassie*, in part because, after the fuss over *The Plough and the Stars*, he had moved to London, where the various distractions of literary life tended to interrupt his writing. He had also tried to write a play that avoided replicating his earlier work. As Lennox Robinson tartly observed, O'Casey 'couldn't go on writing slum plays for ever and ever'.[36] But O'Casey's struggle to achieve a new style, setting and subject-matter made the Abbey's rejection even more difficult to accept, and he complained to Gregory that the theatre had overthrown its original constitution, which had boasted of 'the freedom to experiment'.[37]

In March 1926, roughly two months before O'Casey started work on *The Silver Tassie*, he wrote to Huntly Carter, a proponent of alternative forms of theatre, to declare that 'I was delighted with your Modern Drama in Europe', a recently published volume that examined the effect of the war upon European theatre.[38] Although O'Casey often maintained terrific grudges against critics, here he praised a book that announced of him, 'Unfortunately, he has fallen into the net of middle-class conventional technique – a circumstance which fully illustrates the powerful influence of middle-class out-of-date methods'.[39]

O'Casey nonetheless felt 'delighted' with this description because it chimed with his sense of his own development. O'Casey wanted to avoid being defined by what Carter called 'stark realism' and the 'out-of-date' middle-class methods of naturalism, and so attempted to embrace a more expressionistic style, discovering a model to emulate in Strindberg.[40] Mid-way through O'Casey's writing of *The Silver Tassie*, he watched a production of Strindberg's *The Father* at the Everyman Theatre in London in August 1927, and wrote a rather odd letter of congratulation to Robert Loraine, the actor who had played one of the main parts. O'Casey declared:

> We thank you and your comrades for your and their revelation of *The Father*. Would that I could see you and them playing in *The Dance of Death*.
>
> Kyrie Eleison, Robert Loraine, Christie [*sic*] Eleison.[41]

This 'Kyrie Eleison' is, to say the least, an unorthodox way to sign off, as the phrase derives from the opening of the Catholic Mass, and means 'Lord have mercy, Christ have mercy'. O'Casey had been toying with that particular phrase during this period, and employs the same words in *The Silver Tassie*, where, amidst a ruined monastery, a voice intones '*Kyr. . .ie. . .e. . .eleison. Kyr. . .ie. . .e. . .eleison, followed by the answer: Christe. . .eleison*' (II, 36).

The letter to Loraine that O'Casey wrote mid-way through his work on *The Silver Tassie*, in which he praises Strindberg and includes this chant, reveals something of O'Casey's developing theatrical thinking. The Swedish dramatist showed how a writer might transcend naturalistic modes of composition, and move into an increasingly experimental and fantastic style. By these lights, expressionism might not be the binary opposite of, but an outgrowing from, naturalism, and thus O'Casey's letter praises *The Dance of Death*, a play that sits on the cusp of this development in Strindberg's oeuvre. As Eszter Szalczer puts it, Strindberg's 'title already suggests we should not take everything literally. The environment is highly metaphorical – a projection of the characters' mutual state of mind rather than a realistic setting'.[42] Hence the action of Strindberg's drama occurs in the tower of a former prison on an island known as 'little hell', and perhaps inspired O'Casey to set parts of *The Silver Tassie* in a similar symbolic hell in which everything is a little '*distorted*' from reality (II, 36).

Gabriel Fallon points out that Ernst Toller's play *Masse Mensche* ('masses and man') became another key influence on O'Casey's developing expressionism at this time, although, characteristically, O'Casey denied the connection. In 1935 O'Casey had declared that Ernst Toller's *Seven Plays* was 'in many ways a holy book', but in 1953, after the critic David Krause had spotted Toller's influence on the Irishman, O'Casey wrote that 'Toller has had no influence whatever upon me [. . .] I have never read a play by Toller twice, and admire only his MASSES AND MEN, though I find this too timid and too much of a wail'.[43] Nevertheless, Fallon performed in a production of *Masse Mensche* by the Dublin Drama League in 1925, which O'Casey came to watch, with Fallon claiming that 'it was the form even more than the content of the play that appealed to him'.[44]

Toller's play tells the story of Sonja, who leads a workers' strike during wartime, despite opposition from her husband, a bourgeois capitalist who protests, vainly, against her involvement. A nameless figure tells Sonja that only through violence will justice be achieved, and a brutal insurgency begins; although ultimately the revolutionaries lose and Sonja is executed. Notably the work proceeds by alternating episodes that advance the story with dream scenes that develop the meaning and significance of the action, and each time there is a 'real' part of the plot, there follows a 'fantasy' sequence. For example, in scene three, Sonja comes to understand the need to adopt strong-arm tactics, followed by a dream section featuring dancing and chanting figures. In that latter sequence, dancers represent both sentries and victims, and the interchangeable positioning of these two groups helps develop the meaning of the preceding scene, namely by showing how, if you are willing to use brutality, you are likely to find yourself hoist on your own petard.[45] In this way, Toller explores his theme by using stylized setting, words and movements, disrupting any audience notion that the play might present a linear progression of recognizably real-life situations.[46]

For those who dislike O'Casey's later plays, the absorption of such expressionism is precisely the moment where his career went wrong. According to such thinking, this autodidact was ill-equipped to adopt techniques from Toller and Strindberg, and should have remained within the traditions of melodrama, music hall and Abbey-Theatre naturalism, in which he and his Dublin audience had been more thoroughly schooled. Undoubtedly the Abbey rejected O'Casey's play in part because it emulated alien ideas, with the playhouse's directors feeling bemused by that Toller-ish shift from first-act realism into a fantastical second act where O'Casey sought to develop the meaning of the opening section by abandoning the lifelike setting as well as all of the characters he had just introduced. Lennox Robinson wrote 'I don't think the mixture of the two manners – the realism of the first act and the un-realism of the second – succeeds, and the characters who were Dublin slum in the beginning [of] the play end by being nowhere'.[47]

Toller himself argued against those who criticized him for alternating reality and dream by saying, 'These pictures of "reality" are not realism, are not local colour; the protagonists [. . .] are not individual characters. Such a play can only have a spiritual, never a concrete reality'.[48]

O'Casey too had been moving against the notion that his plays simply portrayed 'reality', and although Toller's work provided a catalyst for a change in dramaturgical strategy, O'Casey's work did not undergo a simple shift from the photographic to the symbolic. Most notably, the second act of *The Plough and the Stars* had already drifted into Toller territory, as J. L. Styan writes, 'In the brilliant act II of this play, the heated patriotic oratory of the shadowy figure outside the pub, heard in counterpoint with the increasingly noisy, drunken voices inside, is halfway to creating a ritualistic effect of the expressionistic kind'.[49] As we saw in Chapter 2, O'Casey's playwriting strategy had always involved blending together a range of non-naturalistic influences, and as early as 1926, the playwright Dennis Johnston had drawn attention to the wrongheaded idea that O'Casey might be an entirely realist dramatist, writing:

> It is becoming more and more clear that as a realist he [O'Casey] is an imposter. He will tell you the name and address of the person who made each individual speech in any of his plays, but we are not deceived by his protestations. His dialogue is becoming a series of word-poems in dialect; his plots are disappearing and giving place to a form of undisguised expressionism.[50]

Thus the second act of *The Silver Tassie* deepened an effect for which O'Casey had already striven, avoiding telling a straightforward story about the protagonists of act one but deepening the symbolic meaning of that initial act through song, rhythmical movements and repetitive chant. During the newspaper furore about Yeats's rejection of the play, the dramatist and former Abbey manager St John Ervine waded into the public debate to declare, 'Mr. O'Casey is experimenting in his new play, and, although his experiment is not entirely successful, it is very impressive [. . .] I am nearly certain that, in performance, it will seize and hold the mind. The Abbey's directors made a grave mistake in rejecting it'.[51] Amidst the swirl of hostile judgements about O'Casey's play, Ervine provided a sound verdict here, and one that continues to stand the test of time. O'Casey had indeed written one of the boldest pieces of twentieth-century Irish drama, creating a script that, although in need of the careful editorial attention given to his earlier works, can still be profoundly affecting when staged by skilled performers.

Meanwhile, in London, O'Casey worked on a 1929 production of *The Silver Tassie* at the Apollo Theatre with Charles Cochran, a producer already known to O'Casey via Huntly Carter's book on drama. Cochran later described the second act as 'without exception the finest symbolic scene I can recall on the London stage'.[52] Yet Cochran's engagement with O'Casey proved fleeting, and the London director ended up urging O'Casey to 'get back to the method of "Juno"'.[53] In this way, then, the rejection of *The Silver Tassie* did mark a shift in O'Casey's career, although hardly because O'Casey lacked the capacity to absorb and incorporate a new set of theatrical ideas from continental Europe. Rather, from that moment onwards he wrote without a regular theatre audience in mind, and missed the kind of careful, if blunt, advice that had shaped his earlier work. He tended to publish his subsequent scripts in advance of performance, without the words having been tested and refined in rehearsal, or understood by an audience in a performance context. In 1949, the year in which he redrafted *The Silver Tassie*, he admitted that the Abbey 'gave me the power through rehearsals, to amend or alter. Since then, all my plays have had to be published before production; I've had no aid from rehearsals, & so each – except "Cockadoodle Dandy," I think – needed touching here and there'.[54]

For consistency and ease of reference, the default setting of this book is to refer to the plays as published in Macmillan's *Complete Plays*, but O'Casey, who felt increasingly divorced from the practicalities of theatre making, certainly did not view those texts as definitive or unalterable, and there exist a number of variant versions of his scripts. For example, the version of *The Silver Tassie* published in 1928 has a completely different ending to the revised version later published by Macmillan in *Three More Plays* and also in the *Complete Plays*. In the 1928 version, after Jessie comments 'Poor Harry!', the nurse Susie Monican comments simply 'Oh nonsense! If you'd passed as many through your hands as I, you'd hardly notice one', before pulling Jessie from the chair towards Barney's embrace.[55] This provides a harsh dismissal of Heegan, and O'Casey later rewrote this passage to foreground a more sympathetic interpretation of why the onstage characters need to move on with their lives and cannot dwell on the distress of the paralysed soldier. In the revised version, Susie gives a longer monologue at this point in the play, reflecting, 'We can't give sight to the blind or make the lame walk. We would if we could. It is the misfortune of war' (II, 103). In the first version of 1928, the characters then dance a tango, before Susie sings a song that explicitly criticizes Harry by declaring 'He is gone, we remain, and so/ Let him wrap himself up in his woe'.[56] But in the revised script, the characters dance a more sombre waltz, and the song criticizes those who are morose in general rather than attacking Harry directly: 'He to whom joy is a foe,/ Let him wrap himself up in his woe' (II, 103). O'Casey thus retreated from the live-and-let-die conclusion that he had originally included, perhaps uncertain about how that might play with audiences still raw from the conflict.

When he wrote his subsequent scripts, O'Casey grew accustomed to flying blind in this way, increasingly distanced from the realm of the playhouse. But of course the rejection of *The Silver Tassie* also had unfortunate consequences for the Abbey Theatre, which bade a sad farewell to its reputation for innovation. The excitement of those early years, during which Synge as well as O'Casey had premiered work in Dublin, now gave way to a mid-century mediocrity, as the playhouse singularly failed to recreate its earlier glories. In 1928, at the time of the *Tassie*'s rejection, the government representative on the Abbey board broke ranks to tell the press 'I should like to see it on the stage'.[57] Lady Gregory soon came to agree, watching *The Silver Tassie* in London the following year and writing in her diary that the Abbey should have produced the play.[58] Even Yeats eventually saw the merits of O'Casey's text, asking to produce it at the Abbey in 1935.[59]

At the time of the play's rejection, Yeats wrote to Gregory, 'The tragedy is that O'Casey is now out of our saga'.[60] Meanwhile O'Casey filled the time by drawing cartoons of himself being barred from the Abbey or of himself adopting a fighting pose. He signed a letter of 11 May to Yeats 'Farewell', and a Parthian shot appeared in the *Irish Times*: 'I feel that the rejection of the play has done more harm to the Abbey than it has done to me, and it would be unhuman of me to say that I was sorry for that. So for the present, good-bye all, and cheerio'.[61]

Within the Gates

From 1930, O'Casey set about writing another play, *Within the Gates*, which he published in 1933 and premiered in London at the start of 1934, winning praise from certain key admirers. G. Wilson Knight, for example, declared that 'O'Casey's experience as a war dramatist enables him to master the far harder task of dramatizing peace through a number of *ritual conflicts*; and the interest never flags'.[62] Meanwhile the US critics spoke highly of the piece, with George Jean Nathan labelling the play 'one of the true masterpieces of the modern theatre', and Brooks Atkinson proclaiming that he had never seen anything so grand in the theatre.[63]

The text itself advances the playwriting style of *The Silver Tassie*, with an expressionistic method dominating the onstage action. We see four highly stylized scenes, set in each of the four seasons at a different time of day, revolving around characters with symbolic names such as 'the Dreamer', 'the Bishop' or 'the Atheist'. Such innovative writing calls to mind the work of other avant-garde writers. For example, O'Casey's placard-bearing characters achieve the kind of effect that would later become widely associated with Brecht; John O'Riordan sees the play as akin to the spiritual paralysis and 'heap of broken images' described in Eliot's 1922 poem *The Waste Land*; while Christopher Murray discerns a Nietzschean influence.[64] Certainly the London-based O'Casey owned a copy of Nietzsche, positioned alongside volumes of Balzac and Shakespeare in such a way as to catch the eye of visiting journalists.[65]

However, the premiere of *Within the Gates* met with generally lukewarm reviews, and O'Casey felt disappointed by the production, which survived for only 28 performances.[66] The *Observer* even hinted that the play would have done better in Dublin, with Ivor Brown writing that 'In a foreign country a new play by a dramatist of Mr. O'Casey's distinction would be produced at a State Theatre, with all its resources'.[67] Indeed, a disillusioned O'Casey had burnt his bridges in Ireland, but now found great difficulty in producing work in London, where the theatrical landscape looked bewilderingly unfamiliar. Admittedly, the play met with better fortunes in the United States, where it was staged for 141 performances before falling victim to religious protestors who forced the cancellation of a regional tour.[68]

Something of O'Casey's dissatisfaction with this play can be deduced from it becoming his most extensively revised work. The original volume published in 1933 differs in many places to the script in the *Complete Works*, with the redrafted version labelled the 'stage version' to distinguish it from the original 'play of four scenes'. Although the broad plot as outlined at the start of this chapter is the same in both cases, O'Casey made considerable changes by adding dialogue, deleting characters and inadvertently making the work less coherent. The platform speakers of Hyde Park, for example, who play a prominent part in the original act three, vanish from O'Casey's revised version, making the need for the play's location less clear. Similarly, in the earlier 1933 script, the war memorial onstage is clearly part of the story. The prostitute's mother marries a soldier who is then killed in the conflict, and the mother's sense of loss leads to alcoholism and the disintegration of the family. We are told that this mother 'began to mourn the memory of 'er husband. She began to manufacture wreaths of laurel leaves en' scarlet poppies, completing a new one weekly en' dumping each on a different memorial'.[69] However, in the revised version, although this mother has again lost a husband in the war, the obsessive form of her grieving is unexplained, and so the onstage memorial becomes a kind of decorative add-on rather than something integral to the story.

After the UK production of *Within the Gates*, the London publisher Jarrolds contacted O'Casey. The recent play had revealed O'Casey's interest in Hyde Park, chiming with Jarrolds' plans to print the autobiography of a real-life orator from that location, Bonar Thompson. O'Casey agreed to write a preface to this autobiographical volume, and found a number of resonances with his own experiences. After all, Thompson describes himself as an Irish exile in London who had worked on the railways as a manual labourer, during which time he educated himself by reading books and pamphlets. However, O'Casey's preface to the volume proved ungenerous, commenting that 'Bonar Thompson hasn't observed things vividly', and continuing:

He must learn to observe instinctively what is worth observing, then look long, and gather into his mind all that can and must be gathered in of the things he sees and of the things he hears. He must think a lot less of himself, and a lot more of others. By his own declaration, he finds it too easy to write. Had he found the gathering of thoughts together a hard thing to do, he would have written a far, far better biography of himself. But he deserves a better abiding-place than a rickety platform in Hyde Park, and I hope the book may be his first step down from that high place to a safer, sounder, if less arrogant place on the paths and in the byways of life.[70]

Ironically, these criticisms anticipate the hostile pronouncements that later reviewers would make about O'Casey's own work, but despite the negative tone, the publisher decided to print O'Casey's comments as the preface to Thompson's work. O'Casey did admit that Thompson's 'reminiscences of his young days, and of all that happened to him in Antrim, are, perhaps, the best things in the book; but the descriptions given are too fitful, as indeed are all those given by the author of what happened to him in Ireland'.[71] O'Casey evidently felt that he could do better, believing that he could describe his own younger days in a less 'fitful' and more 'vividly' observed way.

Autobiographies

O'Casey therefore began to write a similar autobiographical volume, initially feeling spurred into action by the hostility of the Abbey Theatre. He had 'thought of writing a book reminiscent of my experiences' as early as August 1926, but it was not until after the rejection of *The Silver Tassie* that he began to set his ideas down, writing his narrative in the third-person.[72] In an *Observer* interview of 1929 he declared that he had now 'written part of an autobiography', and one of his unpublished notebooks contains an early draft dating from 1929 or 1930, outlining a number of events from his life, such as a fight with his sister, which would disappear from the printed version.[73] He had initially envisaged writing just one book, but in 1938, after he had finished the first volume about his childhood, he told his publisher

Harold Macmillan that two more volumes now required completion. By 1945 O'Casey had admitted that a fourth volume might be needed, and although he referred to that as the 'last' instalment, by 1951 he had to confess that 'I've written a lot of a 5th vol. Of biography, & now fear I shan't be able to end it without another one'.[74] Thus O'Casey eventually composed his autobiography over the course of two decades, publishing six volumes between 1939 and 1954, and describing his life from birth up until the age of 73.

The titles of the individual volumes of autobiography reveal the piecemeal nature of the project. The first three refer to a metaphorical house: *I Knock at the Door*, *Pictures in the Hallway*, and *Drums Under the Windows*. But if O'Casey set about constructing a building, he kept extending that building in unusual and unexpected ways. The name of the fourth volume, *Inishfallen Fare Thee Well*, is taken from a Thomas Moore poem of migration from Ireland ('Sweet Inishfallen, fare thee well'); the penultimate title, *Rose and Crown*, is a pub name indicating O'Casey's residence in England rather than Ireland; and the final volume, *Sunset and Evening Star* takes a cue from Tennyson's 1889 poem 'Crossing the Bar', a poem of Christian piety that begins, 'Sunset and evening star/ And one clear call for me'.[75]

Despite the fact that O'Casey had scarcely planned the volumes as one unified work, a number of features do bind the autobiographies, and one of these is O'Casey's sense of grievance over 1928. As Michael Kenneally observes, 'No other event is returned to more frequently or analysed in such detail; repeatedly, the narrative draws attention to the paramount influence that the *Tassie* controversy had on the life of the protagonist'.[76] O'Casey surely felt the victim of a monumental injustice. Indeed, in *Rose and Crown* he sets out the full production history of *The Silver Tassie* from 1928 until 1951, and concludes:

> The Irish critics have made all the use they could of the Abbey's first rejection of the play, and have pursued it with curious and persistent hatred; but it still refuses to lie down. Peace, be still, heart of O'Casey: It is only Ireland that abuses the play now. Everywhere else, the play has been accepted as a fine and courageous experiment in modern drama. (*Auto* III, 42)

O'Casey emphasizes that the Abbey's rejection simply constituted the theatre's initial reaction, and is at pains to describe how the playhouse, and others, belatedly embraced the play. But he nevertheless demonstrates a sense of persecution so acute that even setting these memories onto the page, many years later, is likely to induce tachycardia.

Indeed, the key details of O'Casey's family life play second-fiddle to the fate of *The Silver Tassie*, giving the books a slightly odd sense of priority. At one point in the autobiographies he describes writing the text: 'He calculated the play would run in the Abbey for at least three weeks, maybe four, and the royalties he'd get would about cover the expenses of the birth of his child' (*Auto* III, 23). But up until this point in the autobiography, O'Casey has conspicuously failed to mention his courtship and marriage of his wife Eileen, let alone her pregnancy and the arrival of his son Breon. In this way, then, the autobiographies reveal the extent of the injury that had been inflicted on the playwright by the *Tassie* affair, and attest to the long-lasting trauma of 1928.

Joyce

When O'Casey sought a new direction after the fiasco of the *Tassie*, he increasingly considered that the best writer of the age worked primarily as a novelist rather than a dramatist. In 1926, O'Casey 'ferreted out a copy of "Ullyses" [*sic*] at last', and then found himself falling increasingly under the influence of 'the bould [*sic*] & (to me) great James Joyce'.[77]

In the following years O'Casey idolized Joyce, and, although the two men never met, O'Casey felt delighted in 1939 to receive a letter from the novelist that pointed out a misprint in the *Irish Times*, attributing authorship of the newly published *Finnegans Wake* to O'Casey. Joyce wrote, 'I hope it may be prophetical and that we may some day meet. When my wife recovers from an attack of influenza we are going to see your play [*Juno*] at the Theatre de l'Oeuvre and if I find that it is attributed to me I shall certainly send you the programme'.[78] O'Casey responded with warm praise for *Finnegans Wake*:

> A friend here (a painter) and I often read it (or try to) together; and I, it is fair to say, am better than he, and lead him into many a laugh and into the midst of wonder and wonderland. It is an amazing book; and hardly to be understood in a year, much less a day. I've had constant contact with you in 'Dubliners' and 'Portrait of the Artist'; and in 'Ulysses' – that great and amazing work.[79]

O'Casey viewed himself as being exiled and despised just like Joyce, and derived comfort from the idea that Dublin's literary clique had put them both beyond the pale.

An increasingly Joycean tone is therefore found in the autobiographies. For example, when O'Casey describes the *Playboy* riots he places himself in the midst of a protesting crowd, which consists of a list of fictional figures including the music-hall character of 'the man who broke the bank at Monte Carlo' (*Auto* II, 107). This section recalls a distinctly Joycean asyndeton, with the Cyclops chapter of *Ulysses* even including the same listed reference to Monte Carlo's celebrated gambler.[80] But as a result, a number of reviewers noted that O'Casey affected an artificial voice, and the writer felt particularly riled by George Orwell, who unsheathed a vorpal sword on *Drums Under the Windows* because 'large portions of it are written in a simplified imitation of the style of "Finnegan's [*sic*] Wake," a sort of Basic Joyce, which is sometimes effective in a humorous aside, but is hopeless for narrative purposes'.[81]

This review can scarcely be remembered as Orwell's finest hour. He misreads both O'Casey and Yeats, includes a bitter attack on O'Casey's right to live in England, and compares Irish writers to fleas.[82] But O'Casey could never forgive and forget such animadversions, however giddy, and responded to Orwell's charges by writing a letter to the *Observer*, which the newspaper refused to publish.[83] Instead, O'Casey included a stinging attack on Orwell in the later autobiographical volume *Sunset and Evening Star*, mocking Orwell's 'self pity' and the Englishman's desire 'to drag all life down with himself to his own stony despair' (*Auto* III, 294). O'Casey felt particularly riled by Orwell's accusation that the autobiographies emulated Joyce, and responded with the declaration:

> Basic Joyce! Bad or good; right or wrong, O'Casey's always himself. Of course Sean did this and did that, because he was alive, and will go on doing this, doing that till something called death stops him. Everybody's doing it, doing it, doing it. The low note about cogging from Joyce is particularly ironical, seeing that in his first venture, sent to Sean for an opinion, Orwell himself tried to imitate Joyce, not here and there only, but in whole scenes as near to the genius as Joyce as Sean's few verses are near to the poetical genius of Shakespeare. (*Auto* III, 298)

O'Casey added, 'Orwell has as much chance of reaching the stature of Joyce as a tit has of reaching that of an eagle' (*Auto* III, 299), and in personal correspondence wrote even more caustically, describing Orwell as 'like a wolf mad with the mange, as Hitler was a wolf mad with a jaundice against the Jew'.[84]

In a more fair-minded assessment of O'Casey, Hubert Nicholson commented that the Dubliner 'has been accused lately of imitating (I suppose "imitating badly" is meant) James Joyce. He is certainly no Daedalus, no maze-maker, as Joyce is; but to me he seems the one completely natural inheritor of some of the Joyce techniques'.[85] Nevertheless, the clash with Orwell made O'Casey wary of acknowledging that Joycean influence, declaring in 1962:

> I wasn't influenced by James Joyce any more than all who read him were. I was too old to be influenced by him . . . The glimpses of influence given in the biography were more a desire to show my admiration for this great writer [. . .] Joyce's influence was like a bugle call, loud and clear at first, fading away as it was being heard . . . very soon forgotten.[86]

Of course, as with so many of O'Casey's statements about his life and work, that Petrine denial can scarcely be taken at face value.

In Memoriam

Although this chapter has so far described O'Casey's autobiographies as a six-volume enterprise, the writer did in fact produce a seventh autobiographical work. On his death in 1964, his family discovered a diary among his papers, but withheld the text from publication until 1991, when Calder press published the slim volume under the title *Niall*. The journal dates from a sad, late time in O'Casey's life, in the period after his second son, Niall, died at the age of only 21 at Christmas in 1956. At this point, the playwright felt utterly bereft, left in an apartment he described as 'quiet, & full of echoes', with a wife who made a despairing, although thankfully unsuccessful, attempt at suicide.[87]

Niall therefore contains a number of stark, poetic and profoundly moving descriptions of O'Casey's loss. Indeed, in 1992 the *New Theatre Quarterly* declared 'It records an intensely private grief and clearly should have remained private'.[88] Christopher Murray agrees that 'It would be an obscenity to intrude too far upon such a text not written for publication'.[89] Nevertheless, O'Casey's widow carefully edited and approved the volume, and O'Casey himself thought of the work in consciously literary terms, citing a telling range of writers from Tennyson to Hardy and Blake. In any case, O'Casey produced a chapter-length version of these reflections in his 1963 volume *Under a Coloured Cap*, and this earlier publication is scarcely any less grief-stricken. He evidently thought of the full diary as a coda to the six-part published autobiography, which had concluded with his thoughts about raising children in the nuclear age. The sixth volume had argued that money should be spent on cures for child-killing diseases rather than on weapons, but nevertheless concluded with a sunny view of life, with the concluding word being 'Hurrah'. The writing of *Niall* forced him to revisit these ideas about the illness and death of children, and to reassess his upbeat conclusion:

> At the end of the biographical volume, *Sunset and Evening Star*, I wrote a 'hurrah for life!' It was meet and right so to do. From one of seventy and over, it was but a fair tribute to the many years life had given.

But could a young lad of twenty-one say the same thing when he knew he was about to die? Could he give such a tribute to life which had given him so little; denied him so much?[90]

Like the earlier volumes of the autobiographies, *Niall* cannot be read as a straightforwardly factual account. For example, the date of his son's death is often wrong, with O'Casey describing how 'on the last day of the year, he died'.[91] In editing the book for publication Eileen O'Casey assiduously noted on each occasion, 'An error of memory: Niall died on 30 December, 1956', but of course, as so often in the earlier autobiographies, the author concerns himself with the symbolic rather than the literal truth.

After the torrent of words that we find in the earlier autobiographies, *Niall* shows how O'Casey has become aware that language is quite inadequate for describing his lived experience. Much as Lear grieves his dead daughter through wordlessness, so O'Casey's written lament begins:

30 December. 1956 Niall died.
 5 January 1957
12   "
19   "
26   "
 2 February
 9   "
16   "
23   "
 2 March
 9   "
16   "
23   "
30   "
 6 April
13   "

Oh, God, to think of it; I buried a father when I was a little boy, and a son when I was an old, old man.[92]

The earlier autobiographies, which begin with that death of his father, allow little room for doubt. O'Casey always knows who his enemies are, knows whose arguments are right and wrong, and knows how to set about justifying his own ideas and actions. But in the lament there is little of this surefootedness. Here language begins to break down, to confront the reader with a terrible sense of uncertainty: about the universe, the purpose of life and about the process of writing itself, a 'foolish' and 'useless practice'.[93] Here O'Casey becomes something like the voice of Beckett's *The Unnamable*, realizing the folly of continuing to narrate, yet compelled to continue: 'I can't go on, I'll go on'.[94]

Of course, the character of Niall himself remains a void at the heart of the diary. The mourning parent simply cannot represent the boy in anything other than frozen, saintly terms, and so, despite the title, the book paradoxically displaces Niall to become a record about the writer himself. In O'Casey's own eyes the project therefore becomes an increasingly self-indulgent example of *Weltschmerz*, ending with the bald declaration that 'These weekly tributes to him are trifling and useless, bringing him no nearer, nor easing the ache of the sorrow of his going. I thought they might, but still each day he comes into my mind; and always will till I go too'.[95]

The text displays a hypnotic, repetitive and rhythmic quality, as O'Casey revolves monodic utterances about his loss again and again, never able to move on or feel that his pain has dulled, even though all about him is changing. One of the final entries in the lament declares, 'I see the senseless futility of war; of the shameless waste of energy and thought preparing for it, thought and energy that could be used in the destruction of the damned things that kill our young'.[96] Here O'Casey is revisiting his long-term preoccupations, still in the realm of Harry Heegan, Paddy Tobin, Johnny Boyle and the other dead sons and brothers cut down during the world war and the Irish revolution. For all the innovations in form and style, then, O'Casey ultimately returns to a long-term set of thematic interests, and had, in a way, indeed been correct to assert in response to Orwell that 'Bad or good; right or wrong, O'Casey's always himself' (*Auto* III, 298).

CHAPTER 4
COMMUNISM, 1936–46

The Star Turns Red (Published and Staged 1940)

It is Christmastime during a period of revolution, in a family home where two brothers clash over politics. The first sibling, Jack, joins the freedom-loving communists, but his brother Kian sides with fascist paramilitaries called the 'Saffron Shirts', who are supported by a repressive Catholic organization named the 'Christian Front'. Two clergymen arrive: a mean-spirited purple priest who helps the fascists, and a brown priest who supports the poor. These clerics try persuading Jack to abandon communism before the 'Saffron Shirts' threaten him, led by Kian. The fascists deem Jack's girlfriend Julia immodest, and drag her away for a flogging, and, when Julia's father objects, Kian shoots him dead, with Kian's name thus echoing that of history's first murderer. Meanwhile, a group of squabbling and corrupt union men, who are under pressure from the fascist purple priest, decide to abandon the charismatic workers' leader, Red Jim. But when Red Jim appears he refuses to stop urging revolution. The purple priest overreaches his authority by demanding that the workers remove a red flag from display over Julia's dead father. Red Jim arrives and defies the cleric, supported by a group of Red Guards who raise their fists, strike up drums and begin a chant. After a battle, the communists seize control of power. But Jack is killed during the fighting, and is borne in by Julia and by the brown priest, who has joined the communists. Kian finally realizes that Jack has been right, and, despite the purple priest's protestations, abandons fascism. At the end of the play, the onstage silver star of Christmas turns into the glowing red star of communism.

Purple Dust (Published 1940)

This comedy revolves around two self-satisfied Englishmen, the fat, city businessman Cyril Poges and thin, Oxford graduate Basil Stoke. Both have arrived in Ireland, accompanied by their Irish girlfriends, Souhan and Avril, in order to escape the Second World War. While the fighting rages, Poges and Stoke plan to renovate an old Tudor house in the Irish countryside, even though the local workmen believe this plan insane. Poges seeks to profiteer from the war by investing in a cement company, on the basis that shares will jump when the German bombing intensifies. The evident cowardice of the Englishmen contrasts with the bravery of the play's hero, the workers' boss Jack O'Killigain, an Irishman who has fought for the communists in Spain's Civil War. Avril, Souhaun and the maidservant are all attracted to Jack, with Avril even riding naked on horseback with him. The Englishmen hold patronizing and colonialist views, but are themselves revealed as buffoons, particularly when terrified by a stray cow that they think is a wild bull. Jack outwits the pretentious Poges, mocking the Englishman's sense of history and taste in poetry. Meanwhile Avril and Souhaun, having wheedled a yearly allowance of £500 from the Englishmen, flee to join Irish lovers. The building project itself descends into the chaos and 'purple dust' of the title. Poges and Stoke conclude that it might be dangerous to live in such a 'crazy' community, and the play ends with a cod-Wagnerian conclusion as the house is engulfed by a river that rises all around it.

Red Roses for Me (Published 1942)

Red Roses for Me revolves around Ayamonn Breydon, a 22-year-old Protestant socialist who lives in a Dublin tenement with his mother. Their neighbourhood is full of pious Catholics, for whom Ayamonn shows tolerance and fondness, and with one of whom, Sheila Moorneen, he is in love. However, Sheila is short-tempered and urges him to give up his 'foolish things': namely painting, Shakespeare and the cause of the workers. She tells him that a strike is going to take place, and urges him to distance himself from it. But he vehemently refuses, and agrees to speak at a socialist meeting, even though he knows of plans for violent repression of the event, where strikers will sing the song 'Red Roses for Me'.[1] Ayamonn then moves into the centre of Dublin, where 'bright and lovely' colours cover the set and the previously naturalistic scenery takes on a heroic aspect. Ayamonn sings and dances, and members of the Dublin crowd join in, before they are all interrupted by the ominous tramp of soldiers. The final part of the play is set at a church at the time of the Easter vigil, and the offstage noise of galloping horses and rifle fire can be heard. Some of those attacked by the soldiers plead to enter the church for sanctuary, before the news arrives that Ayamonn has been killed. His body arrives at the church, despite some opposition from his Protestant enemies, and the kindly rector leaves the lights up, declaring 'He's not so lonesome as you think, dear friend, but alive and laughing in the midst of God's gay welcome' (III, 227).

Oak Leaves and Lavender (Published and Staged 1946)

This play revolves around a manor-house in the west of England, owned by Dame Hatherleigh. During a prelude, the spirits of Hatherleigh's eighteenth-century ancestors dance around the stage and observe that the country is in danger. The rest of the action then takes place amid the Battle of Britain, during which the Irish butler of the house, Feelim, acts as Head Warden of the district. Feelim's English-born son, Drishogue, has fallen in love with Monica, the daughter of a local farmer. At the same time, another romance is blossoming between Dame Hatherleigh's son Edgar and a local land-girl, Jennie. But Edgar and Drishogue have become RAF (Royal Air Force) pilots, the 'hearts of oak' who will defend England, and both men join the squadron after spending time with those lovers. Ominously, the characters left in the house repeatedly smell lavender, which they associate with death, and see flames outside. Feelim defends himself against criticism that he is part of the 'selfish' Irish nation that remains neutral during the war, and his sacrifice becomes clearer when news arrives that his son Drishogue has crashed and died nearby. Edgar has also been killed in this burning plane, as well as his girlfriend Jennie, who vainly attempted to rescue the pilots. Nevertheless, the play ends on a note of optimism. The Red Army joins the battle, the great house is converted into a tank factory, and Monica reveals that she and Drishogue secretly married before his death, leaving her now pregnant with his child. Jennie, Edgar and Drishogue are all buried together, before finally the ghostly dancers return to receive the dying Hatherleigh.

O'Casey at the Barricades

On 17 July 1936 Spain's right-wing nationalists rose against a left-wing government that they found repressive, and the country's Civil War began. For the rest of Europe, this clash provided a chilling premonition of future conflict, as the Spanish right allied itself with international fascism, drawing support from Mussolini and Hitler, and inviting the Luftwaffe to use parts of Spain for target practice. Inexorably, only four months after this conflict ended, German troops invaded Poland, thus ensuring that, by May 1945, Europe had been engaged in total war, or in a dress rehearsal for that total war, for at least nine years.

Seán O'Casey was of course the great playwright of war. His early plays dealt with the conflict in Ireland; his first English plays tackled the fighting and aftermath of the First World War; and he now felt profoundly affected by events in Spain. For him, this latest battle crystallized the key conflicts of the age, with the hostilities not simply concerning the Azaña government and Spain's nationalist opposition, but the broader European tussle between left and right. As Frederick Benson points out, a whole host of particular circumstances unique to Spain in the 1930s meant that fighting occurred in that location: the country had a feudal system of landownership, a powerful Church, a decadent aristocracy, an anarchist tradition and irreconcilable political parties.[2] But, from the viewpoint of Devon, the Spanish conflict demonstrated whether fascists or communists would gain the upper hand in Europe, and whether the justice of left-wing politics or the injustice of the right would dominate world history.

Other cultural figures shared O'Casey's attitude toward the fighting. During Spain's Civil War, many international writers came out in support of the left-wing, republican side, with some, such as George Orwell, even enlisting as combatants. Others, such as E. M. Forster, H. G. Wells and Virginia Woolf, signed open letters of support for the republicans, and in the summer of 1937, O'Casey himself felt drawn into making a similar public pronouncement.[3] The poet and radical, Nancy Cunard, distributed a questionnaire for British and Irish authors to complete, which stated:

> To-day, the struggle is in Spain. To-morrow it may be in other countries – our own. But there are some who, despite the martyrdom of Durango and Guernica, the enduring agony of Madrid, of Bilbao, and Germany's shelling of Almeria, are still in doubt, or who aver that it is possible that Fascism may be what it proclaims it is: 'the saviour of civilisation'.
>
> This is the question we are asking you:
>
> Are you for, or against, the legal Government and the People of Republican Spain?
>
> Are you for, or against, Franco and Fascism?

The responses appeared in a book, *Authors Take Sides on the Spanish War*, published by the *Left Review* later that year. Unsurprisingly, the volume revealed that most respondents sympathized with the left. Ezra Pound and T. S. Eliot joined the handful who declared themselves neutral, while Evelyn Waugh liked neither option but declared that, if pushed, he would join the four who favoured the right.

O'Casey gave a less ambiguous response, writing: 'I am, of course, for a phalanx unbreakable round those who think and work for all men, and I am with the determined faces firing at the steel-clad slug of Fascism from the smoke and flame of the barricades'.[4] In a letter to George Jean Nathan, O'Casey declared in similar language, 'I'm still doing all I can to speed on the good work in Spain where the workers & thinkers & poets are alive in the flames of the barricades'.[5]

O'Casey primarily sought to 'speed on' the republican cause through the power of his writing. Shortly before the outbreak of the Spanish war, O'Casey admitted that, although he had an idea for another drama, creatively he had hit a brick wall. He told Nathan that the title of 'The Star Turns Red' sounded appealing, but 'I haven't started a new play yet. I am a little tired of all the rows that my plays caused'.[6] The events in Iberia, of course, sparked O'Casey back into life, and he completed this work between 1937 and January 1939, making the script into a forthright condemnation of fascism.[7] Originally, O'Casey planned an even more radical effect in this drama, envisaging a final scene in which a left-wing song would be 'commenced by one, by two, by three, then by ten. Carried on by a hundred, till the whole audience joins in'.[8]

Location

In O'Casey's previous plays, the writer had created settings that could be recognized as specific historical places, such as Dublin's tenements during the Irish revolution, the Western Front or post-war Hyde Park. But in *The Star Turns Red* O'Casey moves his action to a non-specific, mythical location. Here the battle parallels that of Spain, but other places and times are invoked too. The setting is 'tomorrow or the next day' (II, 240), something that scarcely coheres with the present tense of the title, 'the star *turns* red', nor with those aspects of the play that recall the Dublin lockout of 1913. Furthermore, although the play is inspired by the Church-fascist relations of the Spanish Civil War, the communist forces come to resemble the Russian Bolsheviks as depicted by Eisenstein in his 1927 film *October*.

In addition, certain aspects of *The Star Turns Red* recall what O'Casey had seen in contemporary London. O'Casey had noticed the newspaper controversy generated in March 1937 when an MP had asked a parliamentary question about a communist-party recruiting campaign, which used artwork showing a hammer and sickle superimposed upon a crucifix.[9] The poster transpired to be a fascist fake, designed to alienate London's Catholic workers from Spain's left-wingers. But O'Casey found a kind of inspiration in this image, and constructed a play in which comradely singing repeatedly drowns out Christian hymns, and in which the star of Bethlehem is ultimately displaced by the red star of communism.

The malevolent fascist paramilitaries of the play are called the 'saffron shirts', a name that echoes the Nazi paramilitary brownshirts who had played an active role in Germany during the 1920s and 1930s, as well as Mussolini's fascist blackshirts who had marched on Rome in 1922. But the saffron shirts look most similar to an organization that O'Casey had seen at closer quarters. O'Casey claimed to use the English newspaper the *Daily Mail* 'as I use the Bible – takes what I wants out of both, & leave the rest standing where it is', and in 1934 that journal came out in strong support of the blackshirted British Union of Fascists.[10] 'The Blackshirt Movement', declared the *Daily Mail*, 'is the organised effort of the younger generation to break the stranglehold which senile politicians have so long maintained'. 'Hurrah for the Blackshirts!' ran the publication's infamous headline, yet even after the newspaper abandoned this position, and Hitler invaded Austria, the British blackshirt leader Oswald Mosley could still attract 11,000 supporters to an indoor rally at Earl's Court.[11] Thus, when O'Casey jotted down his earliest ideas for *The Star Turns Red*, he considered the fascist 'apes' of his drama in terms of 'Mosley & his crew', and repeatedly thought of the fictional right-wingers as 'blackshirts'.[12] Unsurprisingly, in the published play, the fascist Kian wears the close-cropped moustache of Hitler and Mosley, and employs the greeting, 'Hail, the Circle and the Flash', an allusion to the lightning-in-a-circle emblem adopted by Mosley's followers. In real life, Mosley's enemies mocked this swastika-like symbol as 'a flash in the pan', and O'Casey accordingly puts this phrase into the mouth of a character who feels cynical about politics (II, 253).[13] O'Casey himself described Mosley as 'that peacock-feathered jay', and wanted to show in *The Star Turns Red* that despite all of the fascists' efforts to convey an impression of orderliness and discipline, the truly unified and well-trained force of revolution might come from the left.[14]

A range of European influences evidently affected O'Casey as he worked on his play, but the playwright continued to pay close attention to the political situation in Ireland, and, ultimately, the setting of *The Star Turns Red* looks more like some nebulous Irish place than anywhere else. In his homeland, the blueshirt movement boasted some 30,000 members in early 1933, connecting with the kind of populist Catholicism that saw Irish bishops leading the flock in noisy denunciations of Russian atheism. In March 1933 Dublin experienced a series of anti-communist protests during which right-wing crowds sang 'Faith of Our Fathers', something that would inspire the denouement of O'Casey's later play *Behind the Green Curtains*.[15] By August 1936 an organization called the Irish Christian Front had been established in order 'to help the stricken people of Spain in their struggle against the forces of international Communism', and the leaders of this loosely organized movement saw the fight against communism as akin to a crusade, which, *à la* George W. Bush, therefore justified violence.[16] As the Christian Front put it, 'we want the advance guard of the anti-God forces stopped in Spain and thereby from reaching our shores'.[17] In August 1936 the organization held a meeting of around 15,000 in Dublin, and crowds of over 40,000 turned out for rallies in Cork and Dublin later that year.[18] At the high-point of the Christian Front's support for Franco, the leader of Ireland's Blueshirts even took a brigade of 600 volunteers to fight for the nationalist cause in Spain.[19]

O'Casey illustrates what he felt to be the dangers of such a development. In *The Star Turns Red* the saffron shirts are paired with a nefarious organization called by the real-life name of the 'Christian Front'. During the play, this Christian Front opposes communism, holds a rally, and is described as a growing power (II, 285). The ideas propagated by the Catholic organization are parroted by the poor, who are unable to see the communists as liberators rather than bullies. However, the play relies so heavily on such references and allusions to contemporary political events that the piece looked somewhat dated when eventually performed. After all, the real-life Christian Front had petered out amidst financial controversies in mid-1937, while the eyes of Europe turned from Spain to another set of battles after 1939.

Frank Ryan

When O'Casey wrote *The Star Turns Red* he kept in close contact with an acquaintance who was both an old friend and a combatant in the Spanish conflict. Of course, the vast majority of those from Ireland who participated in the Spanish Civil War fought on Franco's side. But on 11 December 1936 a group of about 80 volunteers left to battle for the republicans under the leadership of the one-time IRA hero, Frank Ryan, who declared: 'Our fight is the fight of the Spanish people, as it is of all peoples who are the victims of tyranny'.[20]

However, Ryan received a bullet wound to the arm, which forced him home to recover, and during his recuperation he visited O'Casey in London on several occasions, with the playwright greatly enjoying their convivial discussions. O'Casey tried to persuade Ryan to avoid returning to the dangers of Spain, although Ryan refused to countenance such an idea, declaring that he 'couldn't think of leaving the boys by themselves'.[21] Ultimately, Ryan did trek back to Spain, to act as the most senior Irishman in the conflict, the adjutant of the Fifteenth Brigade. But O'Casey's warnings proved correct, and his friend never returned home. Spanish right-wingers captured and imprisoned Ryan for two years, before transferring him into the hands of German intelligence, leading to accusations that he acted as a collaborator with the Nazis before his death in Dresden in 1944.[22]

Frank Ryan's visits to O'Casey had an obvious impact on *The Star Turns Red*, which features a communist commander who is shot by the fascists, and also affected several of O'Casey's subsequent plays, which include Irish heroes who have fought for the left in Spain (in *The Bishop's Bonfire*, which will be discussed in the following chapter, the character of Manus also owes much to Ryan). After all, Ryan and O'Casey had a long association, having played hurling together when young, then finding themselves on opposite sides during the row over *The Plough and the Stars*, before being united once again in the 1930s by the fight against Franco. Indeed, such was O'Casey's feeling of reconciliation that he even felt happy to submit *The Star Turns Red* to the Abbey, commenting on the earlier riots, 'The Leader of the attack then [Frank Ryan] has now become one of my friends – I was never an enemy of his [. . .] He is really a splendid fellow'.[23]

This rebooted friendship may explain why parts of *The Star Turns Red* appear to rewrite the play that Ryan had once picketed, *The Plough and the Stars.* In both works, O'Casey repeats the same offstage action, with insurgents seizing a communications centre, and a child in the neighbourhood dying of consumption. Some specific stage business is also recycled, with soldiers invading a building at the end of both plays, and O'Casey redeploying same jokes, such as when unlikely figures declare themselves socialists. There are other indications in *The Star Turns Red* that O'Casey thought about the rebellion of 1916 when imagining what future communist revolution might look like. Most notably, O'Casey echoes Yeats's line about one of the Easter-week insurgents, 'Because I helped to wind the clock/ I come to hear it strike', although in *The Star Turns Red* the bewildered Lady Mayoress responds to such a suggestion with absurd literalism, 'What clock/ Which clock? Whose clock? [*To the old man*] What clock were they talking about?' (II, 339).[24]

O'Casey's renewed amity with Frank Ryan had helped emphasize communism's potential as a reconciling force, healing personal as well as wider social rifts. So when O'Casey updated the ideas he had explored in *The Plough and the Stars,* he could reject that earlier play's notion that political enthusiasm provided a problem, and instead assert that only the direction of that commitment could bring difficulties. Creating the character of Jack in *The Star Turns Red* provided the chance to rewrite the character of Jack Clitheroe from *The Plough and the Stars,* who fights and is shot in the Easter Rising, and who last appears in a display of callousness and violence, as his spouse tries to hold him back from the conflict. Clitheroe's commitment to politics thus causes him to disdain the comfort of home for battle, and to become a kind of wife-beater in the cause of nationalism, as she begs, 'Please, Jack. . . . You're hurting me, Jack. . . . Honestly. . . . Oh, you're hurting . . . me!' (I, 236).

The character of Jack who appears in *The Star Turns Red* provides the antidote. This time, sacrifice for a political cause is entirely commendable, and news of Jack's death is greeted with cheering and the sound of 'The Internationale', rather than the noise of slaughterhouse and madhouse. The characters onstage receive the announcement in the following way:

> **Jim:** (*to the silently crying Julia.*) He's not too far away to hear what's happening. You'll nurse, now, a far greater thing than a darling dead man. Up, young woman, and join in the glowing hour your lover died to fashion. He fought for life, for life is all; and death is nothing!
>
> (*Julia stands up with her right fist clenched. The playing and singing of 'The Internationale' grow louder. Soldiers and sailors appear at the windows, and all join in the singing. The Red Star glows, and seems to grow bigger as the curtain fails* [. . .]). (II, 353–4)

This later passage comes very close to endorsing the very notion of blood sacrifice that O'Casey had so lambasted in his earlier work, and wins *The Star Turns Red* the distinction of being O'Casey's most polemical play. O'Casey, having renewed his acquaintance with Frank Ryan, now found that this old antagonist from 1926 had become a leader of Irish troops in the Spanish Civil War, and so the playwright decided to revisit the themes of the drama that had driven a wedge between them. Ultimately O'Casey's later work endorses the notion that, if sacrifice is made in the cause of communist revolution, then that sacrifice will prove worthwhile.

Jack in the Books

In the play that O'Casey wrote next, *Purple Dust*, he employs a comic form that differs greatly from the utopianism of *The Star Turns Red*, but again the most attractive character onstage is a communist called Jack who has fought in Spain. With each of the previous incarnations of Jack having met a sticky end, O'Casey could scarcely resist giving the character of Jack in *Purple Dust* the punning surname O'Killigain ('kill again'), and once more, this latter Jack re-enacts a version of the climactic scene from *The Plough and the Stars* in which Nora had shouted 'Please, Jack. . . . You're hurting me':

> **O'Killigain:** [. . .] While you were livin' your lesser life, an' singin' your dowdy songs, I was fightin' in Spain that you might go on singin' in safety an' peace. (*He grips her arm*) I've come for you, now, me love.

> **Avril:** (*emotional and anxious.*) I cannot go where things are said and things are done, for love has had no voice in the beginning of them! (*She tries to free her arm*) Oh, Jack, let me go – you're hurting me! (III, 107)

However, this time all ends happily. In *Purple Dust*, O'Killigain has survived revolution and is returning home to seek romance, a reversal of Jack Clitheroe's storyline in *The Plough and the Stars*. Although Avril speaks Nora's lines about being hurt by Jack, this time the lovers end up running away together, and Jack serenades Avril with a climactic song about the need to 'Come away from the dyin' (III, 119). Political commitment and a loving family life prove incompatible in *The Plough and the Stars*, but in *Purple Dust* communist enthusiasm only increases the protagonist's virility and personal contentment.

Yet another version of Jack appears in O'Casey's World-War-Two drama *Oak Leaves and Lavender*, although this time he appears briefly, only speaking a short part of the script. His intervention nevertheless marks a decisive shift of tone in the play, helping to make that familiar O'Casey gear-change from naturalistic to expressionistic register. After the cry of 'Come on in, Jack!' a roughly dressed figure in tweed cap arrives to request help for the working-class victims of the Blitz, demanding angrily, 'Damn your eyes, give us shelters!' (IV, 77). This short and sturdy figure scarcely resembles the communist sex-symbol of *Purple Dust*, but does again defend the ordinary rights of the working people, and in response a proletarian crowd takes up his slogans as a chant. Meanwhile a younger and physically attractive figure, the character of Drishogue, explains that he will battle the Nazis because he is still haunted by the Spanish Civil War. As Drishogue explains:

> I'm fighting for the people. I'm fighting against the stormy pillagers who blackened the time-old walls of Guernica, and tore them down; who loaded their cannon in th' name of Christ to kill the best men Spain could boast of; who stripped the olive groves and tore up orange trees to make deep graves for men, heaping the women on the men, and the children on the women. I was too young then to go out armed for battle, but time has lengthened an arm long enough to pull the Heinkels and Dorniers out of the sky, and send them tumbling down to hell! (IV, 61)

In *Oak Leaves and Lavender*, then, the socialist sentiments are split between that older, cloth-cap-wearing Jack, and the second-generation Irishman, Drishogue. It takes little imagination to see a link here with O'Casey's hopes for real life. As the playwright moved towards second childishness, his eldest son, who faced British-army conscription, had world enough and time to continuing fighting on O'Casey's behalf.[25]

Two last characters with the autobiographical name of Jack appear briefly in the late plays that we will encounter in the following chapter. In *The Bishop's Bonfire* a worker is killed by a priest, after which the audience learns that the dead man is 'poor Jack' (IV, 195). Then finally, in the play that O'Casey wrote as an octogenarian, *The Drums of Father Ned*, the characters pause to listen to offstage footsteps going by. 'That's Jack the Cantherer', one of the characters reveals, before another declares that the noise of such footsteps will soon end: 'The little sounds we make on this earth, an' then we go: we whistle an' sing, we hammer an' saw, talk in anger an' talk in love, say a few prayers in a hurry; then we go, an' the little sounds cease' (V, 213).[26]

Red Roses for Me

Overall then, those left-wing plays of the 1930s and 1940s consistently spend time introducing a communist hero called Jack, who is often a veteran of the Spanish Civil War, and who serves to rebut the most famous character with that name in the oeuvre, the nationalist figure presented in *The Plough and the Stars*. But the best of O'Casey's plays from this period, *Red Roses for Me*, seems to deviate from this pattern, as here the main character is Ayamonn rather than Jack. However, *Red Roses for Me* is a revised and much improved version of a script from 1919, *The Harvest Festival*, which did indeed revolve around a character called Jack, a charismatic union man who is killed when a strike becomes violent. More than two decades after the Abbey had rejected *The Harvest Festival*, O'Casey recycled much of the plot and some of the same lines in *Red Roses for Me*. Thus, in both works, offstage gunfire and disturbance signify the violence of the strike, and in both plays the worker-hero dies at the end; although if the earlier version is an apprentice piece, the later play is a substantial achievement that has clearly benefitted from O'Casey's extensive editing and redrafting.

So why did Jack become Ayamonn in the revised play? O'Casey's early notes for *Red Roses* reveal how he originally considered the protagonist so autobiographical that the character's title alternates between 'Jack' and 'Sean', while the mother figure is labelled 'Mrs Casside'.[27] But when O'Casey worked up his drafts into the final version of *Red Roses for Me* he decided to incorporate elements from his autobiographical volume *Pictures in the Hallway*, where tram conductor called Ayamonn O'Farrel attends an anti-Boer-War protest and attacks a member of the mounted Dublin Fusiliers (*Auto* I, 368).[28] O'Casey presumably wanted to imbue *Red Roses for Me* with something of this gung-ho spirit, and so included Ayamonn's name in the play.

Nevertheless, despite bearing a different moniker, the leading figure of *Red Roses for Me* echoes all those other left-wing Jacks by showing just how praiseworthy it might be to sacrifice yourself for the correct political cause. *Red Roses for Me* thus shows Ayamonn being asked by an anonymous railwayman to speak on a platform at a socialist meeting, and when Shelia tries persuading him to avoid going for the sake of self-preservation, Ayamonn remains adamant about attending. The play does not present onstage this convocation of workers, where Ayamonn is killed by police, but does show him on his way there, when the orator is pictured in a scene of the 'finest colours God has to give', singing and dancing for joy. His lyrics and movements are then taken up by those around him, as he declares:

Fair city, I tell thee our souls shall not slumber
Within th' warm beds of ambition or gain;
Our hands shall stretch out to th' fullness of labour,
Till wondher an' beauty within thee shall reign. (III, 198–201)

Socialism, then, offers a kind of vibrant, life-giving energy, associated with song and light and fertility. Indeed, the orator here is the very opposite of the nationalist demagogue that O'Casey had once depicted in *The Plough and the* Stars, who uses Patrick Pearse's words to praise only the dead and the possibility of death. Ayamonn, by contrast, sees hope in burgeoning life, in those 'young ones at play' (III, 200). Although the final act of *Red Roses For Me* is set during the Easter vigil, then this is a consciously different paschal vision than that presented in *The Plough and the Stars*. In *Red Roses for Me*, just as in O'Casey's other major plays of this period, the playwright seeks to reverse the earlier cynicism that he had shown towards politics. In this later period he is still willing to lambast those who embrace the wrong cause, but shows that true believers in communism might nonetheless reach a kind of Elysium.

Shaw

When O'Casey received his copy of the *Authors Take Sides* questionnaire about the Spanish Civil War in 1937, he read the introductory material that declared, 'It is clear to many of us throughout the whole world that now, as certainly never before, we are determined or compelled, to take sides. The equivocal attitude, the Ivory Tower, the paradoxical, the ironic detachment, will no longer do'.[29]

In the period after completing this questionnaire, O'Casey indeed decided to avoid equivocation, and nailed his colours to the mast by supporting communism as a sweeping global force. But, in doing so, O'Casey declined to follow the example of agitprop writers, who scripted inexpensive works that might easily be transported to working-class audiences.[30] By contrast, O'Casey wrote politically committed plays that required well-resourced playhouses that could provide complex sets, musically-gifted actors and relatively large casts.

If O'Casey disregarded agitprop, he did pay close attention to his good friend G. B. Shaw, who, like O'Casey, felt increasingly impressed by the USSR, and who, like Yeats, spoke with all the authority of a Nobel laureate. Indeed, the communist government had invited Shaw to visit in the summer of 1931, when, as Stanley Weintraub notes, Shaw had been introduced to 'seemingly efficient factories, model schools, bustling collective farms, and even sanitized prisons'. A meeting with Stalin formed the centrepiece of the carefully stage-managed trip. 'He was charmingly good humoured', Shaw reported delightedly, 'There was no malice in him, but also no credulity'.[31] After his visit, Shaw wrote an article for the newspaper that Jim Larkin edited, the *Irish Worker*, declaring that 'In Russia there is no unemployment, the people are healthy and carefree and full of hope, going a bit short and working a bit hard'. He continued, telling readers that Russia had:

> factories with full modern equipment, modern American machinery and several Americans on the technical staff who deliberately prefer life in Russia to life in America, working at full pressure without a single parasite [. . .] There are no millionaires nor ladies and gentlemen there. Priests are so scarce that unless you go into a church where they are actually officiating you will not notice their existence. There are no streets of luxury shops and no mendacious commercial advertisements but nobody seems a penny the worse. There is no idolatry; the soldier and his officer hobnob on terms of perfect equality off duty.[32]

O'Casey read this article and agreed wholeheartedly, commenting, 'of course, what he says about what he saw and what he heard there is so simple and so charged with commonsense, so necessary to the vital welfare of man, that no-one in power or in place will hear, or hearing, will refuse to understand'.[33]

After that visit, Shaw made clear his support for left-wing dictatorships in the play *On The Rocks*. Shaw set this piece in the near future, revealing the inadequate and shambling response of democratic governments to the demands of the people. In *On the Rocks* a British prime minister is faced by crowds protesting in the street, but his only response is to try dispersing this mob rather than solving the underlying problems. Shaw's characters give a pessimistic view of the role of the democratic electorate here, with the prime minister declaring that the people 'know very well that they dont govern and cant govern and know nothing about Government except that it always supports profiteering'.[34] Instead, the prime minister considers becoming a dictatorial leader who will implement a radically socialist programme, but ultimately backs down, realizing he is ill-suited to the job.

O'Casey shared Shaw's enthusiasm for Stalin, treasuring a picture of the communist leader and boasting that 'Stalin is becoming a household name in Totnes'.[35] O'Casey also enjoyed reading *On the Rocks*, and published a review of it in 1933 for the *Listener*.[36] Consequently, when he wrote his first play about the polarized politics of the 1930s, *The Star Turns Red*, he echoed Shaw's near-future setting, depiction of mass unrest offstage and view of the inevitability of violence. O'Casey also borrowed some specific details from *On the Rocks*, which similarly describes a political landscape of 'black shirts, or brown shirts, or red shirts'.[37] Shaw's work concludes with an unemployed mob attacking Downing Street, smashing windows, and singing 'England, Arise!', while, inside, the prime minister and his wife refer to one another as 'darling'. Likewise, the final section of O'Casey's play shows the lord and lady mayor calling each other 'darling' while, outside, a crowd of workers is rising up and singing 'The Internationale' (II, 347).[38]

One correspondent from New Jersey asked O'Casey, 'If you think Communism so wonderful, why don't you go to Russia and take George Bernard Shaw with you [?]'.[39] But although O'Casey emulated Shaw, there does exist an important difference between those concluding scenes of *On the Rocks* and *The Star Turns Red*. Shaw's play finishes with a mob marching on Downing Street but being dispersed by police, giving the drama a rather ambiguous and anti-climactic ending:

Hilda: Oh! Here come the mounted police.

Sir Arthur: Theyve splendid horses, those fellows.

Hilda: The people are all running away. And they cant get out: theyre in a cul-de-sac. Oh, why dont they make a stand, the cowards?[40]

O'Casey, in rewriting a version of this scene, creates a less supine conclusion in which the crowd does make a stand and manages to repel the forces of oppression, recalling the famous, real-life attack by Irish rebels on British forces at Mount Street Bridge during 1916:

Joybell: (*excitedly.*) The mounted police flying hell for leather down the street!

Old man: And five of them toppling from their saddles! [. . .] Look! oh, look! – they're firing at the police from the foundry windows! (II, 345)

Shaw believed that democratic governments had failed, but actually felt fairly indifferent about whether fascism or communism would provide the replacement. After all, he had befriended Oswald Mosley as well as Stalin, and his play describes how a strong and dictatorial leader, of whatever stripe, would be preferable to the muddle and mish–mash of the current democratic arrangements. But O'Casey thought differently, wanting his audience to understand that communism, and certainly not fascism, provided the political vigour of the future. Shaw's play ends at a point when the characters have identified that a Coriolanus is needed, but are unable to discern who exactly might play that role. O'Casey's drama, by contrast, concludes by portraying a strong, communist leader in action. The idealized character of 'Red Jim', who is part-Stalin and part-Jim Larkin, takes to the stage to declare: 'We fight on; we suffer; we die; but we fight on' (II, 352).

Can't You Listen?

However, O'Casey's enthusiasm for the USSR led him to an unquestioning dogmatism that he would scarcely have tolerated in his opponents. The worst example of this attitude, and the most morally repugnant moment in O'Casey's playwriting, occurs in *Oak Leaves and Lavender*, a play designed to celebrate the point at which the USSR enters World War Two. O'Casey ignores the part played by the United States in the conflict, and his play revolves around the help offered to the Allied cause by Stalin's troops, whose entry into the war occurs at the climax of the play, with much cheering, singing and flag waving. The script concludes with the idea that 'Hearts of oak don't last; so hearts of steel we are!' (IV, 107), an allusion to the fact that those 'hearts of oak', the British forces fighting Hitler, needed reinforcement from the 'man of steel', Joseph Stalin.

In order to convey the political message more clearly, the play introduces a harridan called Deeda Tutting, who wishes to argue with the heroic Drishogue because of his support for the USSR. In real life O'Casey had encountered Freda Utley, a London-born socialist who had once, by her own admission, been a 'passionate defender of the Soviet Union', and who had settled in that country for nine years. There she married a Russian-Jewish husband, Arcadi Berdichevsky, a western-educated member of the Jewish Social Democratic party in Russian Poland.[41] However, in 1936, Berdichevshy fell foul of the secret police, whose officers arrested him on a trumped-up charge of import irregularities, sentenced him without trial and condemned him into a Stalinist concentration camp. A distraught Utley, alone in Moscow with the couple's two-year-old son, had little choice but to retreat to England, where she campaigned against the USSR, writing in 1949 that 'the Russian government could be even more cruel than the Nazi Government. For the Nazis did at least allow communication between prisoners and their relatives, and informed the latter when a concentration camp victim died or was shot'.[42]

As part of her campaign to raise awareness of her husband's fate, Utley met with O'Casey, confronting the playwright with some discomforting truths about Stalin's regime. But after this discussion,

O'Casey singularly failed to alter his beliefs, and now, instead, used *Oak Leaves and Lavender* to satirize his meeting with Utley. Her fictional counterpart is dismissed by Drishogue in the following way:

Deeda: I and my husband worked there on Committees, Comintern and Light Industries, so I know. If you were there, you'd see a look of fear in every sunken eye, misery chiselled on every pallid face, rags trying to cling to every shrunken body, and all steeped in the drab life they have to live.

Drishogue: Others with eyes as clear as yours, lady, have seen brighter and manlier things there. The fear you say you saw may have been the deep, dark fire of courage; the chiselled lines in pallid faces, the insignia of resolution; the ragged garments, the hurried shelter worn by sturdy hope striding down the street. If you want, woman, to see fear in th' eye, the pinched and pallid face, the shrunken figure, the tattered garment, ribbed to welcome every gusty wintry wind, look here at home – you'll find them plentiful in every town and city!

Deeda: (*more shrill and positive.*) Can't you listen? I know! [. . .] My husband worked beside me. He, too, found his dream was false. (*With a shrill and positive whine.*) He suddenly disappeared like thousands of others – perhaps millions – into a concentration camp. (*In a modified scream.*) If it weren't for you and other Liberals here, Stalin daren't have done it!

Drishogue: (*mockingly.*) You'll be telling me in a minute that Stalin himself is the one man left outside a concentration camp! [. . .] (*calmly.*) Well, if the behaviour you're showing now is usual with you, I don't wonder your husband disappeared – it was the wisest thing he could do. (IV, 46–9)

O'Casey often denounced the failings of the democratic governments of Ireland and Britain, yet when he analysed communism he remained happy to accept the worst violations of individual liberty. Indeed *Oak Leaves and Lavender* proves willing to excuse, and even joke about, gulags, forced starvations and executions. O'Casey had clearly absorbed accounts of the USSR from Shaw, and consequently felt that the country offered hope to the workers of the world, turning a deaf ear to all the bone-chilling evidence to the contrary. After all, O'Casey knew of Shaw's assurances that only 'parasites' received brutal treatment under the generally lenient Soviet system, with Shaw having praised the efficiency of Stalin's justice: 'if they find that you have been speculating or exploiting the labour of others, your relatives will presumably miss you and you will not turn up again. And there will be no visible jury to intimidate, no visible patrolman to corrupt, no visible magistrate or judge with an interest in your booty'.[43]

Over the matter of the USSR, O'Casey clashed openly in the press with Malcolm Muggeridge, who accused the playwright of throwing in his lot with 'Communist sycophants'.[44] In turn, O'Casey questioned Muggeridge's knowledge of the country, but O'Casey remained on a sticky wicket here. After all, Muggeridge had been Moscow correspondent for the *Manchester Guardian*, whereas the playwright's arguments relied on little more than a personal faith in Stalin and a set of doubtful second-hand reports from Shaw. Nevertheless, O'Casey declared, 'I have always stood for the U.S.S.R. and I stand for her now, and for Stalin, too: and it will be a wise day for England when she lines up beside this great country'.[45] Not even the disappearance of Arcadi Berdichevsky could change O'Casey's mind. The writer always felt frustrated by those whose experience of the USSR contradicted the version that he imagined, and so, in the passage quoted above, he sought to reduce the horrors of the European bloodlands to a misogynistic joke. Unsurprisingly, when O'Casey premiered *Oak Leaves and Lavender* in 1947, after images of the holocaust had revealed the cancer at the heart of Europe, the production proved a critical and commercial flop.

Oak Leaves and Lavender does of course include admirable elements. The comic bungling of O'Casey's Home Guard predicts the popular BBC comedy *Dad's Army*, while the playing of Wagner's 'Ride of the Valkyries' during a scene of aerial warfare points forward to Coppola's *Apocalypse Now*. Besides which, O'Casey had written one of the few plays to detail the sacrifices and discomforts of the numerous migrants from 'neutral' Ireland who found themselves in Britain between 1939 and 1945.

Ultimately, however, it is difficult to derive pleasure from a play that repeatedly uses the gulag and concentration camp as a source of easy punch lines. At one point in the play a prissy English liberal worries about the arrival of the Germans, fretting that the invading Nazis will have taken note of his letters to *The Times*, and that this will mean 'torture and the concentration camp for me!' (IV, 76). O'Casey may have expected this to raise a snigger, but these passages feel even more troubling when we remember that, in the mid-1930s, O'Casey had again been influenced by Shaw into supporting the sort of eugenic policy that would provide the *raison d'etre* for the Nazi death-camps. As O'Casey wrote in 1934:

> We can't go on bolstering up and covering with down the hopelessly unfit and the incurably useless, but rather we must learn to eliminate the waste products of humanity [. . .] the unfit and the useless are not only cared for, but pampered with the attention of philanthropic and Christian Societies and people. To get sensible help one must almost always first be in a condition when help is practically useless. To keep the fit fit and the healthy healthy must be the first care in an intelligent community. And to do this less time or no time can be wasted on the hopelessly unfit, and the incorrigibly incompatible [. . .] We must have a standard for the common good of all. If a man or a woman sink below this standard, then he or she must be eliminated.[46]

To be fair, once the older O'Casey discovered more about the horrors of World War Two he avoided such glibness. In 1963, shortly before his own death, O'Casey published a moving essay about his dead son Niall, in which he described how Niall had visited the Nazi charnel houses after the war. O'Casey wrote:

> I remember how he shuddered telling me about a visit to Belsen Camp while the regiment was on manoeuvres, a place where thousands of bearded Jews, wrinkled women, handsome young Jewesses and vigorous lads, and crowds of little Jewish children died; destroyed so exclusively and terribly that even remembrance

died with them: nothing there now but the wind to tell of the sorrow and the gloomy silence to cover the dead.[47]

As a result of such reports, O'Casey became strongly pro-Israeli in his later years, repeatedly condemning anti-Semitism, and feeling that Israel was 'threatened and tormented by the surrounding Arab governments'. He felt that the Jews needed a national home with protected borders, because 'I cannot forget the dreadful holocaust of Jewish people blasted and burned by the savage fascist powers'.[48]

Yet, although O'Casey may have revised his views about the comedic potential of the concentration camps, he failed to withdraw his support for Stalin and for the repressive policies of the USSR. Indeed, in that same tribute to Niall, O'Casey describes being troubled by a final argument with his ailing son. Niall expressed revulsion at the Soviet Army's quashing of the 1956 Hungarian Uprising, rushing home to argue 'vehemently' against his father's pro-communist viewpoint.[49] Where Niall saw the brutal obliteration of a genuinely popular student and people's movement, his father saw only the necessary destruction of a hateful group that had sought to establish a fascist regime and to mete out 'bitter revenge' to communists.[50] The events of 1956 had no effect on Seán O'Casey's commitment to the Soviet system, and even after Khrushchev's denunciations of Stalin, O'Casey continued to insist that people 'forgot the many times Stalin made no mistake; and they have but to look at the USSR to see the amazing achievements of the Man'.[51]

Yeats

Paradoxically, just as O'Casey maintained his admiration for Stalin, he also continued to respect W. B. Yeats, whose views lay at the other end of the political spectrum. Yeats and O'Casey had been reconciled in 1935, when the younger man finally received an invitation to stage *The Silver Tassie* at the Abbey Theatre, and in later years, O'Casey sought to forgive Yeats by locating the blame for 1928 in other places. In the 1940s, O'Casey suspected that Yeats's wife had been responsible for the *Tassie*'s rejection, and by the 1950s he fingered a jealous Lennox

Robinson because 'R[obinson] was annoyed at L[ady] Gregory's liking for me'.[52]

Unlike O'Casey, Yeats had little interest in the Soviet Union, and disliked the very notion of communism. In 1933, Yeats had told Olivia Shakespear 'I find myself constantly urging the despotic rule of the educated classes as the only end to our troubles'.[53] Yet, by 1946, O'Casey repeatedly used Yeatsian words for parts of his pro-Soviet play. Indeed, O'Casey finally called the script *Oak Leaves and Lavender: A Warld on Wallpaper*, and that subtitle, originally planned as the main title, had been cribbed from a phrase used by Yeats in correspondence over *The Silver Tassie*.[54]

As we have seen, in 1928, Yeats condemned O'Casey for writing *The Silver Tassie* about a war in a faraway place. Yeats felt that his protégé should have continued to write about the Dublin slums rather than the unknown horror of the trenches, and that if O'Casey insisted on invoking the fighting, the subject should have been used simply as contextual 'wallpaper'. But O'Casey disagreed with that verdict at the time, and continued to disagree in the 1940s. When he scripted *Oak Leaves*, his new play about global conflict, he knew more of the wartime experiences about which he wrote. Bombing raids, soldiers billeted in nearby countryside and conscription had become all too familiar to O'Casey in the early 1940s, and he felt now, more than ever, that wars and revolution should be central to the dramatist's art.

Thus Yeats continued to function as a contrarian inspiration for the Devonian playwright, with numerous allusions to Yeats's writings appearing in O'Casey's plays during this period.[55] O'Casey felt particularly affected by Yeats's late play *Purgatory*, a short and peculiar text with a distasteful message.[56] The chief protagonist of *Purgatory* describes how his high-born, Anglo–Irish mother conceived him as the result of a liaison with a low-born stable-hand, and has thus corrupted her lineage and destroyed the family's great house. The main character then stabs his own son to death in an attempt to stop this pollution being transmitted any further in the family bloodline.

In *Purple Dust*, O'Casey provides a comic coda to Yeats's dark work. *Purgatory* revolves around a ruined house in a terminal condition, symbolizing the despoiling of ascendancy culture across Ireland. But

Purple Dust shows the comic antics of two Englishmen who attempt to arrest that decline. In O'Casey's play the restoration is of course hopeless. The house is just as doomed as in Yeats's work, and the only real ways for men to find success are by pursuing communist politics and attractive women. O'Casey may also, of course, have been enjoying another joke at Yeats's expense here. Yeats had spent time after 1917 renovating the ruined tower of Thor Ballylee in rural Galway, a construction that Ezra Pound gleefully labelled 'ballyphallus'.[57] Accordingly, in *Purple Dust*, the men who are concerned with such restoration work are notably those who catastrophically fail to satisfy their partners.

From 1940, O'Casey had lived in Totnes, a Tudor market town full of historic buildings, which doubtless helped inspire the descriptions of such architecture in *Oak Leaves and Lavender*. However, the author continued to think back to Ireland, and described a building that recalls the Irish home of his real-life friend Lady Gregory, who had lost her only son in wartime skies just like the grand dame described in the play.[58] In real life, Lady Gregory's fine residence at Coole Park had been torn down in 1941 after ending up in the care of the Irish state. O'Casey himself had visited this house in 1924, where he had carved his name in the autograph tree, and he learned about the property's destruction in 1942.[59] At the end of *Oak Leaves and Lavender* Lady Hatherleigh's ancestral home has been equally deprived of its heir, and will make way for the needs of the technological, and potentially communist, future. As one character rousingly declares: 'Now, ladies and gentlemen, murmur your last farewell, and take your last look at the house of your fathers; for in a few minutes' time we link this with the other factory turning out tanks for the Red Army, and tanks for our own' (IV, 104–5). The old dame herself dies, joining a terpsichorean union with the ghosts of her ancestors, and closely emulating the Noh-style dance-dramas that Yeats had written and that O'Casey had thought 'funny' (*Auto* II, 497). By the end of *Oak Leaves and Lavender*, then, just as at the end of Yeats's play *Purgatory*, the grand ancestral house must be destroyed because the family line has ended, but the arrival of the Red Army in O'Casey's drama shows how this destruction might be transmuted into something triumphant.

Notably, after Yeats's death, O'Casey wrote commemorative pieces about the poet for distribution in the countries where the communist struggle most concerned Totnes's foremost Stalinist. In 1939 O'Casey scripted an essay on Yeats for the USSR, and in 1946 O'Casey wrote a tribute for broadcast in Spain, proclaiming the Nobel laureate 'the greatest poet of his generation'.[60] Such writing showed O'Casey's desire to reconcile his love for the poetry of the Abbey director with an abiding left-wing political commitment of the sort that Yeats cordially despised. In earlier life O'Casey had affiliated with all kinds of different organizations, including the Gaelic League, the Protestant Church, the IRB, the Citizen Army and the Gaelic Athletic Association. But the cause of communism stuck with him most thoroughly and most enduringly. As Bernice Schrank has insightfully shown, even in 1960 he was still writing to left-wing veterans of the Spanish Civil War, addressing them as 'comrades' and praying for their 'success'.[61]

In a number of his private letters O'Casey expresses his distance from a dry and lifeless kind of Marxist theorizing as well as from left-wing notions of art, and never actually became a member of the Communist Party. Yet, all too often, his plays of the Second World War present communism as an uncomplicatedly Good Thing. If O'Casey had allowed more uncertainties into these dramatic writings, then the scripts may have acquired a richer and more complex texture. As we have seen, the plays of his Dublin trilogy include many moments of authorial doubt and self-questioning, but his later work endorses the emancipatory opportunities of just one political philosophy, and lacks much of the humanitarian concern expressed by the younger writer. When O'Casey had prepared to defend *The Plough and the Stars* in 1926, he had written the note, 'There is one great difference between Mrs S[heehy Skeffington] and me, a difference that gives to me the power of seeing vividly the things that she sees through a glass, darkly, and that difference is this: she sees everything with the eyes of a political partisan, while I see everything with the eyes of a Dramatist'.[62] By the time he came to write his later plays, he could scarcely claim to have maintained that distinction.

CHAPTER 5
THE CHURCH, 1946–64

Cock-A-Doodle Dandy (Published and Staged 1949)

Michael is a farmer who owns a lucrative bog, but is in dispute with Mahan, who owns the lorries that transport Michael's turf. Michael refuses to pay higher transport costs, and so Mahan's men threaten to strike. Meanwhile, Michael feels suspicious of his own daughter, Loreleen, who has recently returned from England. She and two other energetic young people, Robin and Marion, are closely associated with a human-sized bird, 'the Cock', who arrives intermittently to dance and terrify the older residents. A repressive priest, Father Domineer, attempts to purge the community of the Cock's influence and corral the locals into docile Catholic piety. He sends Michael's paralysed sister-in-law Julia off to the Marian shrine at Lourdes, organizes a book burning and a march against paganism, and even hits and kills Mahan's best lorry driver for cohabiting. Loreleen attempts to escape this repressive environment in Mahan's car, which he provides after becoming disillusioned over the death of his employee. But Domineer's acolytes catch the duo. Loreleen is dragged to the priest and Mahan dispatched home to his wife. However, Robin commands that Domineer release Loreleen, and the priest exiles her, although her stepmother vows to keep her company. Robin and Marion also decide to leave voluntarily rather than staying in this stultifying environment. Finally, Julia returns from Lourdes, uncured, and Michael is left with only his rosary beads for company.

The Bishop's Bonfire (Published and Staged 1955)

Councillor Reiligan is an influential figure who is preparing his home to receive a visit from the local bishop. A kindly priest, Father Boheroe, is unimpressed by all the fuss being made for this arrival, and realizes that Reiligan's 25-year-old daughter Keelin is in love with Daniel, who has returned from Britain in order to see her. Boheroe sees the couple kissing and blesses them. However, a less kindly cleric, Canon Burren, teams up with Reiligan to berate Daniel and successfully divides the lovers, with the Canon encouraging Keelin to marry a 58-year-old farmer instead. The Canon also acclaims the arrival of a religious figurine, which is brought into the house as part of the preparations for the bishop, but which disarms some of the characters by displaying the magical ability to blow a horn. Meanwhile, Reiligan's other daughter, the 27-year-old Foorawn, has opted to become a nun. Her former lover, Manus, reappears in the town, where he declares his undiminished feelings of affection. However, she refuses him, saying that she now belongs to God. As the others go to welcome the bishop, Manus breaks into Reiligan's house and is discovered by Foorawn. She threatens to call the police and in response he shoots her. Nevertheless, she has time to declare her love for him, and with a final flourish she grabs his gun and writes a suicide note so that he will escape the charge of murder.

The Drums of Father Ned (Staged 1959)

McGilligan and Binnington have grown up in a small town, attended the same school, and have married a pair of sisters. But the men have a longstanding antipathy towards one another, and have fought on opposite sides in the Civil War. Since then, however, they have become prominent local figures, with McGilligan becoming deputy mayor and Binnington the mayor. They are now willing to put aside their differences for the sake of business and moneymaking, particularly when a cultural festival (*An Tóstal*) is being organized in the local area. The young people of the district, including Binnington's son and McGilligan's daughter, Nora, are eagerly preparing and rehearsing for this event, and are being encouraged by Father Ned, an unruly offstage presence who is never actually seen by the audience. Ned is cordially despised by the local parish priest Father Fillifogue, who tries to destroy the young people's enthusiasm for the festival. Nevertheless, Ned repeatedly confounds Fillifogue's decrees. Nora declares that the young are fed up with restrictive rules, and reveals to both families that she and Binnington's son are lovers who regularly share a bed. These two young people decide to stand for election to the Irish parliament, and although Fillifogue and their fathers try to stop this, the reactionary forces are unable to mobilize. Instead, the young people announce that 'Father Ned is on the march!' (V, 236), and the drama concludes with a rumbling of the clergyman's drums.

Behind the Green Curtains (Published 1961)

The play begins in a churchyard, shortly before the funeral of a well-liked Protestant playwright.[1] A group of Catholics loiters uneasily outside the church, and their archbishop confirms by telephone that it would be a grave sin for them to enter, although an attractive 26-year-old woman called Reena and a working man of nearly 30 called Beoman defy the cleric. The scene then shifts to the house of Senator Dennis Chatastray, a businessman and patron of Irish writers, who innocently provides a home for his young maid, Noneen, in order to protect her from an abusive alcoholic father. Chatastray is confronted by the conservative Catholic leader, Kornavaun, who feels outraged that Noneen and Chatastray should live together without being married. Kornavaun is further aggravated by a 'mixed marriage' between a Catholic and a Protestant at Chatastray's factory, as well as by the senator's support for banned writers, and by Chatastray's refusal to join a forthcoming demonstration against communism. Kornavaun consequently brings the factory to its knees with a strike, while his goons kidnap Noneen and hospitalize Chatastray. On the day of the anti-communist protest, Reena arrives at Chatastray's house to care for him, eventually kisses him, and wonders if they can find somewhere to live together. But when Chatastray hears the hymn 'Faith of our Fathers' emanating from the demonstration, he dons sackcloth and rushes to join the Catholic marchers. The worker Beoman arrives. He now kisses Reena, declares his love for her and they decide to join Noneen in leaving Ireland.

Catholic Protests

At the end of his writing career, O'Casey wrote four plays that contrast with the early Dublin trilogy. In these late works the playwright presents interchangeable locations in small-town, provincial Ireland, a static and unchanging country rather than one in the midst of political upheaval. If the early scripts focused on the poor of the tenements, the late plays are located in and around the houses of the new Irish state's Catholic bigwigs, who work hand-in-glove with the clergy, and are desperately interested in making money above all else. Members of this prosperous Catholic class spend their time creating stage-sets for themselves, with rooms and decorations designed for ostentatious display rather than use. As a result, the momentum of the original Irish revolution has petered out, with all of those radical ideas about social progress leading to nothing but a beggar-my-neighbour attitude, and a country dominated by reactionary old men who sap the vigour of the young. The Irish revolution may have begun with hopes of cherishing all of the children of the nation equally, but, as O'Casey shows, it ends with those children emigrating to avoid a stultifying country where power is held by those wearing the starchiest dog-collars or carrying the heaviest wallets.

O'Casey had an acute sense that post-revolutionary Ireland needed a second wave of decolonization. As one of O'Casey's characters declares in *The Bishop's Bonfire*, 'You've escaped from the dominion of the big house with the lion and unicorn on its front; don't let yourselves sink beneath the meaner dominion of the big shop with the cross and shamrock on its gable' (V, 81). In response to such writings, O'Casey endured harsh criticism from those who considered him either anti-Catholic or removed from the reality of mid-twentieth-century Ireland.

By this stage of his career, of course, Seán O'Casey had grown accustomed to the brickbats of Catholic groups, and wrote his late plays in reaction to a sustained period of hostility that had caused him financial headaches as well as creative frustration. Until the 1930s, objections to his plays had mainly been made on the grounds of indecency or because of a perceived insult to Irish patriotism. Indeed, between 1917 and 1920 he had enjoyed a romance with the Catholic Máire Keating, and at the end of the 1920s he felt happy about marrying another Irish Catholic, Eileen Carey, in the church of All Souls and the Redeemer in Chelsea.

However, in 1935 opposition to his writings increasingly emerged on devotional grounds, both in the United States and in Ireland. During this year, he gave the US premiere of what was then his most religiously provocative play, *Within the Gates*, which revolves around an unrepentant prostitute whose real father is a bishop. Here O'Casey condemns the abuses of Catholic residential institutions, allows atheist characters to explain their viewpoint and broadens his attack across the Christian denominations. At one stage, before the prostitute's identity has become clear, the bishop even shows a sexual attraction to his own offspring, and his former lover tells him, 'your religion's as holy as a coloured garter round a whore's leg' (II, 218). The dying daughter does end the play by making the sign of the cross, but, for some Christians, this scarcely redeemed the production. At the start of 1935 Father Russell M. Sullivan, the head of the Boston College Council of Catholic Organizations, and active member of the 'Legion of Decency', a cinema-censorship board, denounced the play. He pointed out the 'sympathetic portrayal of the immoralities described', and put pressure on the Catholic mayor of Boston to prevent the show from arriving in the city. The mayor dispatched his censor to see the New York production, who confirmed the priest's view, and the mayor then declared the play 'nothing but a dirty book full of commonplace smut' and 'requested' that the work not be offered for the scheduled week-long run at the Shubert Theatre, something that amounted to a de facto ban.[2] The producers refunded thousands of dollars that had already been paid for tickets, and griped about the methods that caused the cancellation, before a planned tour of 11 other cities then collapsed.[3]

In a statement justifying this turn of events, the mayor of Boston listed the advice he had received from three churchmen: Father Sullivan, Bishop Charles W. Burns of the Methodist Episcopal Church and the Rev. John Van Schaick of the Mennonite church.[4] This ecumenical alliance irked O'Casey, who sent a telegram to New York, declaring, 'I don't write plays to please priests'.[5] Years later, when the Cork

Drama Festival banned *The Plough and the Stars*, he would still reflect on the Boston ban as marking a particular turning point, telling one correspondent that 'I am quite used to this sort of thing now. I had a tour of a play of mine stopped in America by the combined agitation of the Jesuits and the Methodists. And they talk about censorship in the Soviet Union!'[6]

O'Casey could perhaps have regarded this setback with equanimity. After all, he knew that he had written something provocative, and the cancelled US tour of *Within the Gates* ensured that a second New York run later in the year became even more profitable than the first.[7] But shortly after the Boston ban, protests took place closer to home against *The Silver Tassie*, a development that, for the playwright, must have felt far more bewildering. For sure, O'Casey deliberately included in *Within the Gates* elements that some Christians might find offensive, but such an intention had not primarily motivated the writing of *The Silver Tassie*, which dwells on the futility and horror of warfare, has nothing hostile to say about any religious denomination and contains at its heart a message of peace.

Nevertheless, protests occurred in Dublin at least partly because of what O'Casey himself had come to symbolize. The only Catholic among the directors of the Abbey Theatre, Brinsley MacNamara, objected to Yeats's reconciliation with O'Casey, and when Yeats declared his intention to produce *Within the Gates* at the Abbey, MacNamara vetoed the idea because the piece was 'objectionable' and 'unsuccessful'. An undaunted Yeats then selected instead *The Silver Tassie*, which MacNamara began to find inappropriate too, telling the press that he found a 'travesty of the Sacred Office in the second act', where O'Casey includes chanted words from the Latin Mass in order to convey the profundity of the experience of trench warfare. MacNamara declared that when he finally saw the piece at the Abbey he felt that 'an outrage had been committed', compounded by the fact that 'the majority of the players taking part in the production were Catholic'.[8] When the rest of the board asked MacNamara to retract his complaints, he refused and instead publicly resigned his position.[9]

MacNamara received a great deal of support from a Sligo priest, Father Michael Gaffney. In the week before the Dublin production, the clergyman described how *The Silver Tassie* 'may possibly have been filled from a sewer', sending his warning to the Catholic newspaper the *Standard*, a publication that O'Casey came to despise.[10] The *Standard* published Gaffney's comment that: 'In attempting to analyse this play, I have fallen into despair. I have no hope of conveying any adequate idea of its deliberate indecency and its mean, mocking challenge to the Christian Faith'.[11]

Gaffney's reasons for objecting to such an innocuous drama derived from the earlier brouhaha over *The Plough and the Stars*, when O'Casey had lampooned the Irish patriot Patrick Pearse. Gaffney knew Pearse's mother, Margaret, and had been asked by her to adapt Patrick's short stories for stage presentation.[12] The resultant plays are little more than Catholic kitsch, presenting a portrait of the patriot that reverses O'Casey's satirical depiction by foregrounding Pearse's piety and prayerfulness, and O'Casey himself joked, 'I shall never forgive Father Gaffney for his bad plays'.[13] When Gaffney heard that the Abbey planned to produce *The Silver Tassie* he saw an opportunity to return to the fray and continue battling on Pearse's behalf, and although the *Tassie* could scarcely be considered sectarian, the priest knew of earlier grumbling by the Catholic *Universe* newspaper when the play premiered in London during 1929, with Gaffney now revisiting and magnifying those complaints.[14] The *Standard* took its cue from the clergyman, and demonized the play as a 'Revolting Production', 'sheer trash' and 'An Outrage on our Faith'.[15] According to this newspaper, the Abbey 'has decided to permit the Church to be mocked, the name of God to be insulted, immorality to be flaunted as a matter of course, and the foulest language of the gutter to be used before audiences which are overwhelmingly Catholic'.[16]

Gaffney's protest began in the Catholic press but soon reverberated more widely. The priest delivered an address to the Academy of Christian Art in Dublin, stating that *The Silver Tassie* had been 'staged in the full panoply of blasphemous crudity' and lamenting that 'There had been no riot in Dublin to mark its passing'.[17] The *Irish Independent* then reproduced Gaffney's words, giving him a broader national platform, and forcing the Abbey Theatre to make an official response, with the playhouse's secretary declaring Gaffney 'misinformed'.[18] With distinctly less restraint, the former director of the Abbey, St John Ervine, observed that Father Gaffney's criticisms had the hysterical tone of 'a kitchenmaid who had seen too much of Mr. Clark Gable'.[19] Eventually the row generated enough heat for O'Casey's London-based mother-in-law to learn about it, which can scarcely have delighted the writer himself. For many years she recycled comments from Ireland's press in order to reinforce her own personal dislike of the author, informing her daughter, 'It's not only me – look what other people are saying'.[20]

O'Casey told a friend, 'there is no value to me or to you in wasting time & sacred thought with Father Gaffney'.[21] But despite such sound advice, after 1928 O'Casey found it increasingly difficult to shrug off such disparagement of his work. He retained copies of Gaffney's articles in the *Irish Press* and the *Standard*, and penned an extensive rebuke to the priest, which he sent to the Abbey but which Yeats diplomatically refrained from having published.[22] In this article, O'Casey expressed bewilderment at Gaffney's main criticism, pointing out that 'there is no travesty of the Mass, stated clearly or furtively implied, from one end of the play to the other'. O'Casey claimed to have included parts of the Mass 'to imply the sacred peace of the Office compared with the horrible cruelty and stupidity of the war', and stated that in any case he disliked only conservative versions of Catholicism rather than the broader faith, elements of which he had long found beautiful.[23]

Nevertheless, the reaction against *The Silver Tassie* meant that the Abbey curtailed the first Irish run of the play, and in the following years the playwright increasingly excoriated the figure of the repressive priest who sets about suppressing innovative and original thinking.[24] Following that clash with Father Gaffney, O'Casey converted the scrapbook that contained press clippings about his own Catholic wedding into a resource for satirizing Catholicism, adding cuttings from newspapers about groups such as the Knights of St Columba or the Legion of Mary, whose members would be targeted in O'Casey's late plays.[25] One newspaper article in particular had a catalysing effect on the writer. He kept the story, 'Month in Gaol for a Kiss', which *Irish Press* reported in 1944, to remind himself of the seemingly introspective battles that Ireland fought while the rest of humanity engaged in world war.[26] For O'Casey such a case typified the dismaying attitudes promoted by the Catholic Church in Ireland, and he dramatized this story in *Cock-A-Doodle Dandy*, where the young characters of Robin and Marion, who appropriately bear the names of the heroic outlaws of English folk myth, have been respectively imprisoned for a month and fined 40 shillings for kissing in a public place.

From 1929, the Irish Censorship of Publications Board had the power to ban books, and throughout the country, assiduous religious activists, particularly those of the Catholic Truth Society, pored through libraries in order to seek out and report indecency. Accordingly, O'Casey found his collection of stories, poems and short plays *Windfalls* banned in 1934, as well as the first two volumes of his autobiography in 1939 and 1942. The board lifted the prohibition on the autobiographies in 1947, although the Irish Customs Office mysteriously impounded all copies of his essay collection *The Green Crow* for a year during the following decade, leading O'Casey to tell correspondents in the 1950s that 'most of my books have been banned in Ireland' and to denounce the Vatican as 'the enemy, not only of Ireland, but of the world'.[27]

These clashes led O'Casey to script a set of late plays that repeatedly revolve around ill-tempered, irrational and censorious clerics. In *Cock-A-Doodle Dandy* O'Casey presents Father Domineer, who, after killing a worker, learns that another parishioner is reading books, and responds by roaring that such volumes must be destroyed. In *The Bishop's Bonfire*, O'Casey shows how a group of parishioners might welcome the local bishop into their midst by lighting a bonfire of literature and art. Similarly, *The Drums of Father Ned* depicts a priest revealing that he has 'cleaned' the library by organizing the incineration of those holdings he dislikes (V, 231). O'Casey's final play, *Behind the Green Curtains*, refrains from showing any clergymen onstage, but indicates that they are still pulling the strings: the bishops decide whether Catholics can attend a Protestant funeral; which books can be read; and how to cajole subversive writers into repentance. By the end of the play, the liberated characters simply decide to draw the green curtains down on the whole scenario, in a mirror image of the famous scene in *The Wizard of Oz*. In that film, Dorothy and Toto bring freedom to Oz by opening the emerald drapes and uncovering the truth about the country's dictatorship, but in O'Casey's play there is no hope for Ireland but to close the curtains again and leave this merry old land in the stranglehold of the bishops.

Serious God-Baiter?

However, O'Casey's late works have little interest in defaming the historical character of Christ, and do convey broadly Christian themes about the blessedness of the poor and the hypocrisy of the outwardly pious. O'Casey may have described himself as an unbeliever, and have triggered paroxysms of outrage in religious newspapers like the *Standard*, but, as Kenneth Tynan concluded after seeing *The Bishop's Bonfire*, 'As a serious God-baiter O'Casey is a non-starter'.[28] The practising-Catholic poet Patrick Kavanagh, with his tongue perhaps in his cheek, even told O'Casey 'I am about as good a Catholic as yourself', and described the playwright as the author of 'intensely Irish Catholic books'.[29]

O'Casey sought to distinguish between the lamentably authoritarian leaders of the Church, and Catholicism's moral philosophy and poetic tales, which he praised and admired.[30] Perhaps the best articulation of O'Casey's approach is given by Julia in the earlier play *The Star Turns Red*, who looks at a crucifix and observes, 'Against you, dear one, we have no grudge; but those of your ministers who sit like gobbling cormorants in the market-place shall fall and shall be dust' (II, 315). Accordingly, O'Casey's late plays make the broad argument that God is found in places other than ecclesiastical buildings, and that the things which the Vatican condemns as sinful might in fact contain their own kind of spirituality. The face of a beautiful woman, the music of Mozart, a starlit sky, or the tender embrace of a lover, might be viewed suspiciously by Rome as inspirations towards 'evil' (IV, 125), but the more sympathetic voices of O'Casey's late plays explain that such everyday wonders in fact provide evidence of God's handiwork. Thus the renegade priest, Father Boheroe, and the like-minded Catholic characters in these dramas tend to speak like Gerard Manley Hopkins, finding manifestations of Christ in the natural world of Creation rather than the 'gilded foolishness' of orthodox religious worship (V, 30).

O'Casey felt that conventional devotion deserved to be mocked for being wrongheaded, but also because, all too often, modern Christians had concentrated their energies on such pious distractions rather than living up to the ideals of the religion's founder. Allusions to the King James Bible are all-pervasive in O'Casey's writings, but some of the most entertaining examples occur when O'Casey contrasts the religion's ascetic origins with the worldliness of modern Christians. For instance, in *The Bishop's Bonfire* a mason argues with his workmate by adapting the words of St Paul's famous letter to the Corinthians. Paul writes: 'Charity suffereth long, and is kind; charity envieth not; charity vaunteth not itself, is not puffed up'. But in *The Bishop's Bonfire*, the workman physically wrestles with his colleague and shouts, 'True religion isn't puffed up, you bastard; it's long-sufferin' an' kind, an' never vaunts itself like you do; true religion doesn't envy a man a brick, you rarefied bummer!' (V, 13–14).

Furthermore, O'Casey co-opts such theological language in order to justify the communist cause. In *The Drums of Father Ned*, Michael Binnington feels particularly frustrated by the divisions and sectarianism of small-town Ireland, and argues that God is not the property of any particular group, but something altogether more radical: God might be the 'shout of th' people for bread in th' streets, as in th' French Revolution; or for th' world's ownership by th' people, as in th' Soviet Revolution' (V, 226). Such a phrase, which begins with the quasi-Eucharistic and ends with the Marxist, shows that there might be something sacred about the communist desire for equality, with O'Casey presenting the avowedly atheist philosophy of the USSR in a language that Christians might understand and find appealing. O'Casey's late plays try to realign those two Jewish heresies, Marxism and Christianity, not wishing to alienate and offend Christians, but to use the rhetorical tropes and philosophical ideas associated with their faith in order to redirect attention to the more worthwhile goal of achieving global justice and personal fulfilment in this world rather than the next.

Thus the historical Christ emerges, in the late plays, as a figure who might help fuse Christianity with communism. In *The Drums of Father Ned*, Jesus is implied to be a rather likeable socialist agitator, familiar with the symbols of communism from his day work, yet also appreciative of fun and beauty (V, 166–7). Accordingly, carpentry and manual labour carry a Christological resonance for O'Casey, and repeatedly appear in the late plays as potentially elevating the ordinary man in the contemporary world. During *The Bishop's Bonfire*, Father Boheroe explains to a nun that the building-site employee 'has helped to build hospitals where the sick shelter, homes where we live, churches even where we worship; he serves God as a mason better than I do in my priesthood, or you in your chastity' (V, 117). Similarly, in *The Drums of Father Ned*, Irish Catholics worry about whether to accept imported wood from communist Russia, but Father Ned preaches that the cargo should indeed be distributed and utilized, employing the Eucharistic language of 'Take it, and be thankful' (V, 231).

Real-Life Inspiration

In any case, a number of real-life clergymen had inspired O'Casey to write these late plays. For example, *Cock-A-Doodle Dandy* had occupied O'Casey's mind for a long time, with one of his earliest surviving notebooks mulling over a character called 'Cock Codger or Hen Codger', and his personal letters since 1928 dwelling on 'The Red Cock'.[31] But O'Casey finally set down his ideas after renewing his acquaintance with Reverend Harry Fletcher, who, years before, had been curate of St Barnabas's Church in Dublin. In their correspondence of 1945, Fletcher described the old rhyme 'Kilcock', which tells of a resident of the Irish town of Kilcock who dies and meets St Peter at the gates of heaven. The saint has never heard of the Irish location, and thinks that the poem is a needling reference to his notorious denial of Christ, before finally realizing that the Irishman is not teasing, and concluding:

'O I see you're the better of me
Tho' I thought you were trying to mock
Come in' – said the Saint with a grin
'You're the first that has come here from Kilcock'.[32]

Fletcher included this rhyme in his letters to O'Casey, and helped to focus the writer's thoughts on how that avian image might have a subversive effect upon religious authority.

Similarly, the liberating clerics of the late plays, Father Boheroe and Father Ned, had been based on a number of real-life Catholic churchmen. O'Casey felt most impressed by Father Walter McDonald, a professor of theology who clashed with the Church hierarchy in an attempt to reconcile science and religion, suffering official censorship and recording these struggles in *Reminiscences of a Maynooth Professor*, which appeared in 1925, five years after McDonald's death.[33] The book had a profound effect on O'Casey, who transcribed parts of the *Reminiscences* almost verbatim in the autobiographies, and, for decades, would obsessively recommended the priest's memoirs to friends and acquaintances.[34] In the autobiographies, O'Casey also set about embellishing the professor's story, imagining McDonald's college at Maynooth as a silent and isolated Catholic community, with the rebel priest standing outside and shouting truth at the inhabitants. Here, the Catholic world, with its lack of questioning, its oppressive hierarchy and its stultifying commands to obedience, is shaken by McDonald's yelling from without the gates. McDonald thus inhabits that same spatial zone as Father Ned, and provides a trial run for the latter priest, whose liberating noise also threatens an enclosed world dominated by Rome's favoured clerics.

Another real-life priest who inspired O'Casey's writing was the Sligo clergyman Michael O'Flanagan, who in 1915 had led his poor parishioners to commandeer fuel that they had been officially denied. O'Flanagan carried his own spade to the Cloonerco turf bogs, after telling his congregation at Mass that:

What I would advise the people to do is for every man and boy who wants a turf bank and who can work a turf spade to go out to the waste bog tomorrow, and cut plenty of turf. You need not be the least afraid. God put that bog there for the use of the people [. . .] Are we going to let our poor little children shiver to death with cold next winter for want of a fire?[35]

Such actions deeply impressed O'Casey, who recycled O'Flanagan's words in the introduction to *The Drums of Father Ned*, praising the priest's concern for 'his poor flock [who] were shivering through a black winter' (V, 130). O'Flanagan also suffered suspension from the priesthood when he acted as Vice President of Sinn Féin, and further enhanced his reputation with O'Casey in 1938 by lauding those Irishmen who joined the left-wing International Brigades in Spain.[36] Hence O'Casey looked back to O'Flanagan in devising the setting for *Cock-A-Doodle Dandy*, in which the main character of Michael is greedily profiteering from a turf bog, and refusing to pay his workers a decent wage. Michael's private ownership of this land is the result of chicanery: he bought it for next to nothing from an elderly relative who failed to see the value of the peat, and thus O'Casey follows O'Flanagan in critiquing the notion of such a resource being privately owned and exploited.

However, O'Casey also took inspiration from Catholic priests who, in real life, differed significantly from his own broader agenda. Walter McDonald, for example, was no Father Ned. Although McDonald worked hard as a man of principle and decency, he had no intention of fomenting outright rebellion against the Church, and after the Irish bishops banned McDonald's book *Motion: Its Origin and Conservation*, the author himself strove to withdraw the volume from circulation.[37] Similarly, O'Casey admired John Hayes, a canon who had founded the Irish community organization *Muintir na Tíre* ('the people of the land') in the 1930s, and the playwright also praised Peter Yorke, a San Francisco cleric who supported striking workers in the early twentieth century. However, both Hayes and Yorke had been motivated by Pope Leo XIII's encyclical *Rerum Novarum* ('Of New Things'), which condemns socialism and which O'Casey repeatedly derides in *Cock-A-Doodle Dandy*. Indeed, Yorke told striking workers that Leo had been 'the greatest moral authority in the world', and Hayes even gained the support of Mussolini, who declared 'an interest in activities in Ireland'.[38] When O'Casey used such priests in order to inspire the late plays, then, he needed a selective memory about what these figures had actually done and said. Meanwhile, in his personal notebook, O'Casey imagined a still more radical or subversive kind of priesthood, jotting the names of: 'The Right Rev. James Joyce[,] The

Venerable Bernard S.[haw] Order of Divinity of Secular Life. The most Reverd. W. B. Yeats'.[39]

Protests

As a result of O'Casey's antipathy towards institutional Catholicism, this deeply spiritual and inquisitive man found himself condemned by many as simply a cantankerous, anti-religious crank. When Dublin witnessed the first production of *The Bishop's Bonfire* in February 1955, the *Standard* judged and condemned the play prior to performance, declaring that 'Sean O'Casey's hatred of the Catholic Church permeates all his writings'. The newspaper dusted down its 20-year-old criticisms from the *Tassie* affair, arguing again that 'O'Casey has prostituted his undoubted ability in the cause of anti-God and anti-Clericalism', and asking, 'Where is the nation's self respect?'[40] Meanwhile Kenneth Tynan travelled to the packed Gaiety Theatre for the production and reported that 'Catholic militants paraded outside the theatre, bearing signs that urged Sean to go back to Moscow, while within there was a mild persistent hubbub, punctuated now and then by the gentle popping of stink-bombs'.[41] The right-wing Catholic association *Maria Duce* took a leading part in organizing protests outside the playhouse, with demonstrators lighting bonfires or holding banners that defamed O'Casey, and the Irish police arriving to maintain order.[42] *Maria Duce* also managed to disrupt the action inside the auditorium, with members hollering 'This is blasphemy' and scattering pamphlets over the other spectators.[43] However, these remonstrations scarcely caused the author himself to worry. He felt more annoyed by the generally negative reaction of the Irish critics, whose vitriol contrasted with the broadly positive reviews of those writing for the UK newspapers. *The Times* of London declared that 'To better Mr. Sean O'Casey's latest play we should need to go some way back in his theatre, as far back as *The Silver Tassie*'.[44] Yet the *Irish Times* proclaimed:

Whether or not he likes it, O'Casey must face the fact that his yardstick as a tragi-comedian is 'The Plough and the Stars'.

Nobody who has known and reverenced the greatness of this 29-year-old play could fail to weep at the feeble echo and image of its greatness seen in the Gaiety Theatre last night.[45]

In response, O'Casey denounced the Irish reviews as 'a bewildering mass of dismissals, denials, denunciations, declensions, and deviations', and his subsequent volume of essays, *The Green Crow*, condemned the 'Irish critics who hint or shout that O'Casey knows Ireland no longer', claiming, 'I know her so well that they clap their hands over their dull ears, so that they may not have to hear'.[46]

One commentator, Thomas Hogan, now noted sadly that O'Casey 'sees his native country through a haze of press cuttings, and he does not appreciate that, apart from a lunatic fringe, most of his audience at the first night of his play desperately wanted it to turn out to be a good play'.[47] O'Casey's former friend, the Catholic theatre-critic Gabriel Fallon, wrote an open letter, which the *Irish Press* published, asking, 'why should the unfavourable opinions of a few Dublin critics upset you? Well, I'll tell you, Sean O'Casey. In the first place it is because your overweening vanity is severely hurt. You don't like criticism, Sean O'Casey, you only like praise'.[48]

Then, in October 1958, *Cock-A-Doodle Dandy* received its professional world premiere in Toronto, almost a decade after the first amateur production in the United Kingdom. In Canada, a few members of the audience left in outrage at every performance, and at one point, four audience members interrupted the show to demand censorship. 'Does the church know about it?' they yelled at the actors, before urging the rest of the audience to leave at the interval. Eventually they started shouting 'You're a liar' until escorted from the building.[49] Worse still, in the United States the American Legion, an organization of army veterans, threatened the play on the grounds that O'Casey sympathized with communism. When Arthur Miller tried to persuade the Dramatists' Guild to fight such intimidation he encountered apathy and opposition, leaving the financial sponsors of the play to withdraw and the US production to remain unopened.[50]

O'Casey reached the end of his tether when he attempted to premiere *The Drums of Father Ned* in Dublin. He submitted this work to the organizers of the 1958 festival *An Tóstal* ('a gathering'), a tourist-friendly cultural event that had run for five years, and which had initiated the Dublin Theatre Festival from 1957. O'Casey initially felt positive about *An Tóstal*, thinking that it might be an expression of Ireland's enthusiastic youth.[51] He scripted *The Drums of Father Ned* in praise of the event, with Irish conservatism painted as the natural enemy of such life-affirming festivities. But unfortunately for O'Casey, the plot, revolving as it does around Catholic attempts to censor *An Tóstal*, ended up proving all too prophetic.

In real life, *An Tóstal* originally boasted an impressive line-up of plays. The festival had been due to open on 11 May 1958 with O'Casey's *The Drums of Father Ned*, three new mime plays by Beckett and a dramatized version of Joyce's *Ulysses*. However, when the Archbishop of Dublin, John McQuaid, saw O'Casey's potential peccancy on the programme he refused permission for a special service in Dublin to mark the opening of *An Tóstal*, a Mass that had been said in previous years. The panic-stricken organizers asked for 'structural alterations' to O'Casey's play, but this request predictably appalled the author, who decided to withdraw rather than mutilate his work. Shortly afterwards, the Joyce adaptation *Bloomsday* also disappeared from the bill after members of the *Tóstal* organizing council worried about heaping further controversy upon the festival. When O'Casey heard about this he must have reflected ruefully on how, in his play, Father Domineer shows a particular enthusiasm for destroying an edition of Joyce's *Ulysses*. Certainly Samuel Beckett felt unimpressed, and withdrew permission for his own work to be staged at *An Tóstal*.[52] O'Casey also sought to respond in kind.[53] From now on, rather than waiting for the country to ban his work, he would provide his own prohibition in advance. To those in Ireland who sought permission to produce his works in the subsequent years he wrote the following sort of response:

> I had banned performances of my plays in Ireland following the ban placed on my work by the Catholic Archbishop of Dublin in 1958; all but amateur productions. Over the latter I have no control, unfortunately; but those who perform my plays as amateurs are going contrary to my wishes.[54]

Indeed, the Dublin premiere of O'Casey's final full-length play *Behind the Green Curtains* was delayed for more than a decade after the playwright's death, and in 1975 met with a response of muted disappointment rather than open hostility.[55]

Religion of the Credulous

A number of observers have argued that O'Casey always retained something of the autonomic anti-Catholicism of his childhood. Paul Johnson, for example, writing in the 1980s, observed that O'Casey held 'to the end of his days a hatred of Roman Catholicism as the religion of the credulous, the uneducated and the socially inferior'.[56] Similarly, in the 1960s, Kenneth Tynan observed that 'we do well to remember' O'Casey's Protestant upbringing when watching the late plays.[57] Such arguments are predicated on something akin to Raymond Williams' distinction between 'commitment' and 'alignment'. According to Williams, commitment is intentional, something that we can adopt or set aside, whereas alignment is a set of deeper social formations that form an individual's entire system of observation and judgement. As Williams puts it, 'our own actual alignment is so inseparable from the constitution of our own individuality that to separate them is quite artificial'.[58] If we believe such arguments, O'Casey may have been free to commit himself to various positions throughout his life, but he could never extricate himself from the religious alignment that he was born into, and which formed his normal mode of being in, and viewing, the world. Accordingly, figures such as Gabriel Fallon and Alan Simpson asserted that O'Casey's underlying Protestantism had been masked by an atheism 'adopted for the sake of annoying the Irish clergy'.[59]

O'Casey himself had little time for such notions, feeling that during his years in Dublin he had grown closer to working-class Catholics than to Ireland's generally wealthier Protestants, and in his final years he expressed tremendous admiration for two of the twentieth century's greatest Catholic icons, Pope John XXIII and John F. Kennedy. The playwright even sent a personal message of sorrow to one of Robert Kennedy's friends after the president's death.[60] Yet in O'Casey's earlier life, he found inspiration on the sectarian bookshelf. His early volume *The Sacrifice of Thomas Ashe* has an obvious linguistic affinity with 'The Sacrifice of the Mass', a phrase long used by Roman Catholics to describe their religious ceremony of the Eucharist, but also by Protestants in order to mock that ceremony.[61] Elsewhere, O'Casey's *The Story of the Irish Citizen Army* recalls the title of Alex Dallas's volume *The Story of the Irish Church Missions*, and O'Casey's book emulates something of the earlier work's structure.[62] Many nationalists, of course, viewed the Irish Church Missions with the deepest suspicion. The *Nation* referred to the organization as 'that most pestilent of frauds' and 'an impudent failure', which attracted support from only 'foolish fanatics' and from the 'de-nationalised Irishman of about the worst type'.[63]

The Irish Church Missions was of course the organization to which O'Casey's father, the inspirational figure of O'Casey's early autobiographies, devoted an entire working life. In fact, the first published volume *I Knock at the Door*, to which O'Casey considered giving the Wordsworthian title 'Father of the Man', argues that the playwright's intellectual formation owed almost everything to the bibliophilia of Casey *père*. As Michael Keneally has pointed out, 'The image of his scholarly father, reinforced by the presence of his books in the home, is thus presented as the most significant factor in directing Johnny's introduction to the world of letters'.[64] Towards the start of the autobiographies, O'Casey describes the library that surrounded him as a child:

> Marshalled tightly together, there they were, the books he [O'Casey's father] used to read, pore, and ponder over: a regiment of theological controversial books, officered by d'Aubigné's *History of the Reformation*, Milner's *End of Controversy*, Chillingworth's *Protestantism*, holding forth that the Bible, and the Bible alone, is the religion of protestants, with an engraving of the fat face of the old cod stuck in the front of it; Foxe's *Book of Martyrs*, full of fire and blood and brimstone [. . .]. (*Auto* I, 27–8)

The books that O'Casey remembers here, and which helped to inculcate his love of reading, are, aside from Milner's volume, resolutely anti-Catholic. The first book that O'Casey cites, d'Aubigné's *History of the Reformation*, describes the oppositional stance of Martin Luther, portraying the young reformer as living in 'extreme poverty', with a father who consistently procured books even though 'books were then rare'.[65] Accordingly, O'Casey describes his own childhood in the same vein, and his late plays follow Aubigné's scathing descriptions of venal Catholic clerics. As Aubigné writes:

> Men sighed for deliverance from the tyranny of the priests. The priests themselves were sensible that if they did not devise some remedy, their usurped power would be at an end. They invented indulgences. The priests said, 'O penitents, you are unable to perform the penances we have imposed upon you. Well then, we, the priests of God, will take upon ourselves this heavy burden. But the labourer is worthy of his hire. We must be paid'. Some courageous voices were raised against this traffic, but in vain![66]

In *Cock-A-Doodle Dandy*, O'Casey describes the Catholic Church as inhabiting the same moral realm, where the wealthy use their lucre to secure a place in heaven. Michael says, 'Me own generous gift of fifty pounds for th' oul' bog'll be rewarded', and wonders about how to 'get th' higher saints goin'' (IV, 157). A few moments later, another character confirms that 'Honour be th' clergy's regulated by how much a man can give!' (IV, 159). In the version of *The Bishop's Bonfire* that appears in O'Casey's *Complete Plays*, he toned down some of the anticlericalism of the early drafts, but those first iterations had focused on the parishioners hoarding cash for the priests, and on the cleric who 'is always pleased to take money'.[67]

In the books that O'Casey remembered his family owning in the late 1800s, the Catholic priest is repeatedly described as a bogus fraud, whose role as intercessor between God and laity had been dreamt up in order to bolster the power of the organization, and who could be avoided by Protestants returning to the bible alone. William Chillingworth's influential volume *The Religion of Protestants*, which O'Casey remembered seeing on the paternal bookshelves, set forth these arguments and asked Catholics to re-examine their scriptures before answering the question, 'how know you that there is any Church Infallible [?]'[68] In the mid-1950s, O'Casey returned to these ideas, using *The Bishop's Bonfire* to pour scorn on the mediating role of priests:

Foorawn: [. . .] How could I ever possibly know that God wouldn't be angry with me for breaking my vow?

Father Boheroe: How did you know that God was pleased when you took it?

Foorawn: The Canon told me, the Bishop told me.

Father Boheroe: Oh, yes, the Bishop and the Canon. I forgot them. They hear everything that God says. (V, 116)

Boheroe's sarcasm means that, as the play goes on, he is a Catholic priest only in the sense that Martin Luther was a Catholic priest in about 1520.

O'Casey also remembered seeing *Foxe's Book of Martyrs* during his childhood, and if the young writer had indeed encountered those volumes then he could scarcely have avoided being struck by the publication's vivid woodcuts of Protestant martyrs being burned to death. For someone schooled in such acts and monuments, the primrose way to the 'Bishop's Bonfire' was scarcely likely to be described as a positive notion, and perhaps also explains why the image of offstage flames is a recurring and ominous image in O'Casey's work.[69] Furthermore, *Foxe's Book of Martyrs* advocates the kind of iconoclasm that the mature O'Casey would find appealing. In Foxe's book, the Protestant martyr John Maundrel declares that 'wooden images were good to roast a shoulder of mutton, but evil in the church; whereby idolatry was committed'.[70] O'Casey emulated such humour in *The Bishop's Bonfire*, where he blows a raspberry at 'the population of stone an' wooden saints' by including the periodic horn-blasts of 'St Tremolo' (V, 56). Similarly, in *Cock-A-Doodle Dandy* a statue of St Patrick tries to swat Michael's supposedly evil daughter with a crozier, while *Behind the Green Curtains* includes an extended and mocking meditation on supposedly weeping statues of the Virgin Mary (V, 260).

The broader absurdities of Marian devotion are also skewered by O'Casey's late plays. He eagerly digested information about religious apparitions at Lourdes and elsewhere, collecting clippings that reported, for example, that 'A young man appeared to be healed. He died'.[71] Indeed, the playwright had good reason to feel grimly cynical about miracle cures, having witnessed the agonies of his own dying son in 1956.[72] Accordingly, in *The Drums of Father Ned*, the name of the saint who saw the Marian vision at Lourdes, Bernadette, belongs to a young character who does a provocative dance, 'jutting her bottom out in an excited way' (V, 191). In *Cock-A-Doodle Dandy*, the paralysed Julia pilgrimages to Lourdes, but returns without any cure. And in *Behind the Green Curtains* the characters repeatedly mock the 'useless prayers' of the Pyrenean grotto (V, 258).[73]

Of course, whether or not such writings provide evidence of a deep-rooted religious alignment, a great deal of O'Casey's judgement on Irish Catholicism in the mid-twentieth century also happened to be true. Since 2005 a series of official enquiries have exposed the secrecy and oppression of Catholic institutions, as well as the self-serving nature of the ecclesiastical hierarchy. Today, many devout Catholics in Ireland would tend to agree with O'Casey about the noxious intersection of state and clerical power that long existed in the country. During the summer of 2011, even the Mass-going Irish prime minister denounced 'Roman clericalism' as 'devastating' and declared that Irish law would from now on 'always supersede canon laws that have neither legitimacy nor place in the affairs of this country'.[74] Of course, O'Casey had made precisely this argument half a century earlier, with the sympathetic character of Beoman in *Behind the Green Curtains* declaring that priests 'must submit to the laws of the land they live in; where they move an' have their being. They must be subject to the State, without any cod benefit or privilege of priesthood' (V, 291).

O'Casey's late writing also prefigures some of the successful work written by subsequent dramatists in Britain and Ireland. The basic idea behind *The Bishop's Bonfire* involves a nervous community awaiting the arrival of an authoritarian prelate, and provides the template for a Rabelaisian episode of the acclaimed TV comedy *Father Ted* in the 1990s, entitled 'Kicking Bishop Brennan up the Arse'. Another writer who moved from London to Devon, Jez Butterworth, premiered his hit play *Jerusalem* in 2009, conjuring up similar Dionysiac energies to *Cock-A-Doodle Dandy* by presenting the character of Johnny 'Rooster' Byron. 'Rooster' first appears barking like a dog, moves like '*a dancer, or animal*' and influences a group of young acolytes despite facing hostility from sometimes violently repressive opponents.[75] Meanwhile, in Dublin, O'Casey's *The Drums of Father Ned* may have been rejected at the Dublin Theatre Festival of 1958, but the festival itself continued in subsequent years, and more recently O'Casey's work has appeared on the bill alongside new performances that excoriate aspects of mid-twentieth-century Irish Catholicism. In the Dublin Theatre Festival of 2011, *Juno and the Paycock* could be seen at the same time as Brokentalkers' *The Blue Boy*, a harrowing, multimedia portrayal of child abuse in the Artane Industrial School, as well as Anu Theatre's devastating site-specific work *Laundry*, which condemned the Magdalene Laundry on Gloucester Street by encouraging audience members to interact with a cast recreating the suffering experienced by women and children. These theatrical events explored exactly those ideas about institutional bullying, brutality and misogyny of which O'Casey had been so well aware. In 1947, for example, he met one survivor of abuse, Desmond Brannigan, and noted, 'He was reared up in an Irish Industrial School – a place, governed by Christian Brothers, where little is learned, and boys are knocked senseless'.[76] Nothing could be further from the progressive educational ideals that O'Casey had discovered in the work of Patrick Pearse. However, in the mid-twentieth century, Irish popular opinion failed to embrace O'Casey's ideas about Catholicism, and the writer himself did little to dispel the notion that he had become a wilful controversialist, if not a downright sectarian blowhard. In 1949 Austin Clarke pointed out that Catholic theology 'now seems to have a morbid fascination for him', and in the 1950s even Flann O'Brien, writing satirically for the *Irish Times*, criticized O'Casey's hieratic obsession as being 'all very tiresome indeed'.[77]

Emigration

As a result of this theological kerfuffle, other significant aspects of O'Casey's late works have tended to remain in the shade. For one thing, the elderly O'Casey is one of the great Irish writers of emigration, and these mature writings are permeated by the theme in a similar way to the output of a playwright like Tom Murphy. After all, O'Casey wrote his late dramas at a time when Ireland had set about shedding its population at the most rapid rate since the 1800s. As Robert E. Kennedy points out, in the decade from 1951 an average of 409,000 abandoned Ireland every year, leaving the country in 1961 depleted by 2.8 million people or one-seventh of the total population.[78]

Consequently, each of O'Casey's late plays is set in an Ireland that is wracked by emigration, where the country is ossifying into conservatism because some of the brightest and most energetic citizens are being leached away. By the end of *Cock-A-Doodle Dandy*, O'Casey presents a stage denuded of its key characters, as the key figures decide to travel to 'a place where life resembles life more than it does here' (IV, 221). The same atmosphere of loss pervades *The Drums of Father Ned*, where the end of *An Tóstal* sees ten workers leaving the local factory for England, and where the title character enacts his own form of exile by declining to appear on the stage. Similarly, at the conclusion of *The Bishop's Bonfire*, Daniel plans to leave for England as soon as the flames have died down, Manus makes his escape, and the very final words of the play are those of the song 'Bring Back my Bonnie to Me' (V, 125). Likewise, O'Casey's last full-length play, *Behind the Green Curtains*, concludes with the three most liberated characters leaving for England, trailing the 'Tens of thousands, boys an' girls, [who] have done it' (V, 323). In the years since O'Casey drafted these lines, Ireland has repeatedly looked to such a solution in times of economic crisis, potentially giving O'Casey's late plays a continuing thematic relevance to members of the most recent 'generation emigration'.

At the time O'Casey wrote these scripts, a number of Dublin's politicians and journalists worried that the Irish abroad would embarrass the country, potentially highlighting the poor conditions that existed at home and confirming anti-Irish stereotypes. Éamon de Valera made a well-known speech in Galway in 1951 in which he pointed to the undesirable nature of English 'digs' and warned that those who inhabited such lodgings risked diminishing 'the prestige of our people generally'.[79] Of course, O'Casey had long been accused of disgracing Ireland in this way. As early as the 1920s, St John Ervine reported hearing an English spectator saying of *Juno*, 'If I were a patriotic Irishman I should refuse to act in that play outside Ireland! [. . .] Such people! *Such* people! I'd hate to expose my country like that!'[80] Yet for all O'Casey's criticisms of his homeland, he remained fiercely loyal to Ireland. He declared 'I wouldn't think of surrendering my Irish citizenship', and always considered his British-born children as Irish, writing: 'I'd like Breon & Niall & Shivaun to see their own countrie [*sic*], "its glory and its shame" as Connolly wrote; though, on the whole, sardonic critic as I am, I'd say more glory than shame; far more glory'.[81]

Girls are Fleein'

One of the most striking features of Irish emigration has always been the number of women who have left the country. Elsewhere in Europe, men have typically formed the majority of migrants, but, as Bronwen Walter points out, 'Irish women have left in greater numbers than men in most decades since 1871 when reliable statistics were first recorded', identifying the underlying trend that 'the ratio of women to men in emigration streams increased steadily from 1,010 women per 1,000 men in 1871–81 to a high point of 1,365 in 1946–51'. This meant that, of the women living in the Irish republic in 1946, one in three had departed abroad by 1971.[82]

Heather Ingman points out that women often left Ireland because of 'dissatisfaction with their life and status'. Push factors included the poor social and working conditions that existed on isolated farms, the 1937 constitution that lavished attention on the role of women within the home, and the fact that the Irish Free State had introduced a marriage bar in 1923, preventing anyone with a husband from remaining employed in a number of occupations. This rule remained in place until 1973.[83]

In *Cock-A-Doodle Dandy* the question of emigration is focused on Loreleen, who points out that 'th' girls are fleein' in their tens of thousands' (IV, 194), and O'Casey shows a particular sensitivity to the reasons why women might feel compelled to leave. A word that repeatedly occurs in the late plays is 'bitch', the term used so evocatively by O'Casey in his earlier play *The Plough and the Stars* at the moment when Bessie Burgess, who has been gently caring for Nora, is shot. When Bessie curses Nora, the play refuses to move towards reconciliation or redemption, and O'Casey returns to this word with similarly jolting effect in his late work, with Michael using the term to refer to his wife and daughter in *Cock-A-Doodle Dandy*, and Manus describing his ex-lover as a 'bitch' in *The Bishop's Bonfire*, immediately before shooting and killing Foorawn in a death scene that explicitly recalls Bessie's in *The Plough and the Stars* (V, 123).[84]

Such terminology indicates the atmosphere of misogyny that, for O'Casey, characterized the conservative, male-dominated and repressed Ireland of the mid-twentieth century, and he graphically illustrated this theme by including scenes of attempted sexual assault in his late plays. In these works, a middle-aged Irishman usually attacks an unwilling woman of roughly half his own age, after which she is blamed for incitement. For example, in *Behind the Green Curtains*, the obnoxious Catholic leader, Kornavaun, tries to molest Noneen, and although she pushes him away, he observes, in language that combines John Donne and St Patrick's Breastplate, 'You're damned pretty before, behind, an' below, as I seen when I folleyed you upstairs' (V, 277), later blaming her for being a 'little whorish tantaliser' (V, 317). The same dynamic recurs between Mahan and Loreleen in *Cock-A-Doodle Dandy*, Rankin and Keelin in *The Bishop's Bonfire*, and Skerighan and Bernadette in *The Drums of Father Ned*. In this environment, where misogyny dominates, it is little surprise that women feel compelled to escape.

Unstaged

Ironically, although O'Casey's late plays dwell on migration and loss, they have themselves been banished from the stage, consistently failing to find a place in the dramatic repertoire. O'Casey himself declared *Cock-A-Doodle Dandy* 'my favourite play; I think it is my best play', and hoped that time might vindicate his positive feeling about the work.[85] But in reality such assertions have scarcely been tested one way or the other in the English-speaking world, where the late texts are so little known, and so rarely performed, that few people have had the opportunity to evaluate his writing.

For some critics, the fundamental problem of O'Casey's later works is that he tries to deal with the real-life issues facing Ireland and Catholicism, but bases his attack upon an assortment of remote memories and second-hand reports. Perhaps more fundamentally, however, O'Casey's late playwriting is hindered by a related problem that affects the overall construction of these scripts, namely that as he tried to write these dramatic works he increasingly knew about practical theatre-making only as a detached outsider. As a result of his distance from the living world of the playhouse, the plots tend to stutter, with moments of transition between the folkloric and the contemporary becoming awkward and self-conscious. Many of his inclusions are inventive and *sui generis*, and there is nothing bankrupt about the elderly playwright's imagination. But some closer collaboration with editors, actors and directors may have helped to rid the plays of what are, at times, rushed denouements, one-dimensional characters and simplistic moralizing. After all, when O'Casey wrote his masterpieces, *The Plough and the Stars* and *Juno and the Paycock*, he had an intimate knowledge of the acting company. The character of Fluther Good would have been inconceivable without the skills of Barry Fitzgerald, just as Juno could never have gained theatrical life without Sara Allgood. When, in 1997, the Abbey Theatre unearthed the promptbook for *The Plough and the Stars*, researchers could see just how collaborative the process of staging that work had been. The promptbook reveals, quite aside from the changes that Yeats requested, further additions and suggestions in the hand of both O'Casey and the director Lennox Robinson.[86] Similarly, Gabriel Fallon recalled that, in *Juno*, O'Casey had originally included what must have been a somewhat clunky scene that depicted the roadside execution of Johnny Boyle. The Abbey directors insisted on this being cut from the production, leaving O'Casey feeling 'rather aggrieved', and leading Fallon to reflect 'that the directors were perfectly right and that the shooting of Johnny Boyle was in the imagination of the audience infinitely more terrible [. . .] the artist is not always the best judge of his work'.[87] As Paul O'Brien writes:

> With the help and encouragement of Lennox Robinson and especially Lady Gregory, O'Casey worked to develop his style and technique. Robinson thought his early plays were too didactic, though well conceived, and encouraged him to move away from stereotypical characters and 'replace them with characters drawn from his own experience'. Lady Gregory convinced him to 'throw over my theories and work on my characters' and it was this character-based technique that brought him success [. . .] that he took Yeats's advice seriously is evident from the inscription in the presentation copy of *Juno and the Paycock*: 'The man who by the criticism of a bad play of mine made me write a good one'.[88]

When O'Casey and the Abbey parted company he lost this network of noisy and sometimes meddlesome assistants, and his late plays consequently bear the signs of a dramatist who has been writing for too long in solitary confinement.

Yet the elderly playwright continued, admirably, to engage with the immediate problems facing the young people of modern Ireland, and scorned the idea of simply replicating the earlier style of his most commercially successful works. Furthermore, his late plays point forward instructively to later theatrical successes. Companies such as Theatre Workshop, 7:84 Scotland, and Kneehigh would, in the twentieth and twenty-first centuries, integrate societal critique, popular music, symbolic staging and the youthful energy of dance and disruption into engaging theatrical presentations. These companies of course worked hard to bring writers into close contact with actors and directors, so that semi-improvised moments could become part of the warp and weft of the performance text.[89] As we shall see in the following chapter, O'Casey's works outside the Dublin trilogy have often gained their best reputation in the non-Anglophone world, where relatively free translations and adaptations of the scripts have identified what is best within his theatrical vision, while straying from many of the specific details of O'Casey's writing, in effect providing through posthumous production the kind of collaborative and creative approach to the scripts that the living writer failed to find after 1926.[90] What is so striking about the Abbey promptbook for *The Plough and the Stars* is O'Casey's awareness of proxemics and physicality, with the dramatist focusing not simply on the words spoken but on specific ideas about how the bodies should move and be positioned upon the stage. Hence, we find him adding details about how exactly Nora ought to take her hat off, or how Rosie should adjust her shawl.[91]

However, in old age, O'Casey had lost his connections with practical theatre makers, and felt dubious about the 'tampering' approach of groups like Theatre Workshop.[92] Indeed, when away from his contacts at the Abbey, he may always have felt something of this suspicion. After he first arrived in England in 1926, the drama reviewer for the *Daily Express* noted the playwright's reticence about actually seeing the production of *Juno and the Paycock* then onstage in London, with the journalist subsequently reporting, 'O'Casey admitted that he had not visited his own play on the previous night. Indeed, it was not until a week later that [James] Fagan [the director] persuaded the shy and highly strung Dubliner to see his first English audience'.[93] O'Casey grew still more wary of watching live versions of his work in later years, leading to the Dublin rumour that he felt too afraid to attend the opening of *The Bishop's Bonfire*.[94]

The bombast of O'Casey's public pronouncements might imply that his out-of-touch attitude revealed little more than pig-headedness. But a more fair-minded critique must acknowledge that O'Casey continually sought new ways of expressing a theatrical vision that would escape some of the hidebound assumptions of the contemporary stage. Like Brecht, O'Casey saw that dominant modes of theatre had a number of limitations that writers ought to expose and transcend. But whereas Brecht always felt at home in the rehearsal room, O'Casey increasingly felt like an interloper here and suffered at times from a crippling social awkwardness. O'Casey came to believe that he belonged hunched over the typewriter rather than in the world of improvisations and warm-up exercises, and in the late 1930s he positively fled from the invitation to work in collaboration with the director Michael Chekhov and the actors at Dartington Hall. At times O'Casey revealed his lack of confidence in his own work, such as when the *New York Times* anthologized two of his articles in 1954, triggering 'a slap of fright. I usually wonder if they be worthy of selection'.[95] On another occasion he admitted to finding his early work 'commonplace & immature' before adding, 'not that my present or early-past is so amazingly good either'.[96]

When the dramatist reflected on the process of writing *The Bishop's Bonfire* and *The Drums of Father Ned* he confessed that, although he usually proved capable of making friends in a few moments, 'I find it difficult, and have always done so, to talk or write about my work; what I have done, what I intend to try to do. I am what is called a shy fellow, dreading to meet a new acquaintance'.[97] O'Casey is rarely considered a writer with a lack of self-assurance, and yet his splenetic outbursts mask a genuine vulnerability, with the author feeling insufficiently confident to engage in the inevitably rough-and-tumble debates, confrontations and compromises of the rehearsal process. As a result, his late plays fail to make up in execution what they achieve in imagination and ambition, and rather than providing the end of his career with a ringing note of accomplishment, leave us with a tantalizing collection of 'what ifs'.

CHAPTER 6
CRITICAL RESPONSES, 1923–2013

O'Casey and T. C. Murray

Seán O'Casey could scarcely have hoped for a better reaction to his first professionally produced play. At the end of that first version of *The Shadow of a Gunman* in 1923, the onlookers applauded generously and brought O'Casey onto the Abbey Theatre stage for a curtain call. The following day, the *Evening Herald* declared the play 'brilliant, truthful, decisive' and 'flawless'.[1]

In later years, O'Casey helped foster the impression that Ireland had rejected him, but in actual fact *The Shadow of a Gunman* has remained a staple of the Irish theatrical repertoire, along with the two other plays of O'Casey's Dublin trilogy, up until to the present day. This remarkable onstage endurance is perhaps best demonstrated by comparison with a rival playwright who originally shared the auditorium with O'Casey. On 12 April 1923 *The Shadow of a Gunman* appeared as the first part of a double bill, followed by the comedy *Sovereign Love* by the well-established Cork writer, T. C. Murray. Murray was only seven years older than O'Casey, but had already achieved considerable literary success, seeing six of his plays performed at the Abbey since 1910. O'Casey saw Murray as his main rival, cutting out newspaper clippings about the Corkonian and gluing them into a notebook, as well as jealously reading the comments of reviewers who implored the Abbey to revive Murray's work more frequently, because such 'true to life' depictions of rural Ireland made Murray's output 'rank with the Abbey masterpieces'.[2] *Sovereign Love* had already been staged there for 99 performances, and many of those in the large crowd who came to watch the first night of *The Shadow of a Gunman* had doubtless purchased tickets in anticipation of seeing Murray's work.[3] In the event, however, O'Casey's unknown play made the old favourite by Murray

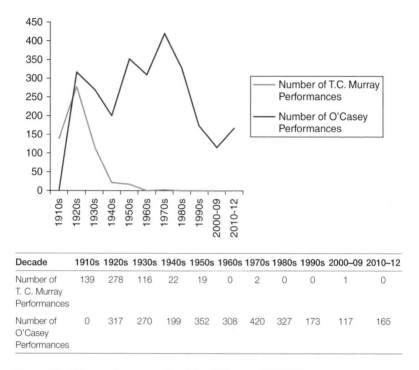

Decade	1910s	1920s	1930s	1940s	1950s	1960s	1970s	1980s	1990s	2000–09	2010–12
Number of T. C. Murray Performances	139	278	116	22	19	0	2	0	0	1	0
Number of O'Casey Performances	0	317	270	199	352	308	420	327	173	117	165

Figure 6.1 Abbey performances of work by O'Casey and T. C. Murray

feel plodding and predictable. In the ensuing years, as shown by the graph in Figure 6.1, the two writers enjoyed quite differing fortunes.[4]

The flatlining of Murray's 13 plays owes much to the public's waning taste for peasant plays, as well as spat between Murray and the Abbey management.[5] But by contrast, the 17 performed plays of O'Casey grew, unsteadily, in popularity towards the 1970s, when, as we shall see, a series of flattering obituaries of the playwright as well as the advocacy of Tomás Mac Anna meant that the Abbey gave special attention to the writer.

Poverty Porn

At the time of O'Casey's second major production, *Juno and the Paycock* in 1924, he sealed his reputation and eclipsed all other rivals in Dublin.

Only a few months after his debut, O'Casey could boast of being the most popular writer at the Abbey Theatre, with his first two successful plays being revived so often that during 1924 roughly one in five Abbey performances, or 78 shows, boasted O'Casey as their author.[6] Furthermore, unlike many other dramas at the Abbey, O'Casey's plays usually filled the house.[7] In 1926, the *Irish Times* described the first performance of O'Casey's third major play, *The Plough and the Stars*, as 'The high-water mark of public interest in the work of the Abbey Theatre', and although the Abbey box office took only £179, £181 and £188 in the three previous weeks, it made more than £434 in the six days of *The Plough and the Stars*. The week afterwards, the theatre took only £156, yet when *The Plough and the Stars* reappeared later in the year the playhouse again recouped over £421.[8]

In the 1920s, O'Casey's appeal relied partly upon the perception that, as the *Irish Times* explained, 'Mr. O'Casey lived among the people he portrays, and he makes his audience live among them, too'.[9] Middle-class theatre patrons could now experience a vicarious thrill in safely touring the tenements with O'Casey, witnessing at one remove the conditions described by the press following the Dublin Housing Inquiry's stomach-churning reports of slum life in 1914. In the twenty-first century, critics have labelled certain movies about the poor as 'poverty porn', in the belief that Western filmmakers and audiences exploit the underclass of the developing world by treating the suffering of other people as a fit subject for 'entertainment' without any critical or moral stance being taken.[10] O'Casey, of course, avoided such charges by claiming to speak of the slums, from the slums. After the success of his second major play, he told Lady Gregory that alongside his writing, he continued as a manual worker, and the *Manchester Guardian* reported that O'Casey 'had stood in a labour exchange queue only last week'.[11]

Lady Gregory, whose childhood had been spent amidst the 4,000 acres of her father's estate at Roxborough, had difficulty in comprehending tenement life, and felt fascinated by O'Casey at least partly as a result of this incomprehension.[12] In conversations during 1923–4, O'Casey effectively rehearsed the first draft of his autobiographies with her, downplaying his middle-class origins and emphasizing his more recent struggles with poverty. Such a strategy

as one of the poor among the poor' and those 'years of life in the slums and in the capricious destinies of the working man in Dublin, always sure of small wages and not always sure of employment'.[17] The influential American critic, Brooks Atkinson, read O'Connor's article, and then conveyed O'Casey's penniless upbringing to the United States in the pages of the *New York Times*, repeating O'Connor's view that O'Casey had been strengthened by experiencing years of poverty.[18] Indeed, when O'Casey first arrived in London, numerous English newspapers reported the apocryphal story that an unrecognizing butler had ejected the congenitally down-at-heel writer from a smart literary soiree being given in the Irishman's honour.[19] Through this process of Chinese whispers, by the end of 1927 O'Casey had become known across two continents as the slum writer who, against all the odds, had developed a precocious literary talent.

At times, O'Casey's identity as a slum dramatist provided a useful defence mechanism. During the riots over *The Plough and the Stars* in 1926, he sidestepped criticism about his mockery of Ireland's dead heroes by claiming that he wished only to write 'about the people that he knew – the bone and sinew of the country'.[20] St John Ervine, a unionist who abhorred the Easter Rising, argued that O'Casey had offered tenement life 'without any middle class palliation or contempt – a fact which no doubt accounts for the hysterical wrath of the refined ladies who kicked up a hullabaloo in the Abbey'.[21] Ervine knew full well that O'Casey's harsh interpretation of the 1916 rebels provided the real reason for the protest, with female relatives of the dead demonstrating against O'Casey. But Ervine preferred to use an argument that dovetailed with O'Casey's public image as the tenement underdog whose honest and untutored bark might silence the noisy pretentions of middle-class life.

Nevertheless, O'Casey's early reputation as a slum writer hindered his later career. W. B. Yeats believed that O'Casey excelled at writing in an autobiographical vein, and after seeing *Juno* in 1924 declared, 'Casey [*sic*] was bad in writing of the vices of the rich which he knows nothing about, but he thoroughly understands the vices of the poor'.[22] Yeats refused to believe the younger man capable of writing about the middle classes, and when O'Casey submitted *The Plough and the Stars*,

Yeats initially felt that 'What is wrong is that O'Casey is writing about people whom he does not know, people he has only read about'.[23] As Nicholas Grene has shown through analysis of the Abbey promptbook, Yeats then persuaded O'Casey to rewrite the play in order to delete those bourgeois elements.[24] The very early notes on the play, now held in New York Public Library, confirm that O'Casey originally conceived Jack Clitheroe as a character who would wear a trilby hat and dark coat, which is the uniform of Adolphus Grigson, the solicitor's clerk of *The Shadow of a Gunman*, rather than that of the labourer Clitheroe would become.[25] Yeats, of course, believed that O'Casey came from the tenements and wished to restrict him to looking back in anger towards that situation.

More widely, the notion that O'Casey wrote directly out of his own experience also won him the label of 'realist', with the critic A. E. Malone, for example, describing O'Casey in 1929 as a 'photographic artist'.[26] In this context, as Bernard Benstock puts it, being a 'realist' might mean little more than that O'Casey 'was well versed in describing the basics of a tenement room'.[27] But such a label could tell only a half-truth, affixed awkwardly onto a set of plays that had been influenced so thoroughly by Shakespeare, melodrama and music hall. As early as 1924, O'Casey told Joseph Holloway of being 'amused when he hears people say, who never were in a tenement, that his plays are photographic of the life he depicts. They not knowing anything at first hand of what they are talking'.[28] Nonetheless, for those who followed Malone's train of thought, O'Casey's later works would inevitably prove disappointing. After all, if you are expecting a photographic impression of Dublin's slums by a writer who has grown up among them, you are likely to feel bemused by plays that include a utopian soviet revolution, an offstage statue that keeps blowing a horn, and the onstage dancing of a human-sized chicken.

Worse still, after O'Casey's death in 1964, a number of biographers exposed the more complex circumstances of his childhood. The writer had not simply been born a slum child, but had lived cheek by jowl with poverty in a middle-class family whose circumstances suffered an unnerving dip after the death of his father. For hostile critics, such revelations made O'Casey look, at best, an unreliable narrator, or, at worst, a charlatan who engaged in a lifelong version of Monty Python's 'we were so poor' sketch. In 1966, the Dubliner Anthony Butler declared starkly that 'foreign scholars have been misled'. Butler's own family lived close to O'Casey's last residence in Ireland, 422 North Circular Road, so Butler knew it 'would be grossly absurd to draw any comparison between the houses there and real tenements'.[29] On further investigation, Butler found that O'Casey's family had never settled anywhere other than in respectable houses, and that even the playwright's short time at tenement-like lodgings in Mountjoy Square had been spent in an area that also housed doctors, solicitors and a hotel proprietor.[30] Butler concluded, in a reversal of what Yeats had once claimed, that O'Casey in fact knew next to nothing of the slums, and that the onstage tenement characters should be thought deeply unconvincing as a direct consequence of O'Casey's alleged lack of actual experience.[31]

Four years after Butler published his findings, the American researcher Martin Margulies published the short and insightful book *The Early Life of Sean O'Casey*. Where Butler exploded the myth that the playwright had inhabited the slums, Margulies emphasized that O'Casey had not been the Dickensian illiterate presented in the autobiographies. Margulies showed that O'Casey's father, earning 5 pounds, 15 shillings and 8 pence a month, had a wage of 'approximately twice what the Dublin manual laborer could expect to earn'.[32] Margulies found that the dramatist's education had affinities with that of G. B. Shaw, and that O'Casey's sister had provided 'more formal education than he acknowledged in the autobiographies'. Margulies also examined O'Casey's school records to show that the would-be author had a rather good history of passing exams and receiving academic prizes from the age of seven.[33]

By the time that Garry O'Connor published his biography, *Sean O'Casey: A Life* in 1988, the dramatist could be introduced as someone who maintained 'contempt for factual truth'. O'Connor stated that O'Casey's 'assumption of poverty was, like a saint's, ultimately an act of will. He fashioned out of actual materials the image, part fact, part fiction, by which he came to be recognized. He saw the opportunity to become the poetic symbol of the Dublin slums: he seized it'.[34] In previous years, O'Casey's time on the breadline had provided a way of excusing the weaker parts of his writing. As John Jordan put it:

> There are occasions, in reading O'Casey, when one loses patience with his lads and lasses, so ardent, so selfconsciously gay, so ostentatious in their pursuit of culture. And then I think of the first three volumes of his great autobiography, and am humbled by that record of mind and imagination and above all enthusiasm, surviving the bitter and bloody arena of the slums in Victorian and Edwardian Dublin.[35]

When scholars reassessed O'Casey's background after his death, they ceased to think in this way, and his self-presentation began to look either evasive or deliberately dishonest. But such judgements are unfair. O'Casey's own home had not been among the worst in Dublin, but he had teetered on the edges of poverty, knew the ragged districts well and faced the prospect of blindness, fatherlessness and a spiral of ever-worsening material deprivation from early in his life.

Walking Away

During his lifetime, O'Casey also faced the insistent allegation that he had betrayed Ireland. He left Dublin for London in 1926, after *The Plough and the Stars* had provoked ructions in the Irish capital and *Juno and the Paycock* had enjoyed a successful run in London's West End. From that point onwards, some Dubliners felt suspicious of the dramatist, who looked like he might be stirring up controversy at home in order to win his day in the sun overseas. Dublin's *Evening Herald* warned darkly that 'by far the worst kind of play is that which shows Irishmen up to the ridicule of foreigners', and when the Abbey revived *The Plough and the Stars* in May 1926, some republican demonstrators duly attempted to recreate the initial protests that had occurred in February by arming themselves with placards and stink bombs.[36]

However, at the performances in May the number of appreciative audience members dwarfed the protestors, and the box office enjoyed a record week. After the police evicted O'Casey's opponents from the revival, the remaining audience members applauded the officers, cheered the show and smoked cigarettes to mask the lingering smell of stink bombs.[37] *The Plough and the Stars* would still stir up controversy on the east coast of the United States, but the play lost its ability to cause protest in Dublin relatively quickly, perhaps in part because the Abbey actors took to editing away some of the potentially controversial material, deleting references to Nora and Rosie's sexuality, erasing phrases that referred to God, and completely eviscerating the scene in which Nora begs Jack to abandon the fighting.[38] The only hint of future riotousness occurred in 1947, when the poet Valentin Iremonger used an Abbey performance of the work to denounce the theatre's conservative programming.[39] Indeed, by 1928 the Dublin press reported of the play that 'It was difficult to think that it was once the cause of a "scene"'.[40] In the immediate aftermath of the 1926 riots, then, O'Casey's work continued to generate generally positive commentary in Dublin. The *Irish Times* observed that the May 1928 production of *Plough* saw the actors returning to the stage half a dozen times to thank the spectators, who clapped and stamped in approval, and who turned out in such great numbers that the auditorium could have been filled twice.[41]

If anything, the riotous reaction to *The Plough and the Stars* had probably assisted O'Casey in the short term, helping to sell tickets for his much-publicized show. But London newspapers had started reporting some distinctly unflattering comments that the writer had supposedly uttered about his homeland, such as 'Ireland isn't good enough for me'.[42] The real turning point came when Yeats rejected *The Silver Tassie*, crystallizing the earlier reservations that some Dubliners felt, with O'Casey's decision to publish the related correspondence simply promulgating Yeats's opinion that O'Casey 'has left his material here in Dublin, and will, in all likelihood, never find it anywhere else'. Cue a *volte face* from the previously supportive *Irish Times*, which now stated that 'Those who shook their heads over Mr. Sean O'Casey's future when they heard that the playwright was going to take up residence in London will find some confirmation of their fears in the fact that the Abbey Theatre directors have rejected his new play'.[43]

Yeats's widely disseminated words only heightened the public's awareness that *The Silver Tassie* had been the first O'Casey work composed in England, well away from the grinding poverty that Yeats pronounced the only begetter of O'Casey's plays. Later critics would follow Yeats in believing that this geographical shift marked a dividing line in O'Casey's oeuvre. As one reviewer put it, 'When Mr. O'Casey shook the dust of the Dublin tenements from his shoes, he shook with it a great deal of his power to write moving plays'.[44] In reality, of course, there is good reason to suspect that O'Casey's decoupling from the Abbey Theatre rather than his removal from the slums had the greatest effect on his writing. However, for a number of commentators, his physical distance from Ireland's tenements became one of the defining features of his later work. For example, by the middle of the twentieth century, Clifford Odets described the sad feeling that O'Casey had given up speaking for the parish, and was instead attempting to speak in a generalized way to the world.[45] However, O'Casey himself had a keen sense of the injustice of such criticism, pointing out that the man who instigated this line of attack, W. B. Yeats, 'conveniently forgot that he himself was educated in his youth in Hammersmith, London; that he lived as a young man there for twenty-five years', and that the Abbey director used Ireland only 'as a pied de terre' [*sic*].[46]

From *The Silver Tassie* onwards, O'Casey's reception in Ireland and Britain tended to diverge. Admittedly, O'Casey's plays struggled to find life on the British stage. But when the new texts appeared in published form, London-based commentators usually reacted in broadly positive terms to material from a writer whose talent had been recognized with the Hawthornden Prize in 1926 and by Hitchcock's decision to film *Juno and the Paycock* at Elstree in 1930.[47] In Ireland, by contrast, although the Abbey continually revived O'Casey's works, pundits often wrote scathingly about the new material by a writer who had emigrated from the country and who espoused anti-Vatican views. For example, the London-based *Times Literary Supplement* dealt with O'Casey's autobiographical writings in the manner described in Table 6.1.

Table 6.1 *TLS* comments on O'Casey's autobiographies

Title of volume	Date	Reviewer's comment
I Knock at the Door	1939	These swift glances back at things that made him and at the peculiar circumstances of his childhood will explain why his tragic comedies have delighted and infuriated Dublin audiences.[48]
Pictures in the Hallway	1942	This prose of his is so manifold, so rich, so bursting with vitality, that it greatly increases respect for the control that moulds such ebullience into the dialogue of the plays.[49]
Drums Under the Windows	1945	A great deal of innocent exhilaration.[50]
Inishfallen, Fare Thee Well	1949	An intolerable deal of rhetoric to a few plain facts, and it is here that Mr O'Casey gives expression to his distrust of priests, his impatience with social reformers and his hopes of Communism.[51]
Rose and Crown	1952	His exuberance is as unfailing as ever; his humour as captivating and preposterous; his pity an enormous tear, in which we find ourselves, like Lilliputians, swimming for dear life.[52]
Sunset and Evening Star	1954	There is to be drawn from Mr O'Casey's dramatized version of himself the same quality of exhilaration that playgoers draw from the pick of his stage characters.[53]
Collected Autobiographies	1963	Excellent value – more than 1,000 pages of prose in a continuous state of excitement.[54]

By contrast, the reviews of O'Casey's autobiographical writings that appeared in the *Irish Independent* tended to dismiss the autobiographies, and to condemn O'Casey's religious views (Table 6.2).

This hostile critical reaction, to say nothing of the official censorship, felt particularly galling for O'Casey, who assiduously took delivery of the Irish newspapers at his house in Devon. He had not abandoned

Table 6.2 *Irish Independent* comments on O'Casey's autobiographies

Title of volume	Date	Reviewer's comment
I Knock at the Door	1939	The book, in my opinion, is unsuitable for youthful Catholic readers.[55] *Two months after publication the censorship board banned the book in Ireland, only lifting the restriction in 1947.*
Pictures in the Hallway	1942	*No review: the Irish censorship board again banned the book between 1942 and 1947.*
Drums Under the Windows	1945	The writing is a queer mixture [. . .] It is a book which, I think, no Irish Catholic could read without feelings of pity and disgust.[56]
Inishfallen, Fare Thee Well	1949	*Appears in 'books received' section, without comment on content.*[57]
Rose and Crown	1952	The more one reads of Mr O'Casey's autobiography the more one is sorry that he did not stick to his last. His reputation as a dramatist will hardly be enlarged by his venture into this other field of English [. . .] He has few good words to say of any person or institution mentioned, and needless to say his choicest sneers and jibes are reserved for the Christian churches in general and the Catholic Church in particular.[58]
Sunset and Evening Star	1954	It is scarcely autobiography in the true sense; it is more an occasion for the author to spread and sprawl in print his virulence, prejudices and contempt for the world in general and the Catholic Church in particular [. . .] he is bitter, bumptious and a terribly boring word-spinner. What is worse, he is tiresome.[59]

Ireland, but returned to it obsessively in his writing, knowing, as any admirer of James Joyce would do, that exile could provide a creatively liberating view of home.

However, if Joyce gained a reputation for literary experimentation and innovation, O'Casey's émigré status scarcely provided the same opportunity. As Andrew Gibson points out, Joyce's decision to settle in Paris in the 1920s brought the novelist to an artistic and intellectual hub, replete with opportunities to meet Ernest Hemingway, Djuna Barnes, T. S. Eliot, and Wyndham Lewis.[60] But if Joyce had the opportunity to 'make it new' among numerous avant-garde admirers in the cosmopolitan centre of Europe, the Devon-based O'Casey could be dismissed as retreating away from innovation into the anonymity of a conservative, English backwater.[61] O'Casey scarcely lived among the leading experimentalists of the age in Totnes, and his literary visitors tended to be committed academic acolytes. After 1941, while the safely dead Joyce could be praised for maintaining a forensic knowledge of Dublin's streets, the living O'Casey received criticism for being out-of-touch.[62]

In the 2010 novel *Ghost Light*, Joseph O'Connor satirizes Irish reaction to O'Casey in the mid-twentieth century:

> They say he lives someplace on the south coast of England (*Jaysus*), is grown shrivelled with his hatreds, has been blind many years. He wears a skullcap and seaboots and a filthy Aran sweater he stitched from dead critics' hair. A face like an elephant's bullock, one of the stagehands once chuckled, and that was neither today nor yesterday, God knows. Poor Johnnybags Casey and his harem of perceived slights. What must they make of him, the villagers and their children, as he shambles the fogs like a poisoned old dosser on his way to sign fraudulently at the Labour?[63]

As we shall see, for many international audiences, O'Casey has proven himself a master-craftsman of slapstick comedy, but O'Connor's writing highlights an Irish tendency to focus instead upon O'Casey as a creator of inadvertent comedy, with the playwright himself as the butt of the joke. From the perspective of much of Dublin, then, both Joyce and O'Casey may have jumped ship, but only one had jumped successfully.

My New-Found Land

If O'Casey's new work met with an increasingly hostile reaction in mid-twentieth century Ireland, his reputation enjoyed an entirely different fate in the United States. The exciting news of his initial Abbey plays had travelled to New York by 1926, where in March of that year, two of the most important twentieth-century drama critics attended the continent's initial production of his work. The first reviewer, George Jean Nathan, co-edited the *Smart Set* magazine, founded the *American Mercury* magazine, and found himself described by H. L. Mencken as 'the *only* American dramatic critic worth reading'.[64] The second, Brooks Atkinson, acted as theatre critic of the *New York Times* for 31 years, and 'presided over Broadway' according to Arthur Miller.[65] Both Nathan and Atkinson actually felt slightly disappointed with the United States' first O'Casey production, a version of *Juno and the Paycock* given at the cramped Mayfair Theater in New York, but they nevertheless praised O'Casey's text and prepared the ground for the Abbey players, who embarked on three long tours of North America from late 1931, with the Dublin actors showcasing O'Casey's work and cementing his reputation as the best-known living Irish playwright in the English-speaking world.[66]

During the following decade, Nathan and Atkinson reacted with delight when the author himself visited their city. Nathan witnessed the New York production of *Juno*, and then travelled to England to watch James Fagan's production of *The Plough and the Stars*, which the critic praised in the *American Mercury* as London's major theatrical event of the year.[67] Nathan asked O'Casey himself to contribute something to the *American Spectator* magazine, and the playwright, who had already read and admired Nathan's book *The Critic and the Drama*, submitted the new play *Within the Gates*. Nathan relished this script so much that he helped secure a production on Broadway in 1934, and invited O'Casey to attend rehearsals.[68] Such zeal proved a much-needed tonic for O'Casey, still smarting from the Abbey's rejection of *The Silver Tassie*, and in his autobiographies O'Casey describes spending time in New York with Nathan as being something like a Wordsworthian love affair: 'A joy-ride: the pair of them were young again, and heaven was all around them' (*Auto* III, 169). The homoerotic subtext of such descriptions is clear, and is perhaps why O'Casey made such strenuous efforts to demonstrate his homophobia in correspondence with Nathan following this visit.[69] Still, in the following years, Nathan would remain reliably boosterish, writing so exuberantly that the envious St John Ervine snapped: 'stop talking about Sean O'Casey as if he were heaven's only light. He is superb music-hall with a hint, now and then, but rarely, of a poet – that's all'. Nathan responded by declaring that O'Casey is 'at his best the best of all living Irish playwrights but even at his worst so much better than three-quarters of them at their best'.[70]

O'Casey also met Brooks Atkinson during this 1934 trip to New York, and although O'Casey would never return to the United States, Atkinson visited England and proved a consistent friend and champion during the following three decades. Unlike O'Casey's detractors in Ireland, Atkinson was keen to promote the idea that there had been no falling off in O'Casey's output, and that the playwright proved friendly and respectful to a range of different people.[71]

Perhaps it had simply been good luck that O'Casey established such enduring friendships with Atkinson and Nathan in 1934, but this wooing of American critics may also have been a canny move for a writer who had notably failed to cultivate supporters in London. In 1957 he reflected, 'the London patrons of the theater dont like O'Casey, and the literary critics, I fear, don [*sic*] like him very much either. It is a matter of indifference to me, for over many years now, I have fixed mine [e]yes on the hills – that is to say, the theater patrons of New York'.[72] Similarly, in his autobiographies he reflected, with surely faux naivety, on his newfound closeness to the reviewers in the United States (*Auto* III, 191–2), and by 1937 Hollywood had acknowledged O'Casey's significance with John Ford filming *The Plough and the Stars*.[73]

Nevertheless, despite winning praise from Nathan and Atkinson, O'Casey's reputation for atheism and communism made the playwright suspect in the eyes of many in the United States, particularly with the onset of the Cold War. After Boston's clerics had forced the cancellation of *Within the Gates* in the 1930s, the 1940s saw Macmillan refuse to publish *Cock-A-Doodle Dandy* in New York, and the early 1950s witnessed *Red Roses for Me* opening to protests in Houston, Texas. In California, the McCarthyite Tenney committee labelled O'Casey as a 'dangerous subversive', and Arthur Miller later observed that 'Caution set in among critics and commentators toward the work of a man who, it was said, still wore a hammer-and-sickle badge on his lapel'.[74]

Paul Shyre

In this climate, O'Casey risked being permanently muzzled if not for an enthusiastic young producer called Paul Shyre, who at first viewed the playwright with a kind of religious reverence.[75] Perhaps surprisingly, Shyre refrained from staging the Dublin trilogy, but, in 1954, first asked O'Casey for permission to stage *Purple Dust*. The playwright's rejection of this request was virtually autonomic, but Shyre persisted and instead adapted and presented the first volume of O'Casey's autobiographies, which in 1956 appeared as a kind of pared-down, public reading.[76] Shyre's work initially emerged as a low-key event, given during a snowstorm in the spring at New York's Kaufmann auditorium, but Shyre remained determined, and staged a similar version of the second volume in May.[77] He then toured the material to Harvard and Massachusetts Institute of Technology in the summer, before returning to give the shows again in New York.[78] Audiences proved so appreciative that longer runs soon commenced at other venues off and then on Broadway.[79] Predictably, Brooks Atkinson threw his weight behind the productions, endorsing the work in the *New York Times*.[80] Shyre then catered for popular demand by recording a Tony-nominated LP of the second volume of the autobiographies, and producing an onstage version of the tricky third volume, which has a more diffuse storyline.[81] New York spectators watched revivals of Shyre's shows many times between 1956 and the early 1970s, with the adaptations drawing positive attention to O'Casey by revealing the Irishman not as a problematic communist figure, but as a writer who had lived a version of the American dream, overcoming unpromising beginnings through resourcefulness, determination and sturdy self-sufficiency.[82]

After the critical and financial success of the staged autobiographies, Shyre then turned to O'Casey's unfamiliar play-texts, particularly *Purple Dust*, a script written almost two decades earlier but not yet seen anywhere in the United States. The director Sam Wanamaker had sought to bring the piece to New York in 1953, but after a loss-making and poorly received UK tour Wanamaker ditched his plans. O'Casey had then refused permission for Shyre to direct this piece in 1954, but when the writer eventually acceded, Shyre's production ran for 480 performances during 1956–8 at the Cherry Lane Theater in Greenwich Village, thus providing the longest-lasting production of any O'Casey drama, and the playwright's only sustained theatrical success since *The Plough and the Stars*.[83]

In the light of such triumph, the composer Marc Blitzstein and writer Joseph Stein created and staged O'Casey's earlier work in a truly Broadway form: the musical 'Juno' opened in 1959, and although the show lasted for only 16 performances, it did later win admirers through an original-cast recording, and revivals in 1992 and 2008.[84] Theatres in London and Dublin also requested that Shyre bring his shows to those cities, although O'Casey's professed distrust of English and Irish audiences scuppered any such plans.[85] Nevertheless, at the end of 1957 O'Casey felt deeply grateful for Shyre's work in the United States, 'for the weekly dollars are very welcome'. The director hosted O'Casey's daughter in New York, staged a short-lived version of *Cock-A-Doodle Dandy* in Toronto and New York, and twice rendezvoused with O'Casey in Devon, causing the Irishman to declare that 'it was a good day for me when a lad named Paul Shyre came into my vision over the hills'.[86] In September 1957 O'Casey even wrote to the then Prime Minister of Britain, Harold Macmillan, to pass on a copy of an article that Shyre had written in the *New York Times*.[87]

O'Casey evidently felt thrilled by Shyre's achievements with the autobiographies, jotting in a notebook:

> Between the writing of plays, in the dead vast middle of the night, when our children & their mother slept, I often sat down and let my thought wander back in time, murmuring the remembrance of things past with the listening ear of silence; fashioning them

into unspoken words, & setting these down upon the sensitive tablets of the mind [. . .] Now the characters have stepped out of the pages, and American actors have breathed life into them the heart of Dublin life, have shown on the New York Stage the wonder of a growing child.[88]

However, the success of the dramatized autobiographies also encouraged other producers to look afresh at O'Casey's work, and Shyre became concerned that the writer might grant the rights to the plays in a willy-nilly fashion that could damage Shyre's own interests. Most troubling of all was the spectre of Hollywood sniffing around the texts that Shyre had popularized. After all, Shyre himself harboured an ambition to use O'Casey's writing to break into film, planning an ill-starred celluloid version of *Purple Dust*, which never appeared despite O'Casey's confession to a neighbour that 'I'm more interested in that than anything the B.B.C. can do with my work'.[89] Shyre afterwards directed a television version of *Juno and the Paycock* which O'Casey learned had been 'pretty bad', despite Shyre's own boast of having made 'a very good production'.[90] At about this time, O'Casey also realized that Shyre's theatrical version of *Cock-A-Doodle Dandy* had been 'mishandled very badly – a shocking production, & it deserved nothing but a quick retirement'.[91] So O'Casey instructed his US agent to decline Shyre's requests to tackle *Within the Gates* and *The Silver Tassie*, feeling that the director ought to handle something less ambitious.[92] Meanwhile, O'Casey had been wooed in person by two other would-be movie producers, one of whom had impressed O'Casey so much that the playwright started to refer to the potential filmmaker as 'our son'.[93] These competitors ruined Shyre's prospects, as they, rather than him, gained permission to adapt the autobiographies as the film *Young Cassidy* in the early 1960s. This MGM version of O'Casey's story followed Shyre's approach, removing political radicalism from the dramatist's priorities, and instead advertising the movie with the tagline: 'Bellowing, Brawling, Womanizing Your Way! He's in action morning, noon and night – after every woman and wonder in sight!'[94]

Meanwhile, Paul Shyre felt justifiably aggrieved. In the 1950s, at a time when O'Casey received little by way of royalties from anywhere else, the Broadway success of *Purple Dust* provided much-needed cash, as well as helping to rekindle interest in O'Casey, who was shortlisted for the Nobel Prize in 1960 and offered an OBE in 1962.[95] The communist playwright who was once *persona non grata* in the United States had, partly as a result of Shyre's tenacity, gained such a loyal following in the country that by 1962 the arts editor of the *Irish Times* could write the following parody, comparing O'Casey's transatlantic popularity with that of Joyce:

> Yesterday – June 25th 1995 – a black flag with a green crow on it was unfurled from a Dublin building to mark the 71st anniversary of Boylesday and the opening of the Sean O'Casey museum [. . .] A group of 235 American O'Casey students attended the opening ceremony together with a number of fashion and gossip writers [. . .] The minister for Culture and Tourism, in his address of welcome, said [. . .] such were the numbers of American tourists who were coming to this country in search of O'Caseyiana that his department was considering reviving the defunct Abbey Theatre in some years' time to coincide with the falling-in of copyright of the author's work.[96]

Yet, for Paul Shyre, O'Casey's decision to grant the movie rights to MGM felt like a slap in the face. If Shyre had played things more cannily, he might still have forged a career in film, as the elderly playwright had won a promise from the producers of *Young Cassidy* that they would employ Shyre if at all possible.[97] However, the wounded American remained unaware of this commitment, and made a calamitous mistake by threatening O'Casey with court action. Shyre should have known better, as he had no grounds for claiming rights to the autobiographies, and his *bêtise* predictably slammed the door on the friendship, with O'Casey angrily eviscerating Shyre's legal claims in a lengthy set of letters. The dramatist also contacted his US agent Jane Rubin, to declare: 'There has been too much of Paul must do this, Paul must have that altogether; you and he demand a bit too much; but Paul will never handle anything of mine again'.[98] In turn, Shyre criticized O'Casey for 'holding a grudge so long and answering me the way some petulant child would'.[99] The rift could scarcely be healed now. In fact, in O'Casey's correspondence, he deliberately took to misspelling Shyre's name, a belittling tactic that Yeats had once employed with the young O'Casey.

Of course, Shyre had overstepped the mark in assuming that his efforts gave him a proprietorial claim over O'Casey's creative works. Yet there could be little doubt that Shyre had done more than anyone since Lady Gregory to popularize O'Casey through performance. Perhaps appropriately, O'Casey's friendship with these two supporters ended in similar acrimony, even if, after the dramatist's death, Shyre himself started to suffer a selective amnesia about the relationship, describing only a 'long and happy acquaintance with Sean O'Casey's work'.[100] Less than a month after the playwright died, Shyre even co-directed a New York tribute-show, *Hurrahs! And Faretheewells*, a specially adapted version of the first two autobiographical pieces, starring a remarkable cast that included Martin Sheen, Lillian Gish and Brooks Atkinson, as well as the Clancy Brothers and Tommy Makem.[101] Shyre himself never again enjoyed the kind of Big-Apple triumph that he had experienced when working with O'Casey's texts, and the director spent his later career attempting to recapture those past glories.[102] Yet his versions of O'Casey's autobiographies would long be remembered in New York, with the first two adaptions being revived most recently at the city's New Globe Theatre in November 2007 under the direction of the company's founder Stuart Vaughan, who had directed the premieres 50 years before.[103]

O'Casey and the Academy

Following the labours of Brooks Atkinson, George Jean Nathan and Paul Shyre in the United States, the country's university system provided a talented generation of O'Casey researchers who came to dominate scholarly discussion of the playwright during the 1960s and 1970s.

During the Second World War, O'Casey had befriended the literature teacher David Greene, who had been billeted with the US navy near Plymouth, and who later sought O'Casey's help for a book about J. M. Synge.[104] Greene taught a gifted student, David Krause, who followed in his tutor's footsteps by visiting O'Casey frequently, and who hoovered up O'Casey's letters for publication.[105] According to O'Casey's wife, Krause 'would spend the days at the flat and we looked upon him as one of the family'.[106] This favoured academic later wrote *Sean O'Casey: The Man and His Work*, a volume that owes much to the insights provided by the O'Casey household, but which struggles to find an appropriate critical distance from the playwright, seeking to please O'Casey by avoiding any contradiction with the more improbable details of the autobiographies.[107] As Krause told O'Casey, the project sought 'to awaken everyone to the full significance of your plays' so that 'men of good will the world over' will 'be able to find strength and courage and hope in your powerful and dramatic dramatizations of human spectacle'.[108] Krause, like Paul Shyre, also sought to breathe theatrical life into the autobiographies, and between 1965 and 1972 joined with Patrick Funge, the founder of the small-scale Lantern Theatre, to stage versions of the first three volumes in Dublin. In July and August 1972 the Lantern Theatre gave a back-to-back staging of all three parts, in a show lasting for almost seven hours and which the Dublin *Evening Herald* hailed as a world record.[109] This adaptation provided a part-staged reading of an edited version of O'Casey's work, with a handful of actors playing many parts, and so perhaps inevitably called to mind Paul Shyre's earlier version, with Funge and Krause's private correspondence revealing their anxiety about rivalling Shyre.[110] Still, Funge and Krause incorporated Dublin street songs and actors with genuinely Dublin accents, and so, according to the reviewer Patrick O'Connor, 'this version has managed to avoid most of the stage-Irishisms that vulgarized the Paul Shyre adaptation'.[111]

Another US scholar, Robert Hogan, proved his loyalty to O'Casey by writing a PhD about the playwright's experimental dramatic techniques, and then directing the premiere of *The Drums of Father Ned*.[112] In the subsequent book-of-the-thesis, *The Experiments of Sean O'Casey*, Hogan agrees that O'Casey is 'a great man', confirms without any caveat that the playwright is 'a product of the Dublin slums', and declares that critics have been wilfully obtuse in dismissing much of O'Casey's later drama.[113] Indeed, Hogan absorbed something of O'Casey's own rhetorical style, attacking those who had denigrated the Irishman's work by declaring, 'Drama critics, myself included, have perennially been shiftless, dense, incompetent, argumentative, pompous, self-appointed Brahmins [. . .] the modern practitioners have added the invaluable quality of deafness to their vocational blindness'.[114]

Alongside Hogan and Krause, a third influential academic voice, that of Ronald Ayling, also began to speak on O'Casey's behalf. Ayling first made the pilgrimage to Devon when studying in Leeds, and, although later based at universities in South Africa and Canada, he continued to pay an annual visit to O'Casey until the author's death, and to fight O'Casey's corner in numerous newspapers. So, for example, when a piqued O'Casey banned his work from professional production in Ireland, Ayling contacted the *Manchester Guardian* to declare that this was 'a very worthwhile stand to have made', and when Ireland's press attacked O'Casey, Ayling adopted a Yeatsian persona and told the *Irish Times* that the country's newspapers relied on 'hacks and amateurs'.[115] In addition, Ayling's critical writings aimed to redeem the playwright's later works, declaring: 'In plain words, O'Casey soon outgrew the playwriting possibilities of the Abbey directorate, the practical as well as artistic resources of the theatre's production team and the physical limitations of what was, before 1966, a very tiny theatre'.[116]

Throughout Ayling's career, he continued to defend O'Casey, becoming the literary advisor to the O'Casey estate, and complaining about the 'excited prurience' of Garry O'Connor's biography in the late 1980s. Krause also continued to collect and publish four massive volumes of O'Casey's collected letters between 1975 and 1992. But in 1970, the third of those musketeers, Robert Hogan, fell out of love with the cause, after, according to him, the playwright's wife threatened to sue him for plagiarism and for invasion of privacy. Eileen O'Casey apparently felt upset by a biographical play that Hogan had written called *What Is the Stars?*, and he in turn grew disillusioned with the playwright's estate, reflecting on his earlier enthusiasms:

In the late 'fifties or early 'sixties, Ayling, Krause and, I suppose, myself were constantly in armed and vehement combat against any benighted wretch who assaulted Sean's person or works. And although we were probably more often right than wrong (as there was a lot of stupidity rampant), we may have set an unfortunate pattern. It was a pattern that we were emulating from the Great Man himself, but it was the worst of his influence.[117]

By the 1970s, Hogan may have lost the will to promote O'Casey with such vigour, but books continued to emerge from academics whose thinking and mode of argument had been influenced by him, Ayling and Krause.[118]

Robert Lowery

In particular, one more US-based critic, Robert Lowery, played an influential role in promoting the playwright. In 1974 Lowery had enrolled as an undergraduate in European history at Hofstra University, and unlike the earlier generation of scholars, never had any personal contact with Seán O'Casey.[119] Despite this potential disadvantage, Lowery proved an intelligent and enthusiastic academic supporter, persuading Hofstra to host an O'Casey Festival which he would organize, and to print a new journal which he would edit, called the *Sean O'Casey Review*. He secured the endorsement of O'Casey's widow for his ventures, ambitiously aimed to develop what he called 'O'Casey Studies', and succeeded in producing a regular publication full of fascinating articles.

Lowery demonstrated enviable energy in these endeavours, but could be excessively defensive about O'Casey's reputation and status. For example, in 1978 Katharine Worth published the intelligent study *The Irish Drama of Europe from Yeats to Beckett*, which is scarcely an attack on O'Casey. Indeed, the playwright emerges from Worth's book as a key influence on Beckett.[120] However, Lowery disliked the way Worth identified O'Casey's debt to Yeats, and wrote to O'Casey's widow to warn about Worth's claims.[121] Eileen O'Casey tried to curb Lowery's enthusiasm, and when he set about organizing O'Casey's centenary celebrations in Ireland, she wrote, 'I think it really should be left to the Irish people to do it themselves. I am quite sure the Abbey will do something'.[122]

Lowery then set up a major anniversary event in the United States, organized by his 'American Committee for Sean O'Casey's Centenary', which boasted the support of Ayling, Krause and Hogan, as well as luminaries such as Lynn Redgrave and Pete Seeger. The *New York Times* pronounced Lowery the chief among O'Casey enthusiasts, and he told the newspaper that he had been attracted to O'Casey's work by the playwright's own faith in the goodness of people.[123] Such a viewpoint accounts for the adulatory tone of the *Sean O'Casey Review*, which, according to the editor in the first volume, celebrates 'an exceptional soul' who 'sought to erase from the soil of the earth the plague and pestilence of poverty', and whose death meant 'the world lost a part of its conscience'.[124]

By 1980, Macmillan had decided to publish a set of literary annuals, one on Yeats and one on O'Casey. Lowery's *Sean O'Casey Review* at Hofstra came to an end, and instead he moved to editorship of Macmillan's better-produced *O'Casey Annual*. But although Macmillan's sister journal, the *Yeats Annual*, survives to this day, the O'Casey publication appeared only four times between 1982 and 1985. Ultimately the *O'Casey Annual* perhaps found it difficult to speak to those who had only a passing interest in O'Casey, although the volumes did contain some excellent examples of literary scholarship and formed part of a distinct attempt to revive interest in O'Casey by Macmillan, with the company printing the five-volume complete plays of O'Casey in 1984.[125]

O'Casey's Death

At the start of the 1960s, Ireland followed the US example and started to reappraise O'Casey in a friendlier way. For his eightieth birthday, the *Irish Times* celebrated the writer, criticizing the 'ingratitude, malevolence, jaundice of O'Casey's countrymen to O'Casey', and allowing figures such as Micheál MacLiammóir and Samuel Beckett an opportunity to praise the octogenarian.[126]

The New York success of O'Casey's work in the late 1950s was followed by renewed interest among London producers, and some plays that Paul Shyre had staged in the United States subsequently enjoyed a debut on the English stage. *Purple Dust*, having succeeded on Broadway, now appeared for the first time in London as part of an 'O'Casey Festival' in 1962, more than two decades after the work was written, and in 1959 London saw the British premiere of *Cock-A-Doodle Dandy*, 11 years after O'Casey had composed the piece.[127] Television audiences in Britain and the United States watched O'Casey being interviewed, with NBC broadcasting from his home in Torquay in 1956, and the BBC's *Omnibus* giving a sympathetic presentation of the writer in 1968.[128] In addition, throughout 1964, Irish newspapers excitedly recounted stories about the production of *Young Cassidy*, the cinematic version of O'Casey's autobiographies that, when filmed on location, sprinkled some Tinseltown glamour upon Dublin.

Admittedly, antagonism towards the playwright still existed. On St Patrick's Day in 1960, Ed Sullivan decided to cut from his popular US-television show an interview with O'Casey, after Irish–American leaders contacted Sullivan to protest. The TV host ended up condemning O'Casey as 'rather a shabby expression of Ireland'.[129] Similarly, in 1966, the Irish government committee responsible for co-ordinating the Golden Jubilee of 1916 requested that no O'Casey play should appear at the Abbey Theatre during Easter Week, as the dramatist showed the heroes in an improper light.[130] The Irish Prime Minister Seán Lemass wrote to his minister for posts and telegraphs to warn that the state broadcaster, RTÉ, ought to produce 'suitable' programmes during the anniversary, adding 'This means in particular no O'Casey'.[131] But such conservative paranoia may actually have helped to bolster the playwright's reputation. After all, the Irish Academy of Letters strongly condemned Ed Sullivan's decision as a 'triumph for Yahooism'; while the verdict of the 1916 committee was denounced as 'quite absurd' by the managing director of the Abbey Theatre, Ernest Blythe, and mocked by the *Sligo Champion* as 'possibly the most stupid statement to be issued in the Jubilee year'.[132] Both the Abbey and RTÉ scheduled *The Plough and the Stars* later in 1966.

Furthermore, Brendan Behan's death in March 1964 allowed Ireland to rehearse its reaction to the loss of O'Casey, with Behan's obituarists celebrating 'an exceptional playwright, perhaps the greatest since Seán O'Casey'.[133] O'Casey himself reflected, 'It is a sad thing that Brendan failed to care for, and nourish the talent he undoubtedly had, and sought his last rest far too soon'.[134] When O'Casey died six months after Behan, at more than twice Behan's age, Irish and British newspapers accordingly published an even more laudatory set of eulogies. The *Sunday Telegraph* called O'Casey 'the greatest playwright of the twentieth century' and 'far more experimental and original than Brecht'.[135] The *Irish Times* meanwhile praised O'Casey for producing work that had escaped the restrictive confines of naturalism, crowning him both a 'genius' and one of the 'immortals'.[136]

Accordingly, in the 1960s and 1970s, Irish producers turned their attention to O'Casey's less-familiar works. Despite the dramatist's ban on productions in Ireland, in 1962 Telefís Éireann gained permission to show his one-act sketch, *The Moon Shines on Kylenamoe*.[137] The Dublin director Alan Simpson attempted to stage the equally short *Figuro in the Night* in London in 1963, until forbidden by the British censor.[138] Meanwhile, in 1966, RTÉ supported the idea of presenting the Irish premiere of *The Drums of Father Ned* at the Olympia Theatre, which advertised the drama as 'the O'Casey play that Dublin never saw'.[139]

The director of the Olympia premiere, Tomás Mac Anna, had been a long-term O'Casey enthusiast, although the relationship between the two men had initially looked unpromising. In the 1950s, Mac Anna had taken charge of producing plays in Irish at the Abbey Theatre, and had written somewhat tactlessly to O'Casey to ask 'for your recent one-acts not knowing whether they will be good, bad or indifferent'. In England, O'Casey proudly continued to write letters in enthusiastic if ungrammatical Irish, praised cultural organizations that promoted the language, and described feeling 'rather elated' that Galway audiences would see an Irish-language version of the *Plough* in the 1940s.[140] But he felt peeved by being contacted by 'only' the 'Gaelic element' at his former stomping ground of the Abbey, and declared, 'I have no desire to have my plays done into Irish, so, even had I copies, there would be no use of sending them to you'.[141] O'Casey disliked being reminded that the Abbey management no longer considered him a writer of new work for the main house. When he saw Peter Kavanagh's 1950 volume *The Story of the Abbey Theatre* the dramatist drew a large cross next to Kavanagh's suggestion that after *The Silver Tassie* 'O'Casey wrote no more plays for the Abbey Theatre'.[142] Despite the inauspicious correspondence with O'Casey, Mac Anna acted in the Abbey's version of the *Tassie* at the Queen's Theatre in 1951, and then worked with the Berliner Ensemble on a version of *Purple Dust* in 1966. Mac Anna wanted Ireland to follow Germany's willingness to associate O'Casey with theatrical experimentation, and he suggested that the Abbey ought to produce *The Drums of Father Ned*. The directors returned the script to Mac Anna almost immediately with one word in Irish scrawled on the fly-leaf, 'Truflais!' ['rubbish'], and so the 1966 premiere of *Drums* occurred instead at the Olympia.[143]

Admittedly, O'Casey had continued to launch sallies on the Abbey Theatre towards the end of his life, for example, by telling the *Irish Times* in 1964 that the playhouse had been dead for years.[144] Yet in practical terms he proved more supportive. Three months before his own death, O'Casey relaxed the Irish ban on his work, jokingly telling one indomitable theatre group in Kerry that 'I suppose the best way to get rid of you is to give in to you'.[145] He also allowed the Abbey to produce the Dublin trilogy to mark the four-hundredth anniversary of Shakespeare's birth, and even granted a special extension to the theatre's 1964 run of *The Shadow of a Gunman*.[146] After O'Casey's death, Tomás Mac Anna at the Abbey became the dramatist's greatest Irish champion, directing a remarkable number of unfamiliar works at the playhouse between the late 1960s and the mid-1980s.[147] Indeed, Mac Anna even caused an O'Casey-style controversy with a script of his own about Northern Ireland in 1970, a play that Mac Anna had inevitably named *A State of Chassis*.

Some critics have complained that O'Casey's later plays have been disgracefully neglected by theatre directors and never really given a chance on the stage, and yet in the Ireland of the 1970s, these dramas did appear at the Abbey on a regular basis.[148] Indeed, for a brief period, under Mac Anna's influence, O'Casey's later works appeared at the Abbey with greater frequency than the early pieces (Figure 6.2).

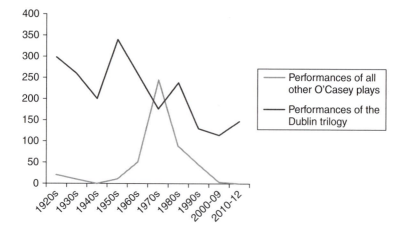

Decade	1920s	1930s	1940s	1950s	1960s	1970s	1980s	1990s	2000–09	2010–12
Performances of *The Shadow of a Gunman*	123	74	25	78	96	40	156	0	0	0
Performances of *Juno and the Paycock*	125	70	59	120	61	30	18	88	0	48
Performances of *The Plough and the Stars*	49	115	115	142	101	106	65	40	114	99
Performances of all other O'Casey plays	20	11	0	12	50	244	88	45	3	0
Performances of the Dublin trilogy	297	259	199	340	258	176	239	128	114	147

Figure 6.2 Abbey performances of O'Casey's Dublin trilogy and his later work

However, just as O'Casey's later plays began to gain a hearing in Dublin, Broadway's estimation of the writer began to change. By the mid-1960s, the *New York Times* had seen its critic Brooks Atkinson replaced by Walter Kerr, which scarcely boded well for O'Casey's reputation. When the *Times* appointed Kerr a number of critics noted his tendency, in his previous work as reviewer at the *New York Herald*, to ignore contemporary avant-gardists, to enthuse mainly over musicals and light comedy, and to show little interest in playwrights such as Strindberg, who O'Casey deeply admired. For example, the *New Republic* critic and dean of the Yale School of Drama, Robert Brustein, observed that Kerr was 'consistently opposed to every experimental play. The fact that Walter Kerr will be the only drama critic of importance and will determine the success or failure of every production dooms the theater to 25 years of mediocrity'.[149]

In previous years, Kerr and Atkinson had clashed over *Red Roses for Me*, a play that Atkinson admired but which, for Kerr, showed how O'Casey had an unfortunate 'bent toward abstraction, the fondness for the giant term rather than the significant detail' and so 'has washed his characters clean of character'. He similarly rejected O'Casey's *Cock-A-Doodle Dandy* for being 'despairing in content'.[150] At the *New York Times*, in 1966, Kerr declared that none of the plays except the Dublin trilogy and *Purple Dust* could be revived, adding caustically that 'revive' was the wrong word for plays that had never found an audience, that O'Casey's entire career had gone wrong, and that the playwright's talent had lapsed into deafness.[151]

The *New York Times*, which had been so supportive of O'Casey during his lifetime, now published harsh criticism of the writer. For example, when David Krause unveiled the first volume of *The Letters of Sean O'Casey* in 1975, the newspaper printed a review declaring that O'Casey could not bear the weight of an enormous publication like this, because his plays were generally so weak.[152] In earlier years, Brooks Atkinson had taught the United States to value O'Casey, but by the 1970s the *New York Times*, so influential in determining the commercial success of playhouse productions, had renounced such judgements.

In this atmosphere, although Krause's compilation of such a comprehensive set of letters provided a treasure trove for committed O'Casey devotees, and did reveal many unknown instances of the playwright's generosity, the publication may ultimately have diminished the playwright's reputation by showing how O'Casey, like most of us, had often spent his time engaged in petty squabbles and passing controversies. In addition, the vast majority of these letters came from outside the period of his most frequently revived plays, as only about one twentieth of the 3,500 pages dates from before or during the premiere of the Dublin trilogy. Those who already found O'Casey's autobiographies repetitive and narcissistic would scarcely look more kindly at the further publication of four massive volumes of letters, and even Krause himself admitted 'A collection of letters that gives only one side of a natural dialogue can be frustrating to the reader'.[153] Broadway neglected O'Casey from the 1960s, and by 1992, when the final volume of the letters appeared, covering just the final five years of O'Casey's life, the publisher's claim that the book was 'surely a necessity for every scholar of Irish drama' looked somewhat wishful.[154]

Non-Anglophone O'Casey

Nevertheless, the significance of O'Casey, and the most important plays within his oeuvre, look quite different when assessed from a variety of international perspectives. In the twentieth century, O'Casey had become a globally recognizable writer, with Ronald Ayling and Michael Durkan tracing translations of O'Casey's work into 26 languages, from Afrikaans to Chinese.[155] Since Ayling and Durkan's survey, the non-English-speaking world has often provided a corrective to the Anglophone theatre in terms of the parts of O'Casey's oeuvre that are generally remembered and celebrated. For example, in the summer of 2010 the National Theatre Bucharest staged its premiere of *The End of the Beginning* ('S-a sfârşit cum a-nceput') in its main auditorium, a 1,155-seat hall in the Romanian capital, and the play remains in the theatre's repertoire at the time of writing in 2012. O'Casey drafted this one-act play in about 1932, after his arrival in London, as a kind of music-hall sketch for Arthur Sinclair, but it took five years before the Abbey produced the piece, and it has rarely been seen on the English-speaking stage since then, even though Samuel Beckett expressed his admiration.[156] The play revolves around the antics of two men, Darry Berrill and Barry Derril, after Darry swaps jobs with his wife because he thinks he can do the housework better than she can. Of course, all goes wrong for Darry. In a premonition of the bovine antics of *Purple Dust*, he decides to tether his cow to a chair, and ends up lodged inside a chimney.

Unlike the Dublin trilogy, *The End of the Beginning* revolves around determinedly agricultural concerns. The housework in question involves caring for pig, heifer and hens, and so the play may have had a particular resonance in modern Romania, where some 32 per cent of the population works in farming and forestry (compared to the EU average of 4.9%).[157] However, the setting alone does not explain the appeal of *The End of the Beginning*, particularly as modern Bucharest can scarcely be considered a rural idyll. Rather, Romanian critics responded favourably to what they identified as the 'Laurel and Hardy' style of clowning demonstrated by the central duo, and such comedy may explain the wider appeal of this piece in the non-English-speaking theatre world.[158] After all, in regions where Ireland's anti-colonial struggle remains unfamiliar, *The End of the Beginning* relies on little reference to Irish political history, but allows audience members to enjoy the observations of a writer who, when in London, visited the Camden Town Music Hall and Metropolitan Music Hall on Edgware Road, and chuckled over the work of artistes including Little Titch, Harry Lauder, Dan Leno, George Roby, Vesta Tilly and Marie Lloyd.[159] This is the kind of variety style that O'Casey had channelled in his characters of Darry and Barry in *The End of the Beginning*, and O'Casey's version of this humour has often proven popular in continental Europe. At the time of writing, as well as the Romanian version, in Austria the Volkstheater in Vienna is scheduled to give its new production of the play in May 2012, and the theatre has again marketed the production as involving the comic style of Laurel and Hardy.[160]

The Austrian Volkstheater and Romanian National Theatre Bucharest, in bringing *The End of the Beginning* to the stage, have followed the example of Germany, where O'Casey's farce has long remained popular. Versions of *The End of the Beginning* ('Das Ende vom Anfang') were given at Berlin's Forum-Theater in 1966; at Schaubühne am Hallenschen Ufer, Berlin, in 1975; and at Theater der Stadt, Brandenburg, in 1976.[161] In 1986, B. K. Tragelehns directed an acclaimed production starring Heinz Werner and Michael Altmann Kraehkamp, which premiered in Munich but then ran for more than a decade (and 500 performances) in venues including Berlin's Schiller-Theater, Hansa-Theater and Volksbühne; leading the German press to hail the play a 'slapstick classic'.[162] Since then, this piece has become a staple of the country's theatre, and at least one recent German critic, Eva-Maria Magel, has pointed out the British music-origins of the play's humour, acknowledging how the joking recalls not only Laurel and Hardy, but also the English comedian Freddie Frinton.[163] The work of Frinton, like *The End of the Beginning*, has been largely forgotten in his homeland, but is widely known in Germany through the now traditional rebroadcasting of his skit 'Dinner for One', on New Year's Eve each year. Hence German audiences retain an affection for the energies of the British music hall, even if those energies have suffered neglect in the English-speaking world.

However, the roots of Germany's affection for O'Casey go deeper than simply a love of O'Casey's revitalized *zanni*. As early as 1931, the *Irish Worker* reported that 'The plays of Sean O'Casey are having a wonderful success in Germany', and before the fall of the Berlin Wall, O'Casey's unequivocal political commitment and his insistence on overturning the old, bourgeois order made him extremely popular with audiences in the communist German Democratic Republic (GDR).[164] The best source for describing the texts available for production in East Germany is the one-time monopoly publishing house in Berlin, Henschelverlag, and one of the last of their catalogues before 1989 lists some 22 plays by O'Casey. Only Shakespeare has more entries.[165] In terms of performance, there were 62 productions of 18 pieces by O'Casey in the former GDR, meaning that audiences here could see his plays that had been largely forgotten elsewhere.[166] For example, in the mid-1960s Eileen O'Casey travelled to East Germany to see the Theatre Der Stadt in Cottbus perform the one-act farce *The Hall of Healing* ('Halle der Heilung'), and wrote the programme notes when the same theatre performed *Behind the Green Curtains* ('Hinter den grünen Vorhängen').[167]

O'Casey also found audiences in West Germany, at least in part because of the advocacy of the director Peter Zadek. Zadek had been born in Berlin, but from the age of eight grew up in Britain, where he first forged his theatre career. However, in his early thirties, he returned to Germany, where he spent the rest of his life, and where he promoted numerous writings first encountered in Britain. As a result he proved one of O'Casey's greatest champions, identifying the Irishman as a writer like Shakespeare who 'sees the people as they are – and loves them as they are: big, small, stupid, dirty, funny, logical or illogical'.[168] Zadek initially staged *The Shadow of a Gunman* ('Der Rebell, der keener war') at Ulm Municipal Theatre in 1960 and at Hamburg's Thalia Theatre in 1961, before in 1967 staging a controversial version of *The Silver Tassie* at the Wuppertal Opera, which angered some because of Zadek's pacifism and the director's provocative assertion, before the premiere, that 'everyone who takes part in the war, is an asshole'.[169] Critics pointed out that such pacifism would have left Hitler in place, but Zadek scarcely felt cowed by the debate, and instead went on to make a somewhat psychedelic television film of the play, under the title *Der Pott*.[170]

Of course, the division between East and West Germany made O'Casey's plays particularly piquant, and at times brought riotous interruptions to the performances. When Berlin's Maxim Gorki Theater staged a first East German performance of *The Star Turns Red* ('Der Stern wird rot') in 1968, the premiere was soon followed by a rival West German version at the Wuppertal Opera, where a noisy auditorium saw a number of prominent audience members walking out, with the Christian Democratic Union mayor denouncing O'Casey's endorsement of communism and demanding that the production should halt straight away.[171] More serious protests occurred in 1953, when Fritz Kortner directed *The Silver Tassie* ('Der Preispokal') at Berlin's Schiller-Theater. Like Peter Zadek, Kortner was a Jewish exile, who had returned to his homeland to work in the theatre, and who did a great deal to bolster O'Casey's reputation in West Germany. In June 1953 Kortner premiered his version of *The Silver Tassie* in the Schiller-Theater, but three days before the performance, a workers' strike in East Berlin had triggered a widespread rebellion against the GDR government, providing the communist bloc with a first major uprising, and bringing about violent suppression by Soviet troops. The Western Allies failed to do anything about the Soviet brutality, leaving O'Casey's anti-war message looking misplaced. Numerous audience members stood up, some made speeches, while others marched out. As the protests grew more boisterous, some audience members even began to express disturbingly Nazi sentiments. 'Back with Werner Krauss' shouted some of the rioters, referring to a notoriously anti-Semitic actor who had won praise from Goebbels and Hitler; while 'go to Munich' shouted others at Kortner, who had fled from Germany for the duration of the war. One Jewish reporter noted that 'No doubt, the scandal had an anti-Semitic flavour' and that 'it was the worst theatre scandal we can remember. Nobody showed the least respect for the actors who had to wait until the riots died down'.[172]

Nevertheless, despite such protest, O'Casey's formal experimentation meant that German critics in the West as well as the East admired the writer, often noting his affinity with Bertolt Brecht.[173] Berlin's Deutsches Theater underlined this connection in a 1986 version of *Cock-A-Doodle Dandy* ('Kikeriki'), which starred Brecht's granddaughter, Johanna Schall, in the part of Julia.[174] Two decades earlier, the Berliner Ensemble (the company that Brecht himself had founded) staged an acclaimed version of *Purple Dust* ('Purpurstaub'), which ran in repertoire for 12 years and was again watched by Eileen O'Casey. She told the *Berliner Zeitung* that 'It makes me very happy to experience the way in which O'Casey is honoured and loved here'.[175] The *World Stage* reported that:

> The Berlin Ensemble performed *Purple Dust*, as it were, like a posthumous meeting between O'Casey and Brecht. Both have a lot in common: they were social realists as well as real socialists; both left behind a lifetime's work, full of intellectual energy and lyric beauty, which places them at the top of the dramatic world literature of our century.[176]

German audiences gave similar acclaim to O'Casey's prose works.[177] A number of foreign-language publishers produced the autobiographies (Ayling and Durkan tracked down versions in languages including Bulgarian, Czech and Finnish) but the German translation published by Diogenes Verlag proved the most enduring. The German version first appeared in instalments between 1957 and 1963; a collected edition reappeared in the 1960s, 1970s and 1980s; and Verlag then produced a cassette recording in 1973 as well as reissuing the first part ('Ich klopfe an: Autobiographie') again in 2008, at a time when no version of the English original remained in print.[178]

Meanwhile, in France, O'Casey enjoyed popularity during what was known as the 'décentralisation' movement. This took place from around 1959 to 1969 under the auspices of the minister for cultural affairs, André Malraux, and aimed to generate a cultural renewal by encouraging regional theatre companies to produce original work, instead of allowing French theatre to remain dominated by those companies set up to cater for the Parisian bourgeoisie.[179] During this time, O'Casey's work appeared in numerous Centres dramatiques, or regional state-subsidized theatres, notably Georges Goubert's direction of *Juno and the Paycock* ('Juno et le paon') for the Comédie de l'Ouest in Rennes in 1960.[180] As David Bradby explains, 'A government enquiry in 1951 had concluded that "the success of the provincial dramatic centres would seem to show that the theatre must go out to the popular public in the workers' suburbs, that it is possible to interest them in either classical or modern works of a high quality"'.[181] In Paris itself, the actor-director Jean Vilar became director of the Théâtre National Populaire (TNP) in 1951, believing that theatre should be 'a public service in exactly the same way as gas, water or electricity', and using his contacts with unions and factories to encourage workers into the venue.[182] O'Casey's socialist politics chimed with this climate of engagement, and accordingly Vilar's TNP staged *Red Roses for Me* ('Roses rouges pour moi') in 1961, with Vilar's replacement Georges Wilson directing *Purple Dust* ('Poussière pourpre') in 1966. In 1973, after Wilson in turn had left, the government moved the TNP's title to one of the country's most innovative playhouses, the Théâtre de la Cité at Villeurbanne, run by the highly influential director Roger Planchon, which had been a particularly militant playhouse, and had staged a notable production of *Purple Dust* in 1965.[183] In France, then, the desire to watch O'Casey and the drive to 'décentralisation' went hand in hand.

Since that time, productions of O'Casey in France have been rare, but when his work has been performed, French playhouses have tended to stage a more eclectic range of O'Casey's plays than that usually performed in English-speaking theatres. For example, in the 1970s, French audiences warmed to the anarchism of *Cock-A-Doodle Dandy* ('Coquin de coq'), with the play produced at the Théâtre de Nice in 1971, the Festival d'Avignon in 1975, and the Théâtre de l'Est Parisien in 1976. In more recent times, audiences at the Théâtre de Gennevilliers watched *Nannie's Night Out* ('Nannie sort ce soir') in 2002, the Paris Conservatoire produced *The Silver Tassie* (retaining the English title) in 2006, and the Comédie-Française followed Germany in staging *The End of the Beginning* ('La fin du commencement') during 2007–8. When the Théâtre Dijon Bourgogne produced a version of *The Plough and the Stars* in 2008–9, and toured the production to cities including Lille and Geneva, *Le Figaro* praised O'Casey as 'popular, political, poetic', and criticized the French theatre for not staging more frequently this 'great piece' full of 'humanity, vitality, and insight'.[184]

If the modern German theatre led the way in showing the popularity of O'Casey's one-act sketch, *The End of the Beginning*, the Czech dramatic world has shown the potential of O'Casey's other short pieces. At about the same time that he had written *The End of the Beginning*, O'Casey had written another one-act sketch, *A Pound on Demand*, which is again little known in the Anglophone theatre. *A Pound on Demand* is a slapstick piece about a drunken man, and his inevitable music-hall sidekick, ineptly attempting to withdraw some money from a counter at the post office. In 1963 Czech television broadcast a 35-minute film version, 'Usporená libra', starring the well-known actor, Jan Werich, as the downtrodden Sammy, the central character who is refused access to his savings and is wearied by the forces of officialdom and police, and whose constrained position is emphasized in the film by the fact that he is often framed by a wire cage.[185]

Werich's daughter, Jana Werichová, then translated another of O'Casey's one-act plays, *Bedtime Story*. This play – a rewritten version of an O'Casey short story entitled 'I Wanna Woman' – shows the pious bachelor Mulligan in a state of post-coital anxiety, having sneaked Angela Nightingale back to his all-male lodging house. Mulligan forces Angela to leave, and she takes some of his money and possessions in revenge for her shabby treatment, leaving him so bewildered and annoyed that a policeman and medics are called to the scene. Jana Werichová's translation attracted the attention of the director Jiří Krejčík, who in turn spent time in the 1960s developing *Bedtime Story* first as a TV drama, and then as a theatre piece.[186] This Czech stage version ('Penzion pro svobodné pány') does retain much of the original plot and characterization, but Krejčík included additional scenes and a considerable amount of new dialogue, producing the piece at the Činoherní Klub Theatre in Prague, where it ran for 16 years, and providing a script that, to this day, continues to enjoy great popularity among Czech acting groups of varying quality. Krejčík also adapted the script into a feature film with Barrandov Studies in 1967.[187] According to him, the drama remains popular in the Czech Republic because, although some of O'Casey's dialogue is obsolete, the male–female relationship at the centre of the work has an 'eternal' dynamic, and enjoys a particular resonance in the former Czechoslovakia, where, in the interwar years, if a man vowed to marry a woman after sex, that promise was taken extremely seriously and might be legally enforced.[188]

Further east, in Cold-War Russia, the communist regime also wished to promote O'Casey. Somewhat predictably, the government newspaper *Izvestia* declared:

The principal danger that faces our literature is revisionism, which takes many forms, from reviling everything we have done and attempting to dance subjectivistic rock and roll on the backs of the dead and the living to the sly introduction of corrosive theories into the very foundation of our literature, its Marxist-Leninist aesthetics [. . .] the sympathies of Sean O'Casey, Katharine Prichard, Frank Hardy and the 92-year-old writer Mary Gilmore are on our side, not theirs.[189]

Accordingly, the 1976 Soviet higher education textbook *Stylistic Analysis* includes an excerpt of *The Hall of Healing*, and articles in the Soviet *Literatura Radziecka* from the 1950s praise O'Casey as 'Writer-Fighter' and as a 'Writer-Citizen' who continued 'to march in the avant-garde of fighters for peace'.[190] During the mid-twentieth century, critics in the USSR such as Boris Isakov and A. Anikst insisted that Russian theatre producers ought to devote energy to bringing O'Casey's works to public attention.[191] Indeed, Ayling and Durkan describe a relatively extensive list of Russian translations of O'Casey's texts, but in terms of playhouse performance the dramatist remained unknown, and only *The Bishop's Bonfire* had been staged by 1965.[192]

During the post-Soviet era, O'Casey's communist ideas have lost some of their immediacy in Russia, and his writings appear onstage infrequently, although his work was nevertheless evoked in the context of contemporary political events in 2008. That year, the prestigious Maly Drama Theatre in St Petersburg premiered in its 50-person studio a version of *The Shadow of a Gunman* ('Ten' Strelka'). The director Lev Dodin, who ran the playhouse, had staged earlier work that responded to contemporary politics, dramatizing Dostoevsky's *The Devils* in 1991 during a post-coup period of food shortages, and staging Abramov's *Brothers and Sisters* during two wars in Chechnya.[193] In 2008, the Russian government both supported an independence movement in South Ossetia and opposed an independence movement in Kosovo, adding a particular frisson to *The Shadow of a Gunman*, a play that manages to mock both those who strive for political independence and the brutal soldiers of the anti-independence forces. The director of the Maly Drama Theatre's production, Oleg Dmitriev, when asked about whether the Kosovan situation made his production 'prophetic', tactfully decided to demur, emphasizing simply that Donal Davoren is a kind of hollow figure, who is keen to 'be regarded as a hero' but ultimately 'lacked the courage'.[194]

Paradoxically, however, O'Casey's Dublin trilogy has long been admired for precisely the oppose reason in Korea, for providing uplifting national ideas rather than for conveying cynicism about politics. In 1910, Japan annexed Korea and became the colonial ruler, encouraging Korean dramatists and critics to find a connection between their country's situation and Ireland's status as a British colony, with the later partition of Korea extending the analogy. For such writers, O'Casey could be seen as a playwright who, in articulating the distinctiveness of the Irish experience under colonialism, provided a heroic exemplar for Korean drama to follow. For example, the Korean literary critic,

Sin Seok-yeon, in an essay of 1929, described O'Casey during the Easter Rising as being 'in hospital at that time. He was arrested by the British army and rescued in a volley by the Irish revolution army just before he was shot'.[195] Korean critics such as Gim Yong-su and Gim Gwang-seop have similarly recommended the study of O'Casey, and the Dublin trilogy accordingly played a key role in the development of the work of Yu Chi-jin, the Korean playwright who contributed to the establishment of realist drama in Korea, and whose so-called peasant trilogy of plays depicts the impoverishment of rural communities under Japanese colonialism.[196]

Such international perspectives point to a different and more complex kind of O'Casey than the playwright who is remembered in the Anglophone world. In translation, O'Casey is a writer whose legacy does not simply rely upon the Dublin trilogy, but whose wider body of work has found multiple audiences and varying interpretations in different countries around the globe.

Revisionism and the 'Troubles'

However, in the English-speaking world, from the late 1960s, the situation in the North of Ireland provoked a new set of criticisms about the politics of O'Casey's work, focusing particularly on the Dublin trilogy, which by this time had inspired a host of Irish imitations including Brendan Behan's 1958 play *An Giall*, Denis Johnston's 1958 drama *The Scythe and the Sunset*, and Hugh Leonard's 1966 television mini-series *Insurrection*.[197]

Between 1969 and 1998, the North of Ireland found itself riven by particularly severe sectarian violence, with the IRA claiming legitimacy from the Easter Rising.[198] For many in Southern Ireland who felt appalled by the modern IRA's activities, the earlier revolution suddenly appeared a less glorious and more complicated business, with O'Casey's cynicism about violent nationalism acquiring a fresh if often somewhat spurious relevance. For example, the *Sean O'Casey Review* published David Krause's article 'Some Truths and Jokes about the Easter Rising', which praises O'Casey's 'intention to nauseate the die-hard nationalists'.[199] Similarly, Brooks Atkinson and Al Hirschfeld wrote of *Juno and the Paycock*, 'The date is 1922, but the play is still pertinent a half century later. In Ulster temperament still overwhelms reason and hatreds still result in the murder of neighborhood people'.[200]

By March 1972, the British government had imposed direct rule on the North, a situation that recalled Ireland during the Anglo-Irish War. Accordingly, at the Abbey Theatre in 1976 Tomás Mac Anna gave Ulster accents to the Dublin Protestant characters of *The Plough and the Stars*, something that quickly became the theatrical norm, despite making little sense in the context of the play. There followed major revivals of *The Plough and the Stars* throughout 'The Troubles': the British National Theatre staged a version in 1977 and the Abbey followed in 1984, with Joe Dowling directing memorable productions of *Juno and the Paycock* and *The Plough and the Stars* in Dublin during the 1980s. As if to show how O'Casey's mindset now dominated popular understanding of the Irish revolution, in 1991 the Irish government celebrated the seventy-fifth anniversary of the Easter Rising in a maladroit and low-key way, while London's Young Vic and Dublin's Abbey Theatre staged expensive revivals of *The Plough and the Stars*. By the year 2000, the Ulster Unionist minister in charge of culture in Northern Ireland, Michael McGimpsey, claimed O'Casey as his 'favourite dramatist', declaring 'I have a passion for him'.[201]

However, a number of critics questioned the tendency to graft O'Casey's historical trilogy onto the contemporary crisis in the North of Ireland. Such commentators took inspiration from Raymond Williams, who in 1969 attacked the ethics of O'Casey's first two Dublin plays:

> This people's dramatist writing for what was said to be a people's theatre at the crisis of this people's history, is in a deep sense mocking it at the very moment when it moves him. The feelings of the fighters, in that real history, are not dramatically engaged at all; all we see and hear is the flag, the gesture, the rhetoric. The need and the oppression are silent, or at best oblique in some consequent action. What is active and vociferous is a

confusion: the victims trapped in their tenements and abusing or flattering each other.[202]

This passage expresses a Marxian suspicion about the form in which O'Casey had chosen to write the Dublin trilogy. Williams felt that these plays share a naturalistic mode that foregrounds domestic action, and that, while this kind of drama can therefore express the comforts of home life perfectly well, such plays cannot offer a fair critique of the broader political situation in which that home life is located. So, for example, a domestic drama would be inadequate to describing the struggles of the ANC (African National Congress) in South Africa, or the independence-era relationship of North America and Britain. The 'need and the oppression' cannot be drawn convincingly in such drama, where those who are fighting for a political cause will always look less persuasive than those who refuse to engage in any kind of political critique, and where the comforts of the domiciliary are inevitably more realized and more attractive on the stage.

Williams's argument was taken up and expressed most brilliantly by Seamus Deane, a poet and literary critic from the Catholic community of Derry. In 1972–3, the British army patrolled the streets of his hometown, and those two years saw over a quarter of all killings from political violence during the 30 years of 'Troubles', with Catholic civilians making up 254 and Protestant civilians 125 of the 759 deaths.[203] In this context, Deane felt dismayed by those who now found parallels between the situation in the North and O'Casey's Dublin trilogy. For Deane, O'Casey's work offered a false dichotomy between a contented domestic life, controlled by women, and a violent political world, dominated by men. Deane pointed out that staying at home is not really an alternative to political engagement, and in the 1970s those homes might in any case be attacked and incinerated by sectarian or neo-colonial forces. He therefore insisted, 'it would be wrong, especially in present conditions, to take him [O'Casey] as our paradigm of a dramatist who made political preoccupation central to his work'.[204]

Deane's essay, when reprinted in modified form in his volume *Celtic Revivals*, proved a pivotal critique for Irish literary and cultural studies, and Deane returned to his thoughts about the playwright during the following three decades, in part because he wanted to warn that O'Casey had provided a wrong turning down which a large number of subsequent Irish writers had followed. For example, in 1999 Deane identified Roddy Doyle's novel *A Star Called Henry* as a dispiriting 'rerun of O'Casey', while in 2001 Deane defended Ronan Bennett's television drama *Rebel Heart* by stating that 'Almost all drama and much fiction about the Irish political situation, and especially about the northern situation, has structured itself around the narrative of a collision between the private and public life that turns out to be catastrophic'. Such a manoeuvre, according to Deane, 'inevitably assigns politics to the bigots and fanatics, and the private world to the emotionally wounded or the sensitive'.[205]

Deane felt compelled to reiterate his case because, as Ireland moved into the Good-Friday era, O'Casey's Dublin trilogy remained well-thumbed by writers and directors. In 1995 the BBC screened a high-profile version of *The Shadow of a Gunman* starring Kenneth Branagh and Stephen Rea, and in 1999 Declan Croghan staged an updated version of the play, in which a bed-sit in Kilburn replaces O'Casey's urban slum in Dublin, with disaffected anti-ceasefire republicans of the 1990s taking the place of those fighting the Anglo-Irish War in 1920.[206]

For Deane, such examples showed O'Casey's malign but pervasive influence, and other influential Irish critics followed Deane's way of thinking. In *Inventing Ireland* Declan Kiberd notes with approval Deane's view that 'all of O'Casey's gunmen are shadows' and adds that in *The Plough and the Stars* 'not even for twenty minutes of a two-and-a-half hour play are the rebels allowed to state their case'.[207] Meanwhile, George Watson, in *Irish Identity and the Literary Revival*, writes, 'I agree with much of what Mr Deane has to say; it may not be without significance that he, like the present writer, is of Northern Irish Catholic background'.[208] More recently, Joe Cleary's important book *Outrageous Fortune* shows how Deane's view has acquired the status of academic orthodoxy, with Cleary endorsing the view that 'O'Casey's trilogy has no intention whatever of seriously addressing the issues involved'.[209]

Of course, Seamus Deane also wrote game-changing reappraisals of other writers, most notably attacking W. B. Yeats for expressing 'the pathology of literary unionism'.[210] Yet in response to these latter arguments, a group of theoretically informed Yeats scholars challenged Deane in forums such as the *Yeats Annual* and the Yeats summer school.[211] No similar academic community had developed around O'Casey, partly due to the uneven quality of some of the oeuvre, and partly due to the playwright's own general hostility to critics outside his handful of preferred admirers. As a result, an intelligent critique of Deane's views about O'Casey emerged more gradually from isolated writers rather from a recognizable group of dedicated O'Casey experts. Hence Nicholas Grene, in his book *The Politics of Irish Drama*, argues that the concern of O'Casey's Dublin work 'is not, as Deane maintains, a matter of promoting a sentimental humanity represented by women and the family over against a stigmatised but unexamined politics of the men'.[212] Grene asks us to look again at O'Casey's women, and to question whether the violence, vanity and vitriol we find there is really an endorsement of stable home life and of family values.

Rónán McDonald takes Grene's idea one step further, arguing that Deane is mistaken in discussing O'Casey as a writer who pits the positive realm of domestic life against the negative realm of politics, because there is something profoundly pessimistic about the entirety of the Dublin trilogy as well as *The Silver Tassie*. McDonald takes his cue from Samuel Beckett's 1934 review of *Windfalls*, in which Beckett praises *Juno* as O'Casey's best play because 'it communicates most fully this dramatic dehiscence, mind and world come asunder in irreparable dissociation – chassis'.[213] Ultimately, McDonald argues that O'Casey's early plays were Beckettian *avant la letter*, as they show mankind bound upon a wheel of fire, continually subject to the painful and the irrational. Two decades earlier, prior to the publication of *Niall*, Brendan Kennelly had described O'Casey's career as a 'journey into joy', which concludes with the final 'Hurrah!' of the six autobiographical volumes.[214] But McDonald argued precisely the reverse: that a deep pessimism lurks at the heart of O'Casey's writing. McDonald concludes, 'It is not, as O'Casey's detractors often maintain of the Dublin trilogy, simply a failure to give politics a fair hearing; his fraught confrontation with his writings in recent years. After the death of Eileen O'Casey, the O'Casey estate swapped publishers from Macmillan to Faber in 1995, but Faber wished only to reprint a selection of the dramatic works, and refrained from making the autobiographies available until 2011. This meant the neglect of major plays, particularly from the second half of O'Casey's career, as well as the short farces that have proved popular with international audiences.

Yet O'Casey himself retained a popular fascination in the final years of the twentieth century and into the first years of the twenty-first. In 1992, the producer of *Phantom of the Opera*, Hal Prince, dramatized a version of O'Casey's autobiographies in an off-Broadway show, *Grandchild of Kings*. This production emphasized O'Casey's struggles with poverty rather than his attraction to Larkinism or communism, with the Dubliner ending the play as a go-ahead, self-made man, vowing 'to start now doing things for himself'.[219] Unfortunately, New York had already seen a similar version of O'Casey in the work of Paul Shyre, and reviewers tended to consider Hal Prince's piece either a dutiful exercise in excerption or else a pale emulation of Shyre's staging.[220] Perhaps a play that dealt honestly with some of the writer's political affiliations might have felt more engaging.

During the same year, a more nuanced version of O'Casey appeared in the unlikely setting of the ABC television series *Young Indiana Jones*.[221] Hollywood last dealt with O'Casey in 1965, when the playwright emerged as the bare-chested, muscular womanizer of *Young Cassidy*. By contrast, in 1992, the slight actor John Lynch portrayed O'Casey as a bespectacled and hunched thinker. The earlier portrayal looked increasingly distant as *Young Indiana Jones* depicted O'Casey's distaste for 'capitalist gain', and showed how, far from relishing fighting, he shied away from the nationalist battlefield.

Indeed, *Young Indiana Jones*, by focusing upon the writer's 1916 incarnation, encouraged audiences to dwell on his youthful failures rather than his subsequent successes. Instead of showing O'Casey as the author of the Dublin trilogy, the television programme portrayed a down-at-heel scribbler who had yet to compose anything of note, condemned by a fictional Yeats for writing about 'political ideas [that] are seldom dramatic'. In 2004, Colm Tóibín gave a similar emphasis to his play, *Beauty in a Broken Place*, which the Abbey Theatre staged as part of the celebrations to mark the playhouse's centenary. Tóibín's work is largely set during the riots over *The Plough and the Stars* in 1926, but begins by showing Lady Gregory rejecting O'Casey's early work because, although the writing gives a 'remarkable sense of character', O'Casey needs to 'keep away from ideas'.[222]

At the end of *Beauty in a Broken Place*, the fictional Lady Gregory asks about O'Casey's compositional technique, and he replies by describing the important role played by the playhouse rather than by giving an autobiographical statement.[223] In this way, Tóibín emphasizes the place of O'Casey within the broader story of the collective. Drama is inevitably a collaborative and communal process, and *Beauty in a Broken Place* highlights the difficulty of assessing O'Casey without knowledge of his complicated relationship with the Abbey.[224] Similarly, at the turn of the millennium, chronological studies by writers such as Christopher Morash and Robert Welch emphasized O'Casey's position within the narratives of the Abbey Theatre and of Irish drama more broadly.[225]

Nonetheless, in the same year as Tóibín's play, Christopher Murray took a different approach, publishing a meticulously researched biography of O'Casey that placed the playwright within a set of wider contexts, particularly those relating to London and Devon as well as Dublin. Other biographies had of course been published in earlier decades, including volumes by Saros Cowasjee, David Krause and Gary O'Connor. Yet none of these earlier volumes had been able to rely on the depth of archival research that was conducted by Murray, who located unfamiliar material in a range of international libraries, and whose judgements therefore rest on a wealth of material that had not been consulted by the earlier writers. Reviewers praised Murray's work on publication as potentially inaugurating a 'new era' in the study of O'Casey by doing what Richard Ellmann had once done for Joyce: and just like Ellmann, Murray proves a sympathetic and intelligent reader of the subject's life, adeptly managing to convey insightful insights from manuscripts and from personal testimony, while also proving able to reach a series of independent and original conclusions.[226] If this was a new era for O'Casey biography, then it was one in which scholars could also rely on the new Seán O'Casey archives at the National Library of Ireland, the acquisition of which in 2001 was followed by the arrival of Eileen O'Casey's papers in 2006.

Towards 2016

In the English-speaking world, the Dublin trilogy continues to dominate discussion of O'Casey, but the play that has been subject to the greatest reassessment in recent years is *The Silver Tassie*, largely because of the script's successful adaptation into musical form. Earlier in the twentieth century, composers had made ill-fated efforts to convert O'Casey's writings into music dramas. Blitzstein's musical 'Juno' had run for less than three weeks in New York in 1959, and in the following decade Elie Siegmeister had written an operatic version of *The Plough and the Stars*, which played only at Louisiana State University in 1969 and to a largely bemused audience in Bordeaux in 1970.[227] However, in the year 2000, English National Opera redressed these failures by premiering Mark Anthony Turnage's excellent operatic adaptation of *The Silver Tassie*.

Turnage had seen the Abbey Theatre's interpretation of the play in 1990, which strikingly included music throughout the entirety of the second act, and he had then worked alongside the librettist Amanda Holden to produce a shortened version of the story, with his efforts in some respects improving upon the script of 1928. Whereas the transition between first-act naturalism and second-act expressionism can feel jarring in O'Casey's drama, Turnage employed a form where naturalism would never get a look-in, and used some of the most powerful moments of orchestration to suggest profound continuities between the scenes on the home front and those in the trenches. In the year after this English premiere, Patrick Mason directed a version of the opera at Dublin's Gaiety Theatre, highlighting a resonance with contemporary political arguments. In the preceding months, Irish politicians had debated how best to commemorate the Irish dead of the Great War, and so Mason took the decision to rain poppies down on the auditorium, covering spectators with a symbol that had long proved contentious in Ireland.

In the wake of Mason's production, which gained a great deal of media attention in Dublin, the director of the Druid Theatre company, Garry Hynes, announced plans to stage O'Casey's original version of *The Silver Tassie*. She had already masterminded an acclaimed version of J. M. Synge's complete works, and so began to consider the idea of producing a similar O'Casey cycle, which would incorporate the Dublin trilogy as well as *The Silver Tassie*. Hynes apparently felt willing to see Druid and the Abbey collaborate on such a venture: the Abbey was, after all, the country's national theatre, and she felt that some of the plays could open in Dublin rather than at Druid's Galway base. According to the *Irish Times*, she approached the Abbey in 2006 to propose the project, but soon discovered that the national theatre had taken the rights to both *The Plough and the Stars* and *Juno and the Paycock*, making her scheme impossible. In her newspaper comments, Hynes declared, 'We were gazumped by the Abbey. It was pretty disturbing. We were in the middle of negotiation. We were very much taken by surprise to find that the Abbey had purchased the rights to two of the plays, therefore making our plans untenable. And they had done that in the full knowledge of our plans'.[228] The director of the Abbey, Fiach MacConghail, declared himself 'bemused' by these allegations, as the national theatre had been negotiating with the O'Casey estate since early 2006.[229]

In summer 2010, Irish audiences had the chance to compare the work of both rival companies, with the Abbey producing *The Plough and the Stars* under the direction of Wayne Jordan at the same time as Druid produced their version of *The Silver Tassie* directed by Hynes. Druid toured to the Gaiety Theatre in Dublin for five nights, thus allowing audiences to contrast the two productions directly. In the event, both companies had taken a broadly similar approach to O'Casey's work. Both attempted to avoid naturalistic elements, and both tended to downplay the comic turns scripted by O'Casey. Instead, the Abbey's 2010 version of *The Plough and the Stars* confronted its audience with a scene of broken and rusted metal girders. If in 2007 Hynes had used the language of property speculation when describing being 'gazumped', by 2010 the Abbey set for the *Plough* looked something like a half-abandoned construction site, a reminder of all those Celtic-Tiger dreams that had disappeared in Ireland's recent economic meltdown, and potentially implying that the republic heralded in 1916 had still not been built. Druid's production also began with a bare and far-from-realistic setting, with the bleak opening view of an impoverished Dublin scene, where domestic abuse takes place, offering resonances with the country's prevailing political and social concerns. In these similar, stark productions, the Abbey and Druid companies both emphasized that O'Casey might continue to speak to the present moment: he might not simply be the playwright of the revolutionary period, but also of the Ryan report and the ghost estate.[230]

By this time, for those at the Abbey, the writings of O'Casey had become bound up in a set of existential questions about the national theatre itself. Since the end of the 1990s, the Irish government had been considering the prospect of providing the players with a larger home, but the process had been complicated by vacillating property prices, political prevarication and economic recession. After a protracted debate about different sites, the Joycean scholar, senator and would-be presidential candidate, David Norris, argued that the state should take the opportunity to re-found the Abbey inside Dublin's GPO, the headquarters of the Easter Rising.[231] In 2009, Norris asked readers of the *Irish Times* to imagine a celebration of the centenary in 2016 which would have at its heart 'the Abbey Theatre reopening in the GPO with a revival of Seán O'Casey's great Dublin trilogy including *The Plough and the Stars*, in which Pearse himself appeared as a character, a red carpet issuing from that heroic portico as European heads of state arrive'.[232] Fleetingly, the Irish government adopted this plan, before abandoning it in the face of dwindling funds and opposition from critics such as Fintan O'Toole. O'Toole argued that *The Plough and the Stars* is 'sceptical and subversive', that O'Casey's work forms part of a theatrical culture that seeks to challenge the state and its myths, and that Ireland should avoid entombing the theatre within a building that symbolizes the state's official culture.[233]

More than a century after O'Casey's birth, then, the author remains central to Irish drama and to Irish identity in a way that is true of no other playwright. It is inconceivable, for example, that a debate about the location of the country's national theatre could revolve around his Abbey contemporaries such as T. C. Murray, Brinsley MacNamara or even Lady Gregory. It is equally difficult to imagine that Ireland's best acting companies would tussle over scripts by O'Casey's rivals such as Edward McNulty, George Shiels or Lennox Robinson. Yeats may have rejected O'Casey's work, but today Yeats's own plays are largely forgotten by performers and directors, while O'Casey's first dramas are continually revived, with the best-known quotations recycled by Irish journalists, radio presenters and political commentators alike.[234] Indeed, O'Casey's three early scripts are still helping to bankroll the Abbey, with the *Irish Times* running a headline in 2011 – some nine decades after those tenement dramas first helped to keep the Abbey solvent – that declared, 'O'Casey Play Helps Abbey Return to Profit'.[235] More widely, one only has to look at the beguiling tat sold today on Dublin's tourist trail to see that O'Casey has secured a popular place in the literary pantheon alongside Yeats, Synge, Joyce, Beckett and Shaw.

Of course, after the critical and commercial success of the Dublin trilogy, the trajectory of O'Casey's writing career proved a disappointment. Like other long-lived literary figures of the twentieth century such as Arthur Miller, John Osborne and Alan Sillitoe, O'Casey enjoyed preternatural success with early work, but continued to write prolifically into old age for diminishing returns, often falling victim to political and aesthetic faddishness, while suffering the barbs of critics and rival writers intent on father-killing. Yet, in the final analysis, O'Casey stands apart from almost all of his contemporaries. Although his critical reputation may have waxed and waned during the past 90 years, his best-known work has consistently been a touchstone for Irish directors and actors. In addition, the posthumous O'Casey has found appreciative audiences in an assortment of non-Anglophone contexts, where spectators have often shown enthusiasm for the experimental aspects of his work, and have greatly relished the one-act farces. O'Casey himself would undoubtedly have been pleased by this. Much of his international success came after his death, but his correspondence reveals his eagerness to communicate with letter-writers around the world, and the final piece that he wrote, six days prior to his death, was an article for the *New York Times*.[236] Meanwhile in his homeland today, just as in 1926, O'Casey's work ignites new debates and new controversies, and refuses to go gentle into the good night of literary history.

PART 2

NEW PERSPECTIVES

CHAPTER 7
DIRECTING O'CASEY

Garry Hynes, in conversation with James Moran

Garry Hynes founded the Druid Theatre Company in Galway in 1975, and acted as its Artistic Director until 1991. From 1991 to 1994 she worked as Artistic Director of the Abbey Theatre in Dublin, where she staged a landmark production of O'Casey's *The Plough and the Stars.* In 1995 she returned to the post of Artistic Director of Druid, where she worked on a version of *The Silver Tassie*, as well as an abortive attempt to stage a cycle of O'Casey's works. In 1999, she directed a production, at the Gaiety Theatre in Dublin, of *Juno and the Paycock*, with Michael Gambon, Cillian Murphy and Marie Mullen in lead roles. She has also directed internationally, including the musical, 'Juno', by Mark Blitzstein and Joe Stein.

JM I'd like to begin by asking if you can remember when you first encountered the work of Seán O'Casey. Which of his works did you first come into contact with? Did you first read the text or see a production?

GH I would definitely have read the work. I remember seeing the 1990 Abbey version of *The Silver Tassie* and I remember that it didn't quite make sense to me. But I remember being excited by the theatrical power of the piece, it made quite an impact. And then, you know, I suppose from the 1980s on[wards] I would have been looking for an opportunity to do some O'Casey, but the resources required were too large for a company like Druid, so I really didn't have the opportunity. So then I decided to do *The Plough and the Stars* as my first production at the Abbey when I became artistic director, probably with a conscious sense of the place of O'Casey in the Abbey's history. I wanted to look at those plays, I wanted to find a way to look at those plays that tried to recover some of the shock of the new that must have been felt when they first went on at the Abbey, because I think, like Synge and like playwrights connected with any institutions, the productions can become institutionalized.

JM You speak of being excited by the 'theatrical power' of *The Silver Tassie*. Can you be a bit more specific about what exactly you mean?

GH I think it's the sheer boldness of its theatricality. He has such a striking vision for the second act. By every account, including its own, it's an imperfect play. But the boldness of it, the sheer embrace of theatricality really drew me to it.

JM I'd like to ask you some specific questions about your relationship with O'Casey's Dublin trilogy. Fintan O'Toole has recently argued in the *Irish Times* that any director of O'Casey's Dublin trilogy in modern Ireland needs to take notice of the high-profile production of *The Plough and the Stars* that you staged at the Abbey in 1991. First, can you tell us a bit about the background to that production? Why did you end up directing that particular play, in that place and at that particular time?

GH There were a number of things involved there. First of all, I would have been aware, and acutely aware from my experience of Synge, that the Dublin plays had almost become kind of victory runs for the theatre. They had become associated with their major roles, they had become very separated from the fierce, political outsider that was O'Casey himself. I was also aware that these three plays were looked on as great pillars of naturalism, and *The Silver Tassie* as his break from naturalism, and I felt that's just absolutely not true. These plays are not pieces of naturalism, they are as ferociously theatrical – perhaps more resolved pieces of theatre than the *Tassie* – but the same person who wrote the *Tassie* wrote those three plays in the preceding six years, so these plays are connected, and I wanted to explore that. I was also conscious of wanting to explore something that I had missed from O'Casey productions a lot of the time, the sheer poverty, the brutal violent poverty that is at the heart of the plays.

JM There was of course a strong reaction to that production: could you say a bit about that reaction? I think this may have had something to do with what Hans Robert Jauss calls the 'horizon of expectation' of the audience, but I wonder if you agree. Do you think the response was generated by the striking aesthetics of your production, by the pre-existing notion of what an Abbey O'Casey should be, or with the fact that Ireland was celebrating the seventy-fifth anniversary of the Easter Rising? Or was it something else entirely?

GH Well there was also the context that I was the first new artistic director of the Abbey who had come from the outside, who hadn't grown up through the Abbey. There was even within the institution itself, as I only discovered later, a sense that I was not quite entitled to be artistic director of the Abbey. That was part of the response as well.

JM Where would that internal opposition to you within the Abbey have been articulated?

GH You have to remember that at the time I became AD, I entered into a situation where a large majority of the staff had been there for a long time and there was an acting company on life contracts. In fact, the only individual who changed with any regularity was the AD. I was the seventh in six years, and the twelfth since the late 1960s. I, however, was quite unprepared for the understandable apprehension that greeted my appointment within the organization and being fair, strategically, it probably wasn't such a good idea to go into the house and start smashing the china straight off. But I did. And I sort of deliberately did it. So that was also part of the context. I've absolutely no doubt whatsoever that if that particular production had been done in the Project [Arts Centre in Dublin] that it would have generated nothing like that response, and possibly would have generated quite a positive response.

JM Did you anticipate the response, which included some high-profile and sometimes negative comment in the press?

GH No. It was interesting and odd that the UK press more favourably reviewed it and the Irish press generally didn't. But everything was interpreted not for itself but as a kind of message. Creative decisions were seen as insults and slurs on the national theatre, our nationhood, our great icon. 'Imagine taking a bunch of actors and asking them to shave their heads'. The response in Ireland took place, I think, at the interface of culture and politics, and I think that for me that's why the controversy grew. It was good in a way. I remember Tomás Mac Anna, being the mischievous character that he always was, coming into my office at the Abbey and saying 'you won't really be blooded as an artistic director until you have your first controversy'. And the controversy was great, but in retrospect, I think it may have served to reinforce an image of me as an enemy of the institution.

JM To me it seems like certain versions of O'Casey's Dublin trilogy that have followed in the wake of your 1991 production have emulated something of what you have done in terms of a stark and anti-naturalistic presentation, while others have set themselves against your approach. At the Abbey, for example, Wayne Jordan's version of *The Plough and the Stars* in 2010 seemed to follow what you had done, but directors such as Ben Barnes [who directed the *Plough* in 2005] and Howard Davies [who directed *Juno* in 2011] seem to have aimed instead for what we might label a 'heritage' approach. Is that a fair observation?

GH I can't comment on that other than to say, I don't know how you can do O'Casey and not try to connect with the cantankerous, epic, throw-everything-in kind of writer he is. His politics were all over the place, but they were fiercely felt, and fiercely, passionately believed. But notwithstanding the controversy, I don't believe my production [in 1991] was fully achieved.

JM What were the failings?

GH I'm just not sure that everybody was in the same play, which is one of the things that a director needs to do. So I would have loved to have gone back to it, and to have been able to produce it again a year later or a year after that, using the basic same elements.

JM   Yes, you didn't return to O'Casey for a while afterwards.

GH   Well I would have liked to do more O'Casey in the Abbey, but I was only three years there as it turned out, and obviously, combined with then trying to run Druid, to go back to O'Casey was just not something that was strategically available to me.

JM   Would you have done more O'Casey at the Abbey if you had stayed on?

GH   Yes. That was the plan originally.

JM   Of course, you did direct O'Casey again in Dublin, when you opened an acclaimed version of *Juno and the Paycock* at the Gaiety in 1999. Perhaps some people might have expected that after the brouhaha over the *Plough* you might have wanted to stay away from this writer in this city. Why and how did you decide that you were going to return to the Dublin trilogy in this venue?

GH   It was a Noel Pearson production and he asked me to direct it with Michael Gambon in the lead role. I don't think the experience with *Plough* put me off directing O'Casey, I don't think anything would. I was lucky to put together a tremendous cast with Michael Gambon, including John Kavanagh (who had previously played Joxer for Joe Dowling alongside Donal McCann), Marie Mullen, Cillian Murphy, Dawn Bradfield, David Wilmot, Declan Conlon, Bríd Brennan and Pat Leavy. However, it didn't turn out as well as I'd have liked it to. On reflection, certain decisions I made approaching the production were not good ones and this had an effect.

JM   Can you tell us a bit more about those problems? As you say, you had the most amazing cast for this production. Were the actors wary of certain aspects of O'Casey's work, or did you need to twist a few arms to get these actors on board in the first place?

GH   I didn't have to twist any arms. You usually don't when it comes to casting O'Casey. I had problems in the design. It got in the way when I got on the rehearsal floor. This had nothing to do with Francis O'Connor's design but with my own decisions for the production.

JM Did you discover things about the play in rehearsal that you hadn't seen beforehand?

GH It is not as clear-cut as that. Every play, when you go into rehearsal, will fundamentally be discovered with the actors. The thing with O'Casey is that you have to strike a balance between contrasting elements, between the comedy and the grim poverty, between the heroic and the domestic and the sheer ugly and sometimes you don't live up to it. You can't, for instance, fall into the trap of having Juno as a hero from the beginning because you miss the beautiful detail of the quotidian awfulness of her life. I think with Juno's character, we more or less got the balance right, but we were not so successful elsewhere.

JM If you were to revisit *Juno and the Paycock*, how would you change your approach?

GH When you revisit any play, the foremost considerations are the present context, the time and place of performance. Saying that, putting together an ensemble company, working over a number of O'Casey plays together and becoming steeped in the man, the writer and the plays is fundamental to any approach I take to doing O'Casey in the future.

JM But on this occasion what were you seeking to achieve with your interpretation of the play?

GH I wasn't trying to do anything else but serve the great play, that it is for the audiences at that time.

JM Did you have a sense that critics and audiences were comparing your *Juno* with your earlier version of the *Plough*?

GH No. Not at all. I think the controversy earlier [with the *Plough*] was more a critical thing and rolled over into criticisms of me and my time at the Abbey. Audiences are not usually bothered with who the director is, particularly if they are having a good time.

JM Of course, this time, your production was onstage at exactly the same time as another high-profile revival of exactly the same play in the United Kingdom. Colm Meaney was starring in John Crowley's production of *Juno* in London [at the Donmar Warehouse]. Did you know about this clash in advance, worry about it, or feel the need to distinguish your approach from that of Crowley?

GH I don't remember being aware of it at the time. I saw his production later in New York.

JM Perhaps one of the more surprising decisions of your career was your next encounter with O'Casey, when you turned to a revival of Marc Blitzstein's musical version of *Juno and the Paycock*, 'Juno', in New York in 2008. That musical had originally closed after only 16 performances when first produced in 1969, and O'Casey himself said he never had faith in its success from the start. How did you end up deciding to direct this piece, and what were the challenges?

GH Jack Viertel is a friend of mine who runs 'Encores!' [reviving American musicals in New York]. He started talking to me about the musical. It had been a pet project of his for years. I looked at it, and I said, what's not to like about doing this?

JM Blitzstein is of course one of the great and neglected composers of modern America.

GH Absolutely, and I had never done a musical, and this was doing it in great circumstances with 'Encores!'. So I threw myself into it and I was thrilled to have done it.

JM What were the challenges of doing the musical?

GH The challenges were very particular, because with 'Encores!' you are supposed to do it in a week with actors on-book. But it was fantastic for me, I enjoyed doing it so much, although I think ultimately the musical doesn't quite work, but I had some very interesting experiences. I met Joseph Stein, who wrote the lyrics, and he was thrilled about it going on again. We had a question-and-answer session at the theatre, with Stein speaking. I think basically O'Casey saw Shaw have a big hit with *Pygmalion*, and then along came Stein and said 'I'd like to do a musical': O'Casey thought, 'good stuff'. Stein said he had gone over to O'Casey in Devon and had sent the book to O'Casey for approval and O'Casey commented, 'it's so good I could have written it myself'. Now Stein told that story to imply that O'Casey had given him incredible praise. But I just sat there and thought, I can hear O'Casey's voice and he's saying, 'it's so good, I *did* write it myself'.

JM   Do you view O'Casey as a particularly musical writer? There are a lot of songs and, for me, there's a sense with the later works that he does move into an increasingly musical mode. The works perhaps aren't as tightly plotted, but instead we find elaborations on a theme, which often remains unresolved.

GH   Someone should look at the later O'Caseys and apply a kind of rigorous musical approach. He grew up with Boucicault, and the general approach of 'look, if it works, throw it in'. I think that's what really appealed to me, doing O'Casey in that big way with a full orchestra and everything, applying a new mix of elements to the plot. Finally though I think the musical ['Juno'] fails because unfortunately both the music for, and the writing of, the Captain and Joxer is unsuccessful. They turn into cartoon characters. So, I think no, it's not a good musical, because it fails to represent that central relationship that O'Casey so brilliantly achieved.

JM   One of your great successes with the Druid theatre company was your version of J. M. Synge's complete works [DruidSynge], and in about 2005–6 you began to think about producing a similar O'Casey cycle, which would incorporate the Dublin trilogy as well as *The Silver Tassie*. Could you explain some of your thinking here? Why do these four plays deserve to be seen together?

GH   Well, these four plays present an extraordinary record of a time when the temperature of life was raised to impossible levels and so much that reaches into our own time was formed. It is one of the few series of plays written within ten years of the events they refer to, whose status as world literature is guaranteed. The plays respond to the events as they were experienced and remembered but they also pull back to see bigger movements and patterns, and ideas and themes, working through those events. But you know, however you come to look at them, they are great plays, and the opportunity to do them with a company of actors is something that, by definition – if the productions are in any way successful – will help us to look at the plays in a new way.

JM Did you just want to produce the Dublin trilogy and *The Silver Tassie*? Or were you tempted to think of a broader cycle that might include later plays too?

GH Certainly we had ideas in terms of promoting other events alongside the production, which would see some versions and readings and discussions of O'Casey that provided some larger context to examine him within. And certainly there would have been the thought that, if we discovered something through doing this, then that would have given us a platform for looking at the later plays. I would have had at the back of my mind the idea that by doing the first four we might fashion an engine for going into the later plays. Then we would have a viewing platform for those plays, we would have earned and learned a reason through the process of doing all these earlier plays together.

JM Were you initially thinking of staging the cycle to coincide with the centenary of 1916?

GH No, I absolutely wasn't and had the cycle been produced at that time, there is no way the plays would have remained in repertoire in 2016.

JM There was an assumption in the press that such a cycle would be explicitly connected to the centenary.

GH My intention was solely to do with O'Casey and coming to know the man and the scale and uniqueness of his achievement through seeing his plays together, and it had nothing to do with the timing or with doing productions to coincide with centenaries. An ensemble whose members come together over a long period of time to work on more than one play offers a way to look at those plays in ways that doing individual productions can't. This is not just speculation. We have the experience with audiences, so we know this for real. I would love to see the Dublin plays in the performance context of an ensemble and also see this context as a route into the later plays, which offer up particular challenges when it comes to contemporary audiences. With the later plays, the challenge is to find for them a context in the present in which they make absolute sense, and I think that to come at the later plays on the back of a cycle of the Dublin work is to find for them as good a context as any.

JM It's deeply unsatisfying that, so far at least, we haven't seen your idea of an O'Casey cycle translated into the reality of performance. I understand that there are a number of sensitivities involved here, but are you able to say anything about why such plans have been frustrated?

GH It is a matter of public record that as a result of the Abbey theatre acquiring the rights of all three Dublin plays we were unable to continue with our plans, at that time.

JM Do you hope it might be possible to resurrect your plans for an O'Casey cycle at some point in the future?

GH I continue to hope it will be possible and, indeed, it is my most passionate ambition to do this project.

JM In the meantime, you have carried on with your work of bringing O'Casey's plays to the stage, producing a version of *The Silver Tassie* with Druid in 2010. What drew you to that project?

GH As a result of my disappointment of not being able to continue with any of the Dublin plays, I initially decided not to continue with any of the plays. But then, as a director I wanted to go back into that O'Casey world and so, despite the fact of the *Tassie's* original inclusion in the broader O'Casey project, we decided to produce that play [as a standalone piece] in 2010.

JM This production of the *Tassie* toured widely, across Ireland, the United Kingdom and United States. What, if anything, did you notice from the way that different audiences engaged with the play?

GH I do remember audiences being stunned by the scope and ambition of the play, even the sheer existence of it. It kind of knocked people out and that applied everywhere, Galway, New York, London.

JM But, of course, the *Tassie* is far less well known and potentially has less cultural cachet than the Dublin trilogy. You're introducing a play as much as introducing an interpretation, so how did you approach that?

GH Just as you approach any production. It's a question of creating the best possible context for it to be seen within, and trying to solve some of the problems. And one of the problems is the second act. I decided that the chant and the dirge and all that kind of thing are just quite simply terribly boring, so we decided to commission new music. Then, you know, the Augustus John design is so brilliant, and so incredibly fantastic, and has now become such a part of the imagery of the First World War that we knew we could not go there. So we were trying to figure out how to represent the brutality of war, the monolith, the hugeness of it and the smallness of the people against it, but in a way that doesn't rely on earlier imagery. And we came up with the tank. A tank that was almost too big for the stage. Another issue is the first act. Yeats said – or at least he wrote to O'Casey – that the first act is great, but I have a problem with it. There's this kind of faux naturalism. So the decision came, by working with the two actors, that they were really a music-hall double act, and we would lift them out so that naturalism was literally only a painted background.

JM Were there any other problems?

GH Yes, one of the problems with doing the *Tassie*, you have to then shrug off the imagery of *Oh What a Lovely War*. Another of the issues is that Harry Heegan is the hero, and yet Heegan often remains at the margins. So that led to the decision to have Harry Heegan play the Croucher in Act Two.

JM In that way, for me there felt like a set of continuities between your 1991 *Plough* and your 2010 *Tassie*. In both cases, you were trying to divorce O'Casey from a lingering sense that he might be a naturalistic writer.

GH Well I'm quite sure there are continuities. I mean I'm the same person who directed both plays, and I have strong ideas about O'Casey, so I'm sure there are continuities, but there were certainly no deliberate connections. It was part of the attempt to get at this writer who I think has, for all sorts of reasons, historically and politically, become difficult to produce on the modern stage.

JM One of the things that I noticed in your 2010 version of *The Silver Tassie* was that the domestic abuse in the early scene chimed with a series of horrendous reports that had recently been released about institutional abuse in twentieth-century Ireland. Similarly, during the Irish banking collapse, I kept recalling the line that Brennan o' the Moor says in *Red Roses for Me*, where he worries about his money in the Bank of Ireland, and says that the cash must be safe and sound. Does the Irish theatre approach O'Casey's plays in order to find a way of analysing contemporary politics?

GH Productions of plays do, by definition. For instance, I did [John B. Keane's play] *Big Maggie* in 2001 at the Abbey, at a time when that play from 1969 was still available as an old-fashioned but still ultimately benign play. With the events of the last ten years, that interpretation is absolutely no longer available. There's a black void between us and that time in Ireland. That sense of re-evaluation over the last decade would be applicable not just to O'Casey but generally. I think, as a theatre director, you always read things politically. But then you have to balance your political reading with your first function as a director: to make that play live on stage for a present-day audience. If your political reading is too intense, and is towards some sort of tract or commentary, then you may cut the reading off from the process of exchange with a present-day audience, and at that point you have failed.

JM   So in order to thrive in the twenty-first century, O'Casey's plays really need careful directors?

GH   Well, all plays need careful directors. But I think what's really missing for O'Casey's career is a context. O'Casey is a writer who needs a new assessment, and you won't be able to do that from a disjointed series of single productions. I still believe that O'Casey needs a set of productions sharing an overall approach and an ensemble company over a period of time.

CHAPTER 8
O'CASEY'S POSTCOLONIAL DRAMATURGY

Victor Merriman

Victor Merriman is Professor of Performing Arts at Edge Hill University, United Kingdom. He is the author of *Because We Are Poor: Irish Theatre in the 1990s* (2011), and edited a Special Issue of *Kritika Kultura* on Radical Theatre and Ireland (2010). He was a member of *An Chomhairle Ealaion*/The Arts Council of Ireland (1993–98), and chaired the Council's Review of Theatre in Ireland (1995–96).

In Colm Tóibín's play, *Beauty in a Broken Place*, commissioned by the Abbey Theatre for its centenary celebrations in 2004, Seán O'Casey is a metaphorical spark enflamed by repressive winds blowing across contested landscapes of class, race, gender, religion and nation in the Irish Free State. Postcolonial critical practice is especially concerned with state power – both how it operates in people's lives, and how it is resisted – during and after the colonial moment. In evaluating the efficacy of oppositional cultural production – especially in the theatre – the systems and practices through which work is mediated must also be addressed. The stakes are high in contests over culture, as W. E. B. Dubois understood, 'It is one thing for a race to produce artistic material, it is quite another for it to produce the ability to interpret and criticise this material'.[1] For Gerry Smyth, 'Irish culture cannot express, reflect, embody – or any of the other favoured metaphors – the decolonizing nation until it is so constituted by an enabling metadiscourse: criticism'.[2] Accordingly, postcolonial theorists seek to recover cultural practices and artefacts which have been written to the margins of cultural and political histories, in order to evaluate their potential for intervention in the struggles of today. For these reasons, this essay dissents from influential schemae which canonize a youthful

O'Casey at the expense of an O'Casey who 'was cut off and cut himself off from Irish theatre' and who 'did not take root elsewhere'.[3] In such schemae, O'Casey's dramas cluster round a perceived 'cut off' point: W. B. Yeats's rejection of *The Silver Tassie* (1928), the fallout from which shaped subsequent critical views, with a charge of unsuccessful 'experimentalism' dogging the reputation of his later plays, implying a double loss – of dramaturgical facility and of engagement with actually existing Ireland.

Not the least of the problems attending a narrative of decline into empty experimentalism is that it normalizes a view of the Dublin trilogy as not 'experimental' – in the sense of risky and challenging – enabling their domestication to the cultural barrenness of a Free State of which O'Casey was always a stern critic: 'Sophisticated and successful, the [Abbey] actors scored a comfortable popular success with O'Casey's plays, when they ought to have gone for an uncomfortable popular success [. . .] [the] first three plays were widely performed by amateur companies in the same emasculated manner'.[4] Tomás Mac Anna's productions restored interest in a group of later plays (Abbey Theatre, 1970s and 1980s), and recent productions of Abbey productions of *Juno and the Paycock* by Ben Barnes (1997), and *The Plough and the Stars* by Garry Hynes (1991), drew out with great impact the political in the personal present in the dramatic action. Nonetheless, O'Casey's creative trajectory is still obscured among critical and historiographical emphases on rejection, exile and subsequent decline to which Yeats's letter written in 'splenetic age' has given rise.[5] The controversies, with their extraordinary cast of characters, and their amenability to popular tropes of brittle artistic egos and temperamental spats, are of undeniable interest, but lead, ultimately, to critical distortion. The act of reading them as but one episode in a lifetime of engaged cultural work, brings the plays themselves into focus as cultural interventions for a new audience, living through new traumatic circumstances. This critical strategy exposes to view, not 'later failures' in O'Casey's work, but aspects of a long dramaturgical journey, remarkably consistent in theme and intent.

An influential Anglophone critical consensus did real damage to O'Casey's reputation, and James Simmons reveals the nature of that consensus while drawing attention to the problems created for academic critics by O'Casey's works:

> Most literary discourse in my generation has dwelt on self-expression. The essence of this mainstream approach to literature [*sic*] is that, whatever the apparent subject of a work of art, what we are relishing is the sensibility of the author; but it has been uneasily realised that this doesn't work for folk music and even popular songs which are so largely made up of conventional passages that they seem to be composed almost communally. In the theatre, miracle plays, mysteries, pantomimes and melodramas (the forms we invoke to describe O'Casey's special quality) have this quality or, as we find ourselves saying, lack of 'quality'.[6]

In other words, the critical tradition through which O'Casey's plays were filtered is 'a very controlled conversation among a very controlled number of people'.[7] For participants in that conversation, dramatic literature enjoyed the authority of textuality, even though its artefacts are clearly not texts, but 'pre-texts' for performance. Simmons can acknowledge collective creation of popular forms, but cannot admit this feature of theatre practice in evaluating works of 'literary merit'. Simmons describes a view of art as that which is 'relished' by an initiated elite, and from which popular taste, as John McGrath had previously argued, was – at best – something to be explained away.[8] McGrath might have had Simmons's faint praise for O'Casey in mind:

> I believe that something like bad taste was the inspiration that made O'Casey mix the modes of comedy and tragedy so radically. His later lack of development suggests that luck and accident are more likely explanations of his achievement than perception and ingenuity. He was not ingenious or perceptive; but he had loads of experience that we more fortunate need our noses rubbed in.[9]

Such a critical project is far from innocent, enforcing the exclusion from authorized accounts of the world and the work, much of the reality of people's lives, and the actual dynamics of playwriting and theatre-making in the twentieth century. Within the terms of the literary criticism described by Simmons, many of O'Casey's plays simply cannot be read as having any merit. Simmons is left nonplussed, for instance, by the popularity of later plays – especially *Purple Dust* – in the repertoire of the Berliner Ensemble, post-1965: 'despite the respect one must have for so advanced and universally acclaimed a theatre, I suspect the Germans are creating their own play out of O'Casey's wordy text'.[10]

As we saw in Chapter 2, *The Shadow of a Gunman, Juno and the Paycock* and *The Plough and the Stars* reveal O'Casey working with dramatic structures and stagecraft drawn from melodrama and the music hall: forms indigenous to the Dublin stage during his formative years. Christopher Fitz-Simon points up the continuity of performers between 'popular Irish melodrama [and] the Abbey Theatre's radical artistic agenda', citing, specifically, F. J. McCormick, who created key roles in each play of the Dublin trilogy, and Fitz-Simon is explicit on the influence of Boucicault on O'Casey: 'Boucicault [. . .] specifically prefigures O'Casey's tragic satire'.[11] Melodrama accommodated with ease stories of foreign war and domestic loneliness, of local villainy and virtue, frequently by drawing from such narratives the material for grand romantic epics. As the barbarism of twentieth-century urban warfare manifests itself, representation, including dramatic form, comes under increasing pressure, leading to formal disruptions of such realistic episodes as exist in the plays; examples include Mrs Tancred's biblical incantation and black mourning dress disrupting the Boyle's revels. The endings both of *Juno and the Paycock* and *The Plough and the Stars* are codas to tragic action: the drunken dissolution of Captain Boyle and Joxer Daly in *Juno and the Paycock*, and, in *The Plough and the Stars*, two tea-drinking Tommies singing 'Keep the Home Fires Burning', as the Dublin skyline which frames the action flares into deep scarlet. Both episodes are replete with irony, and the latter anticipates *The Silver Tassie*'s dramaturgy of war as unmitigated catastrophe for the working class. The ending of *The Plough and the Stars* develops the ironic gesture deployed in *Juno and the Paycock* toward an epic stage poetry, where sound, lighting and setting express the crises and struggles of the inhabitants of the dramatic world. This strategy is further developed in responding to the transnational calamity of the trenches of World War I. The people staged in *The Silver Tassie* are O'Casey's fellows – the Protestant working class – and not to have developed the thematics of *The Plough and the Stars* to engage with their experiences in the British Army in World War I would have been somewhat unusual. In this way, *The Silver Tassie* did, of course, open up a fault line around official state nationalism, Yeats's account of the Abbey's cultural project, and O'Casey's place within it.

In their exemplary study, *Writing Ireland: Colonialism, Nationalism and Literature*, David Cairns and Shaun Richards summarize O'Casey's complex attitude to questions of class and nation:

> Knowledge which does not empower action, and action which does not represent need, are at the heart of O'Casey's critique of a political movement which embraced abstraction and denied reality. It would be erroneous, however, to conclude that O'Casey abjured nationalist politics *per se*, rather it was a question of the concept of the nation which informed the call to sacrifice.[12]

It was precisely the consciousness of the existence of competing nationalisms that opened O'Casey's work to state disapproval. On one basic question, however, his developing dramaturgy is consistent: the clash of Capital and Labour is the defining confrontation of the twentieth century, underpinning equally indigenous struggles and global conflagration, and its dynamics are visible even in intimate relationships and domestic settings. The latter point is crucial, as it focuses critiques of O'Casey's work by the British Left, from the Workers' Theatre Movement (1930s) to Raymond Williams (1952 and 1968).[13] In the Dublin trilogy colonialism is neither more nor less than the frame of a social order confronted by the crises of European humanity in the early twentieth century. The plays are internationalist rather than nationalist; hence O'Casey's provocation of an emergent state nationalism grounded in fantasies of *Sinn Féin Amháin*: Ourselves Alone. In this light, *The Silver Tassie* is not only not an exceptional experiment, but an inevitable development in a search for form adequate to the representation of traumatic reality. This analysis enables revaluation of plays including *The Star Turns Red* (1940), *Red Roses for Me* (1943) and *Purple Dust* (1945).[14]

In commissioning *Beauty in a Broken Place*, the Abbey centred the O'Casey of the Dublin trilogy in its centenary celebrations. In sharp contrast, as the centenary of the Great Lockout of 1913 approaches, no production of *Red Roses for Me* is programmed in Dublin's theatres. This probably indicates the enduring hegemony of a poor critical view of the later plays, but the loss to public reflection on the meaning of Labour activism, its contested place in Irish history and its significance for Irish crises a century later is considerable. This play extends the expressionism of Act II of *The Silver Tassie* towards a more developed epic form, in which almost every one of the *dramatis personae* has both a narrative and a choric function. It includes an extraordinary transfiguration scene (Act III), in which options unavailable in reality are experienced in opulent excess in dramatic action. Viewed as an enduring struggle for form, the dramaturgical journey from *Juno and the Paycock* via *The Plough and the Stars* and *The Silver Tassie* to *Red Roses for Me* may be grasped, not as a decline from fine craftsmanship into 'experimentalism', but as a broad trajectory from Melodrama, through Expressionism, toward a developed postcolonial aesthetic of Disrupted Realism.[15]

This trajectory is evident also in two plays completed in the early months of World War II, and first published in 1940: *The Star Turns Red* and *Purple Dust*. *The Star Turns Red*, set 'tomorrow or the next day' (II, 240), stages revolutionary social transformation and anticipates *Red Roses for Me* in theme, dramaturgy and historical focus. *Purple Dust* mischievously parodies Yeatsian transcendence and revisits Shavian impatience with 'the torturing, heartscalding, never satisfying dreaming, dreaming, dreaming, dreaming', but is much more than an extended frivolity.[16] O'Casey's play takes up a theme common to Edwardian musicals, such as *The Arcadians* – unease at modernity's encroachment – and, recalling Shaw, filters the trope through a lampoon of Irish and English national characteristics. However shrill the comic exchanges, they turn on the reciprocal dependency of colonial tropes of fair play and efficiency (III, 67) and nationalist mythologies of historical exceptionalism and inherent racial nobility (III, 68). The metaphor of purple dust speaks both of colonial nostalgia for aristocratic order and the unseen, but present spirit of anti-colonial rebellion.

At the end of the play, local workmen, dreamers or not, have absconded with the lovers of the English owners of the Big House, Stokes and Poges. Both local women returned from London, each holds a legal document settling £500 per annum for life on her, signed by her hapless cuckold. Poges utters his final line, wishing to be in England, as green waters tumble into the room from the hall (III, 119). Thus, natural forces and local people combine to vanquish a project to restore symbolically imperial privilege in a landscape which although not decolonized, will literally not give ground to attempts to re-colonize it. The cuckolding and routing of the wealthy English dupes, and their ludicrous attempts at rural living is the stuff of broad comedy throughout. However, with more than an echo of Peter Keegan's bitter valediction in *John Bull's Other Island*, and Yeats's 'September 1913', the play excoriates the Irish Free State:

> **2nd Workman:**   Them that fight now fight in a daze o' thradin'; for buyin' an' sellin', for whores an' holiness, for th'image o' God on a golden coin; while th' men o' peace are little men now, writin' dead words with their tiny pens, seekin' a tidy an' tendher way to the end. Respectable lodgers with life they are, behind solid doors with knockers on them, an' curtained glass to keep the stars from starin'! (III, 72).[17]

The stark consequences of the Free State's loss of moral and social purpose are dramatized in *The Star Turns Red*, dedicated those who fought during the Dublin Lockout of 1913 (II, 239). Produced at the Unity Theatre in London, within weeks of its having been written, the play shares with *Purple Dust* (published in 1940), a narrative conflict of binary opposites; in this case, Fascism and Socialism. Here is a political project shared with the Workers' Theatre Movement, and with Bertolt Brecht's *The Mother* (1931), and *Fear and Misery of the Third Reich* (1938), but the collision of forces devastating Europe, and laying waste to London, is played out in Dublin, among the impoverished working classes. The lethal clash of fascist Saffron Shirts (SS) and Christian Front with Red Jim's Union plays out at domestic level in the implacable opposition of socialist protagonist, Jack, and his fascist brother, Kian. If binaries multiply as the play develops, they do so in ways that expose contradiction, and foreground personal moral choice. As the action progresses, the Brown Priest of the Poor experiences a crisis of service to a religion indicted in incandescent rhetoric by Red Jim:

> **Red Jim:** (*passionately*) If your God stands for one child to be born in a hovel, and another in a palace, then we declare against him [. . .] once and for all and for ever we declare against your God, who hath filled the wealthy with good things and hath sent the poor empty away! (II, 324–5)

When reminded by the Purple Priest of the Politicians of his duty to obey, the Brown Priest, standing beside Red Jim, responds:

> **Brown Priest:** (*In a low voice*) I serve my master here.
> In the loud clamour made by war-mad men
> The voice of God may still be heard;
> And, in a storm of curses, God can bless.
> The star turned red is still the star
> Of him who came as man's pure prince of peace;
> And so I serve him here. (II, 351)

The play culminates in an image of workers' victory in class warfare consistent with the ending of Piscator's 1925 play *Trotz Alledem!* ('In Spite of Everything!'), commissioned for the tenth congress of the German Communist Party:[18]

> *Julia stands up with her right fist clenched. The playing and singing of 'The Internationale' grow louder. Soldiers and sailors appear at the windows, and all join in the singing. The Red Star glows, and seems to grow bigger as the curtain falls.* (II, 354)

Once again, the struggles of Dublin's poor are internationalized. As Cairns and Richards argue, nationalist sentiment is not traduced in this play; rather, O'Casey stages the relative merits as guarantors of the good life of competing political and cultural models, against the decisive struggle of Capital and Labour.

Red Roses for Me revisits the urban sites of the Dublin trilogy, with significant development of purpose. Where the plays of the trilogy, and *The Silver Tassie*, explore sites of armed conflict, in *Red Roses for Me* Dublin is a battleground in an economic war – a fight to the finish, in the case of Ayamonn Breydon, the play's protagonist. The time of the play is given as a little while ago (III, 126), and, as in *The Silver Tassie*, the narrative foregrounds members of the Protestant working class among the tide of great historical events. If the grand contest is that of Capital and Labour, its representation is both localized and enriched by emphasizing the engrained reality, long before national independence, of Catholic neighbours in thrall to an autocratic church. This thraldom produces both a present obstacle with which Labour militancy must contend, and a genealogy for theocratic repression in the nationalist Ireland.[19] Interestingly, a mob's assault on Ayamonn's atheist friend, Mullcanny (Act II), recalls the expulsion of Martin and Mary Doul in Act III of in J. M. Synge's prophetic drama, *The Well of the Saints* (1905). When Mullcanny seeks refuge in Ayamonn's tenement rooms, the mob stones the windows. Immediately afterward, a group of Catholic neighbours enters, celebrating the apparently miraculous return of a missing statue of Our Lady of Eblana to a niche in the tenement hallway. Their Protestant landlord, Brennan, has had the statue secretly removed, re-painted and restored under cover of darkness, but neighbours vie with each other in improbable accounts of the miraculous return of the icon:

Mullcanny: I'll go; there's too many here to deal with – I'll leave you with your miracle.

Ayamonn: You can stay if you wish, for whatever surety of shelther's here, it's open to th' spirit seeking to add another colour to whatever thruth we know already. Thought that has run from a blow will find a roof under [*sic*] its courage here, an' a fire to sit by, as long as I live an' th' oul rooms last!

Sheila:[20] (*with quiet bitterness*) Well, shelter him, then, that by right should be lost in the night, a black night, an' bitterly lonely, without a dim ray from a half-hidden star to give him a far-away companionship; ay' an' a desolate rest under a thorny and dripping thicket of lean and twisted whins, too tired to thry to live longer against the hate of the black wind and th' grey rain. Let him lie there, forsaken, forgotten by all who live under a kindly roof and close to a cosy fire! (III, 178)

Synge's play anticipates that a predominantly Catholic Ireland will place those 'out of step' at enduring risk of destitution, with Ireland's 'cosy homesteads' closed and barred against them. *Red Roses for Me* opened in Dublin two days before Éamon de Valera's notorious St Patrick's Day speech glorifying frugal comfort was broadcast on national radio in 1943. The drama stages with hindsight, the playing out of Synge's dystopian vision. In O'Casey's dramatic narrative, as in Paul Vincent Carroll's *Shadow and Substance* (1932), triumphalist clerical authoritarianism feeds sectarianism, closes down intellectual space and is the bitter enemy of the material progress of working people.[21] Tóibín articulates this narrowing, of culture and opportunity as an encroaching cultural crisis:

Lady Gregory: It is why I wonder what our legacy will be, that there are young men and women out there who risked everything for Ireland, and still they do not believe that Casey's right to speak comes before their right to silence him. What have we achieved if that is not understood?[22]

In *Red Roses for Me*, O'Casey forges a poetics of class struggle for a collective utopian vision, extending a dramaturgical engagement with the condition of working people in Dublin. A version of that vision is dramatized in the remarkable Act III of *Red Roses for Me*, a dramatic episode disruptive of the popular realism that characterizes the developed melodramatic dramaturgy of Acts I, II and IV. The scene is set at a bridge over the river Liffey that flows through the heart of

Dublin city. The people are figured as expressionless crowds of a variety of men and women, who, among the tall houses of Dublin, are sadly in search of a home. The streetscape is dominated by emblems of Church and Imperial State – a silver spire reaches into the sky and Nelson stands atop his pillar – and there is no sign of sun where the people are (III, 185).

The Rector and Inspector of Police cross the bridge into this limbo:

> **Rector:** Things here are of a substance I dare not think about, much less see and handle. Here, I can hardly bear to look upon the same thing twice.
>
> **Inspector:** There you are, and as I've said so often, Ayamonn Breydon's but a neat slab of similar slime.
>
> **Rector:** You wrong yourself to say so: Ayamonn Breydon has within him the Kingdom of Heaven. (*He pauses.*) And so, indeed, may these sad things we turn away from. (III, 191)

Ayamonn, who has been rousing transport workers to strike action, enters and invokes a transfiguration of the city and the people: 'No-one knows what a word may bring forth' (III, 197). Dublin is bathed in a glorious sunset, people are transformed, with the listless now standing *'stalwart, looking like fine bronze statues, slashed with scarlet'* (III, 199). Finnoola and Ayamonn dance an exultant duet, she bathed in a gold light, he in purple, and occasionally swapping to one another's colours. Ayamonn ends the dance, and breaks the spell, as the noise of distant marching in unison can be heard, and Act III closes with a reprise of Ayamonn's hymn to the Fair City:

> We swear to release you from hunger and hardship,
> From things that are ugly and common and mean;
> Thy people together shall build a great city,
> The finest and fairest that ever was seen. (III, 204)

Act III is difficult to stage, requiring scenographic ingenuity, and not only actors, but contemporary audiences are challenged by the stylized hyperbole of its language. It is rhetorically promiscuous, as Ayamonn mobilizes glories of Irish mythology and the Celtic race, biblical imagery, socialist exhortation and an intoxicated sentimentality of place, at the centre of a sustained utopian epiphany which yields only to militant action. And therein lies the script's particular theatrical promise; its impact derives from the combination of frequently incompatible gestures, discourses and images. In Edward Said's terms, it is an exemplary postcolonial artefact, as 'in the cultural forms of decolonization, a great many languages, histories, forms, circulate'.[23] Formally, the postcolonial aesthetic of Disrupted Realism serves the imperative to represent that desired reality which, under domination, it is barely possible to imagine. Among the chaos and damage of colonial and neo-colonial conditions, to demand aesthetic consistency is a critical folly: as in the urban riot, or the popular theatre itself, sense will emerge from among the collisions and contradictions of frequently incoherent, often incompatible forces. Even more significant is the fact and experience of the 'riotous event' itself. As it is dramatized in *Red Roses for Me*, the epiphany in Act III which accompanies the confrontation between Labour and Capital has a double impact: it casts that confrontation as a 'riotous event', and is itself a repeatable, inhabitable, representation of that 'event', which, in Alain Badiou's terms:

> *makes possible the restitution of the inexistent* [. . .] of the world [. . .] a *change of world* is real when an inexistent of the world starts to exist in this same world with maximum intensity [. . .] That is why we refer to *uprising*: people were lying down, submissive; they are getting up, picking themselves up, rising up. This rising is of existence itself: the poor have not become rich; people who were unarmed are not now armed, and so forth. Basically, nothing has changed. What has occurred is restitution of the existence of the inexistent, conditional on what I call an *event*.[24]

In concluding these notes on O'Casey's postcolonial dramaturgy, it may be useful to consider Christopher Morash's characterization of the Irish Free State (1922–48) as a post-utopian society:

> If there is no one answer to the question of how to create a theatre for a post-utopian society, it can be said that there are few Irish plays written in the years after Independence in which there is not some form of mourning for the loss of a utopian future [. . .] the trend becomes glaringly obvious with the overwhelming popularity of the plays in O'Casey's Dublin trilogy, which between them made up three of the top four most frequently performed works at the Abbey between 1925 and 1948.[25]

Perhaps, as Ireland's people are re-colonized by indenture to the transnational banking system, and its political enablers in Europe's former imperial centres, it is time to look again at the questions posed, not only by O'Casey's later plays, but by the systematic marginalization of these works over many decades. The contested reputation of the plays exposes critical prejudice entrenched around class, history, politics and the subordination of performance events to normative qualities owned and canonized by an elite social group. The plays' potential to expose the contemporary revival of parasitic Capital is real, if – as in all dramatic scripts – latent. As Tomás Mac Anna's advice on directing *Purple Dust* suggests – they must be 'directed with invention, judiciously cut, and taken in the right spirit' – that potential can only be realized in performance.[26]

CHAPTER 9
O'CASEY AND CLASS

Paul Murphy

Paul Murphy teaches in the Brian Friel Centre at the School of Creative Arts, Queen's University Belfast. He is former President of the Irish Society for Theatre Research and currently Secretary General (Communications) for the International Federation for Theatre Research. His publications include *Hegemony and Fantasy in Irish Drama, 1899–1949* (2008) and (with Melissa Sihra) *The Dreaming Body: Contemporary Irish Theatre* (2009).

In Seán O'Casey's autobiographical play *Red Roses for Me* the flower seller Dympna comments on the forlorn situation that she and her fellows must endure: 'Ah, what is it all to us but a deep-written testament o' gloom: grey sky over our heads, brown an' dusty streets under our feet, with th' black an' bitter Liffey flowin' through it all' (III, 191). The play is set loosely against the backdrop of the 1911 railway workers' strike and depicts the misery endured by Dublin's unskilled labourers.[1] There is no small irony in the fact that nearly a century later the working people of Dublin and the rest of Ireland endure the despondency concomitant with the near collapse of their economy following the 2008 banking crisis.[2] One should of course be wary in drawing parallels between contexts a century apart, but the consequences of decisions made by greedy plutocrats on the lives of ordinary people are as blatantly evident in the early twenty-first century as they were in the early twentieth century.[3] What the boom of the Celtic Tiger period from the early 1990s up to the bust following the 2008 banking crisis highlighted was the uncomfortable fact of class disparity which, while different in obvious ways, was nonetheless as stark as the gulf that separated rich from poor during O'Casey's formative years.[4] While class as a descriptive term has become unfashionable during the rise of global capitalism since the early 1990s, the difference in lifestyles between rich and poor is more pronounced than ever.[5] Indeed it is the difference in lifestyles which marks the difference between social classes and is the focus of this essay in terms of its manifestation in O'Casey's life and his plays.

O'Casey's status as the working-class playwright who represented in theatrical form the proletarian life he knew since childhood, was enshrined in the various editions of his autobiography and taken as given until biographical scholarship following his death in 1964 called that image into question.[6] In light of such research Nicholas Grene contends that: 'On closer examination it appears that rather than the working-class autodidact from the slums of his self-representations, O'Casey belonged to that commoner type, the writer from a middle-class family gone down in the world'.[7] Grene goes on to state that:

> O'Casey, then, was not, technically, working class in origins; he did not grow up illiterate or undereducated; he did not come from the tenements. Yet the exposed position of his family on the very margins of the lower middle class, and the physical proximity of the places they lived to the actual slums made of O'Casey's social consciousness something quite different from that of a Synge or a Shaw, a Yeats or a Joyce. His was no case merely of vie en Boheme or shabby gentility. He did at times endure real poverty and the menace of the tenements was readily before him. It is out of this experience that the three plays of the Dublin trilogy were created, and they are informed by the complex emotions and attitudes of that identity.[8]

The key issue then in understanding O'Casey's class status is his putative middle-class provenance and the lifestyle he led in his early and later years. As is often the case with those born into humble circumstances, little is known of O'Casey's parents' background other than that provided in his autobiography. Seán's father Michael Casey was born c.1838 just before the onset of the Great Famine to a farming family in

County Limerick, and apparently received little in the way of formal education. Michael was drawn into the Protestant evangelism which moved across the west of Ireland in the decades subsequent to the Famine and became a member of the Irish Church Missions society. As James Moran notes in this volume, many of the books that would have graced the shelves of the Casey household were consequently theological in nature, as well as some of the canonical works of English literature. But Michael was by no means born into wealth nor did he earn a remarkable salary as a clerk in the Irish Church Missions. O'Casey was born in 1880 at 85 Upper Dorset Street, the same street indeed as Richard Brinsley Sheridan, but the neighbourhood had become somewhat déclassé since the heyday of the Augustan Age. It would seem that Michael was the landlord of the three-storey address for a short time, but that proved to be an unsuccessful business venture as his son refers to 'an apartment house kept by me da which nearly ruined him'.[9]

Where 85 Upper Dorset Street was a tenement it was so only in the sense of it being a multiple occupancy dwelling, and O'Casey did not live in the same conditions as those he represented in *The Plough and the Stars*. Indeed he spent only two of his earliest years in the property until the family moved around the corner in 1882 to 9 Innisfallen Parade, a small terraced property built principally to house manual labourers. Michael Casey died barely four years later in 1886 and thereafter his family slipped gradually into poverty. Consequently the young O'Casey experienced little of the kind of lower middle-class lifestyle his parents and elder siblings may have enjoyed. Whatever middle-class aspirations the Casey family had were focused on their eldest daughter Bella, whose promising career as a teacher was cut short by an extra-marital pregnancy and subsequent ruinous marriage to the alcoholic Nicholas Beaver, in spite of her mother Susan's warning that: 'You will sup sorrow if you marry him'.[10] Bella gained sufficient qualifications at the Central Model School on Marlborough Street to begin immediately her short-lived career at St Mary's Infant School, Dominick Street, where she taught her younger brother John (who would later be known as Seán). While he would perhaps have benefitted from his sister's attentions, nevertheless he did not enjoy the same overall quality of teaching provision as the rest of his siblings who, along with G. B. Shaw, attended the Model School, with the latter reporting that he 'at once lost caste outside it and became a boy with whom no Protestant young gentleman would speak or play'.[11]

One can imagine the indignation Shaw would have felt had he been consigned to the same kind of schools as young O'Casey. Bella's early beneficence would be thrown into sharp relief by the brutality demonstrated by John Hogan, principal of St Barnabas's Boys School, which O'Casey would later attend. Hogan's teaching methods, typical of those predominant during the late-Victorian period, relied more on harsh discipline than on building a relationship and treating each child in terms of their individual needs. O'Casey could not flourish in such an environment and his education was hampered further due to the severe conjunctivitis he contracted at an early age that impacted negatively on his ability to attend school and led to bullying by teachers and fellow students alike. He would consequently develop a keen interest in education, particularly more progressive teaching methods, which would later be manifested in an article published in 1918 in the left-wing journal *Irish Opinion*. The piece was called 'Room for the Teachers' and O'Casey made the case for all teachers to join with the Labour movement with the aim of abolishing distinction based on 'status'.[12] The issue which O'Casey addresses goes to the heart of social stratification insofar as the education which a child receives largely determines their future career opportunities and quality of life. The differences in education similarly affect the kind of cultural capital and then economic capital which the child will be able to attain that will in turn affect their lifestyle in terms of choice of food, clothing, housing and leisure activities.[13] Such choices are themselves forms of distinction between different kinds of activities which ultimately constitute the differences between social classes.

The challenges that impeded O'Casey's formal education drove him to an intense form of autodidacticism that propelled him eventually to become a dramatist of international acclaim.[14] He devoured whatever literary tomes came his way, from dictionaries and encyclopedias to Shakespeare and Shaw, all of which fed an imagination desperate to grow and find a means of expression. The practice of intellectual self-help evolved into a form of self-fashioning where O'Casey, often clumsily and erratically but nonetheless inexorably, developed a persona and style of deportment that raised his profile as a chronicler of Irish life. This self-fashioning found its ultimate expression in his autobiographies where O'Casey often referred to himself in the third person and variously embellished or diminished the details of his life to suit the type of identity he sought to create. The relative lack of formal education, particularly in contrast to other figures from the Irish Renaissance such as J. M. Synge or James Joyce, determined to a large extent O'Casey's self-definition as an artist. The lack of social refinement that was a consequence of O'Casey's impoverished youth, especially when compared to that of his middle-class peers, drove him to over-compensate both in terms of the fervent consumption of cultural products in his youth and the tenacious performance of the role of public intellectual in later life.

Following the death of their father, O'Casey's older brother Isaac became the breadwinner for the family, working as an office boy for the *Daily Express*, and with wages of 15 shillings per week that would keep the household out of penury. Isaac introduced his younger brother to the world of the theatre, building jury-rigged stage sets for their improvised plays at home, and taking him to the Queen's Theatre to watch Dion Boucicault's *The Shaughraun*. The cost of admission restricted O'Casey's early theatregoing and his poor eyesight undoubtedly reduced the quality of the experience. Nonetheless he performed on stage occasionally and continued his self-education by reading copies of *Dick's Standard Plays*, lovingly anthologized by Isaac, which enhanced O'Casey's 'unappeasable desire' for reading play texts.[15] However his early enthusiasm for the theatre was eclipsed for some time, initially by his renewed interest in religion and subsequently by his developing interest in the Irish language. Around 1905 O'Casey, styling himself Seán Ó Cathasaigh, was a member of the IRB, the Gaelic Athletic Association and the Gaelic League, as attested by Ernest Blythe, a fellow member of the IRB.[16] In terms of the investment in O'Casey's chosen style of cultural nationalism, the playwright, by his own admission, 'worked harder at night than I did in the daytime – teaching Irish, sweeping floors, and lighting fires before classes began; an' all for love!'.[17] The investment in culture was part of O'Casey's larger project of self-fashioning, by elevation through the attainment of cultural capital where such elevation was not possible by economic capital. When O'Casey was in a position later in life to translate his amassed cultural capital as a successful playwright into economic capital, his obsession with increasing his cultural capital persisted nonetheless. In a letter to Lady Gregory following the success of *Juno and the Paycock*, he described his purchase of a bookcase to house the books he had recently bought as well as the desire to buy a painting from Jack B. Yeats.[18] The difference between cultural and economic capital, particularly in terms of the earlier attainment of the former and its link to the latter, is crucial to understanding O'Casey's ambiguous class status and his protean public demeanor.

In 1899 the Casey family moved to 25 Hawthorn Terrace, East Wall, then a solidly working-class area with the northern railway line on one side and the docklands on the other, which would feature heavily in the setting for O'Casey's play *Red Roses for Me*. He would spend the best part of 20 years living in this area and his experiences would permeate O'Casey's writings, particularly his plays. Shortly after the move to East Wall, O'Casey started working for the railway as a bricklayer's assistant on relatively low pay given the status of the job as a general and therefore relatively unskilled labourer. O'Casey's bookish nature at once set him apart from his fellow labourers while simultaneously endearing him to more skilled workers: 'he [O'Casey] above of all of them would [not] be let within touching distance of an engine, for drivers & firemen were well above labourers, & mortal jealous of their precious dignity. But on account of his knowledge, his eloquent tongue, his Irish enthusiasm, nearly every footplate [. . .] from here to Dundalk would welcome him as a visitor [. . .] possessing a knowledge & a dignity in himself that were high above their own'.[19] The subtleties of intra-class distinction manifest themselves here variously in terms of skill level relative to the professional status of the drivers and in the superiority O'Casey assumes based on the cultural capital he accumulated from his self-education and immersion in the Irish language.

The politics of intra-class status would have profound consequences for the 1911 railway-workers' strike, when unskilled Dublin railway labourers protesting against excessively long hours on minimal pay were not supported by the more skilled engineers, with the consequence that the strike was broken after little more than a week. Jim Larkin founded the Irish Transport and General Workers' Union in 1909 and was considered by the majority of unskilled labourers, O'Casey included, to be their redeemer.[20] After meeting Larkin, O'Casey developed an increasingly militant class consciousness that would be at odds with notions of cultural or intellectual superiority with which the playwright would define himself as an artist. His militancy led to O'Casey's sacking from the Great Northern Railway Company which in turn only radicalized him further in terms of his adherence to Larkin's views on Labour relations. O'Casey immersed himself in public debate; whether on the issue of national independence, class struggle or the Irish language, he would speak vociferously and write caustic articles for Larkin's *Irish Worker*. The 1913 Dublin lockout constituted the high water mark for O'Casey in terms of his involvement with organized Labour politics, insofar as it represented 'the coming of age not only of O'Casey (it remained the definitive experience of his life) but of the Irish workers as a class, conscious of itself'.[21] On 26 August, 200 tram workers left their vehicles unattended in Dublin city centre and sparked a wildfire of sympathetic strike action organized largely through Larkin's union. The corporate and civic response led by businessman William Martin Murphy was ruthless, not least in terms of the public meeting led by Larkin on 31 August (at which O'Casey was present) that would become known as 'Bloody Sunday' due to the brutality exercised by the civil authorities. On 3 September Murphy ordered that all members of the Irish Transport and General Workers' Union would be locked out from their work premises. On Larkin's release from prison on 13 November James Connolly declared that the workers were now in a 'state of war' and called for the formation of an army to protect them.[22] After the strike was finally broken in January 1914 O'Casey was one of the leading figures in the formation of the Irish Citizen Army.

O'Casey was elected secretary of the Irish Citizen Army and his militancy for workers' rights left him at odds with the Irish Volunteers which formed in November 1913 largely in response to Edward Carson's Ulster Volunteer Force. The Irish Volunteers were drawn predominantly from the Gaelic League and the IRB, two institutions which O'Casey viewed as increasingly middle-class and uninterested in the plight of Ireland's working-class. His railing against Patrick Pearse for failing to support the workers during the lockout further alienated O'Casey from the nationalist movement. O'Casey's discontent with the Volunteers manifested again in his objection to Countess Markievicz's membership of both the Citizen Army in her capacity as joint treasurer and of *Cumann na mBan*, the women's auxiliary of the Volunteers. In August 1914 O'Casey put forward a motion to the Council of the Citizen Army that Markievicz should resign; however, he had not only underestimated his support but also the Countess's friendship with James Connolly, with the net result that his motion not only lost the vote but also served to strengthen Markievicz's position.[23] At a subsequent general meeting O'Casey resigned from the ICA, and succeeded in estranging himself from the two organizations that would become immortalized in the 1916 Easter Rising. It would seem that O'Casey, the militant socialist, was but another aspect of a more deep-rooted persona – O'Casey the contrarian – whose penchant for dissent would help make a great playwright but a poor politician and ultimately lead to his isolation. The conflict in loyalties between his brand of uncompromising socialism and his style of cultural nationalism manifest most forcefully in his commitment to the Irish language would torment O'Casey in the years to come. The problem is typified in the response O'Casey received from Shaw: O'Casey asked Shaw to write a preface to three essays on Irish nationalism, language and Labour, which Shaw refused and suggested, 'You ought to work out your own position positively and definitively. This objecting to everyone else is Irish, but useless'.[24] That O'Casey was unable to do this goes to the heart of his frustration in subsequent decades and most especially to his representation of class and nationalism in his early plays.

As O'Casey's interest in organized politics waned his interest in theatre waxed anew. In 1912 his friend Delia Larkin, sister of Jim and Labour leader in her own right, founded the Irish Workers' Dramatic Class at Liberty Hall, then headquarters of the Irish Transport and General Workers' Union. O'Casey's frustrated energies found a new release in the theatre at a time when, according to the actress Máire Nic Shiubhlaigh, Dublin was 'drama mad'.[25] Andrew Patrick Wilson's one-act play *Victims*, the first play set in a Dublin tenement dealing with the plight of the urban poor, was produced by the Irish Workers' Dramatic Class and he and O'Casey engaged in a lively debate in the pages of the *Irish Worker*.[26] Wilson's more nuanced socialist position proved more convincing than O'Casey's, and shortly afterwards O'Casey started to write plays in earnest. The renewed interest in theatre was doubly fortunate for O'Casey insofar as the short period during which Ireland came as close as it ever would to having a socialist revolution was drawing to a close. Jim Larkin left for the United States in late 1914 and Delia would soon leave Dublin for an extended sojourn in London following an internal dispute with James Connolly. As the Labour movement became increasingly embroiled with the nationalist movement the possibilities for social radicalism were eclipsed by the possibility, however remote, of an independent Ireland.

The Easter Rising and its aftermath effectively redrew the political map of Ireland, resulting in the rise of Sinn Féin largely at the expense of Labour to the extent that Éamon de Valera, one of the few surviving leaders of the Rising, 'invited Labour to stand aside until national freedom was attained before claiming "its share of patrimony"'.[27] The subordination of class politics to nationalism was confirmed in the general election following the Anglo–Irish War in 1922 in which the Anglo–Irish Treaty was endorsed and the Labour party entered into an alliance with *Cumann na nGaedheal* ('party of the Irish') which supported the Treaty. In essence, this alliance smothered the dying embers of O'Casey's enthusiasm for the Labour movement in Ireland. Where war and politics had failed, O'Casey would employ culture as the vehicle for social change. Lady Gregory later recalled one of O'Casey's visits to her at Coole Park during which he revealed his ambition was to 'lead the workers into a better life, an interest in reading, in drama especially'.[28] When Jim Larkin returned to Ireland in the ill-fated attempt to resurrect his political career, O'Casey's personal loyalty to the man conflicted with the dramatist's sense of realpolitik and the belief that culture not politics was the best hope for the manumission of Ireland's working-class: 'I love the man and am afraid he would bring me into the movement. And I do not believe it will succeed on his present lines, but through art and culture and the people of culture'.[29] The didactic approach to theatre that O'Casey espoused was of course reminiscent of Shaw, but similarly smacked of the patricianism inherent to the simplistic educationalist view of transforming the lower orders by exposing them to high culture. O'Casey (like most people) was the sum of his contradictions, specifically regarding his ambiguous class status as someone raised in poverty who earned his place as a member of Ireland's cultural elite through his self-education and inherent skill rather than inherited privilege. Yet in his case the tension between frustrated militant socialism and the essentially bourgeois belief in the transformative power of culture would manifest itself publicly, not least in terms of his representation of working-class communities in the three Dublin plays that established his reputation.

O'Casey's early, faltering at tempts to dramatize the conflicting issues which concerned him include the agit-prop play *The Harvest Festival* (c.1919), set loosely in relation to the 1913 lockout in terms of a strike that is brutally suppressed and the working-class hero who dies in defence of his socialist principles. The play set the trend for O'Casey in terms of dramatizing recent events and would be recycled later as *Red Roses for Me* in 1943. *The Crimson in the Tricolour* (c.1921) was a take on the struggle for power between Sinn Féin and the Labour movement, and like his earlier play was submitted unsuccessfully to the Abbey. W. B. Yeats read *Crimson* and noted (somewhat prophetically in terms of O'Casey's dramaturgical development) that 'it is so constructed that in every scene there is something for pit & stalls to cheer or boo. In fact it is the old Irish idea of a good play – Queen's melodrama brought up to date [and] would no doubt make a sensation'.[30] The exposure to Boucicault and popular theatre in his youth would resurface in O'Casey's plays and give them popular appeal, specifically in the use of the comic male pair that appears in his 1922 short story

'The Corncrake' and would become a staple part of his Dublin plays, such as Shields and Davoren (in *The Shadow of a Gunman*), Joxer and Boyle (*Juno and the Paycock*), and the Young Covey and Uncle Peter (*The Plough and the Stars*). The Dublin theatregoer Joseph Holloway noted a conversation with O'Casey on the matter of his preference for the comic over the tragic mode: 'He likes his plays with brightness intermingled with sadness. The comedy of life appeals to him most. O'Casey loves Shaw's work because in the very kernel of tragedy he can introduce something to make one laugh its sting away'.[31] The problem with such an approach is that in the final analysis it serves to take the edge off the social critique that was the aim of each of the three Dublin plays, specifically described as tragedies in the first instance.

Christopher Murray, in his comprehensive biography, suggests that 'O'Casey's gift was for telling the tragic truth "aslant" through comedy'.[32] However, this technique is itself a manifestation of O'Casey's inability to reconcile his early militant socialism with the bourgeois didacticism that he later adopted. The iconoclastic manner in which both Labour and nationalist politics are rendered in the three Dublin plays is a consequence of O'Casey's contrarianism, which is in turn the outcome of his inability, as Shaw suggested, to come to a 'position' on such matters. The poet Austin Clarke, writing at the time that O'Casey's plays were emerging, suggested that: 'If one were purely a dramatist and sufficiently aloof one might be able to study the amazing maelstrom [. . .] that has swept the people of every shade of opinion and transformed quiet citizens into bloody-minded disciples of force'.[33] Murray suggests that it 'was this "aloofness" which was O'Casey's greatest strength as a writer of Ireland's tragicomedy'.[34] The distance between playwright and subject matter which the term 'aloofness' implies emerges from the cultural capital that O'Casey had accumulated which separated him from the working-class community of his youth and early career. The problem of class disparity that persisted well after the Irish Free State had been established in 1922 was one that O'Casey's dramatization served to mollify and make palatable for consumption by the newly ascendant Irish middle-class.

As Murray notes: 'Billed as a tragedy, the *Gunman* was accompanied by a one-act comedy [. . .] In spite of the billing *Gunman* was skillfully played as a tragi-comedy. [. . .] The *Irish Times* concurred, and urged O'Casey to call the play a satire rather than a tragedy. Lady Gregory, commenting in her *Journals*, said "all the political points were taken up with delight by a big audience".[35] The comic potential that was realized in the early performances of *Gunman*, *Juno* and *Plough* gradually became the accepted way in which these plays were performed and expected to be performed by audiences in Ireland and abroad. These performance accretions eventually concretized into a tradition that became reinforced over subsequent decades and was rarely challenged on the professional stage. It was not until 1991 that one of O'Casey's plays received its most powerful revision in Garry Hynes's production of *The Plough and the Stars* at the Abbey Theatre, which was met with confusion and even consternation from audiences and critics alike.[36] The shocking element of the first production of *Plough* in 1926, at least for the audience that rioted, was the iconoclastic representation of nationalism and the perceived slight on the leaders of the Rising. The shocking quality of Hynes's production that so perturbed audiences in 1991 emerged from her choice to accentuate the inhuman conditions in which the tenement dwellers were forced to live by the grinding weight of their poverty. It would seem that the burning issue of class disparity that O'Casey chose to salve with comedy, but was later emphasized by Hynes, proved to be more disturbing to audiences at the start of the Celtic-Tiger period. What O'Casey would have thought of such a reaction will remain forever moot, but is a salient question nonetheless.

CONCLUSION

The generally held conception about the work of Seán O'Casey can be summarized as:

1) Dublin Trilogy = Excellent
2) *The Silver Tassie* = Interesting
3) Everything Else = Forgettable

This book has attempted to show that the dramatist's work is more complicated than such a verdict acknowledges. Throughout his career, O'Casey remained a formally experimental, politically engaged, brilliant, but often flawed writer. The urge to identify 1928 as the moment at which his output suddenly turned from gold to lead owes much to Yeats's well-known rejection of *The Silver Tassie*, but takes little account of Yeats's later, and much less famous, attempts to bring *Within the Gates* and *The Silver Tassie* to the Abbey Theatre in the 1930s.

That is not to claim that O'Casey's later writings are as accomplished as his breakthrough work. As his career developed, he appropriated a number of styles and ideas that he found difficult to incorporate fully into his writing, and only a very idiosyncratic critic would rate something like *Behind the Green Curtains* above *The Plough and the Stars*. Following the Dublin trilogy, O'Casey's desire to innovate and create new works of art remained as strong as ever, but he had cut himself off from that group of dynamic and insightful, if tactless, artistic collaborators at the Abbey, who were themselves touched by genius and who helped to turn his early dramatic ideas into pieces of theatre that are fully achieved. The later works, as this book has tried to show, are fascinating for a variety of reasons, and are far from monolithic, but could often have benefitted from being similarly kicked around and mauled in the rehearsal room.

Still, O'Casey's own talent had scarcely vanished overnight in 1928, and directors who have been willing to use O'Casey as a starting point for a set of new theatrical investigations have often found something genuinely rewarding in the writings from outside the Dublin trilogy. Productions including Paul Shyre's adaptation of the autobiographies, Jiří Krejčík's treatment of *Bedtime Story*, and Mark Anthony Turnage's version of *The Silver Tassie* have each seen new artists taking a creative approach to O'Casey's works, sloughing off sections of the printed texts while maintaining and developing significant parts of O'Casey's original vision. Perhaps that is why O'Casey's later scripts have enjoyed greatest success in the non-Anglophone world. Directors and actors who encounter texts that have already been edited and adjusted through translation have possibly felt more willing to continue that vital process of editing and adjustment. This had, after all, been the way in which the early pieces had been treated by Yeats and Gregory.

O'Casey himself, in his tendency to redraft his later plays, seems to have acknowledged that something of this approach was necessary. Although he expressed deep suspicion about theatre directors who might start chopping and changing the words set down by the dramatist, he had himself frequently taken apart familiar phrases from elsewhere (Shakespeare and the bible in particular) in order to reimagine those words and let them breathe afresh in modern contexts. It would be ironic if his own writing was in turn to become a kind of unchanging Holy Writ, particularly when the texts themselves are anything but certain in their formal aspects: his writings are in fact a series of evolving attempts to explore what the page and the stage might be able to do. For O'Casey, the purpose of such theatrical and literary experimentation was to comment upon the most pressing issues of his own day, and where he saw an injustice he felt the need to write a response, whether that was by describing the plight of the urban poor, the inherent unfairness of global capitalism or the abuses propagated by the Catholic Church.

We can assume that he would therefore have been pleased by the judgements reached in this volume by Garry Hynes, Victor Merriman and Paul Murphy, who, while foregrounding very different aspects of O'Casey's work, each affirm the dramatist's continued relevance to audiences in the early twenty-first century. Paul Murphy argues for recognition of class as a key motivating dynamic that roused the young

O'Casey to creative endeavour, with the playwright accreting cultural capital in the absence of economic opportunity. Murphy thus points out the relevance of O'Casey's work to an Ireland that, after 2008, has been shown to contain the kind of enormous class disparities as those that existed during the dramatist's youth. Victor Merriman points out that O'Casey's later writing may also have a particular, unrealized potential in the modern era of 'parasitic Capitalism', identifying the mature playwright as a writer of 'Disrupted Realism', a form that speaks from and of the postcolonial situation. Merriman also asks, suggestively, that we pay close attention to the processes by which O'Casey's political critiques have been sidelined up until now. Meanwhile, Garry Hynes, who has received both praise and blame for her own refusal to bow to tradition in her productions of O'Casey, maintains that the theatre director has the duty to produce O'Casey in a way that allows the drama to 'live on stage for a present-day audience'. She acknowledges that there is work to do in developing the context in which an audience might receive and understand much of O'Casey's oeuvre, but points back to 'the boldness' of his work and his 'sheer embrace of theatricality'.

It is ultimately this 'boldness' that is the consistent feature of O'Casey's writing. One dismissive caricature of his career sees him as turning from a successful form of theatrical naturalism towards a kind of introverted and pointless experimentalism. Yet, right from the start, O'Casey proved himself an avowed experimenter. The Dublin trilogy is a sequence of plays set down by someone who, prior to that point, had been willing to try his hand at journalism, political statement, poetry, prose history and short theatrical sketch. Hence we find that the trilogy is scarcely a mimetic depiction of Dublin life, but a fusion of various literary influences, from nineteenth-century melodrama to the King James Bible. O'Casey first made his mark by applying this generous style to the foundational historical narratives of his home country, and he did so with humour and with humanity. It is for this reason that his work has, justifiably, earned his writing the label 'Shakespearean'. But whereas Shakespeare showed a notorious reluctance about commenting upon the politics of his own day, instead preferring to fictionalize historical events that had occurred many years in the past, O'Casey's boldness meant a compulsion to speak about contemporary struggles and injustices. O'Casey's decision to address such burning issues was a brave one, as it necessarily brought him into conflict with those who disagreed with his analyses, and also left his plays open to adverse historical judgement. After all, he described events that had not yet been resolved or drawn to any conclusion, with the result that later critics could easily point to times at which his reasoning had been premature or awry.

Overall, however, it would be wrong to label O'Casey's writing career as a failure. Those who have ever struggled to write a dramatic script, to interest a director in staging a production, or to attract an audience to a playhouse, will realize just how tremendously unlikely and entirely precarious the whole process of making theatre can be. If this is true in our own day, it was still truer for O'Casey, who, quite aside from the circumstances of his personal background, was writing through periods of Civil War, Great Depression and World War. Furthermore, he felt compelled to say things that would be unpopular with many people, and to use unfamiliar and experimental theatrical forms with which to do so. Yet nonetheless, unlike almost all of us, he created a number of scripts that have lived, and continue to live, on the stage. Today, his name and plays are well known in many parts of the world that he had never seen or visited himself, and his Dublin trilogy enjoys the same kind of status at the Abbey Theatre as *Hamlet* does at the Royal Shakespeare Theatre. For all of the flaws in his writing, then, O'Casey is still able to mesmerize theatre audiences, to make spectators laugh, feel entertained and to wonder at the world in its continuing state of chassis.

NOTES

Prerumble

1. In 1994 the O'Casey estate moved away from Macmillan, the company that had always been O'Casey's publisher and had published 23 plays in the *Complete Plays* in 1984. Instead, the estate moved to Faber, and the new publisher printed a two-volume version of O'Casey's work that included just nine plays, mostly from the early part of the writer's career. Faber included the Dublin trilogy in this two-volume edition, but also printed the Dublin trilogy as a separate volume. O'Casey, *The Complete Plays of Sean O'Casey*, 5 vols. London: Macmillan, 1984. O'Casey, *Sean O'Casey: Plays 1* and *Sean O'Casey: Plays 2*. London: Faber, 1998. O'Casey, *Three Dublin Plays*. London: Faber, 2000.
2. George Orwell, 'The Green Flag', *Observer*, 28 October 1945, p. 3.
3. O'Neill made his comment in a private letter to O'Casey, after seeing O'Casey's play *Within the Gates*, and his remark is quoted in O'Casey, *The Letters of Sean O'Casey*, ed. David Krause, 4 vols. London and Washington: Macmillan and Catholic University Press, 1975–92, I, p. 482. Monroe's feelings are described in 'Blonde No. 1. Makes a Hit', *Irish Times*, 28 July 1956, p. 3, and O'Casey appears to have written his own fan mail back to her. In 1961 she wrote to her psychiatrist Ralph Greenson to declare, 'I'm reading Sean O'Casey's first autobiography – (did I ever tell you how once he wrote a poem to me?)' *Marilyn Monroe: Fragments, Poems, Intimate Notes, Letters*, ed. Stanley Buchthal and Bernard Comment. London: Harper Collins, 2010, p. 208.
4. Seamus Heaney, 'Introduction', in *Sean O'Casey: Plays 1*. London: Faber, 1998, pp. vii–x (p. x).
5. Sean O'Casey, *The Complete Plays of Sean O'Casey*, 5 vols. London: Macmillan, 1984, I, p. 121. Further references to this edition will be given after quotations in the text.

Chapter 1

1. William Grimes, 'Frank McCourt, Whose Irish Childhood Illuminated His Prose, Is Dead at 78', *New York Times*, 19 July 2009, <www.nytimes.com/2009/07/20/books/20mccourt.html>.
2. Frank McCourt, *'Tis: A Memoir*. London: Flamingo, 1999, pp. 154–5.
3. Doyle pointed out that he uses dashes to signify direct speech because of O'Casey's example, something that also characterizes McCourt's writing. Karen Sbrockey, 'Something of a Hero: An Interview with Roddy Doyle', *TLR: The Literary Review*, 42, 4 (1999), pp. 537–52 (p. 547).
4. *Sean O'Casey – Under a Coloured Cap* was first broadcast by RTÉ on 4 January 2005, and rebroadcast on BBC 2 on 6 March 2005. It was then named the Highly Recommended Documentary at the Seventeenth Foyle Film Festival, and nominated at the 2005 FOCAL awards, recognizing the skill with which the filmmakers integrated archive footage and narration.

5. See Garry O'Connor, *Sean O'Casey: A Life*. London: Hodder and Stoughton, 1988, pp. 12–13.
6. O'Casey, *Autobiographies*, 3 vols. London: Faber, 2011, II, p. 495. Further references to this edition will be given after quotations in the text with the prefix '*Auto*'.
7. Christopher Murray, *Sean O'Casey: Writer at Work: A Biography*. Dublin: Gill and Macmillan, 2004, pp. 15, 19.
8. Martin B. Margulies, *The Early Life of Sean O'Casey*. Dublin: Dolmen, 1970, p. 23.
9. 'Slum Child Who Became World Famed Dramatist', *Irish Times*, 19 September 1964, p. 5.
10. Murray Fraser, *John Bull's Other Homes: State Housing and British Policy in Ireland: 1883–1922*. Liverpool: Liverpool University Press, 1996, p. 109.
11. 'Scandal of Dublin Civic Conditions', *New York Times*, 15 March 1914, p. C4. This article reprinted the sentiments already expressed in the *Irish Times*.
12. O'Connor, *Sean O'Casey*, pp. 126–7.
13. NYPL, Berg Collection, Seán O'Casey Papers, Holograph Notebook Vol.1, f.112.
14. For details of O'Casey's Dublin addresses see Anthony Butler, 'The Makings of the Man', in Sean McCann (ed.), *The World of Sean O'Casey*. London, Four Square, 1966, pp. 12–29.
15. Nicholas Grene, *The Politics of Irish Drama: Plays in Context from Boucicault to Friel*. Cambridge: Cambridge University Press, 1999, p. 112.
16. David Krause, *Sean O'Casey: The Man and His Work*. London: MacGibbon and Kee, 1967, pp. 19–20.
17. 'Award of Hawthornden Prize', *Irish Times*, 24 March 1926, p. 7.
18. Sean O'Casey, 'Always the Plow and the Stars', *New York Times*, 25 January 1953, p. BR1.
19. Murray, *Sean O'Casey*, p. 49.
20. O'Connor, *Sean O'Casey*, pp. 39, 59.
21. NLI, Seán O'Casey Papers, MS 37,938, Francis J. Kelly letter of 16 May 1946.
22. De Blaghd, *Trasna na Bóinne: Imleabhar 1 de Chuimhní Cinn*. Dublin: Sáiséal agus Dill, 1957, p. 132, trans. Murray, *Sean O'Casey*, p. 67.
23. O'Casey, *Letters*, I, p. 191.
24. NYPL, Berg Collection, Seán O'Casey Papers, Holograph Notebook Vol. 14, f.5. See also O'Casey, *Letters*, III, p. 64.
25. Robert G. Lowery, 'O'Casey, Sean', in James McGuire and James Quinn (eds), *Dictionary of Irish Biography*, 9 vols. Cambridge: RIA/Cambridge University Press, 2009, VII, pp. 167–70 (p. 168).
26. Written under the name *An Gall Fada* [Tall Foreigner], 'Sound the Loud Trumpet', *The Peasant and Irish Ireland*, 25 May 1907, reprinted in Seán O'Casey, *Feathers from the Green Crow*, ed. Robert Hogan. London: Macmillan, 1963, pp. 2–6 (p. 5).
27. Patrick Pearse, 'The Murder Machine', in Pearse, *Political Writings and Speeches*. Dublin: Maunsel, 1922, pp. 5–50, 40–1.
28. O'Casey, *Letters*, I, p. 27.
29. O'Casey, *Letters*, II, p. 166.
30. D. H. Lawrence, *The Plumed Serpent*, ed. L. D. Clark. Cambridge: Cambridge University Press, 1987, p. 112.
31. O'Casey, *Letters*, I, p. 52.
32. O'Casey, *Letters*, III, p. 304.
33. O'Casey, *Letters*, I, pp. 40–1.

34. *Young Cassidy*, dir. John Ford/Jack Cardiff, MGM, 1965; <www.diogenes.ch/leser/autoren/land/ie/ocasey_sean/biographie>; for Yu Chi-jin's views see Hunam Yun, *Appropriations of Irish Drama by Modern Korean Nationalist Theatre : A Focus on the Influence of Sean O'Casey in a Colonial Context.* Unpublished PhD thesis, University of Warwick, 2010, p. 208.

35. See James Moran, *Staging the Easter Rising: 1916 as Theatre*. Cork: Cork University Press, 2005, pp. 30–52.

36. O'Casey, *Letters*, II, p. 400.

37. Murray, *Sean O'Casey*, p. 68.

38. NYPL, Berg Collection, Seán O'Casey Papers, Holograph Notebook Vol. 3, f.12.

39. After Keating and he had split up, O'Casey reflected that her Catholic piety made the relationship impossible and satirized this aspect of her personality in his later writing (most notably in the character of Sheila Moorneen in *Red Roses for Me*). See Murray, *Seán O'Casey*, pp. 119–20.

40. Paul O'Brien, 'Sean O'Casey and the Abbey Theatre', in *Echoes Down the Corridor: Irish Theatre – Past, Present, and Future*, ed. Patrick Lonergan and Riana O'Dwyer. Dublin: Carysfort, 2007, pp. 69–80 (p. 70).

41. Murray, *Sean O'Casey*, p. 93.

42. Sean O'Casey, *The Harvest Festival: A Play in Three Acts*. Gerrards Cross: Colin Smythe, 1980.

43. Murray, *Sean O'Casey*, p. 124.

44. Lauren Arrington, *W. B. Yeats, the Abbey Theatre, Censorship, and the Irish State*. Oxford: Oxford University Press, 2010, p. 53.

45. Adrian Frazier, *Hollywood Irish: John Ford, Abbey Actors and the Irish Revival in Hollywood*. Dublin: Lilliput, 2011, p. 4.

46. Christopher Morash, *A History of Irish Theatre, 1601–2000*. Cambridge: Cambridge University Press, 2002, pp. 163–71.

47. Moran, *Staging the Easter Rising*, pp. 48–9.

48. See, for example, Bernice Schrank, *Sean O'Casey: A Research and Production Sourcebook*. Westport: Greenwood, 1996, p. 11.

49. David Mamet, *Theatre*. New York: Faber, 2010, p. 18.

50. O'Casey [Sean O Cathasaigh], *Songs of the Wren, by Sean O Cathasaigh, Author of 'The Grand Oul' Dame Brittannia* [sic]*': Humorous and Sentimental*. Dublin: Fergus O'Connor, [1918], p. 5.

51. J. R. White, *Misfit: An Autobiography.* London: Jonathan Cape, 1930, pp. 249–50.

52. Eileen O'Casey, *Sean*. London: Macmillan, 1972, p. 59.

53. NYPL, Berg Collection, Seán O'Casey Papers, Holograph Notebook Vol. 2.

54. 'Mr. O'Casey's New Play', *Irish Times*, 21 April 1928, p. 6.

55. Information calculated from the Abbey takings book, Abbey Theatre Archives, Abbey Theatre Papers, Vol. 17, P8134.

56. Murray, *Sean O'Casey*, p. 211–12.

57. Ibid., p. 203.

58. O'Casey, *Letters*, I, pp. 284–5.

59. O'Casey, *Sean*, p. 89.

60. NYPL, Berg Collection, Seán O'Casey Papers, Holograph Notebook Vol. 9, f.133.

61. *Daily Sketch*, 12 October 1929, cutting in NLI, Seán O'Casey Papers, MS 38,149/1.

62. O'Casey, *Letters*, I, p. 822. Even in the 1950s he spent time copying out in his own handwriting one of Ivor Brown's reviews praising Sherriff's drama as a play that 'will

never be dated'. NYPL, Berg Collection, Seán O'Casey Papers, Holograph Notebook Vol. 14, f.75.

63. Gabrielle H. Cody and Evert Sprinchorn (eds), *The Columbia Encyclopedia of Modern Drama*, 2 vols. New York: Columbia University Press, 2007, II, p. 1236. Kershaw et al. (eds), *The Cambridge History of British Theatre*, 3 vols. Cambridge: Cambridge University Press, 2004, III, p. 145.

64. James Agate, 'Beyond the Agates', in *First Nights*. London: Ivor Nicholson and Watson, 1934, pp. 271–6 (p. 271). Also quoted in O'Casey's Letters, I, pp. 492–6 (p. 493). Agate declared that *Within the Gates* 'reads like *Alice in Wonderland* interleaved with Euclid', but did temper his criticism with the observation that 'O'Casey is a most distinguished craftsman as well as a poet'.

65. O'Casey labelled the English playwright 'above the ordinary opinions and practices of ordinary life' and 'cuddled', as well as asserting, 'Extraordinary things were done in ancient Egypt, in Greece and Rome, in the Middle Ages, and even in the days of Queen Victoria. Indeed, the most extraordinary thing done by people (including the critics) these days seems to be the crowning of Mr. Coward as a first-rate, first-class, front-rank dramatist'. O'Casey, *The Flying Wasp*. London: Macmillan, 1937, pp. 49, 146–7, 156.

66. O'Casey, *Letters*, I, pp. 214, 280.

67. See O'Casey, *Letters*, II, p. 286.

68. Ibid., 221.

69. Ibid., p. 418; IV, pp. 369, 389.

70. Ibid., p. 689.

71. Ibid., p. 895.

72. 'The Best Play', *Irish Times,* 31 July 1945, p. 3. Murray, *Sean O'Casey: Writer at Work*, p. 264.

73. Sean O'Casey, 'A Miner's Dream of Home', *New Statesman*, 28 July 1934, p. 124.

74. NYPL, Berg Collection, Seán O'Casey Papers, + 70B6521, The National Broadcasting Company presents A Conversation with Sean O'Casey and Robert Emmett Ginna (1955), ff.4–5.

75. Murray, *Sean O'Casey*, p. 238.

76. Hugh Hunt, *Seán O'Casey*. Dublin: Gill and Macmillan, 1980, p. 88.

77. M. H. Gaffney, 'Readers' Views: "The Silver Tassie"', *Irish Press*, 12 September 1935, p. 6.

78. Murray, *Sean O'Casey*, p. 251.

79. Christopher Murray, 'O'Casey, Sean', in Gabrielle H. Cody and Evert Sprinchorn (eds), *The Columbia Encyclopedia of Modern Drama*, 2 vols. New York: Columbia University Press, 2007, II, pp. 982–6 (p. 984).

80. NYPL, Berg Collection, Seán O'Casey Papers, + 70B6521, The National Broadcasting Company Presents A Conversation with Sean O'Casey and Robert Emmett Ginna (1955), f.8. O'Casey, *Letters*, II, p. 395.

81. Richard Bradford, *The Life of a Long-Distance Writer: The Biography of Alan Sillitoe*. London: Peter Owen, 2008, p. 245.

82. However, Susan Canon Harris has argued that 'It would perhaps be more accurate – or at any rate, more illuminating, to say that *The Star Turns Red* was produced by the sole theatrical company in London capable of interpreting it. Though the Unity Theatre was closely allied with, and probably bankrolled by, the Communist Party of Great Britain, it was founded precisely in order to move workers' theater beyond

agitprop'. 'Red Star versus Green Goddess: Sean O'Casey's "The Star Turns Red" and the Politics of Form', *Princeton University Library Chronicle*, 68, 1/2 (2007), pp. 357–98 (p. 394).

83. When the third volume was published in 1945, the publisher printed 8,300 copies, four times the size of the first two editions, which were now being reprinted for book clubs in the United States and Britain. See Murray, *Sean O'Casey: Writer at Work*, p. 276.

84. *Sean O'Casey Reading From His Works*. L. P. Caedmon. 1953. *Young Cassidy.* Dir. John Ford and Jack Cardiff. MGM. 1965.

85. Grene, *The Politics of Irish Drama*, p. 113.

86. NYPL, Berg Collection, Seán O'Casey Papers, Holograph Notebook Vol. 21, f.18.

87. *Joseph Holloway's Abbey Theatre: A Selection from his Unpublished Journal*, ed. Robert Hogan and Michael J. O'Neill. London: Feffer and Simons, 1967, p. 248.

88. O'Casey, *Letters*, III, p. 387.

89. I am grateful to Margaret Eaton for locating these quotes by McCourt. McCourt gave the first quote at the John Hersey Memorial Lecture, 'Preserving Our History Through Story', Key West Literary Seminar on Memoir, 13–16 January 2000, recorded by the organizers on disc 13b. The second quote comes from Dave Welch's interview with Frank McCourt, *Staying After School with Frank McCourt* <www.powells.com/blog/original-essays/staying-after-school-with-frank-mccourt-by-dave/>. McCourt repeated virtually the same words as this latter quote in an after-dinner speech at the American Conference For Irish Studies, 'Ireland and the Americas', at CUNY, 18–21 April 2007. Details of Malachy's involvement in the centenary are found in John Corry, 'O'Casey Centenary Fans Flames of His Works', *New York Times*, 26 March 1980, p. C26.

90. Eileen O'Casey confesses to adultery and to an abortion in her 1971 volume *Sean* and the 1976 follow-up, the somewhat repetitive *Eileen* (1976). Nevertheless, we might question some of her admissions, with Harold Macmillan's biographer doubting the veracity of Eileen's claim to have conducted an affair with the prime minister, commenting that 'Macmillan was old-fashioned, very reserved in matters of sex and morality'. Perhaps she, like her husband, learned the importance of the deliberately constructed self-image. See D. R. Thorpe, *Supermac: The Life of Harold Macmillan.* London: Pimlico, 2011, p. 101.

91. Some footage of O'Casey washing the dishes is included in Shivaun O'Casey's film *Sean O'Casey – Under a Coloured Cap.*

92. See, for instance, Brooks Atkinson's description of the play as 'O'Casey's Beautiful Ode to the Glory of Life'. Brooks Atkinson, *Sean O'Casey: From Times Past*, ed. Robert G. Lowery. London: Macmillan, 1982, p. 94.

93. Seán O'Faoláin, 'The Strange Case of Sean O'Casey', *The Bell*, 6, 2 (1943), p. 118.

94. 'Tenement Dust to Purple Dust', *Irish Times*, 14 December 1940, p. 5.

95. Austin Clarke, 'Cock-a-Doodle Dandy', *Irish Times*, 6 November 1954, p. 6.

96. According to Breon O'Casey, in an interview given as part of his sister's film, *Sean O'Casey: Under a Coloured Cap.*

97. See Sean O'Casey, *Niall: A Lament.* London: Calder, 1991.

98. 'No Beckett Plays for Tostal', *Irish Times*, 17 February 1958, p. 1. I am grateful to Shivaun O'Casey for telling me about the telephone calls.

99. David Krause, *Sean O'Casey and His World.* London: Thames and Hudson, 1976, p. 113.

100. *Behind the Green Curtains* first appeared at the University of Rochester, while *Figuro in the Night* premiered at the Hofstra University Playhouse.
101. The Abbey Theatre is also flanked by the now somewhat forlorn former pub, the 'Plough'.
102. O'Casey, *Sean*, p. 296.

Chapter 2

1. Vivian Mercier, 'Literature in English 1921–84', in J. R. Hill (ed.), *A New History of Ireland*, Oxford: Oxford University Press, 2003, p. 491.
2. Murray, *Sean O'Casey*, p. 104.
3. Sean O Cathasaigh, *The Story of Thomas Ashe*. Dublin: Fergus O'Connor, 1917, p. 14. A revised and expanded edition appeared in 1918 under the title *The Sacrifice of Thomas Ashe*.
4. 'England's Conscription Appeal to Ireland's Dead', in Seán O Cathasaigh, *More Wren Songs*. Dublin: Fergus O'Connor, [1918?], p. 5.
5. *Songs of Ireland and Other Lands*. New York: D. J. Sadlier, 1847, pp. 90–2.
6. Fearghal McGarry, *The Rising: Ireland: Easter 1916*. Oxford: Oxford University Press, 2010, p. 287.
7. O Cathasaigh, *More Wren Songs*, p. 6.
8. P. Ó Cathasaigh [Seán O'Casey], *The Story of the Irish Citizen Army*. Dublin: Maunsel, 1919, p. 55.
9. 'Sunshadows' was eventually published in 1934, in O'Casey's *Windfalls: Stories, Poems, and Plays*. London: Macmillan, 1934, p. 25.
10. Percy Bysshe Shelley, *The Major Works*, ed. Zachary Leader and Michael O'Neill. Oxford: Oxford University Press, 2003, p. 233.
11. Even at the end of the play, once something more significant (the shooting of Minnie) has occurred, Davoren's quoting of Shelley's lines feels misplaced. 'Ah me!' (I, 156), Davoren cries in self-absorption, notably not crying 'Ah Minnie'.
12. Shields, for example, realizes that his friend is quoting from *Prometheus Unbound*, and when Davoren subsequently comments 'The village cock hath thrice done salutation to the morn', Shields immediately recognizes the precise act and scene of *Richard III* from which the quote is taken (I, 131). This is a particularly apposite reference to be shared by the two men who will treacherously abandon Minnie: the quotation from Shakespeare's play comes immediately before a terrified Richard's downfall, when the haunted king worries, 'will our friends prove all true?' (Shakespeare, *Richard III*, ed. E. A. J. Honigmann, rev. edn. Harmondsworth, Penguin, 1995, p. 193). Davoren is also mistaken in believing that Douglas's poem about Annie Laurie was by Burns. Alan Bold, *Scotland: a Literary Guide*. London: Routledge, 1989, p. 236.
13. Jerry's poem about the 'Strife with Nature' recalls O'Casey's earlier poetry about 'when Nature says good bye', with both focusing on moon-imagery and including rhyme words such as 'tell'. See 'The Summer Sun is Tightly Folding', in *Songs of the Wren*, p. 5.
14. Murray, *Sean O'Casey*, p. 216.
15. NYPL, Berg Collection, Seán O'Casey Papers, Holograph Notebook Vol. 3, f.52, 66. 'A Walk With Eros' was published much later in O'Casey's *Windfalls*, pp. 5–20.

16. O'Casey, *Windfalls*, p. 20. An earlier draft is located in NYPL, Berg Collection, Seán O'Casey Papers, Holograph Notebook Vol. 3, f.111.

17. William Ganson Rose, *Cleveland: The Making of a City*. Kent: Kent State University Press, 1990, p. 325.

18. O'Casey, Seán, Abbey Theatre Archives, *The Plough and the Stars* Promptbook, 1926/A/6, Act 1, f.21.

19. 'The Garland' appears in O'Casey's volume *Windfalls*, pp. 27–8.

20. Robert G. Lowery, 'The Development of Sean O'Casey's Weltanschauung', in Robert G. Lowery (ed.), *Essays on Sean O'Casey's Autobiographies*, London: Macmillan, 1981, pp. 62–88 (p. 81).

21. Seán O'Casey, Princeton University Library, 'The Cooing of Doves: A Converzatione in One Act', f.15. From manuscript on deposit at Princeton University Library. Courtesy of the owner.

22. 'Playwright and Critics', *Times Literary Supplement*, 15 February 1957, p. 99. 'Another Outbreak by Mr. O'Casey', *Irish Independent*, 20 September 1952, p. 4.

23. 'A Reigning Success', *Irish Times*, 9 July 1884, p. 2.

24. *Irish Times*, 17 November 1921, p. 5.

25. *Irish Independent*, 1 June 1915, p. 6.

26. British Library, Lord Chamberlain's Collection, *Irish Aristocracy*, 53352, fols 6–7. (C) British Library Board.

27. Fintan O'Toole, 'Course of True Theatre Never Should Run Smooth', *Irish Times*, 8 October 2011, <www.irishtimes.com/newspaper/weekend/2011/1008/1224305440357. html>.

28. *Irish Aristocracy*, f.54.

29. Quoted by George Walter Bishop, 'Shakespeare was my Education: Interview with the Author of *The Silver Tassie*', in E. H. Mikhail and John O'Riordan, *The Sting and the Twinkle*, London: Macmillan, 1974, pp. 42–5, pp. 44–5.

30. Letter of 22 January 1964 to Jill Pomlance, in O'Casey, *Letters*, IV, p. 467. O'Casey's dating is uncertain: he may well have seen the version of *Julius Caesar* that Benson's company presented in Dublin for four performances in December 1893, and which returned for three nights in March the following year.

31. 'Gaiety Theatre', *Irish Times*, 19 December 1893, p. 5. '"Julius Caesar" at the Gaiety', *Irish Times*, 6 March 1894, p. 6.

32. 'Gaiety Theatre', *Irish Times*, 19 December 1893, p. 5.

33. William Shakespeare, *Julius Caesar*, ed. T. S. Dorsch, in Richard Proudfoot, Ann Thompson and David Scott Kastan (eds) *The Arden Shakespeare Complete Works*, London: Thomson, 2001, pp. 333–60 (p. 350).

34. Ibid., pp. 350–1.

35. Ibid., p. 349.

36. Ibid., p. 351.

37. Ibid., p. 348.

38. Quoted by Lady Augusta Gregory, *Our Irish Theatre*. New York: Knickerbocker, 1913, p. 9.

39. The play premiered during March 1860 in New York City, where it played to capacity houses before clocking up an impressive run of more than 200 performances in London. The play also proved a favourite with provincial Britain and with Queen Victoria. When Boucicault returned to Dublin, to perform in the play in 1861, he arrived home a celebrity. Townsend Walsh, *The Career of Dion Boucicault*. New York: Dunlap, 1915, p. 202. Morash, *A History of Irish Theatre*, p. 87.

40. O'Casey, *Letters*, IV, p. 339.
41. The Dublin trilogy is not alone in showing such an influence. Boucicaultian moments appear in O'Casey's later plays, most notably *The Drums of Father Ned*, which presents a play-within-a-play 'in the method of the old melodrama' (V, 170).
42. The story remembered by Joxer is William Carlton's novel *Willy Reilly and His Dear Colleen Bawn*, published in 1850–1, and in a revised version in 1855, although Carlton's text has little connection with Gerald Griffin's *The Collegians*, on which Boucicault based his play. See John Jordan, 'The Passionate Autodidact: The Importance of 'Litera Scripta' for O'Casey', *Irish University Review*, 10, 1 (1980), 59–76 (p. 69).
43. Murray, *Sean O'Casey*, pp. 43–4.
44. This theatre would shortly be converted into the Abbey Theatre, where O'Casey would later make his name as a playwright. Murray, *Sean O'Casey*, pp. 42–6.
45. Nicholas Grene has pointed out that *The Shaughraun* points back to 'the winter of 1867–68', with one of Boucicault's characters describing 'The late attack on the police van at Manchester (September 1867), and the explosion at Clerkenwell prison in London (December 1867)'. Grene, *The Politics of Irish Drama*, p. 8.
46. Abbey Theatre Archives, *Shadow of a Gunman* programme, 1923, ATA IMPG, Vol. 19.
47. Kevin C. Kearns, *Dublin Tenement Life: An Oral History*. Dublin: Gill and Macmillan, 1994, p. 1.
48. NYPL, Berg Collection, Seán O'Casey Papers, Holograph Notebook Vol. 3, f.115.
49. O'Casey said little else about Maurice Dalton's drama, although a fleeting reference in his surviving correspondence shows that he still remembered the piece in the 1940s. See O'Casey, *Letters*, I, p. 883.
50. O'Casey, *Letters*, II, p. 438.
51. Clair Wills, *Dublin 1916: The Siege of the GPO*. London: Profile, 2009, p. 174.
52. The quotations are drawn verbatim from three separate parts of the 1922 volume of Pearse's writings (Pearse, *Collected Works of Padraic H. Pearse: Political Writings and Speeches*, pp. 133–8, 89–100, 213–18) . In real life Pearse had only delivered one of these sections of writing verbally, given on 1 August 1915 at the grave of O'Donovan Rossa in Dublin's Glasnevin Cemetery in front of thousands of uniformed nationalists and members of the Irish Citizen Army. Indeed, O'Casey later described Pearse delivering this oration 'at a meeting which I helped to organise' (O'Casey, *Letters*, I, 619). Pearse penned the other two extracts as newspaper articles, but all three had been reprinted after the rebellion and then put onto the stage in edited form by O'Casey. The two articles that had originally been written by Pearse as newspaper articles rather than as speeches were 'The Coming Revolution', *An Claidheamh Soluis*, 8 November 1913, p. 6; and the anonymous 'Peace and the Gael', *The Spark*, December 1915, pp. 1–2.
53. O'Casey, 'The Cooing of Doves: A Converzatione in One Act', f.4.
54. O'Casey, *Letters*, I, p. 28.
55. Quoted by Gabriel Fallon, 'The House on the North Circular Road: Fragments from a Biography', *Modern Drama*, 4, 3 (1961), 223–33 (p. 232).
56. NLI, *The Plough and the Stars* Typescript with MS Annotations, MS 29,407, f.II-2. For example, the demagogue was to begin with the new line: 'Soldiers of Ireland's army of Independence, this is a proud and a splendid moment for us all! Splendid and proud, for it speaks of a power that is, and of a greater power that is to come —'. And after reciting some of Patrick Pearse's more familiar words the speaker was to continue: 'Many are they who are eager to fight for the thing that is evil, and few there be who

will fight for the thing that is good, but in every age will be found Irishmen willing and eager to fight for the sovereign freedom of their counthry'. O'Casey made similar alterations to every speech given by the orator.

57. NYPL, Berg Collection, Seán O'Casey Papers, Holograph Notebook Vol. 8, f.3. In this notebook, O'Casey also adjusted one of the most bloodthirsty sections of Pearse's writings. The published version of *The Plough and the Stars* includes Pearse's words: 'Comrade soldiers of the Irish Volunteers and of the Citizen Army, we rejoice in this terrible war. The old heart of the earth needed to be warmed with the red wine of the battlefields. . . . Such august homage was never offered to God as this: the homage of millions of lives given gladly for love of country. And we must be ready to pour out the same red wine in the same glorious sacrifice, for without shedding of blood there is no redemption' (I, 195–6). However, when O'Casey reflected on his script he regretted including this quote, and in the New York notebook drafted a replacement with the rhetoric toned down: 'Comrade soldiers of the Irish Volunteers & the Citizen Army, no nationhood can be achieved without armed men; no nationhood can be guarded without armed men, and we hear today in Ireland the loud murmur of armed men marching. There is no truth but the old truth; no way but the old way, & I say that before this convention has passed, the Volunteers & the Irish Citizen Army will show the Sword of Ireland! We are young. And God has given us strength & courage & Counsel. May he give us the victory'.

58. Abbey Theatre Archives, *The Plough and the Stars* Promptbook, 1926/A/6.

59. O'Casey, *Letters*, IV, p. 29.

60. In the alternative version, Boyle seeks to assert his independence from his wife by stating, 'If she prances in, she can prance out again! Bounce her out Are you afraid of her, or what? (despairingly). There's ne'er a one left to stand up to anyone!'. NYPL, Berg Collection, Seán O'Casey Papers, Holograph Notebook Vol. 15, 'Joxer & Boyle', f.2.

61. NYPL, Berg Collection, Seán O'Casey Papers, Holograph Notebook Vol. 3, f.121. In all likelihood O'Casey never actually delivered these lines to anyone, as he proved barely able to speak when confronted by his antagonists in the debating hall in 1926.

62. Article for *Irish Freedom*, reproduced in O'Casey, *Letters*, II, p. 46.

63. Article reprinted in O'Casey, *Letters*, II, pp. 298–300.

64. Ibid., p. 312.

65. Ibid., p. 319.

66. Moran, *Staging the Easter Rising*, p. 16. Arthur Shields and J. M. Kerrigan, 'Great Days at the Abbey', in E. H. Mikhail, *The Abbey Theatre: Interviews and Recollections*, Houndmills, Macmillan, 1988, pp. 133–5.

67. O'Casey, *Letters*, III, p. 342.

68. NYPL, Berg Collection, Seán O'Casey Papers, Holograph Notebook Vol. 4, f.143.

69. O'Casey, *Letters*, I, p. 681; I, p. 677.

70. 'The Condemned Irishmen: Appeal for Reprieve', *Manchester Guardian*, 6 February 1940, p. 9. Almost three decades later *The Sunday Times* revealed that O'Casey had been correct about the Coventry 'bombers': the two hanged 'IRA men' had been innocent. 'Wrong Man Hanged', *The Sunday Times*, 6 July 1969, p. 1. O'Casey, *Letters*, II, p. 493.

71. O'Casey, *Letters*, III, p. 405.

72. 'Abbey Theatre Scene', *Irish Times*, 12 February 1926, p. 7. Variants of this speech also appeared in the *Irish Independent*, *Evening Mail* and *Manchester Guardian*, but the *Irish Times* version is probably the most accurate: Yeats personally dashed a copy to this newspaper, which in 1916 had called for the execution of the Easter rebels.

73. Ria Mooney, 'Playing Rosie Redmond', *Journal of Irish Literature*, 4, 2 (1977), pp. 21–7.
74. O'Casey, *Letters*, III, p. 486. Seán Cronin, *Frank Ryan: The Search for the Republic*. Dublin: Repsol, 1980, p. 23.
75. The quote about Ryan's view of O'Casey's work comes from one of the female demonstrators, Sighle Ui Dhonnchadha, who later reflected that Ryan 'had a much keener and deeper appreciation of literary values than most of us had at that time'. Ryan articulated a rather different attitude towards Easter Week than O'Casey in a pamphlet for the twelfth anniversary in 1928, writing: 'Take your revenge now, oh, Empire! Wreck bodies you could not chain, rip hearts you could not buy. But the souls – oh! you damn them fools! – the souls escape you, and new bodies will claim them. And, even already, their tramp is on the hills'. Quoted by Cronin, *Frank Ryan*, pp. 23, 27.
76. Quoted by Wills, *Dublin 1916*, p. 150.
77. NLI, Seán O'Casey Papers, MS 38,019, letter from Owen Sheehy Skeffington of 4 May 1942.
78. See NLI, Sean O'Casey Papers, MS 37,975, letter by Frank Ryan of 20 February 1926.
79. O'Casey, *The Story of the Irish Citizen Army*, p. 64.
80. See Murray, *Sean O'Casey*, p. 179.
81. NYPL, Berg Collection, Seán O'Casey Papers, Holograph Notebook Vol. 3, f.125.
82. Andrew E. Malone, *The Irish Drama*. London: Constable, 1929, p. 119.
83. O'Casey, *Letters*, II, p. 237.

Chapter 3

1. Lennox Robinson, *Ireland's Abbey Theatre: A History 1899–1951*. London: Sidgwick and Jackson, 1951, p. 121.
2. Arrington, *W. B. Yeats, the Abbey Theatre*, p. 63.
3. 'Ploughing the Star', *Manchester Guardian*, 4 June 1928, p. 8.
4. O'Casey, *Letters*, I, pp. 231–2.
5. The first quote was Yeats and Gregory's view of *The Harvest Festival*, the second Gregory on *The Crimson in the Tricolour*, and the third Robinson on *The Seamless Coat of Kathleen*. Quoted in O'Casey, *Letters*, I, pp. 91–2, 95–6, 101.
6. Lady Augusta Gregory, *Lady Gregory's Journals: Volume 1: Books One to Twenty-Nine*, ed. Daniel Murphy. Gerrards Cross: Colin Smythe, 1978, pp. 308, 446.
7. Table compiled from information in the Abbey Theatre Archives, 'Plays Received' File, 10 April 1922–8 June 1932; and 'Plays Received File', 5 January 1912–1 April 1922. I am grateful to Mairéad Delaney for compiling much of this information.
8. The clashes of that month had longer-term consequences for the organization of the theatre. Dolan was replaced as producer by Lennox Robinson with immediate effect (although retained as theatre manager and player), and Yeats was given a casting vote in case of deadlock at any future directors' meeting. I am grateful to Mairéad Delaney for helping me to locate this information in the Abbey Theatre archives, Director's Minute Book 1925–31. See also Robert Hogan and Richard Burnham, *The Years of O'Casey, 1921–1926: A Documentary History* (Gerrards Cross: Colin Smythe, 1992), pp. 283–4.

9. O'Casey, *Letters*, I, p. 104. O'Casey quoted by Gregory, *Lady Gregory's Journals: Volume 1*, p. 512. O'Casey, *Letters*, IV, p. 305.

10. The character of Bentham also allowed O'Casey to take a swipe at the Dublin poet and esoteric thinker George Russell.

11. Gregory, *Lady Gregory's Journals: Volume 1*, p. 446.

12. O'Casey, *Letters*, I, p. 235.

13. In May 1928, the Abbey revived *The Plough* at the same time as the directors composed their letters of rejection over *Tassie*. Lennox Robinson noted the discomfort that this feeling gave him, writing 'I return the M.S. of "The Silver Tassie". As I write this I hear the audience cheering "The Plough"'. O'Casey, *Letters*, I, p. 241.

14. Yeats quoted in O'Casey, *Letters*, I, p. 268.

15. Abbey Theatre Archives, Abbey Theatre Papers, Vol. 17, P8134.

16. Headlines from the *Daily Sketch*, 24 September 1927, and *Westminster Gazette*, 24 September 1927, retained by O'Casey in his personal notebook, NLI, Seán O'Casey Papers, MS 38,149/2.

17. NLI, Seán O'Casey Papers, MS 38,068, Jackson letter of 22 July 1926.

18. Ibid., Jackson undated letter.

19. W. B. Yeats, 'Introduction', in W. B. Yeats (ed.), *The Oxford Book of Modern Verse 1892–1935*. Oxford: Clarendon Press, 1936, pp. v–xlii (p. xxxiv).

20. R. F. Foster, *W. B. Yeats: A Life: II, the Arch Poet*. Oxford: Oxford University Press, 2003, p. 5.

21. 'Mr O'Casey's New Play', *Observer*, 3 June 1928, p. 19.

22. O'Casey, *Letters*, III, p. 304.

23. Murray, *Sean O'Casey*, p. 92.

24. 'Ireland's Roll of Honour', *Irish Times*, 28 August 1915, p. 7.

25. In 1911, when Tobin had been 19 years old, the *Irish Times* had reported on the club's visit to play the North of Ireland side in Belfast, 'the first appearance of a Southern combination in the North'. Tobin played at half-back, and was praised for a 'nice kick'. He continued playing for the Lansdowne, turning out for the second team in 1912, and training with the club in 1913. 'Football', *Irish Times*, 23 October 1911, p. 4. 'Football', *Irish Times*, 2 November 1912, p. 6. 'Football', *Irish Times*, 1 April 1913, p. 4.

26. 'Football', *Irish Times*, 18 October 1913, p. 4. 'Clontarf v. Dublin University', *Irish Times*, 19 January 1914, p. 4.

27. 'Football', *Irish Times*, 27 January 1914, p. 4.

28. Indeed, even before he went into hospital, O'Casey may have known that many branches of sport had lost some of their best-known participants. Newspapers boasted that 'Most of our sportsmen hold junior commissions, and their work is usually that of platoon-leaders. This means that in an advance they take the post of most danger. We know they do not flinch from it'. 'The Great Game', *Irish Times*, 28 June 1915, p. 5.

29. James Joyce, *Stephen Hero*. New York: New Directions, 1963, p. 34. Robert Spoo, '"Nestor" and the Nightmare: The Presence of the Great War in *Ulysses*', *Twentieth Century Literature*, 32, 2 (1986), pp. 137–54 (p. 144).

30. James Joyce, *Ulysses*, ed. Declan Kiberd. London: Penguin, 1992, p. 40.

31. Terence Brown, *The Literature of Ireland: Culture and Criticism*. Cambridge: Cambridge University Press, 2010, p. 83. Owen, *Collected Poems of Wilfred Owen*, ed. Cecil Day Lewis. London: Chatto and Windus, 1963, pp. 66–7.

32. Robert Hogan, 'O'Casey, Influence and Impact', *Irish University Review*, 10, 1 (1980), pp. 146–58 (pp. 153–4).

33. Hogan and Burnham, *The Years of O'Casey*, p. 270.

34. British Library, Frank O'Donnell, *Anti-Christ: A Play in Seven Scenes*, LC Add 66560A, f.73. (C) British Library Board.

35. Ibid., ff.76–7.

36. O'Casey, *Letters*, I, p. 267. For more on expressionism, see O'Casey *Letters*, II, pp. 568–9, 929.

37. O'Casey, *Letters*, I, p. 320.

38. Ibid., p. 182.

39. Huntly Carter, *The New Spirit in the European Theatre 1914–1924*. London: Ernest Benn, 1925, p. 276.

40. Ibid., p. vii.

41. O'Casey, *Letters*, I, p. 218.

42. Eszter Szalczer, 'A Modernist Dramaturgy', in Michael Robinson (ed.), *The Cambridge Companion to August Strindberg*, Cambridge: Cambridge University Press, 2009, pp. 93–106 (p. 100).

43. O'Casey, *Letters*, I, p. 539; II, p. 929.

44. Gabriel Fallon, *Sean O'Casey: The Man I Knew*. London: Routledge and Kegan Paul, 1965, pp. 47–8. See also Murray, *Sean O'Casey*, p. 193.

45. Ernst Toller, *Masses and Man: A Fragment of the Social Revolution of the Twentieth Century*, trans. Vera Mendel. London: Nonesuch, 1923, p. 27.

46. For more on this scene see Malcolm Pittock, *Ernst Toller*. Boston: Twayne, 1979, pp. 52–67.

47. 'O'Casey's New Play Rejected', *Irish Times*, 4 June 1928, p. 8.

48. Toller, *Masses and Man*, p. ix.

49. J. L. Styan, *Modern Drama in Theory and Practice: Expressionism and Epic Theatre*. Cambridge: Cambridge University Press, 1981, p. 121.

50. Denis Johnston, 'Sean O'Casey: An Appreciation', *Daily Telegraph*, 11 March 1926, in Ronald Ayling (ed.), *Sean O'Casey, Modern Judgments*, London: Macmillan, 1969, pp. 82–5 (p. 85).

51. 'The Rejected Abbey Play: Mr. St. John Ervine on "The Silver Tassie"', *Irish Times*, 9 July 1928, p. 8.

52. Charles Cochran, *Showman Looks On*. London: Dent, 1945, p. 226.

53. O'Casey, *Letters*, I, p. 460.

54. Quoted by Ronald Ayling, 'Introduction', *The Complete Plays of Sean O'Casey: Volume 5*. London: Macmillan, 1984, pp. vii–xxvi (p. xvi).

55. Sean O'Casey, *The Silver Tassie: A Tragi-Comedy in Four Acts*. London: Macmillan, 1928, p. 131.

56. Ibid.

57. 'Abbey Play Controversy', *Irish Times*, 5 June 1928, p. 7.

58. Robert Welch, *The Abbey Theatre, 1899–1999: Form and Pressure*. Oxford: Oxford University Press, 1999, p. 107.

59. Foster, *W. B. Yeats: A Life: II*, p. 370.

60. O'Casey, *Letters*, I, p. 260; Murray, *Sean O'Casey*, p. 203.

61. O'Casey, *Letters*, I, pp. 265–6 (p. 289).

62. G. Wilson Knight, *The Golden Labyrinth: A Study of British Drama*. London: Phoenix, 1962, p. 378.

63. George Jean Nathan, *My Very Dear Sean: George Jean Nathan to Sean O'Casey: Letters and Articles*, ed. Robert G. Lowery and Patricia Angelin. Rutherford: Fairleigh

Dickinson University Press, 1985, p. 140. Brooks Atkinson, 'The Play', *New York Times*, 23 October 1934, p. 23.

64. John O'Riordan, *A Guide to O'Casey's Plays: From the Plough to the Stars*. London: Macmillan, 1984, pp. 143, 151. Murray, *Sean O'Casey*, p. 213.

65. George Walter Bishop, 'Shakespeare Was My Education', pp. 42–5 (p. 43). O'Casey himself wanted readers to know that this play had been influenced by the stage-set of Eugene O'Neill's *Mourning Becomes Electra*, and the quasi-theological musings of the *Daily Express* journalist Jimmy Douglas (II, pp. 114, 131).

66. Murray, *Sean O'Casey*, pp. 226–8.

67. Ivor Brown, 'The Week's Theatres', *Observer*, 11 February 1934, p. 15.

68. O'Riordan, *A Guide to O'Casey's Plays*, p. 165.

69. Sean O'Casey, *Within the Gates*. London: Macmillan, 1933, p. 14.

70. Sean O'Casey, 'Preface', in Bonar Thompson, *Hyde Park Orator*. London: Jarrolds, 1934, pp. ix–xiii (p. xiii).

71. Ibid., p. xii.

72. Quoted by Ronald Ayling in 'The Origin and Evolution of a Dublin Epic', in Robert G. Lowery (ed.), *Essays on Sean O'Casey's Autobiographies*. London: Macmillan, 1981, pp. 1–34 (p. 4).

73. Michael Kenneally, *Portraying the Self: Sean O'Casey and the Art of Autobiography*. Gerrards Cross: Colin Smythe, 1988, pp. 1–2. NYPL, Berg Collection, Seán O'Casey Papers, Holograph Notebook Vol. 9.

74. He failed to realize until very late into the project that he was writing a six-volume work. Quoted by Kenneally, pp. 4, 8. Peter James Harris, *Sean O'Casey's Letters and Autobiographies: Reflections of a Radical Ambivalence*. Trier: Wissenschaftlicher Verlag Trier, 2004, p. 4.

75. Quoted by Christopher Ricks, *Tennyson*, 2nd edn. Berkeley/Los Angeles: University of California Press, 1989, p. 296. O'Casey ironically reverses Tennyson's religiosity: by the end of O'Casey's volume we are perhaps more likely to connect his title with the atom-bomb fission explosions and the nuclear fusion of the stars, or the wrongheadedness of the Catholic Church's one-time geocentric conception of the universe: 'moulding the expanding universe into a doll's house' (*Auto* II, p. 455).

76. Kenneally, *Portraying the Self*, p. 69.

77. O'Casey, *Letters*, I, pp. 190, 792.

78. Ibid., p. 799.

79. Ibid., p. 800.

80. Joyce, *Ulysses*, p. 383.

81. Orwell, 'The Green Flag', p. 3.

82. O'Casey felt that the Englishman simply wanted revenge because of O'Casey's refusal to write the jacket puff for the Gollanz edition of an earlier Orwell novel. O'Casey, *Letters*, I, p. 541.

83. Kenneally, *Portraying the Self*, p. 84.

84. O'Casey, *Letters*, III, p. 48.

85. Hubert Nicholson, 'O'Casey's Horn of Plenty', in Ronald Ayling (ed.), *Sean O'Casey: Modern Judgements*, London: Macmillan, 1969, pp. 207–20 (pp. 210–11).

86. Quoted by Robert G. Lowery, 'Introduction', in Robert G. Lowery (ed.), *Essays on Sean O'Casey's Autobiographies*, London: Macmillan, 1981, pp. xi–xviii (p. xvi).

87. O'Casey, *Letters*, III, p. 555. Murray, *Sean O'Casey*, p. 382.

88. Padraig Tolan, 'Sean O'Casey', *New Theatre Quarterly*, 8, 4 (1992), p. 396.

89. O'Casey, *Letters*, III, p. 384. Murray, *Sean O'Casey*, p. 383.
90. O'Casey, *Niall*, p. 64.
91. Ibid., p. 35.
92. Ibid., pp. 14–15.
93. Ibid., p. 82.
94. Samuel Beckett, *Trilogy*. London: Calder, 1994, p. 418.
95. O'Casey, *Niall*, p. 96.
96. Ibid., p. 95.

Chapter 4

1. O'Casey wrote the song lyrics himself, and put them to a traditional Irish air, first including the piece as simply a 'gay Dublin ditty' in his autobiographical volume *Pictures in the Hallway* (*Auto* I, 309). Today, O'Casey's song is probably better known than his play, having been performed widely by balladeer Ronnie Drew, and used as the title of the breakthrough album made by folk-punk group *The Pogues*.
2. Frederick R. Benson, *Writers in Arms: The Literary Impact of the Spanish Civil War*. London: University of London Press, 1968, p. 6.
3. Hugo García, *The Truth about Spain: Mobilizing British Public Opinion, 1936–1939*. Brighton: Sussex Academic Press, 2010, p. 170.
4. *Authors Take Sides on the Spanish War*. London: Left Review, [1937], p. 21.
5. O'Casey, *Letters*, I, p. 676.
6. Ibid., p. 655.
7. Murray, *Sean O'Casey*, p. 258.
8. NYPL, Berg Collection, Seán O'Casey Papers, Holograph Notebook Vol. 14, f.8.
9. Ibid., endpaper. 'Crucifix Poster', *Manchester Guardian*, 5 March 1937, p. 11.
10. Ibid. Vol. 10, f.146.
11. Thomas P. Linehan, *British Fascism, 1918–39: Parties, Ideology and Culture*. Manchester: Manchester University Press, 2000, p. 151.
12. NYPL, Berg Collection, Seán O'Casey Papers, Holograph Notebook Vol. 14, f.16.
13. Martin Pugh, *'Hurrah for the Blackshirts!': Fascists and Fascism in Britain between the Wars*. London: Jonathan Cape, 2005, p. 134.
14. O'Casey, *Letters*, II, p. 153.
15. Maurice Manning, *The Blueshirts*. Dublin: Gill and Macmillan, 1970, p. 50.
16. Fearghal McGarry, *Irish Politics and the Spanish Civil War*. Cork: Cork University Press, 1999, p. 109.
17. McGarry, *Irish Politics*, p. 109.
18. Ibid., pp. 117, 122.
19. Ibid., p. 28.
20. Ibid., p. 50.
21. Quoted by O'Casey, in *Letters*, II, p. 870.
22. McGarry, *Irish Politics*, p. 53.
23. O'Casey, *Letters*, I, pp. 803–4.
24. W. B. Yeats, *The Collected Works of W. B. Yeats: Volume I: The Poems*, ed. Richard J. Finneran, rev. edn. Houndmills, Macmillan, 1991, p. 308, Yeats's poem 'The O'Rahilly' was published in the first half of 1938, mid-way through O'Casey's composition of his play.

25. Murray, *Sean O'Casey*, pp. 286–7.
26. Some of O'Casey's other fictional 'Jacks' failed to find their way into performance. Most notably, the character of Harry Heegan in *The Silver Tassie* had been called Jack in the first preliminary sketch, and John Jo Mulligan in the one-act play *Bedtime Story* had been revised from the character of Jack in the earlier short story 'I Wanna Woman'. Heegan first appears as Jack in NYPL, Berg Collection, Seán O'Casey Papers, Holograph Notebook Vol. 6, f.36. 'I Wanna Woman' is printed in O'Casey's *Windfalls*, pp. 57–90.
27. NYPL, Berg Collection, Seán O'Casey Papers, Holograph Notebook Vol. 7, ff.20–1. O'Casey recycles a number of his earlier lines when writing *Red Roses for Me*. For example, in *The Harvest Festival*, Jack's mother begs him to avoid going to join the strikers: 'I've no one left now but you, Jack. Stop with me tonight son' (O'Casey, *The Harvest Festival*, p. 37). In the later play, Ayamonn's mother pleads, 'Stay here, my son, where safety is a green tree with a kindly growth' (III, 211).
28. During this section we read a number of lines that would be directly copied into *Red Roses for Me*. For example, the autobiographical question, 'Ruskin? Curious name. Irish was he?' (*Auto* I, 356), reappears in the play as 'Ruskin. Curious name; not Irish, is it?' (III, 157).
29. *Authors Take Sides*, p. 1.
30. Jack Mitchell makes this point in *The Essential O'Casey: A Study of the Twelve Major Plays of Sean O'Casey*. New York: International Publishers, 1980, p. 155.
31. Stanley Weintraub, 'GBS and the Despots', *Times Literary Supplement*, 27 July 2011, <www.the-tls.co.uk/tls/public/article707002.ece>.
32. George Bernard Shaw, 'Shaw Visits Russia', *Irish Worker*, 19 September 1931, p. 8.
33. O'Casey, *Letters*, I, p. 435. George Bernard Shaw, 'Shaw Visits Russia', *Irish Worker* (ed. Jim Larkin), 19 September 1931, pp. 1, 8.
34. George Bernard Shaw, *The Complete Plays of Bernard Shaw*. London: Paul Hamlyn, 1965, pp. 1180–219 (p. 1208).
35. Quoted by O'Connor, *Sean O'Casey*, p. 324.
36. Reprinted in Sean O'Casey, *Blasts and Benedictions*. London: Macmillan, 1967, pp. 195–204.
37. Shaw, *Complete Plays,* p. 1209.
38. Ibid., p. 1219.
39. NLI, Seán O'Casey Papers, MS 37,942, letter from Cornelius J. Sweeney of 4 April 1949.
40. Shaw, *Complete Plays*, p. 1219.
41. Frieda Utley, *Lost Illusion*. London: Allen & Unwin, 1949, p. 9.
42. Murray, *Sean O'Casey*, p. 507. Utley, *Lost Illusion*, p. 237.
43. Shaw, 'Shaw Visits Russia', p. 8.
44. O'Casey, *Letters*, I, p. 727.
45. Ibid.
46. 'GBS Speaks Out of the Whirlwind', *The Listener*, 7 March 1934, reprinted in O'Casey, *Blasts and Benedictions*, pp. 198–9.
47. Sean O'Casey, *Under a Coloured Cap: Articles Merry and Mournful with Comments and a Song*. London: Macmillan, 1963, pp. 128–9.
48. O'Casey, *Letters*, III, p. 349; II, p. 981.
49. O'Casey, *Under a Coloured Cap: Articles Merry and Mournful*, p. 122.
50. O'Casey, *Letters*, II, p. 341.
51. O'Casey, *Letters*, III, p. 635.

52. O'Casey, *Letters*, II, pp. 126, 846.

53. Foster, *W. B. Yeats: A Life: II*, p. 473.

54. Yeats had written: 'Dramatic action is a fire that must burn up everything but itself; there should be no room in a play for anything that does not belong to it: the whole history of the world must be reduced to wallpaper in front of which the characters must pose and speak'. Quoted by Heinz Kosok, *Plays and Playwrights from Ireland in International Perspective*. Trier: Wissenschaftlicher Verlag Trier, 1995, p. 138. O'Casey also took a line from Yeats's play *The Dreaming of the Bones* in order to inspire the – unruly and anti-establishment – titular character of his later play *Cock-A-Doodle Dandy*. The idea for 'the Cock' comes from Yeats's line 'Up with the neck and clap the wing, *Red cock, and crow*'. See Yeats, *The Collected Works of W. B. Yeats: Volume II: The Plays*, ed. David R. Clark and Rosalind E. Clark. Houndmills: Palgrave, 2001, p. 311.

55. For instance, Feelim O'Morrigun in *Oak Leaves and Lavender* bears a surname that recalls the Morrigu, a Celtic goddess of war and death who appears in Yeats's last play, *The Death of Cuchulain*. The characters of *Red Roses for Me* allude to *Cathleen ni Houlihan* and to the same Swiftian madness that inspired Yeats's play *The Words Upon the Window-Pane*. And those ghosts '*in the garb of the eighteenth century*' (IV, 6) who haunt the stage of *Oak Leaves and Lavender* recall the way that Yeats repeatedly sought to bring the Ireland of the Augustan era into contact with the Ireland of the Free State.

56. In an unusual move for O'Casey, he added an unsourced epigraph from *Purgatory* to the autobiographical volume *Drums Under the Windows* (1946).

57. Pound is quoted by James J. Wilhelm, *Ezra Pound in London and Paris, 1908–1925*. University Park: Pennsylvania State University Press, 1990, p. 227.

58. Gregory's only son, Robert, had joined the Royal Flying Corps and been killed on the Italian Front in 1918. Similarly, in *Oak Leaves and Lavender*, Lady Hatherleigh has only one son, and he also dies in aerial combat during wartime. O'Casey's play repeatedly echoes the lines of Yeats's poetic tribute to Gregory, 'An Irish Airman foresees his Death', where Yeats had written, 'Those that I fight I do not hate,/Those that I guard I do not love'. Thus in O'Casey's play Drishogue asserts 'I have no love for England!' (IV, 61). W. B. Yeats, *The Collected Works of W. B. Yeats: Volume I: The Poems*, p. 135.

59. O'Casey, *Letters*, II, p. 25.

60. O'Casey, *Blasts and Benedictions*, pp. 178, 186.

61. Quoted by Bernice Schrank, 'In the Aftermath of the Spanish Civil War: A Previously Unpublished Letter from Sean O'Casey to the Veterans of the Abraham Lincoln Brigade', *Canadian Journal of Irish Studies*, 25, 1/2 (1999), pp. 216–18 (p. 218).

62. NYPL, Berg Collection, Seán O'Casey Papers, Holograph Notebook Vol. 3, f.118.

Chapter 5

1. For those who knew Dublin's theatre scene, the dead playwright in O'Casey's drama, Lionel Robartes would most likely recall the recently deceased Lennox Robinson. O'Casey had heard that the Abbey players who wished to attend Robinson's funeral had phoned their Archbishop and been refused permission (see O'Casey, *Letters*, IV, p. 9).

2. Neil Miller, *Banned in Boston: The Watch and Ward Society's Crusade Against Books*. Boston: Beacon, 2010, p. 141.

3. '"Within the Gates" Ends Tour Tonight', *New York Times*, 19 January 1935, p. 8.

4. 'Boston Mayor Bans "Within the Gates"', *New York Times*, 16 January 1935, p. 20.

5. NLI, Seán O'Casey Papers, MS 38,045, copy of O'Casey's cable to the National Theatre, February 1935.

6. O'Casey, *Letters*, II, p. 423.

7. '"Within the Gates," Sean O'Casey's Provocative Play, Suggested for Capital', *Washington Post*, 27 June 1935, p. 16.

8. 'Abbey Production of O'Casey Play: Revelations by a Director of the Theatre', *Irish Independent*, 29 August 1935, p. 5.

9. 'Resignation of Abbey Director', *Irish Independent*, 4 September 1935, p. 9.

10. O'Casey described the *Standard* ironically as 'a weekly journal whose editorial office is in the porchway of heaven's doorway', and satirized it as the 'Catholic Buzzer' in *Behind the Green Curtains*. At another point he commented, 'when in Dublin, I didn't foresee that one day I'd have a son a gunner in the British Army. He could do worse – be on the staff of the Standard'. O'Casey, *The Green Crow*. London: Comet, 1987 [1957], p. 164. O'Casey, *Letters*, II, p. 438.

11. 'Dominican's Protest', *Standard: An Irish Organ of Catholic Opinion*, 16 August 1935, p. 3.

12. M. H. Gaffney, *The Stories of Padraic Pearse*. Dublin: Talbot, 1935.

13. O'Casey, *Letters*, I, pp. 415, 625.

14. The *Universe* had complained that 'the play certainly expresses, if only in particular passages, sentiments from which a Catholic must recoil', 25 October 1929, clipping in NLI, Seán O'Casey Papers, MS 38,149/1.

15. *Standard: An Irish Organ of Catholic Opinion*, 16 August 1935, p. 1, 8. 'Revolting Production', *Standard: An Irish Organ of Catholic Opinion*, 16 August 1935, p. 1, 3.

16. 'Revolting Production', *Standard: An Irish Organ of Catholic Opinion*, 16 August 1935, pp. 1, 3.

17. 'Frank Apology Wanted', *Irish Independent*, 13 September 1935, p. 7.

18. 'The Silver Tassie', *Irish Independent*, 14 September 1935, p. 10.

19. St John Ervine, 'At the Play: Why do Good Plays Fail?', *Observer*, 1 March 1936, p. 15.

20. O'Casey, *Letters*, IV, p. 545. Eileen, *Sean*, p. 236.

21. O'Casey, *Letters*, I, p. 419.

22. 'Dominican's Protest', *Standard: An Irish Organ of Catholic Opinion*, 16 August 1935; and 'The Silver Tassie', *Irish Press*, 14 August 1935, both retained by O'Casey in NLI, Seán O'Casey Papers, MS 38,149/1.

23. Sean O'Casey, 'Blasphemy and *The Silver Tassie*', in Ronald Ayling (ed.), *Blasts and Benedictions*, London: Macmillan, 1967, pp. 108–10.

24. Christopher Murray, *Twentieth Century Irish Drama: Mirror Up to Nation*. Manchester: Manchester University Press, 1997, p. 135.

25. NLI, Seán O'Casey Papers, MS 38,149/2, scrapbook of wedding clippings followed by O'Casey's cuttings of articles such as 'Dr. Heenan Replies to Critcs [sic] of the Legion of Mary', *Universe*, 12 July 1942, p. 8.

26. 'Month in Gaol for a Kiss', *Irish Press*, 15 January 1944, p. 1. The Scottish teenager involved had since returned to her homeland, so the prison sentence she received was intended to be symbolic rather than actually served.

27. David Krause, 'Introduction', in O'Casey, *Letters*, IV, pp. ix–xx, xvi. O'Casey, *Letters*, II, pp. 713, 1065.

28. Kenneth Tynan, 'A Second Look at O'Casey and Osborne', *Observer*, 30 July 1961, p. 20.

29. Quoted in O'Casey, *Letters*, II, p. 499.

30. Ibid., p. 583.

31. NYPL, Berg Collection, Seán O'Casey Papers, Holograph Notebook Vol. 3, f.29. O'Casey, *Letters*, I, pp. 278, 719.

32. NLI, Seán O'Casey Papers, MS 37,312, Harry Fletcher's letter of 24 February 1945.

33. Walter McDonald, *Reminiscences of a Maynooth Professor*, ed. Denis Gwynn. London: Jonathan Cape, 1925.

34. In the *Reminiscences* McDonald describes his clash with a bishop: 'History, I said, proves that laws have been better made and better observed since subjects became free to criticize them' (McDonald, p. 351). O'Casey retells the story and writes: 'History proves that laws have been better made and better observed since subjects became free to criticise them' (*Auto* II, 489).

35. 'Turf-Cutting in County Sligo', *Irish Times*, 19 August 1915, p. 7.

36. 'Fr. O'Flanagan on Spain', *Irish Times*, 12 November 1938, p. 15.

37. McDonald, *Reminiscences of a Maynooth Professor*, p. 132.

38. The Forward to the rules of *Muintir na Tíre* reveals the inspiration for the movement: 'It shall be incumbent on the Society and its individual members to inculcate a love of God and of country and to strive to secure peace and prosperity for all through the observance of the principles (held sacred by everyone bearing the name of Christian) laid down 40 years ago by Pope Leo XIII in his Encyclical *Rerum Novarum*, and today by Pope Pius XI in his Encyclical *Quadragesimo Anno*'. Meanwhile, during the San Francisco strikes of 1901, Yorke was the principal speaker at a strike meeting of over 15,000 people, where he quoted the encyclical teaching of Pope Leo XIII on the freedom of contract and the fair wage, and bolstered his own arguments with papal teaching. John Ryan, 'The Founder of Muintir na Tíre: John M. Canon Hayes 1887–1957', in *Studies: An Irish Quarterly Review*, 46, 183 (1957), pp. 312–21 (p. 315). Bernard Cornelius Cronin, *Father Yorke and the Labor Movement in San Francisco, 1900–1910*. Washington: Catholic University of America Press, 1943, pp. 57–8. 'The People of the Land', *Irish Times*, 23 November 1931, p. 5. 'The People of the Land', *Irish Times*, 31 March 1932, p. 4.

39. NYPL, Berg Collection, Seán O'Casey Papers, Holograph Notebook Vol. 14, f.129.

40. All quoted by Murray, *Sean O'Casey*, p. 359.

41. Tynan, 'A Second Look', p. 20.

42. Murray, *Sean O'Casey*, pp. 359–60.

43. Ibid., p. 361.

44. 'Mr. Sean O'Casey's New Play', *The Times*, 1 March 1955, p. 6.

45. '"The Bishop's Bonfire" in Gaiety Theatre', *Irish Times*, 1 March 1955, p. 4.

46. O'Casey responded in 'Letters to the Editor: "The Bishop's Bonfire"', *Irish Times*, 23 March 1955, p. 5. O'Casey, *The Green Crow*, p. 233.

47. Robert Hogan, 'O'Casey's Court', *Irish Times*, 23 February 1957, p. 6.

48. Gabriel Fallon, 'To Irish Press', 30 March 1955, reprinted in O'Casey, *Letters*, III, p. 98.

49. 'Shouters at Play Chided by O'Casey', *New York Times*, 7 October 1958, p. 40. 'Trouble over O'Casey Play in Toronto', *Irish Times*, 7 October 1958, p. 8.

50. C. W. E. Bigsby, *Arthur Miller: 1915–1962*. London: Weidenfeld and Nicolson, 2008, pp. 402–3.

51. James P. Byrne, Philip Coleman, Jason King (eds), *Ireland and the Americas: Culture, Politics and History, a Multidisciplinary Encyclopedia*. Santa Barbara: ABC-CLIO, 2008, p. 59.
52. 'No Beckett Plays for Tostal', *Irish Times*, 17 February 1958, p. 1.
53. *Irish Times*, 28 July 1958, p. 1.
54. 'O'Casey Bans Festival Production', *Irish Times*, 24 August 1961, p. 6.
55. See Nesta Jones, *File on O'Casey*. London: Methuen, 1986, p. 80.
56. Paul Johnson, 'Genius of the Terrible Tongue', *Times Literary Supplement*, 6 May 1988, p. 495.
57. Tynan, 'A Second Look', p. 20.
58. Raymond Williams, 'The Writer: Commitment and Alignment', in John Higgins (ed.), *The Raymond Williams Reader*, Oxford: Blackwell, 2001, pp. 208–18 (p. 216).
59. Gabriel Fallon, *Sean O'Casey: The Man I Knew*, p. 157. Fallon had been a close friend of O'Casey, but in a letter written in 1952, O'Casey writes about how the two had fallen out with one another. According to O'Casey it was Fallon's Catholicism that became the source of tension between them. O'Casey, 'To Shaemus O'Sheel', 27 October 1952, in O'Casey, *Letters*, II, p. 914.
60. O'Casey, *Letters*, IV, pp. 451, 466.
61. Protestant polemicists published volumes with this title: for example, in one such book from Cork, Rev. W. Thompson criticizes the overweening power of the Catholic priest, who is 'raised to a dignity above all which Kings are able to confer'. W. Thompson, *The Sacrifice of the Mass Considered. A Discourse Delivered at Christ Church, Cork . . . March 17, 1830*. Cork: Bleakley, 1830, p. 8.
62. For example, both O'Casey's story and Dallas's story begin by focusing on the fact that this is a personal testimony by someone involved in the events (in each case the secretary to the organization), and both testimonies are then salted with scriptural allusions. On the final page of Dallas's book we read a reference to the biblical story of the sower, with Dallas describing 'the growth of those plants of prayer'. Alex Dallas, *The Story of the Irish Church Missions*. London: Society for Irish Church Missions, [1867?], p.196. The final section of O'Casey's finishes with the same parable, referring to the 'seeds of a new life' (O'Casey, *The Story of the Irish Citizen Army*, pp. 61–2).
63. *The Nation*, 11 April 1885, p. 8. 'The "Irish Church Missions": At Their Old Game', *The Nation*, 4 April 1885, p. 2.
64. Kenneally, *Portraying the Self*, pp. 5, 52.
65. J. H. Merle D'Aubigné, *The History of the Great Reformation of the Sixteenth Century in Germany, Switzerland, France, etc.* London: Jarrold, 1873, p. 49.
66. Ibid., p. 19.
67. NYPL, Berg Collection, Seán O'Casey Papers, The Bishop's Bonfire Typescript, 70B5694, f.14.
68. William Chillingworth, *The Religion of Protestants: A Safe Way to Salvation*. London: Mary Clark, 1684, p. 85.
69. One of the things that O'Casey is also recycling in the *Drums of Father Ned* is part of the plot of his earlier, and most religiously provocative play, *Within the Gates*. In that play an atheist (called Ned) and a 'dreamer' (also called Ned) had tried to rescue Jannice. The atheist Ned has helped her to escape from incarceration in a Catholic institution, where she was placed because her father was in training for the priesthood. The dreamer Ned helps her to overcome the traumatic memories of that institution, where 'the nuns, being what she was – a child of sin –, paid her special attention'

(II, 123). Little wonder that the repeated 'drum-beat of the Down-and-Out' in that earlier work is recycled as the auditory cue for rebellion in *The Drums of Father Ned*.

70. *Foxe's Book of Martyrs*, ed. John Cumming. London: George Virtue, 1844, III, p. 696.

71. Martial Massiani, 'But nothing happened at new 'Lourdes'', *Universe*, cutting in NLI, Seán O'Casey Papers, MS 38,149/2.

72. See O'Casey, *Letters*, III, p. 632.

73. O'Casey did however think that, in order to avoid controversy, theatre directors should avoid producing *Cock-A-Doodle Dandy* in the centenary year of the Marian visions at Lourdes. O'Casey, *Letters*, III, p. 543.

74. Enda Kenny, 'This is a Republic, Not the Vatican', *Irish Times*, 21 July 2011, <www.irishtimes.com/newspaper/opinion/2011/0721/1224301061733.html>.

75. Jez Butterworth, *Jerusalem*. London: Nick Hern, 2009, p. 9.

76. O'Casey, *Letters*, II, p. 459.

77. Austin Clarke, 'Och, Johnny, I Hardly Knew Ye!', *Irish Times*, 29 January 1949, p. 6. Myles na Gopaleen, 'Cruiskeen Lawn', *Irish Times*, 19 February 1958, p. 6.

78. Robert E. Kennedy, *The Irish: Emigration, Marriage, and Fertility*. Berkeley: University of California Press, 1973, p. 95.

79. 'Mr De Valera Criticises Midland Cities: Irishmen Said to be Living in "Appalling" Conditions', *Birmingham Post*, 29 August 1951, p. 1.

80. 'At the Play', *Observer*, 10 January 1926, p. 11.

81. O'Casey, *Letters*, I, p. 700; II, p. 286.

82. Bronwen Walter, *Outsiders Inside: Whiteness, Place and Irish Women*. London: Routledge, 1998, p. 15.

83. Heather Ingman, *Twentieth Century Fiction by Irish Women: Nation and Gender*. Aldershot: Ashgate, 2007, p. 15. Walter, *Outsiders Inside*, p. 16.

84. Both O'Casey and the critic Bourke MacWilliam noted the parallel between the death of Bessie Burgess and that of Foorawn. See O'Casey, *Letters*, III, pp. 79, 146.

85. O'Casey, *Blasts and Benedictions*, p. 143.

86. Abbey Theatre Archives, *The Plough and the Stars* Promptbook, 1926/A/6. The promptbook was used from the premiere until the 1950s, and was being used onstage on the night that the theatre burned down (in a sadly ironic echo of the situation described in O'Casey's text).

87. Fallon, *Sean O'Casey: The Man I Knew*, pp. 24–5.

88. O'Brien, 'Sean O'Casey and the Abbey Theatre', p. 72.

89. For instance, in 2011, the National Theatre of Scotland staged *The Strange Undoing of Prudencia Hart*, the story of a woman meeting and escaping the devil. This engaging production relied on a number of ideas from traditional Scottish folk culture, and conveyed the plot with an all-singing, all-dancing performance style that combined music that ranged from Céilidh to Kylie. The production integrated the workaday and naturalistic with the deeply symbolic and theological, relying on the fact that the author, David Greig, had worked closely with the rest of the company, and had devised much of the piece when snowed-in with his director and an actor in a remote part of Scotland. David Greig, *The Strange Undoing of Prudencia Hart*. London: Faber, 2011, p. vi.

90. For example, the version of *The End of the Beginning* being staged in Romania's National Theatre Bucharest at the time of writing substantially changes the ending of O'Casey's piece, while the version of *Bedtime Story* often staged in the Czech republic includes a significant amount of new writing by Jiří Krejčík.

91. Abbey Theatre Archives, *The Plough and the Stars* Promptbook, 1926/A/6, Act 1, 24; Act 2, 6.
92. O'Casey, *Letters*, IV, pp. 231, 489.
93. Gordon Beckles, quoted in O'Casey, *Letters*, I, p. 497.
94. Murray, *Sean O'Casey*, p. 360.
95. O'Casey, *Letters*, II, p. 1015.
96. O'Casey, *Letters*, IV, p. 215.
97. O'Casey, *Blasts and Benedictions*, p. 138.

Chapter 6

1. Quoted by Hogan and Burnham, *The Years of O'Casey*, p. 145.
2. NYPL, Berg Collection, Seán O'Casey Papers, Holograph Notebook Vol. 4, ff. 24–5.
3. <www.abbeytheatre.ie/archives/play_detail/SOV01>.
4. These figures include all Abbey Theatre performances in Dublin, but exclude those performances staged elsewhere. I am grateful to Mairéad Delaney for helping me to compile these figures.
5. See Albert J. DeGiacomo, *T. C. Murray, Dramatist: Voice of Rural Ireland*. Syracuse: Syracuse University Press, 2003, p. 160.
6. His nearest rivals, the long-established playwrights Lady Gregory and Lennox Robinson, each saw their solo works performed on 46 occasions that year. Both Gregory and Robinson of course had the potential advantage of being directors of the theatre.
7. 'Abbey Theatre', *Irish Times*, 14 September 1926, p. 3.
8. 'The Plough and the Stars', *Irish Times*, 13 February 1926, p. 5. Abbey Theatre Archives, Abbey Theatre Papers, Vol. 17, P8134.
9. 'Juno and the Paycock', *Irish Times*, 4 March 1924, p. 4.
10. See, for example, Alice Miles, 'Shocked by Slumdog's Poverty Porn', *The Times*, 14 January 2009 <www.timesonline.co.uk/tol/comment/columnists/guest_contributors/article5511650.ece>.
11. Gregory, *Lady Gregory's Journals: Volume 1*, pp. 511–12, 594. 'Plight of the Younger Irish Writers: Lecture by Mr. C. O'Leary', *Manchester Guardian*, 21 October 1924, p. 20.
12. Caroline Walsh, *The Homes of Irish Writers*. Dublin: Anvil, 1982, p. 75.
13. Gregory, *Lady Gregory's Journals: Volume 1*, p. 514.
14. For example, at one stage O'Casey told Gregory that he taught himself to read from primers and from a *History of the Reformation* at the age of 14, although he had previously informed her that he was 16 when he learned to read and write. Gregory, *Lady Gregory's Journals: Volume 1*, pp. 446,547.
15. 'Award of Hawthornden Prize', *Irish Times*, 24 March 1926, p. 7.
16. 'Our London Correspondent', *Manchester Guardian*, 24 March 1926, p. 10.
17. T. P. O'Connor, 'Men, Women, and Memories', *The Sunday Times*, 4 April 1926, p. 9.
18. J. Brooks Atkinson, 'A Coupl'a Irishmen', *New York Times*, 4 December 1927, p. X1.
19. *Liverpool Post*, 22 September 1927, in NLI, Seán O'Casey Papers, MS 38,149/2.
20. 'The Plough and the Stars', *Irish Times*, 2 March 1926, p. 2.
21. St John Ervine, 'At the Play', *Observer*, 16 May 1926, p. 4.
22. Yeats's opinion recorded by Gregory, *Lady Gregory's Journals: Volume 1*, p. 512.
23. O'Casey, *Letters*, I, p. 146.

24. Nicholas Grene, 'The Class of the Clitheroes: O'Casey's Revisions to *The Plough and the Stars* Promptbook', *Bullán: An Irish Studies Journal*, 4, 2 (1999/2000), pp. 57–66. See also his book *The Politics of Irish Drama*, pp. 281–2.

25. NYPL, Berg Collection, Seán O'Casey Papers, Holograph Notebook Vol. 3, f.83.

26. Andrew E. Malone, 'O'Casey's Photographic Realism', reprinted in Ronald Ayling (ed.), *Sean O'Casey: Modern Judgments*, London: Macmillan, 1968, pp. 68–75 (p. 68).

27. Bernard Benstock, *Sean O'Casey*. Cranbury: Associated University Presses, 1970, p. 90.

28. Quoted by Hogan and Burnham, *The Years of O'Casey*, p. 241.

29. Anthony Butler, 'The Makings of the Man', in Sean McCann (ed.), *The World of Sean O'Casey*, London: Four Square, 1966, pp. 12–29 (p. 21).

30. Ibid., p. 21.

31. Ibid., p. 23.

32. Martin B. Margulies, *The Early Life of Sean O'Casey*, p. 12.

33. Ibid., p. 23.

34. O'Connor, *Sean O'Casey*, p. 5.

35. John Jordan, 'Illusion and Actuality in the Later O'Casey', in Ronald Ayling (ed.), *Sean O'Casey: Modern Judgements*, London: Macmillan, 1969, pp. 143–61 (p. 145).

36. Quoted by Grene, *The Politics of Irish Drama*, p. 141.

37. 'Stink Bombs in the Abbey', *Irish Times*, 4 May 1926, p. 7.

38. Abbey Theatre Archives, *The Plough and the Stars* Promptbook, 1926/A/6.

39. See 'Writers Join in Abbey Protest', *Irish Independent*, 10 November 1947, p. 2.

40. 'The Plough and the Stars', *Irish Times*, 10 May 1928, p. 8.

41. Ibid.

42. *Daily Chronicle,* 20 September 1927, cutting in NLI, Seán O'Casey Papers, MS 38,149/2.

43. 'O'Casey's New Play Rejected', *Irish Times*, 4 June 1928, p. 8.

44. 'Tenement Dust to Purple Dust', *Irish Times*, 14 December 1940, p. 5.

45. 'The Parish and the World of O'Casey', *New York Times*, 5 February 1950, p. 178.

46. O'Casey, *Letters*, III, p. 207; IV, p. 398.

47. *Juno and the Paycock* (released as *The Shame of Mary Boyle* in the United States). Dir. Alfred Hitchcock. British International Pictures. 1930.

48. Austin Clarke, 'The Making of a Dramatist', *Times Literary Supplement*, 4 March 1939, p. 131.

49. Harold Hannyngton Child, 'Johnny Casside Grows Up', *Times Literary Supplement*, 7 March 1942, p. 118.

50. Anthony Victor Cookman, 'The Unfulfilled Nation', *Times Literary Supplement*, 17 November 1945, p. 548.

51. Anthony Victor Cookman, 'Vale Atque Ave', *Times Literary Supplement*, 19 February 1949, p. 115.

52. Austin Clarke, 'Mr. O'Casey in London', *Times Literary Supplement*, 1 August 1952, p. 502.

53. Anthony Victor Cookman, 'Self-Expression', *Times Literary Supplement*, 5 November 1954, p. 699.

54. Austin Clarke, 'Tales from Dublin', *Times Literary Supplement*, 6 September 1963, p. 674.

55. 'Mr O'Casey's Latest', *Irish Independent*, 14 March 1939, p. 6.

56. 'Mr O'Casey's Memoirs', *Irish Independent*, 12 November 1945, p. 4.

57. *Irish Independent*, 8 January 1949, p. 4.

58. 'Another Outbreak by Mr O'Casey', *Irish Independent*, 20 September 1952, p. 4.

59. 'O'Casey, by Himself', *Irish Independent*, 30 October 1954, p. 6.

60. Andrew Gibson, *James Joyce*. London: Reaktion, 2006, p. 135.

61. For example, G. A. Olden describes O'Casey's 'sullen retirement in Devonshire', 'Radio Review', *Irish Times*, 28 October 1954, p. 6.

62. 'Sean O'Casey and Yeats', *Irish Times*, 6 March 1962, p. 8.

63. Joseph O'Connor, *Ghost Light*. London: Harvill Secker, 2010, p. 7.

64. H. L. Mencken, 'Preface', in Arnold Leslie Lazarus (ed.), *A George Jean Nathan Reader*, Cranbury: Associated University Presses, 1990, pp. 12–14 (p. 12).

65. Richard F. Shepard, 'Brooks Atkinson, 89, Dead; Times Drama Critic 31 Years', *New York Times*, 14 January 1984, p. 1.

66. See Frazier, *Hollywood Irish*, pp. 59–60.

67. Arnold Leslie Lazarus, ed., *A George Jean Nathan Reader*. Cranbury: Associated University Presses, 1990, p. 15.

68. George Jean Nathan, *My Very Dear Sean*, p. 17.

69. O'Casey, *Letters*, II, p. 895.

70. 'The Best of the Irish', in *Newsweek*, 29 January 1940, reprinted in *My Very Dear Sean*, pp. 148–50 (p. 148).

71. Brooks Atkinson, 'Critic Recalls the Dramatist as "a Darlin" Man', *New York Times*, 19 September 1964, p. 1.

72. O'Casey, *Letters*, III, pp. 386–7.

73. *The Plough and the Stars*. Dir. John Ford. RKO Radio Pictures. 1936.

74. Robert G. Lowery, 'O'Casey, Sean', in *Dictionary of Irish Biography*, p. 169. Miller, 'Introduction', in *Sean O'Casey: Plays 2*. London: Faber, 1998, pp. vii–xi (p. ix).

75. Arthur Gelb, 'Campaigner in the Cause of Sean O'Casey', *New York Times*, 25 September 1960, p. X1.

76. NLI, Seán O'Casey Papers, MS 38,079/1, Shyre letter of 15 September 1954.

77. Paul Shyre, *I Knock at the Door*. New York: Dramatists Play Service, 1958. Paul Shyre, *Pictures in the Hallway*. New York: Samuel French, 1956.

78. NLI, Seán O'Casey Papers, MS 38,079/1, Shyre's 1956 letters to O'Casey.

79. Lewis Funke, 'Theatre: Self-Portrait', *New York Times*, 17 September 1956, p. 23.

80. 'Theatre: O'Casey Reading', *New York Times*, 19 March 1956, p. 27.

81. *Pictures in the Hallway*. LP Riverside. 1957. Arthur Gelb, 'Campaigner in the Cause', p. X1. Paul Shyre, *Drums under the Windows*. New York: Dramatists Play Service, 1962.

82. Mel Gussow, 'Theater: Shyre's Winning O'Casey', *New York Times*, 30 April 1971, p. 50.

83. Somewhat surprisingly, the anti-materialist message of *Purple Dust* has not led to a revival of interest in more recent years, and a production directed by O'Casey's daughter in Dublin in 1989 received poor reviews.

84. Stephen Holden, 'Gentler "Juno" But it Sings', *New York Times*, 6 November 1992, p. C6. Ben Brantley, 'A Mother Whose Life Song Is About Tenement Nightmares, Not Broadway Dreams', *New York Times*, 29 March 2008 <http://theater.nytimes.com/2008/03/29/theater/reviews/29juno.html?ref=garry_hynes>.

85. NLI, Seán O'Casey Papers, MS 38,079/2, letters between Shyre and O'Casey.

86. O'Casey, *Letters*, III, p. 493.

87. Ibid., p. 460.

88. NYPL, Berg Collection, Seán O'Casey Papers, Holograph Notebook Vol. 21, f.18.

89. O'Casey, *Letters*, III, p. 462.

90. *Juno and the Paycock.* Dir. Paul Shyre. WNTA Newark. 1960. NLI, Seán O'Casey Papers, MS 38,079/4, Shyre letter of 6 February 1956 and O'Casey reply in O'Casey, *Letters*, IV, p. 113.

91. O'Casey, *Letters*, IV, p. 22.

92. Ibid., p. 78, 109.

93. NYPL, Berg Collection, Seán O'Casey Papers, + 70B6521, The National Broadcasting Company Presents a Conversation with Sean O'Casey and Robert Emmett Ginna (1955), f.16.

94. *Young Cassidy.* Dir. John Ford and Jack Cardiff. MGM. 1965. Other tag-lines used on posters advertising the film included, 'Brawling, battling, earthy . . . That's Young Cassidy – taking on the world with two fists clenched and every male sense soaring!', and 'He's a brawling, sprawling giant – on the make for fame and fortune and then some'. The posters also make great use of the image of Rod Taylor's torso and Julie Christie's cleavage.

95. Eileen, *Sean*, p. 273. Murray, *Sean O'Casey*, pp. 416–17.

96. Fergus Linehan, 'Boylesday', *Irish Times*, 18 June 1962, p. 8.

97. O'Casey, *Letters*, IV, p. 233.

98. NLI, MS 37,889/10, Sean O'Casey to Jane Rubin, 1 September 1961.

99. NLI, Seán O'Casey Papers, MS 38,079/4, Shyre letter of 13 August 1962.

100. NYPL for the Performing Arts, MWEZ + n.c. 25,398–25,400, #13 Paul Shyre Scrapbook, programme for Hartford Stage Company's Juno and the Paycock, May/June 1973, p. 11.

101. NYPL for the Performing Arts, MWEZ + n.c. 25,398 #8, Paul Shyre Scrapbook, programme for tribute show of 11 October 1964.

102. Shyre attempted to do for Yeats what he had done with O'Casey, by adapting some of Yeats's writings for performance at UCLA in the 1960s, and he later returned to directing O'Casey plays, such as *The Silver Tassie* in 1973 at the United States International University in San Diego. See NYPL for the Performing Arts, MWEZ + n.c. 25,398–25,400, Paul Shyre Scrapbook.

103. Adam Hetrick, 'Tony Winner Shyre's *I Knock at the Door & Pictures in the Hallway* Begin NY Run Nov 24', 24 November 2007, <www.playbill.com/news/article/1129 87-Tony-Winner-Shyres-I-Knock-At-the-Door-Pictures-in-the-Hallway-Begin-NY-Run-Nov-24>.

104. Eileen, *Sean*, p. 183. David H. Greene, *J. M. Synge 1871–1909*. New York: Macmillan, 1959.

105. However, in the mid 1970s Krause and his one-time tutor Greene ended up in a very public spat after Greene angered Krause, who was publishing the collected letters of O'Casey. Greene refused to allow Krause to have access to the 126 letters that O'Casey had written to the union organizer Jack Carney. Greene was planning to edit and publish his own volume of this correspondence, which he had purchased and placed in his university library. Krause then recruited the younger O'Casey scholar, Robert Lowery, and the two wrote open letters to the press asking Greene to release the documents. NLI, Eileen O'Casey Papers, MS 44,742/2, Letter from Greene to Eileen O'Casey, 5 November 1975.

106. Eileen, *Sean*, p. 247.

107. For example, when Martin Margulies questioned how O'Casey could possibly have passed his exams in reading and writing if the illiteracy described in the autobiographies had been real, Krause claimed, rather implausibly, that the autobiographies remained entirely correct. O'Casey had simply memorized vast

passages from the Bible and from school primers that his mother and sister read aloud to him. Krause, *Sean O'Casey: The Man and his Work*, pp. 2–3. Margulies, *The Early Life of Sean O'Casey*, p. 23.

108. NLI, Seán O'Casey Papers, MS 37,849/1 letter by David Krause of June 1954.

109. 'This Dublin Play Sets World Record', *Dublin Evening Herald*, 29 July 1972, located in NLI, Lantern Theatre Papers, MS 34,905/2 fol.128.

110. For a comparison between the Shyre and Funge/Krause adaptations see James Moran, 'Moving-Pictures in the Hallway: Dramatising the Autobiographies of Seán O'Casey', *Irish Studies Review*, 20, 4 (2012), pp. 389–405. See also NLI, Lantern Theatre Papers, MS 40,206/22, unsigned letter from Patrick Funge to David Krause, 19 October 1965, and Krause's reply of 2 November. Eileen O'Casey also seems to have difficulties in distinguishing between the Shyre version and that of Funge and Krause: see NLI, Lantern Theatre Papers, MS 40,206/28, Eileen O'Casey letter to Patrick Funge of 5 July 1967.

111. Patrick O'Connor, 'Theatre', *The Furrow*, 16:10 (October 1965), pp. 631–3 (p. 633).

112. Bernice Schrank, 'Performing Political Opposition: Sean O'Casey's Late Plays and the Demise of Eamon de Valera', *BELLS: Barcelona English Language and Literature*, 11 (2000), 199–206 (p. 204).

113. Robert Hogan, *The Experiments of Sean O'Casey*. New York: St Martin's Press, 1960, pp. i, 145.

114. Ibid., p. 5.

115. Ronald Ayling, 'Sean O'Casey and the Abbey Theatre', *Manchester Guardian*, 5 August 1958, p. 4. 'O'Casey and the Abbey', *Irish Times*, 25 April 1962, p. 9.

116. Ronald Ayling, 'Sean O'Casey and the Abbey Theatre, Dublin' in David Krause and Robert Lowery (eds), *Sean O'Casey: Centenary Essays*, Gerrards Cross: Colin Smythe, 1980, pp. 13–40 (p. 23).

117. Hogan, 'O'Casey, Influence and Impact', p. 157.

118. See, for example, James R. Scrimgeour's study, *Sean O'Casey*. London: George Prior, 1978, which accepts O'Casey's autobiographies as largely factual, and uses them 'to demonstrate that Sean O'Casey was a creative artist of the first rank' (p. 9).

119. Eileen O'Casey did warn Lowery away from the mistrusted Hogan, who had offered his ill-fated play for publication in Lowery's journal: she wrote to Lowery, 'I would be very distressed if any of it were to appear in your magazine. If you read the entire play I am sure you would be in agreement with me; and as I know you think an enormous amount of Sean I really know you would not want to publish any of this play'. Lowery wrote back to say that the play sounded dreadful, and that he never wanted to cause distress to Eileen. NLI, Eileen O'Casey Papers, MS 44,742/2, letters between Lowery and Eileen O'Casey.

120. See Katharine Worth, *The Irish Drama of Europe from Yeats to Beckett*. London: Athlone Press, 1978, p. 221.

121. NLI, Eileen O'Casey Papers, MS 44,742/2, letters between Lowery and Eileen O'Casey.

122. NLI, Eileen O'Casey Papers, MS 44,742/3, Eileen's letter to Lowery, 16 February 1977.

123. John Corry, 'O'Casey Centenary Fans Flames of His Works', *New York Times*, 26 March 1980, p. C26.

124. Robert G. Lowery, 'A Tribute', *The Sean O'Casey Review*, 1, 1 (1974), p. 4.

125. Despite Lowery's enthusiasm, he too eventually quarrelled with O'Casey's widow. Eileen O'Casey grew suspicious of Lowery after reading a play called *Daarlin' Man*, a

biographical piece about her husband which she disliked. She learned that the play's author had asked Lowery for help, but Lowery assured her that he had discouraged the playwright. However, Eileen knew that Lowery had in fact expressed his liking for the play to the author, and had promised to spread the work around. In retaliation, Eileen recommended Krause to edit a version of *Cock-A-Doodle Dandy* even though the press had initially contacted Lowery. (NLI, Eileen O'Casey Papers, MS 44,742/2, letters between Lowery and Eileen O'Casey).

126. *Irish Times*, 30 March 1960, p. 8.

127. The other plays in this festival were *The Plough* and *Red Roses for Me*. 'London Letter', *Irish Times*, 28 June 1962, p. 7. G. A. Olden, 'O'Casey at Home', *Irish Times*, 1 October 1959, p. 6.

128. *A Conversation with Sean O'Casey*. Dir. Robert D. Graff. NBC. 22 January 1956. *The Exile: Omnibus*. Dir. Don Taylor. BBC1. 6 February 1968.

129. Gabriel Fallon, 'Sean O'Casey', *Irish Times*, 18 March 1960, p. 9. 'An Irishman's Diary', *Irish Times*, 17 March 1960, p. 6.

130. 'Attitude to O'Casey Plays "Quite Absurd"', *Irish Times*, 29 January 1966, p. 7.

131. Lemass quoted by Roisín Higgins, *Transforming 1916: Meaning, Memory and the Fiftieth Anniversary of the Easter Rising*. Cork: Cork University Press, 2012, p. 122.

132. 'O'Casey Cut in TV Film Condemned', *Irish Times*, 21 March 1960, p. 4. 'Attitude to O'Casey Plays "Quite Absurd"', *Irish Times*, 29 January 1966, p.7. *Sligo Champion*, 4 March 1966, quoted by Higgins, p. 51.

133. 'Tributes to Behan', *Irish Times*, 21 March 1964, p. 9.

134. NLI, Seán O'Casey Papers, MS 38,050, letter to Henning Risehbieter.

135. *Telegraph* quoted in 'Sean O'Casey', *Irish Times*, 21 September 1964, p. 7.

136. 'Sean O'Casey', *Irish Times*, 21 September 1964, p. 7.

137. 'O'Casey One-Act Play to be Televised', *Irish Times*, 25 June 1962, p. 1.

138. Donal Foley, 'O'Casey Play Withdrawn After Objections by Lord Chamberlain', *Irish Times*, 19 July 1963, p. 1.

139. '"Unseen" Play by O'Casey on Next Week', *Irish Times*, 2 June 1966, p. 6.

140. O'Casey, *Letters*, II, p. 86.

141. NLI, Seán O'Casey Papers, MS 38,042, Mac Anna's letter to O'Casey on 28 January 1951; and O'Casey's reply of 1 February 1951.

142. NYPL, Berg Collection, Seán O'Casey Papers, Holograph Notebook Vol. 18, f.88. See also Kavanagh, *The Story of the Abbey Theatre*. New York: Devin-Adair, 1950, p. 142.

143. Tomás Mac Anna, 'O'Casey's Toy Theatre', in Micheál Ó hAodha (ed.), *The O'Casey Enigma*, Dublin: Mercier, 1980, pp. 7–19 (pp. 16–17).

144. 'Abbey "Deteriorating"', *Irish Times*, 4 July 1964, p. 24.

145. NLI, Seán O'Casey Papers, MS 38,047, letter to Patricia Turner of 12 June 1964.

146. 'O'Casey Agrees to Allow Abbey to Stage his Plays', *Irish Times*, 14 March 1964, p. 12. 'Gunman' to Stay at the Abbey', *Irish Times*, 26 August 1964, p. 4.

147. Mac Anna directed *Red Roses for Me* in 1967, *Purple Dust* in 1975, *Figuro in the Night* in 1975, *The Moon Shines on Kylenamoe* in 1975, *The Plough and the Stars* in 1976, *Cock-A-Doodle Dandy* in 1977, *The Star Turns Red* in 1978, *The Shadow of a Gunman* in 1980 and *The Drums of Father Ned* in 1985.

148. In 1960 Robert Hogan demanded that the late plays should 'have the intelligent and inimitable interpretation that they deserve and demand' (Robert Hogan, *The Experiments of Sean O'Casey*, p. 9). More recently, in 1994, Fintan O'Toole complained of the 'disgrace that O'Casey's later work should be so neglected', and

argued for 'a fundamental re-appraisal of plays like *Cock-A-Doodle Dandy*, *Red Roses for Me*, *Within the Gates*, and *Oak Leaves and Lavender*' (Fintan O'Toole, 'Time to Look Beyond O'Casey's Successes', *Irish Times*, 1 November 1994, <www.irishtimes.com/newspaper/archive/1994/1101/Pg010.html#Ar01002>).

149. Quoted by Roderick Bladel, *Walter Kerr: An Analysis of His Criticism*. Metuchen: Scarecrow, 1976, p. 2.

150. O'Casey knew about the two contrasting reviews: Walter Kerr, 'Theatre: Red Roses for Me', *New York Herald Tribune*, 29 December 1955; and Brooks Atkinson, 'Theatre: Sean O'Casey', *New York Times*, 29 December 1955. See O'Casey, *Letters*, III, p. 241. Kerr is quoted by Bladel, pp. 40, 72.

151. Walter Kerr, 'Where O'Casey's Career Went Wrong', *New York Times*, 2 February 1969, p. D1. The strangest thing about O'Casey that appeared in the *New York Times* after the writer's death was Katherine Coker's article, 'I Knock at Sean O'Casey's Door', *New York Times* 3 December 1972, p. D17. Coker recalled visiting O'Casey in England during 1957, when she claimed to have watched the playwright scrubbing the floor. Suddenly, she had heard the doorbell ring and Samuel Beckett had arrived on an unexpected visited from Paris, and Coker describes this meeting between the two writers. But in reality, although Coker had visited at the Devon house at this time, the meeting between O'Casey and Beckett had never taken place. Eileen O'Casey later phoned Coker to find out why the article had been written in this way, and Coker had said that the fabrications were added to make the article more interesting. I am grateful to Breon O'Casey for his insights here.

152. Richard Gilman, 'The Letters of Sean O'Casey', *New York Times*, 16 March 1975, p. BR1.

153. David Krause, 'Text and Acknowledgments', in O'Casey, *Letters*, IV, pp. xxi–xxvi (p. xxi).

154. O'Casey, *Letters*, IV, flyleaf.

155. Ronald Ayling and Michael J. Durkan (eds), *Sean O'Casey: A Bibliography*. London: Macmillan, 1978, pp. 277–98.

156. Samuel Beckett, 'The Essential and the Incidental', in Samuel Beckett, *Disjecta: Miscellaneous Writings and a Dramatic Fragment*, ed. Ruby Cohn. London: Calder, 1983, pp. 82–3.

157. Mark Redman and Merit Mikk, *Country Profile on Rural Characteristics: Romania*. Frankfurt am Main: RUDI/Seventh Framework Programme for Research and Technological Development of the European Commission, 2008, p. 13. Available at: <www.rudi-europe.net/uploads/media/Romania_WP1_Report.pdf>.

158. See, for example, Adina Ştefan, 'Bucureşti: Comedia "S-a sfârşit cum a început", la Teatrul Naţional', *Adevarul*, 29 May 2010, <www.adevarul.ro/locale/bucuresti/Bucuresti-_Comedia_-S-a_sfarsit_cum_a_inceput-la_Teatrul_National_0_270573079.html>.

159. I am grateful to Shivaun O'Casey for this information.

160. The Volkstheater's advertising declares: 'Das Stück nimmt unübersehbar Bezug auf die frühen Stummfilm-Komödien und ihre Stars, wie etwa Laurel und Hardy, und zeichnet sich durch fulminante Clowneskerien und überbordenden Klamauk aus', <www.volkstheater.at/home/premieren/1017/Das+Ende+vom+Anfang>.

161. Jones, *File on O'Casey*, p. 45.

162. 'Hansa Theater Heiterer Oktober: Komödien, Slapstick, Evergreens', 29 July 2002, *Berliner Zeitung*, <www.berliner-zeitung.de/archiv/chaos-putzt-mit-hansa-theater-heiterer-oktober—komoedien—slapstick—evergreens,10810590,10031630.html>.

See also <www.kraehkamp.webseite.ms/>.'1986: Das Ende vom Anfang', *Berliner Morgenpost*, 19 June 2008, <www.morgenpost.de/printarchiv/infoscan/article571586/1986-Das-Ende-vom-Anfang.html>.

163. Eva-Maria Magel, 'Männer in Schürzen: Sean O'Caseys "Das Ende vom Anfang" in Wiesbaden', *Frankfurter Allgemeine Zeitung*, 17 June 2002, p. 59.

164. 'The Success of Sean O'Casey', *Irish Worker*, 26 September 1931, p. 2.

165. I am grateful to Tony Meech for this information from one of the catalogues in his possession, and to Wolfgang Trautwein for help in researching the German context of O'Casey's work.

166. I am grateful to Stephan Dörschel and the Archiv der Akademie der Künste in Berlin for this information.

167. NLI, Eileen O'Casey Papers, Letters to Eileen from Hans-Herman Liebrecht, MS 44,709 /1.

168. Quoted by Volker Canaris, *Peter Zadek: Der Theatermann und Filmemacher*. Munich: Hanser, 1979, p. 58.

169. Ibid., p. 101.

170. *Der Pott*. Dir. Peter Zadek. Westdeutscher Rundfunk. 1971. The film's visual dimension is strongly influenced by the Belgian pop-artist Guy Peellaert. See also Zadek, *My Way*. Cologne: Kiepenheuer and Witsch, 1998, p. 301. A very full list of German-language productions of O'Casey is produced by Peter Stapelberg, *Sean O'Casey und das Deutschsprachige Theater (1948–1974)*. Frankfurt am Main: Peter Lang, 1979, pp. 516–52.

171. Jones, *File on O'Casey*, p. 48. 'O'Casey: Geballte Faust', *Der Spiegel*, 12 July 1970, p. 209.

172. 'Old Acquaintances: Kortner Scandal in Berlin', *AJR Information: Association of Jewish Refugees in Great Britain*, August 1953, p. 5.

173. See for instance '"Kikeriki" von Sean O'Casey am Deutschen Theater Berlin, Regie Rolf Winkelgrund', *Neues Deutschland*, 2 December 1986, <www.berliner-schauspielschule.de/kikeriki.htm>. Also Gunther Cwoydrak, *The World Stage*, March 1966, quoted by Nesta Jones, p. 57.

174. Alexander Weigel, *Das Deutsche theater: eine Geschichte in Bildern*. Berlin: Propyläen, 1999, p. 390.

175. Eileen O'Casey in *Berliner Zeitung*, May 1966, quoted by Nesta Jones, p. 57.

176. Quoted by O'Brien, 'Sean O'Casey and the Abbey Theatre', p. 78.

177. The translator Heinrich Boell, for example, hailed the autobiographies as 'the Protestant counterpart to Joyce's "Ulysses"', correctly emphasizing just how integral to Irish literature and to Irish revolutionism the non-Catholic experience might be. Heinrich Boell, 'Wilde Poesie Der Flüche', *Der Spiegel*, 24 November 1969, p. 204.

178. *Die komplette Autobiographie in einer Kassette*. Audio tape. Diogenes. 1973. Ayling and Durkan, *Sean O'Casey: A Bibliography*, pp. 277–94.

179. See David Bradby, *Modern French Drama 1940–1990*, 2nd edn. Cambridge: Cambridge University Press, 1991, p. 87.

180. These productions included Antoine Vitez's 1961 *The Drums of Father Ned* in Marseilles; Jean Daste's 1961 *The Plough and the Stars* in Aix-en-Provence; and Andrew Steiger's 1966 *Shadow of a Gunman* in Metz. This is to say nothing of productions in and around Paris such as André Cellier's 1960 *Bedtime Story*, Gabriel Garran's 1962 *The Star Turns Red*, Guy Retoré's 1967 *Silver Tassie*, or Peter Valde's 1968 version of *The Star Turns Red*. I am indebted to Clare Finburgh for her assistance

with researching the French context of O'Casey's work. More details about O'Casey productions in France can be found at <www.lesarchivesduspectacle.net/>.

181. Bradby, *Modern French Drama*, p. 92.

182. Quoted by Ibid.

183. Jones, *File on O'Casey*, p. 53.

184. Armelle Héliot, 'O'Casey, populaire, politique, poétique', *Le Figaro*, 20 February 2009, p. 32.

185. *Usporená libra*. Dir. Ján Roháč/Vladimír Svitáček. Televizní Filmová Tvorba. 1963. Jarka M. Burian, *Modern Czech Theatre: Reflector and Conscience of a Nation*. Iowa City: University of Iowa Press, 2000, p. 71.

186. Krejčík is a fascinating figure in his own right. At the time of writing, the 94-year-old has just released his latest film and taken part in demonstrations against the corruption of the Czech government.

187. Antonín J. Liehm, *Closely Watched Films: The Czechoslovak Experience*. International Arts and Sciences Press, 1974, p. 85. *Penzion pro svobodné pány*. Dir. Jiří Krejčík. Barrandov Film Studios. 1967.

188. I am indebted to Jiří Krejčík for his comments about O'Casey, and also to Jan Culik, for his tremendous help with all of the Czech research and translation for this book.

189. Nikolai Gribachev, 'Literature and the Present', *Izvestia*, 2 April 1958, pp. 32–3.

190. Elena Geogievna Soshalskaya and Vera Iranovna Prokhorova, *Stylistic Analysis*. Moscow: [?], 1976. A. Saruchanian, 'Pisarz-bojownik', *Literatura Radziecka*, 3 (1955), 152–4. A. Yelistratova, 'Sean O'Casey – pisarz-obywatel', *Literatura Radziecka*, 11 (1952), 174–80. All three of these Russian sources are quoted by Robert Looby, 'Looking for the Censor in the Works of Sean O'Casey (and Others) in Polish Translation', *Translation and Literature*, 17, 1 (2008), pp. 47–64 (p. 52).

191. See Boris Isakov, 'About Depraved Tastes and a Sense of Responsibility', *Current Digest of the Russian Press*, 13 February 1957, pp. 9–11. A. Anikst, 'A Most Extraordinary Spectacle', *Current Digest of the Russian Press*, 6 October 1965, pp. 9–13.

192. Ayling and Durkan, *Sean O'Casey: A Bibliography*, pp. 293–4. Looby, 'Looking for the Censor in the Works of Sean O'Casey (and Others) in Polish Translation', p. 52.

193. John Freedman, 'Interview with Dodin', *Moscow Times*, 1 July 2000, available in English translation at <http://afronord.tripod.com/thr/dodin.html>.

194. Tatiana Troyan, 'Олег Дмитриев: «Человек в «обстоятельствах»', Театрал, 1 April 2008, <www.teatral-online.ru/news/1522/>. I am grateful to Cynthia Marsh for her translations and suggestions when researching the Russian context for O'Casey's work.

195. Sin Seok-yeon, 'Daejeon Ihu Gakgeukdan Baldal Gwajeong: Aeran Geukdan', *Dong-A Ilbo*, 23–24 January 1929, English translation in Hunam Yun, *Appropriations of Irish Drama by Modern Korean Nationalist Theatre: A Focus on the Influence of Sean O'Casey in a Colonial Context*. Unpublished PhD thesis, University of Warwick, 2010, p. 207.

196. The peasant trilogy consists of *Tomak* ('The Shack' of 1931), *Beodeunamu seon Dongri-ui Punggyeong* ('The Scene from the Willow Tree Village' of 1933), and *So* ('The Ox' of 1934). See also: Gim Yong-su 'Aeran-ui Singeuk Jakga Sean O'Casey', *Chosun Ilbo*, 2–17 February 1931; and Gim Gwang-seop, 'Hyeondae Yeongmundan-e daehan Joseon-jeok Gwansim', *Joseon Munhak*, 2.1 (1934), 108–14); both of which are cited, along with a discussion of Yu Chi-jin, in Hunam Yun, pp. 223, 262.

197. For full details of how these plays emulate O'Casey see Moran, *Staging the Easter Rising*, pp. 112–16.

198. The province of Northern Ireland had been governed by the implicitly anti-Catholic Ulster Unionist Party and policed by an overwhelmingly Protestant armed force since the 1920s. When 1968 saw radicalism spreading across Europe and the United States, Catholics in the Northern Irish state organized a series of civil rights marches to highlight their own predicament. When riots followed across Derry and Belfast, London politicians felt compelled to act, and by 1969 the British army had deployed to separate the warring communities. Nationalist areas at first welcomed these troops, but the reception soon soured, and by 1971 Northern Ireland saw murders, gun battles, and Protestants and Catholics being forced from their homes. The presence of the British army on the streets served to foster an atmosphere of violence and retaliation, particularly after 30 January 1972, when the British Parachute Regiment ran amok in Derry on 'Bloody Sunday' and killed 14 unarmed civilians.

199. NLI, Eileen O'Casey Papers, MS 44,742/2, Lowery to Eileen, 9 May 1977. David Krause, 'Some Truths and Jokes about the Easter Rising', *Sean O'Casey Review*, 3, 1 (1976), pp. 3–23 (p. 5).

200. Brooks Atkinson and Albert Hirschfeld, *The Lively Years, 1920–1973: A Half Century of the Most Significant Plays on Broadway*. New York: Da Capo, 1985 [1973], p. 159.

201. 'Sharing, Not Scaring is the Aim', *Irish Times*, 7 July 2000, <www.irishtimes.com/newspaper/features/2000/0705/00070500093.html>.

202. Raymond Williams, *Drama from Ibsen to Brecht*. London: Hogarth Press, 1993, p. 149.

203. Paul Bew, *Ireland: The Politics of Enmity, 1789–2006*. Oxford: Oxford University Press, 2006, pp. 506, 508, 510.

204. Deane, 'Irish Politics and O'Casey's Theatre', *Threshold*, 24 (1973), pp. 5–16, 11–12; and 'O'Casey and Yeats: Exemplary Dramatists', in *Celtic Revivals: Essays in Modern Irish Literature, 1880–1980*. London: Faber, 1985, pp. 108–22 (p. 122).

205. Seamus Deane, 'Roddy's Troubles', *Guardian*, 4 September 1999, p. B8. Deane, 'Fact and Fury', *Guardian*, 6 January 2001, p. B3.

206. Like O'Casey, Croghan scarcely sought to avoid controversy: Croghan's play *Paddy Englishman* depicts a hardline republican who walks into a nearby pub and commits murder, leaving 'bodies everywhere', and who also leaves an explosive device with two panicked flatmates. In February 1999 Croghan premiered the work in the Birmingham Repertory Theatre, only a short walk from the site where, in the notorious pub bombings of 1974, the real-life IRA had killed most people in a single incident during the 'Troubles'. Croghan, *Paddy Irishman, Paddy Englishman, and Paddy . . .?* London: Faber, 1999, pp. 55, 59–60.

207. Declan Kiberd, *Inventing Ireland*. London: Jonathan Cape, 1995, p. 228.

208. George Watson, *Irish Identity and the Literary Revival*. Washington: Catholic University of America Press, 1994 [1979], p. 310 n.15.

209. Joe Cleary, *Outrageous Fortune: Capital and Culture in Modern Ireland*. Dublin: Field Day, 2007, p. 143.

210. Seamus Deane, *Heroic Styles: The Tradition of an Idea*. Derry: Field Day, 1985, p. 10.

211. Most notably, Edna Longley clashed with Deane: see Warwick Gould and Edna Longley (eds), *Yeats Annual: XII: 'That Accusing Eye': Yeats and his Irish Readers*. Basingstoke: Macmillan, 1996. Meanwhile, the Chairman of the Yeats International Summer School, Augustine Martin, challenged Deane directly: 'I read Seamus Deane's essay with admiration and unease, and both feelings have survived successive readings [. . .] The commentary that follows is an attempt to clarify for myself a sense

of disagreement that refuses to go away'. Martin, 'What Stalked through the Post Office?', *Crane Bag*, Vol.2, 1/2 (1978), pp. 164–77 (p. 164).

212. Grene, *The Politics of Irish Drama*, p. 148.

213. Beckett, 'The Essential and the Incidental', p. 82.

214. Brendan Kennelly, 'Sean O'Casey's Journey into Joy', in Micheál Ó hAodha (ed.), *The O'Casey Enigma*, Dublin: Mercier, 1980, pp. 98–111.

215. Rónán McDonald, *Tragedy and Irish Literature: Synge, O'Casey, Beckett*. London: Macmillan, 2002, pp. 94–5.

216. T. A. Jackson, *Sunday Worker*, 24 June 1928, p. 8. Quoted by Raphael Samuel, Ewan MacColl and Stuart Cosgrove, *Theatres of the Left: 1880–1935: Workers' Theatre Movements in Britain and America*. London: Routledge and Kegan Paul, 1985, p. 54.

217. Desmond Rushe, 'A Mould Breaking Debut of Courage', *Irish Independent*, 8 May 1991, located in Abbey Theatre Archives, Box 64, Reviews of *The Plough* 1991.

218. Leonard's intervention in turn provoked a response from Hynes herself, who pointed out in the *Irish Times* that Leonard had, by his own admission, watched only the first half of the performance. Leonard, 'Not While I'm Eating', *Sunday Independent*, 19 May 1991, p. 3L. Hynes, '"The Plough" at the Abbey', *The Irish Times*, 23 May 1991, p. 11. Leonard was at this stage making something of a habit of walking out of productions of O'Casey plays, having written in the *Irish Independent* of how he had abandoned Shivaun O'Casey's version of *Purple Dust* at the Abbey in 1989. Hugh Leonard, 'Hugh Leonard's Log', *Sunday Independent*, 11 June 1989, cutting in the Abbey Theatre Archive, Box 52, *Purple Dust* 1989.

219. Harold Prince, *Grandchild of Kings*. London and Toronto: Samuel French, 1993, p. 119.

220. Frank Rich, 'Evoking the Youth of Sean O'Casey in Dublin', *New York Times*, 17 February 1992, p. C13. Maureen Levins Boyd, 'An Interview with Hal Prince on *Grandchild of Kings*', *The Canadian Journal of Irish Studies*, 19, 1 (1993), pp. 79–85. John Simon, 'Pipsqueak's Progress, Playwright's Regress', *New York Magazine*, 9 March 1992, pp. 76–7.

221. *Young Indiana Jones, Chapter 7: 'Love's Sweet Song'*. Dir. Gilles MacKinnon and Carl Schultz. ABC. 11 March 1992.

222. Colm Tóibín, *Beauty in a Broken Place*. Dublin: Lilliput, 2004, p. 4.

223. Tóibín, *Beauty in a Broken Place*, pp. 76–7.

224. Indeed, when Tóibín's play was premiered in Dublin, it generated a newspaper controversy because of the unflattering portrayal of the Abbey actors F. J. McCormick and Eileen Crowe. The son of McCormick and Crowe, David Judge, wrote to complain about Tóibín's play, 'My mother was depicted as superstitious and poorly spoken; but much worse was the treatment of my father, who was portrayed as a truly despicable human being – and an inferior actor as well'. 'Drama and the Reputation of the Dead', *Irish Times*, 2 November 2004, <www.irishtimes.com/newspaper/letters/2004/1102/1097847332631.html>.

225. Morash, *A History of Irish Theatre 1601–2000*; Welch, *The Abbey Theatre 1899–1999*.

226. Michael Kenneally, 'Review of Christopher Murray's *Sean O'Casey: Writer at Work*', *Irish University Review*, 35, 1 (2005), pp. 211–16 (p. 216).

227. Leonard Lehrman, *Marc Blitzstein: A Bio-Bibliography*. London: Praeger, 2005, p. 133. Elie Siegmeister, Edward Mabley and Sean O'Casey, *The Plough and the Stars: Opera in Three Acts*. New York: MCA, 1970.

228. Quoted by Fintan O'Toole, 'Wrestling for O'Casey's Legacy', *Irish Times*, 3 April 2008, <www.irishtimes.com/newspaper/features/2008/0403/1207113944832_pf.html>.

229. Fiach Mac Conghail, 'I am bemused', Irish Times, 3 April 2008, <www.irishtimes. com/newspaper/features/2008/0403/1207113944836_pf.html>.

230. The Abbey's artistic director stated explicitly, 'Ninety four years on, his [O'Casey's] great drama The Plough and the Stars, a play born out of the crucible of the founding of the Republic, still allows Irish theatre artists to comment on society and the manifestation of those ideals today'. Fiach Mac Conghail, April–September 2010 Abbey Theatre Programme. Dublin: Abbey Theatre, 2010, p. 5.

231. At first the theatre's proposed move was to a docklands site on Dublin's southside, then it was to be expanded on its existing site, then moved to O'Connell Street, then Parnell Square and then a docklands site on the city's northside.

232. David Norris, 'Iconic Marriage of Yeats and Pearse in Abbey GPO, Irish Times, 15 October 2009, <www.irishtimes.com/newspaper/opinion/2009/1015/122425 6681742.html>.

233. Fintan O'Toole, 'Finding a new stage for the Abbey is not a question of location', Irish Times, 24 October 2009, <www.irishtimes.com/newspaper/weekend/2009 /1024/1224257356703.html>.

234. In the past two decades, Yeats's plays have, however, been subject to thoughtful treatment by the Sligo-based Blue Raincoat Theatre Company, under the direction of Niall Henry.

235. Irish Times, 12 November 2011, <www.irishtimes.com/newspaper/ireland/2011/1112/ 1224307460318.html>.

236. O'Casey, Letters, IV, p. 509.

Chapter 8

1. Quoted by Luke Gibbons, 'Alternative Enlightenments', in Mary Cullen (ed.), 1798: 200 Years of Resonance. Belfast: Irish Reporter Publications, 1998, pp. 119–27 (p. 119).

2. Gerry Smyth, Decolonisation and Criticism. London: Pluto Press, 1998, p. 52.

3. James Simmons, Sean O'Casey. London and Basingstoke: Macmillan, 1983, p. 164.

4. Simmons, Sean O'Casey, p. 168.

5. W. B. Yeats, 'The Silver Tassie: A Letter (1928)', in Ronald Ayling (ed.), Sean O'Casey: Modern Judgements. London: Macmillan, 1969, p. 87. In rejecting the play, Yeats declared, 'You have no subject', yet signed off, 'Put the dogmatism of this letter down to splenetic age and forgive it'.

6. Simmons, Sean O'Casey, p. 163.

7. Stuart Hall, 'Cultural Studies and the Crisis of the Humanities', October, 53 (1990), pp. 11–23 (p. 15).

8. John McGrath, A Good Night Out: Popular Theatre: Audience, Class and Form, 2nd edn. London: Nick Hern, 1996, p. 63.

9. Simmons, Sean O'Casey, p. 168.

10. Ibid., p. 166.

11. Christopher Fitz-Simon, Buffoonery and Easy Sentiment: Popular Irish Plays in the Decade Prior to the Opening of the Abbey Theatre. Dublin: Carysfort Press, 2011, pp. 37, 184. McCormick played Seumas Shields (Shadow of a Gunman), Joxer Daly (Juno and the Paycock) and Jack Clitheroe (The Plough and the Stars).

12. David Cairns and Shaun Richards, Writing Ireland: Nationalism, Colonialism and Literature. Manchester: Manchester University Press, 1988, p. 129.

13. Samuel, MacColl and Cosgrove, *Theatres of the Left*, p. 54. Williams, *Drama from Ibsen to Brecht*, pp. 147–53.
14. Dates given are for first professional productions, in each case.
15. See Victor Merriman, *Because We Are Poor: Irish Theatre in the 1990s*. Dublin: Carysfort Press, 2011, for a full discussion of this aesthetic.
16. George Bernard Shaw, *John Bull's Other Island*. Harmondsworth: Penguin, 1984, p. 81. See Simmons, pp. 129–32, for an extended dismissal of *Purple Dust*, notwithstanding its popularity with directors and audiences at the Abbey (1975) and the Berliner Ensemble (since the 1960s).
17. Yeats's 'September 1913' includes the lines: 'What need you, being come to sense,/ But fumble in a greasy till/ And add the halfpence to the pence/ And prayer to shivering prayer, until/ You have dried the marrow from the bone?' W. B. Yeats, *The Collected Works of W. B. Yeats: Volume I: The Poems*, p. 108.
18. John Willett, *The New Sobriety: Art and Politics in the Weimar Period 1917–33*. London: Thames & Hudson, 1987, p. 150.
19. See Joseph Lee, *The Modernisation of Irish Society*. Dublin: Gill and Macmillan, 1989, for an account of the reorganization of the Catholic Church as a power in the land from the 1850s.
20. Sheila's aspiration to a loving relationship with Ayamonn is compromised by her strict Catholicism.
21. See Victor Merriman, 'To Sleep is Safe; to Dream is Dangerous: Catholicism on Stage in Twentieth-Century Ireland', in Eamon Maher and Eugene O'Brien (eds), *Breaking The Mould: Literary Representations of Irish Catholicism*. Bern: Peter Lang, 2011, pp. 193–212.
22. Tóibín, *Beauty in a Broken Place*, pp. 55–6.
23. Edward Said, 'Yeats and Decolonization', in Seamus Deane (ed.), *Nationalism, Colonialism and Literature*. Minneapolis: University of Minnesota Press, 1990, pp. 69–95 (p. 86).
24. Alain Badiou, *The Rebirth of History*. London: Verso, 2012, p. 56. Emphases in original.
25. Christopher Morash, '"Something's Missing": Theatre and the Republic of Ireland Act, 1949', in Ray Ryan (ed.), *Writing in the Irish Republic: Literature, Culture, politics 1949–1999* (Basingstoke: Macmillan, 2000), pp. 64–81 (p. 71).
26. Simmons, *Sean O'Casey*, p. 129.

Chapter 9

1. See Philip S. Bagwell, *The Railwaymen: The History of the National Union of Railwaymen*. London: Allen and Unwin, 1963.
2. See Fintan O'Toole, *Ship of Fools: How Stupidity And Corruption Sank The Celtic Tiger*. London: Faber, 2009.
3. See Shane Ross, *The Bankers*. Dublin: Penguin Ireland, 2009. Also Shane Ross and Nick Webb, *Wasters*. Dublin: Penguin Ireland, 2010.
4. Fintan O'Toole provides a critical commentary on the scale of inequality in Ireland's globalized economy in *After the Ball*. Dublin: TASC at New Island, 2003.
5. For an incisive analysis of the rapid expansion of Ireland's middle-class during the Celtic Tiger period and the lifestyles of the rich, see David McWilliams, *The Pope's Children: Ireland's New Elite*. London: Pan Macmillan, 2005.

6. Early biographical work on O'Casey includes Margulies, *The Early Life of Sean O'Casey*, and Sean McCann (ed.), *The World of Sean O'Casey*. London, Four Square, 1966.

7. Grene, *The Politics of Irish Drama*, p. 112.

8. Ibid.

9. O'Casey, *Letters*, I, p. 696.

10. NYPL, Berg Collection, Seán O'Casey Papers, Holograph Notebook Vol. 9, draft MS of *I Knock at the Door*.

11. Michael Holroyd, *Bernard Shaw: Vol. 1: 1856–1898: The Search for Love*. London: Chatto and Windus, 1988, p. 36.

12. O'Casey, *Feathers from the Green Crow: Sean O'Casey*, pp. 7–10.

13. The analysis is informed here and throughout by the work of French sociologist Pierre Bourdieu, in particular *Distinction: A Social Critique of the Judgement of Taste*, trans. Richard Nice. London; New York: Routledge, 1984.

14. See Jordan, 'The Passionate Autodidact', pp. 59–76.

15. NYPL, Berg Collection, Seán O'Casey Papers, 'Articles: Ireland: 7 Typescripts: The Abbey Theatre', f.12.

16. See Earnán De Blaghd (Ernest Blythe), *Trasna na Bóinne: Imleabhar 1 de Chuimhní Cinn*. Dublin: Sáirséal agus Dill, 1957.

17. O'Casey to David Krause, 2 November 1954, in O'Casey, *Letters*, II, p. 1103.

18. NYPL, Berg Collection, Seán O'Casey Papers, Holograph Notebook Vol. 4.

19. Ibid. Vol. 10.

20. See Donal Nevin (ed.), *James Larkin: Lion of the Fold*. Dublin: Gill and Macmillan, 1998. Also Emmet Larkin, *James Larkin: Irish Labour Leader 1876–1947*. London: Routledge and Kegan Paul, 1965.

21. See Padraig Yeates, *Lockout: Dublin 1913*. Dublin: Gill and Macmillan, 2000. Jack Mitchell, *The Essential O'Casey*, p. 19.

22. Cited in Yeates, *Lockout*, p. 394.

23. For O'Casey's perspective see his (writing as P. O'Cathasaigh), *The Story of the Irish Citizen Army*. Also see R. M. Fox, *The History of the Irish Citizen Army*. Dublin: James Duffy, 1943.

24. Shaw to O'Casey, 3 December 1919, in O'Casey, *Letters*, I, p. 88.

25. Máire Nic Shiubhlaigh, *The Splendid Years*. Dublin: James Duffy, 1955, p. 140.

26. See O'Casey, *Feathers from the Green Crow*, pp. 88–100.

27. Brian Farrell, 'Labour and the Political Revolution', in Donal Nevin (ed.), *Trade Union Century*. Cork and Dublin: Mercier Press, 1994, pp. 42–53.

28. O'Casey quoted in Gregory, *Lady Gregory's Journals: Volume 1*, p. 547.

29. Ibid., p. 584.

30. 'Play Critique by W. B. Yeats', 19 June 1922, in O'Casey, *Letters*, I, pp. 102–3.

31. Holloway, *Joseph Holloway's Abbey Theatre*, p. 220.

32. Murray, *Seán O'Casey: Writer at Work*, p. 146.

33. Mary Shine Thompson, Austin Clarke; A Literary Life-Chronology. Unpublished PhD thesis, University College Dublin, 1997, p. 292. Cited by Terence Brown, *The Life of W. B. Yeats: A Critical Biography*. Dublin: Gill and Macmillan, 1999, p. 287.

34. Murray, *Seán O'Casey: Writer at Work*, p. 143.

35. Ibid., p. 142.

36. See Brian Singleton, 'The Revival Revised' in Shaun Richards (ed.), *The Cambridge Companion to Irish Drama*. Cambridge: Cambridge University Press, 2004, pp. 258–70.

CHRONOLOGY

	Seán O'Casey's Life and Work	Broader Historical Events
1880	Seán O'Casey is born on 30 March (as John Casey) in 85 Upper Dorset Street. His parents are Susan and Michael Casey, and he has four older siblings then living: Bella, Mick, Tom and Isaac	Charles Stewart Parnell becomes leader of the Irish Parliamentary Party at Westminster. The 33-year-old Protestant had been an MP for five years, and sought to achieve Irish self-government (Ireland having been assimilated into the United Kingdom by the 1800 Act of Union)
1882	O'Casey's family move to 9 Innisfallen Parade	
1884		Gaelic Athletic Association is founded
1886	O'Casey's father dies	Gladstone presents the first Irish Home Rule Bill: it is defeated in the House of Commons
Mid-1880s– early 1890s	O'Casey suffers at school due to trachoma, is tutored by his sister Bella and taken to the theatre on occasion by brother Isaac, and the family move to 25 Hawthorn Terrace, East Wall	

	Seán O'Casey's Life and Work	Broader Historical Events
1890		William O'Shea, another Irish MP, cites Parnell as correspondent in a divorce case: Parnell loses the support of Gladstone and is deposed as leader of the Irish Parliamentary Party
1891		Parnell dies
1893		Douglas Hyde and Eóin MacNeill found the Gaelic League, an organization that aimed to restore the Irish language. Gladstone's second Home Rule Bill is passed by the House of Commons but blocked by the House of Lords
1894	O'Casey's family move to 4 Abercorn Road, O'Casey leaves St Barnabas's school and takes his first paid job, in a hardware and china firm	
1899		Members of the Irish Literary Theatre, the forerunner of the Abbey Theatre, perform at the Antient Concert Rooms in Dublin
c. 1900	O'Casey joins the Gaelic League	
1903	O'Casey starts working for the Great Northern Railway	

1904	Abbey Theatre opens to the public on 27 December. Arthur Griffiths writes *The Resurrection of Hungary*, arguing for an independent Ireland under a dual monarch, something that formed the basic philosophy of his new *Sinn Féin* movement the following year
c. 1905	O'Casey joins the secret revolutionary group, the IRB
1907	O'Casey publishes his first work, 'Sound the Loud Trumpet', an article about Irish education written under the pseudonym '*An Gall Fada*' [Tall Foreigner]
	The Abbey Theatre's production of J. M. Synge's *The Playboy of the Western World* is greeted by riots. Pope Pius X issues the *Ne Temere* decree, insisting that children of 'mixed marriages' should be raised as Catholics
1910	General election gives the leader of the Irish Parliamentary Parry, John Redmond, the balance of power at Westminster
1911	O'Casey is sacked by the Great Northern Railway, works as casual labourer hereafter, and writes for Larkin's union newspaper the *Irish Worker*
1912	Asquith introduces the third Home Rule Bill to the House of Commons, beginning months of delay and debate

Chronology

	Seán O'Casey's Life and Work	Broader Historical Events
1913	O'Casey works to bring humanitarian assistance to those involved in the Dublin lockout	The Ulster Volunteer Force is established in order to protect Ulster from Home Rule. The Irish Volunteers movement is founded to ensure that Home Rule is implemented. The Dublin lockout takes place, triggered by tram workers who refuse to sign a pledge agreeing not to join the Irish Transport and General Workers' Union: the dispute lasts for half a year and throws 25,000 people out of work. James Larkin and James Connolly establish the Irish Citizen Army
1914	O'Casey acts as secretary of the Irish Citizen Army, but resigns later in the year. His brother Tom dies	First World War declared. At Westminster, Irish Home Rule is simultaneously enacted and postponed until after the conflict. John Redmond urges Irish men to enlist in the British army. Irish Volunteers split, with the vast majority (150,000) forming the National Volunteers who side with Redmond, and the minority (8,000) remaining as the Irish Volunteers under Eoin MacNeill
1915	O'Casey is admitted to St Vincent's Hospital and sees victims of the First World War	Patrick Pearse – a member of the small military council of the IRB, now planning to use the Irish Volunteers for a rising – gives a famous oration at the funeral of the elderly Fenian O'Donovan Rossa, declaring 'Ireland unfree shall never be at peace'

1916	O'Casey submits his first play to the Abbey, *Profit and Loss*. The script is returned within four days	Irish Volunteers and Irish Citizen Army launch the Easter Rising. An Irish Republic is declared, but the uprising is defeated in 5 days, with the death of 450 people
1917	O'Casey publishes the prose pamphlet *The Story of Thomas Ashe*, which he republishes in an expanded version as *The Sacrifice of Thomas Ashe* the following year. He also acts with the drama group at St Laurence O'Toole Club	Russian Revolution
1917–20	O'Casey enjoys a significant romantic relationship with Máire Keating	
1918	O'Casey publishes the poetry pamphlets *Songs of the Wren* and *More Wren Songs*, and writes a play (*The Frost in the Flower*) for the St Laurence O'Toole Club, whose members refuse to produce the work. His mother and sister Bella both die	Armistice agreed between the Allies and Germany to end the fighting in the First World War. In the general election, the *Sinn Féin* manifesto emphasizes Irish resistance to British rule: the party wins a sweeping victory and takes 73 of 105 available Irish seats
1919	O'Casey publishes his most significant work to date, the prose history *The Story of the Irish Citizen Army*	*Sinn Féin*'s elected candidates establish Dáil Éireann (the Irish parliament), and declare independence, electing a leading veteran of the 1916 Rising, Eamon de Valera, as president. The Dáil accepts responsibility for activities of the Irish Volunteers (increasingly known at the IRA)

	Seán O'Casey's Life and Work	Broader Historical Events
1919–21	O'Casey submits three scripts to the Abbey, all are rejected	The IRA fights a guerrilla war of independence, the Anglo-Irish War, against British forces
1920	O'Casey shares a room with Michael Mullen in a Dublin tenement, 35 Mountjoy Square	
1921	O'Casey moves to 422 North Circular Road, his final residential address in Ireland	Anglo-Irish Treaty agreed. Allows for Ireland to have self-governing, dominion status within Britain's empire, but requiring allegiance to the British monarch. Republican critics refuse to accept the treaty as it fails to deliver a republic and involves an oath of loyalty to the British crown
1922	Another of O'Casey's plays, *The Seamless Coat of Kathleen*, is rejected by the Abbey. But O'Casey then submits *The Shadow of a Gunman*, under the title 'On the Run'. It is accepted for production the following year	The Treaty is narrowly ratified by Dáil Éireann: de Valera opposes this, resigns as president, and is defeated after offering himself for re-election. Pro-Treaty candidates win the majority of seats at a general election. The Free State army fights a Civil War against the anti-Treaty IRA ('Free Staters' against 'Irregulars'). The 1916 Veteran, William Cosgrave, is premier of the new Irish Free State. Publication of James Joyce's *Ulysses*
1923	Abbey produces *The Shadow of a Gunman* as well as *Cathleen Listens In*, but rejects *The Cooing of Doves*	End of Irish Civil War with ceasefire of anti-Treaty forces. W. B. Yeats receives Nobel Prize

Year		
1924	Abbey produces *Juno and the Paycock*, to great financial and popular success, also produces *Nannie's Night Out*	Lenin dies; the General Secretary of the Communist Party, Joseph Stalin, manoeuvres to power
1925		G. B. Shaw receives Nobel Prize
1926	Abbey produces *The Plough and the Stars*, there are riots in response. O'Casey leaves Ireland to live in England for the rest of his life, accepts Hawthornden Prize in London, and takes a flat at 32 Clareville Street in South Kensington	De Valera and others found a new republican party, *Fianna Fáil*, out of the embers of the anti-Treaty *Sinn Féin*
1927	O'Casey marries Eileen Carey in Chelsea	
1928	O'Casey moves to 19 Woronzow Road, St John's Wood: the only property that O'Casey would ever own in his life. His first son, Breon, is born. Abbey rejects *The Silver Tassie*	
1929	*The Silver Tassie* is premiered at London's Apollo Theatre. O'Casey admits that he has 'written part of an autobiography'	
1931	O'Casey sells his home in St John's Wood and moves to 2 Misbourne Cottages, Chalfont-St-Giles; then moves again, nearby to 'Hillcrest' on Dean Way. His brother Isaac, who had emigrated to Liverpool, dies	

	Seán O'Casey's Life and Work	Broader Historical Events
1932		Death of Lady Augusta Gregory. *Fianna Fáil* is elected to government for the first time, and de Valera as premier: the party would remain the largest in the Irish parliament at every election until 2011
1934	*Within the Gates* is staged in London's Royalty Theatre and in the National Theatre, Broadway. The latter staging is successful but by the start of the following year a tour of the production falls victim to religious protest. O'Casey moves from Chalfont-St-Giles to 49 Overstrand Mansions, Battersea. The collection of short plays/poetry/stories *Windfalls* is published but banned in Ireland. O'Casey travels to New York, befriending the critics Brooks Atkinson and George Jean Nathan	
1935	Abbey stages *The Silver Tassie*. O'Casey's second son, Niall, is born	
1936–9		Spanish Civil War
1937	O'Casey alienates British theatre critics by publishing *The Flying Wasp*; he describes his support for republicans in Spain	

1938	O'Casey moves to Devon, where he would live for the rest of his life. Rents 'Tingrith', Ashburton Road, in Totnes	
1939	O'Casey publishes first volume of prose autobiography, *I Knock at the Door*. The book is banned in Ireland until 1947. His daughter Shivaun is born	Death of W. B. Yeats. Publication of James Joyce's *Finnegans Wake*. Second World War begins, Ireland declares neutrality
1940	*The Star Turns Red* premieres at an amateur venue, the Unity Theatre in London	
1941		Death of James Joyce
1942	O'Casey publishes the second volume of prose autobiography, *Pictures in the Hallway*. The book is banned in Ireland until 1947	
1943	*Red Roses for Me* premieres at Olympia Theatre, Dublin, and *Purple Dust* at the People's Theatre, Newcastle-upon-Tyne	
1945	O'Casey publishes the third volume of prose autobiography, *Drums under the Window*: this and the subsequent volumes (1949, 1952, 1954) are not subject to official censorship in Ireland	Suicide of Adolf Hitler, surrender of German High Command, end of Second World War. Atomic bombing of Japan
1947	The last member of the original Casey family, O'Casey's brother Mick, dies in Dublin	

	Seán O'Casey's Life and Work	Broader Historical Events
1949		The Republic of Ireland Act passes into law, declaring the country a republic with no constitutional ties to the United Kingdom
1950		G. B. Shaw dies
1951		Abbey Theatre is destroyed by a fire during a production of *The Plough and the Stars*. The company plays at the Queen's Theatre instead (the current Abbey Theatre building opens in 1966)
1953		Premiere of Samuel Beckett's *En Attendant Godot* in Paris (the first English language production appears in London two years later). Death of Stalin
1954	O'Casey moves to his final residential address, 3 'Villa Rosa' Flats, 40 Trumlands Road, Torquay	
1955	*The Bishop's Bonfire* is first performed, to protests, at the Gaiety Theatre, Dublin	
1956	O'Casey's son Niall dies on 30 December	Nikita Khrushchev denounces Stalin during the Twentieth Congress of the Communist Part. Suez crisis confirms Britain's post-imperial status. The Hungarian revolution is crushed by the USSR. IRA begins 'border campaign' for a united Ireland

1957	USSR launches 'Sputnik', the first artificial earth satellite. Harold Macmillan – whose family firm publishes O'Casey's work – becomes Conservative Prime Minister of the United Kingdom
1958	O'Casey submits *The Drums of Father Ned* to the Dublin Theatre Festival, but the organizers – under clerical pressure – ask O'Casey to alter the play. He refuses and withdraws the piece, and the festival collapses when Samuel Beckett withdraws work in support. O'Casey's play premieres the following year at Lafayette Little Theatre, Indiana, and he bans professional productions of his work in Ireland
1959	Éamon de Valera retires from Irish government and assumes the largely ceremonial role of Irish President. A new pope, John XXIII, announces the Second Vatican Council, to consider the relationship between the Catholic Church and the modern world
1960	John F. Kennedy, a 43-year-old of Irish descent, becomes president of the United States of America

	Seán O'Casey's Life and Work	Broader Historical Events
1962	One final flurry of new works in production sees *Figuro in the Night* at Hofstra University Playhouse, New York; *The Moon Shines on Kylenamoe* in Amherst College, Massachusetts; and *Behind the Green Curtains* at the University of Rochester, New York State	Cuban missile crisis. Death of Marilyn Monroe
1963		John F. Kennedy assassinated. Harold Macmillan resigns as Prime Minister following the Profumo affair (a sex scandal that involved the Secretary of State for War whose pillow talk was suspected of passing security information to the Soviet Embassy)
1964	*Young Cassidy*, a Hollywood movie based on O'Casey's autobiographies, is filmed in Dublin. O'Casey dies, aged 84	

BIBLIOGRAPHY

Published Sources

Agate, James, *First Nights*. London: Ivor Nicholson and Watson, 1934.

Arrington, Lauren, *W. B. Yeats, the Abbey Theatre, Censorship, and the Irish State*. Oxford: Oxford University Press, 2010.

Atkinson, Brooks, *Sean O'Casey: From Times Past*, ed. Robert G. Lowery. London: Macmillan, 1982.

Atkinson, Brooks and Albert Hirschfeld, *The Lively Years, 1920–1973: A Half Century of the Most Significant Plays on Broadway*. New York: Da Capo, 1985 [1973]. *Authors Take Sides on the Spanish War*. London: Left Review, [1937].

Ayling, Ronald, 'Introduction', in *The Complete Plays of Sean O'Casey: Volume 5*. London: Macmillan, 1984, pp. vii–xxvi.

——, 'Sean O'Casey and the Abbey Theatre, Dublin', in David Krause and Robert Lowery (eds), *Sean O'Casey: Centenary Essays*. Gerrards Cross: Colin Smythe, 1980, pp. 13–40.

——, (ed.), *Sean O'Casey: Modern Judgements*. London: Macmillan, 1969.

——, 'The Origin and Evolution of a Dublin Epic', in Robert G. Lowery (ed.), *Essays on Sean O'Casey's Autobiographies*. London: Macmillan, 1981, pp. 1–34.

Ayling, Ronald, and Michael J. Durkan, *Sean O'Casey: A Bibliography*. London: Macmillan, 1978.

Badiou, Alain, *The Rebirth of History*. London: Verso, 2012.

Bagwell, Philip S., *The Railwaymen: The History of the National Union of Railwaymen*. London: Allen and Unwin, 1963.

Beckett, Samuel, 'The Essential and the Incidental', in Samuel Beckett, *Disjecta: Miscellaneous Writings and a Dramatic Fragment*, ed. Ruby Cohn. London: Calder, 1983, pp. 82–3.

——, *Trilogy*. London: Calder, 1994.

Benson, Frederick R., *Writers in Arms: The Literary Impact of the Spanish Civil War*. London: University of London Press, 1968.

Benstock, Bernard, *Sean O'Casey*. Cranbury: Associated University Presses, 1970.

Bew, Paul, *Ireland: The Politics of Enmity, 1789–2006*. Oxford: Oxford University Press, 2006.

Bigsby, C. W. E., *Arthur Miller: 1915–1962*. London: Weidenfeld and Nicolson, 2008.

Bishop, George Walter, 'Shakespeare Was My Education: Interview with the Author of *The Silver Tassie*', in E. H. Mikhail and John O'Riordan (eds), *The Sting and the Twinkle*. London: Macmillan, 1974, pp. 42–5.

Bladel, Roderick, *Walter Kerr: An Analysis of His Criticism*. Metuchen: Scarecrow, 1976.

Bold, Alan, *Scotland: A Literary Guide*. London: Routledge, 1989.

Bourdieu, Pierre, *Distinction: A Social Critique of the Judgement of Taste*, trans. Richard Nice. London; New York: Routledge, 1984.

Bradby, David, *Modern French Drama 1940–1990*, 2nd edn. Cambridge: Cambridge University Press, 1991.

Bradford, Richard, *The Life of a Long-Distance Writer: The Biography of Alan Sillitoe*. London: Peter Owen, 2008.

Brown, Terence, *The Literature of Ireland: Culture and Criticism*. Cambridge: Cambridge University Press, 2010.

Buchthal, Stanley, and Bernard Comment (eds), *Marilyn Monroe: Fragments, Poems, Intimate Notes, Letters*. London: Harper Collins, 2010.

Burian, Jarka M., *Modern Czech Theatre: Reflector and Conscience of a Nation*. Iowa City: University of Iowa Press, 2000.

Butler, Anthony, 'The Makings of the Man', in Sean McCann (ed.), *The World of Sean O'Casey*. London, Four Square, 1966, pp. 12–29.

Butterworth, Jez, *Jerusalem*. London: Nick Hern, 2009.

Byrne, James P., Philip Coleman and Jason King (eds), *Ireland and the Americas: Culture, Politics and History, a Multidisciplinary Encyclopedia*. Santa Barbara: ABC-CLIO, 2008.

Cairns, David, and Shaun Richards, *Writing Ireland: Nationalism, Colonialism and Literature*. Manchester: Manchester University Press, 1988.

Canaris, Volker, *Peter Zadek: Der Theatermann und Filmemacher*. Munich: Hanser Verlag, 1979.

Carter, Huntly, *The New Spirit in the European Theatre 1914–1924*. London: Ernest Benn, 1925.

Chillingworth, William, *The Religion of Protestants: A Safe Way to Salvation*. London: Mary Clark, 1684.

Cleary, Joe, *Outrageous Fortune: Capital and Culture in Modern Ireland*. Dublin: Field Day, 2007.

Cochran, Charles, *Showman Looks On*. London: Dent, 1945.

Cody, Gabrielle H. and Evert Sprinchorn (eds), *The Columbia Encyclopedia of Modern Drama*, 2 vols. New York: Columbia University Press, 2007.

Croghan, Declan, *Paddy Irishman, Paddy Englishman, and Paddy . . .?* London: Faber, 1999.

Cronin, Bernard Cornelius, *Father Yorke and the Labor Movement in San Francisco, 1900–1910*. Washington: Catholic University of America Press, 1943.

Cronin, Seán, *Frank Ryan: The Search for the Republic*. Dublin: Repsol, 1980.

Dallas, Alex, *The Story of the Irish Church Missions*. London: Society for Irish Church Missions, [1867?].

D'Aubigné, J. H. Merle, *The History of the Great Reformation of the Sixteenth Century in Germany, Switzerland, France, etc.* London: Jarrold, 1873.

De Blaghd, Earnán, *Trasna na Bóinne: Imleabhar 1 de Chuimhní Cinn*. Dublin: Sáiséal agus Dill, 1957.

Deane, Seamus, *Celtic Revivals: Essays in Modern Irish Literature, 1880–1980*. London: Faber, 1985.

—, *Heroic Styles: The Tradition of an Idea*. Derry: Field Day, 1985.

—, 'Irish Politics and O'Casey's Theatre', *Threshold*, 24 (1973), pp. 5–16.

DeGiacomo, Albert J., *T. C. Murray, Dramatist: Voice of Rural Ireland*. Syracuse: Syracuse University Press, 2003.

Fallon, Gabriel, *Sean O'Casey: The Man I Knew.* London: Routledge and Kegan Paul, 1965.

—, 'The House on the North Circular Road: Fragments from a Biography', *Modern Drama*, 4, 3 (1961), pp. 223–33.

Farrell, Brian, 'Labour and the Political Revolution', in Donal Nevin (ed.), *Trade Union Century.* Cork and Dublin: Mercier Press, 1994, pp. 42–53.

Fitz-Simon, Christopher, *Buffoonery and Easy Sentiment: Popular Irish Plays in the Decade Prior to the Opening of the Abbey Theatre.* Dublin: Carysfort Press, 2011.

Foster, R. F., *W. B. Yeats: A Life: II, the Arch Poet.* Oxford: Oxford University Press, 2003.

Fox, R. M., *The History of the Irish Citizen Army.* Dublin: James Duffy, 1943.

Foxe, John, *Foxe's Book of Martyrs*, ed. John Cumming. London: George Virtue, 1844.

Fraser, Murray, *John Bull's Other Homes: State Housing and British Policy in Ireland: 1883–1922.* Liverpool: Liverpool University Press, 1996.

Frazier, Adrian, *Hollywood Irish: John Ford, Abbey Actors and the Irish Revival in Hollywood.* Dublin: Lilliput, 2011.

Gaffney, M. H., *The Stories of Padraic Pearse.* Dublin: Talbot, 1935.

García, Hugo, *The Truth about Spain: Mobilizing British Public Opinion, 1936–1939.* Brighton: Sussex Academic Press, 2010.

Gibbons, Luke, 'Alternative Enlightenments', in Mary Cullen (ed.), *1798: 200 Years of Resonance.* Belfast: Irish Reporter Publications, 1998, pp. 119–27.

Gibson, Andrew, *James Joyce.* London: Reaktion, 2006.

Gould, Warwick and Edna Longley (eds), *Yeats Annual: XII: 'That Accusing Eye': Yeats and his Irish Readers.* Basingstoke: Macmillan, 1996.

Greene, David H., *J. M. Synge 1871–1909.* New York: Macmillan, 1959.

Gregory, Lady Augusta, *Lady Gregory's Journals: Volume 1: Books One to Twenty-Nine*, ed. Daniel Murphy. Gerrards Cross: Colin Smythe, 1978.

—, *Our Irish Theatre.* New York: Knickerbocker, 1913.

Greig, David, *The Strange Undoing of Prudencia Hart.* London: Faber, 2011.

Grene, Nicholas, 'The Class of the Clitheroes: O'Casey's Revisions to *The Plough and the Stars* Promptbook', *Bullán: An Irish Studies Journal*, 4, 2 (1999/2000), pp. 57–66.

—, *The Politics of Irish Drama: Plays in Context from Boucicault to Friel.* Cambridge: Cambridge University Press, 1999.

Hall, Stuart, 'Cultural Studies and the Crisis of the Humanities', *October*, 53 (1990), pp. 11–23.

Harris, Peter James, *Sean O'Casey's Letters and Autobiographies: Reflections of a Radical Ambivalence.* Trier: Wissenschaftlicher Verlag Trier, 2004.

Harris, Susan Canon, 'Red Star versus Green Goddess: Sean O'Casey's "The Star Turns Red" and the Politics of Form', *Princeton University Library Chronicle*, 68, 1/2 (2007), pp. 357–98.

Heaney, Seamus, 'Introduction', in *Sean O'Casey: Plays 1.* London: Faber, 1998, pp. vii–x.

Higgins, Roisín, *Transforming 1916: Meaning, Memory and the Fiftieth Anniversary of the Easter Rising.* Cork: Cork University Press, 2012.

Hogan, Robert, 'O'Casey, Influence and Impact', *Irish University Review*, 10, 1 (1980), pp. 146–58.

—, *The Experiments of Sean O'Casey.* New York: St Martin's Press, 1960.

Hogan, Robert and Richard Burnham (eds), *The Years of O'Casey, 1921–1926: A Documentary History*. Gerrards Cross: Colin Smythe, 1992.

Holloway, Joseph, *Joseph Holloway's Abbey Theatre: A Selection from his Unpublished Journal*, ed. Robert Hogan and Michael J. O'Neill. London: Feffer and Simons, 1967.

Holroyd, Michael, *Bernard Shaw: Vol. 1: 1856–1898: The Search for Love*. London: Chatto and Windus, 1988.

Hunt, Hugh, *Seán O'Casey*. Dublin: Gill and Macmillan, 1980.

Ingman, Heather, *Twentieth Century Fiction by Irish Women: Nation and Gender*. Aldershot: Ashgate, 2007.

Jones, Nesta, *File on O'Casey*. London: Methuen, 1986.

Jordan, John, 'Illusion and Actuality in the Later O'Casey', in Ronald Ayling (ed.), *Sean O'Casey: Modern Judgements*. London: Macmillan, 1969, pp. 143–61.

—, 'The Passionate Autodidact: The Importance of 'Litera Scripta' for O'Casey', *Irish University Review*, 10, 1 (1980), pp. 59–76.

Joyce, James, *Stephen Hero*. New York: New Directions, 1963.

—, *Ulysses*, ed. Declan Kiberd. London: Penguin, 1992.

Kavanagh, Peter, *The Story of the Abbey Theatre*. New York: Devin-Adair, 1950.

Kearns, Kevin C., *Dublin Tenement Life: An Oral History*. Dublin: Gill and Macmillan, 1994.

Kenneally, Michael, *Portraying the Self: Sean O'Casey and the Art of Autobiography*. Gerrards Cross: Colin Smythe, 1988.

—, 'Review of Christopher Murray's *Sean O'Casey: Writer at Work*', *Irish University Review*, 35, 1 (2005), pp. 211–16.

Kennedy, Robert E., *The Irish: Emigration, Marriage, and Fertility*. Berkeley: University of California Press, 1973.

Kennelly, Brendan, 'Sean O'Casey's Journey into Joy', in Micheál Ó hAodha (ed.), *The O'Casey Enigma*. Dublin: Mercier, 1980, pp. 98–111.

Kershaw, Baz Jane Milling, Peter Thomson and Joseph Donohue (eds), *The Cambridge History of British Theatre*, 3 vols. Cambridge: Cambridge University Press, 2004.

Kiberd, Declan, *Inventing Ireland*. London: Jonathan Cape, 1995.

Knight, G. Wilson, *The Golden Labyrinth: A Study of British Drama*. London: Phoenix, 1962.

Kosok, Heinz, *Plays and Playwrights from Ireland in International Perspective*. Trier: Wissenschaftlicher Verlag Trier, 1995.

Krause, David, 'Introduction', in O'Casey, *The Letters of Sean O'Casey: Volume IV, 1959–64*, ed. David Krause. Washington: Catholic University of America Press, 1992, pp. ix–xx.

—, *Sean O'Casey and His World*. London: Thames and Hudson, 1976.

—, *Sean O'Casey: The Man and His Work*. London: MacGibbon and Kee, 1967.

—, 'Some Truths and Jokes about the Easter Rising', *Sean O'Casey Review*, 3, 1 (1976), pp. 3–23.

—, 'Text and Acknowledgments', in Sean O'Casey, *The Letters of Sean O'Casey: Volume IV, 1959–64*, ed. David Krause. Washington: Catholic University of America Press, 1992, pp. xxi–xxvi.

Larkin, Emmet, *James Larkin: Irish Labour Leader 1876–1947*. London: Routledge and Kegan Paul, 1965.

Lawrence, D. H., *The Plumed Serpent*, ed. L. D. Clark. Cambridge: Cambridge University Press, 1987.

Lazarus, Arnold Leslie, (ed.), *A George Jean Nathan Reader*. Cranbury: Associated University Presses, 1990.

Lee, Joseph, *The Modernisation of Irish Society*. Dublin: Gill and Macmillan, 1989.

Lehrman, Leonard, *Marc Blitzstein: A Bio-Bibliography*. London: Praeger, 2005.

Levins Boyd, Maureen, 'An Interview with Hal Prince on *Grandchild of Kings*', *The Canadian Journal of Irish Studies*, 19, 1 (1993), pp. 79–85.

Liehm, Antonín J., *Closely Watched Films: The Czechoslovak Experience*. International Arts and Sciences Press, 1974.

Linehan, Thomas P., *British Fascism, 1918–39: Parties, Ideology and Culture*. Manchester: Manchester University Press, 2000.

Looby, Robert, 'Looking for the Censor in the Works of Sean O'Casey (and Others) in Polish Translation', *Translation and Literature*, 17, 1 (2008), pp. 47–64.

Lowery, Robert G., 'A Tribute', *The Sean O'Casey Review*, 1, 1 (1974), p. 4.

—, 'Introduction', in Robert G. Lowery (ed.), *Essays on Sean O'Casey's Autobiographies*. London: Macmillan, 1981, pp. xi–xviii.

—, 'O'Casey, Sean', in James McGuire and James Quinn (eds), *Dictionary of Irish Biography*, 9 vols. Cambridge: RIA/Cambridge University Press, 2009, VII, pp. 167–70.

—, 'The Development of Sean O'Casey's Weltanschauung', in Robert G. Lowery (ed.) *Essays on Sean O'Casey's Autobiographies*. London: Macmillan, 1981, pp. 62–88.

Mac Anna, Tomás, 'O'Casey's Toy Theatre', in Micheál Ó hAodha (ed.), *The O'Casey Enigma*. Dublin: Mercier, 1980, pp. 7–19.

Mac Conghail, Fiach, *April–September 2010 Abbey Theatre Programme*. Dublin: Abbey Theatre, 2010.

Malone, Andrew E., 'O'Casey's Photographic Realism', in Ronald Ayling (ed.), *Sean O'Casey: Modern Judgments*. London: Macmillan, 1968, pp. 68–75.

—, *The Irish Drama*. London: Constable, 1929.

Mamet, David, *Theatre*. New York: Faber, 2010.

Manning, Maurice, *The Blueshirts*. Dublin: Gill and Macmillan, 1970.

Margulies, Martin B., *The Early Life of Sean O'Casey*. Dublin: Dolmen, 1970.

Martin, Augustine, 'What Stalked through the Post Office?', *Crane Bag*, 2, 1/2 (1978), pp. 164–77.

McCann, Sean (ed.), *The World of Sean O'Casey*. London, Four Square, 1966.

McCourt, Frank, *'Tis: A Memoir*. London: Flamingo, 1999.

McDonald, Rónán, *Tragedy and Irish Literature: Synge, O'Casey, Beckett*. London: Macmillan, 2002.

McDonald, Walter, *Reminiscences of a Maynooth Professor*, ed. Denis Gwynn. London: Jonathan Cape, 1925.

McGarry, Fearghal, *Irish Politics and the Spanish Civil War*. Cork: Cork University Press, 1999.

—, *The Rising: Ireland: Easter 1916*. Oxford: Oxford University Press, 2010.

McGrath, John, *A Good Night Out: Popular Theatre: Audience, Class and Form*, 2nd edn. London: Nick Hern, 1996.

McWilliams, David, *The Pope's Children: Ireland's New Elite*. London: Pan Macmillan, 2005.

Mencken, H. L., 'Preface', in Arnold Leslie Lazarus (ed.), *A George Jean Nathan Reader*. Cranbury: Associated University Presses, 1990, pp. 12–14.

Mercier, Vivian, 'Literature in English 1921–84', in J. R. Hill (ed.), *A New History of Ireland*, Oxford: Oxford University Press, 2003, pp. 487–536.

Merriman, Victor, *Because We Are Poor: Irish Theatre in the 1990s*. Dublin: Carysfort Press, 2011.

—, 'To Sleep is Safe; to Dream is Dangerous: Catholicism on Stage in Twentieth-Century Ireland', in Eamon Maher and Eugene O'Brien (eds), *Breaking The Mould: Literary Representations of Irish Catholicism*. Bern: Peter Lang, 2011, pp. 193–212.

Miller, Arthur, 'Introduction', in *Sean O'Casey: Plays 2*. London: Faber, 1998, pp. vii–xi.

Miller, Neil, *Banned in Boston: The Watch and Ward Society's Crusade Against Books*. Boston: Beacon, 2010.

Mitchell, Jack, *The Essential O'Casey: A Study of the Twelve Major Plays of Sean O'Casey*. New York: International Publishers, 1980.

Mooney, Ria, 'Playing Rosie Redmond', *Journal of Irish Literature*, 4, 2 (1977), pp. 21–7.

Moran, James, 'Moving-Pictures in the Hallway: Dramatising the Autobiographies of Seán O'Casey', *Irish Studies Review*, 20, 4 (2012), pp. 389–405.

—, *Staging the Easter Rising: 1916 as Theatre*. Cork: Cork University Press, 2005.

Morash, Christopher, *A History of Irish Theatre, 1601–2000*. Cambridge: Cambridge University Press, 2002.

—, '"Something's Missing": Theatre and the Republic of Ireland Act, 1949', in Ray Ryan (ed.), *Writing in the Irish Republic: Literature, Culture, Politics 1949–1999*. Basingstoke: Macmillan, 2000, pp. 64–81.

Murray, Christopher, 'O'Casey, Sean' in Gabrielle H. Cody and Evert Sprinchorn (eds), *The Columbia Encyclopedia of Modern Drama*, 2 vols. New York: Columbia University Press, 2007, pp. 982–6.

—, *Sean O'Casey: Writer at Work: A Biography*. Dublin: Gill and Macmillan, 2004.

—, *Twentieth Century Irish Drama: Mirror Up to Nation*. Manchester: Manchester University Press, 1997.

Nathan, George Jean, *My Very Dear Sean: George Jean Nathan to Sean O'Casey: Letters and Articles*, ed. Robert G. Lowery and Patricia Angelin. Rutherford: Fairleigh Dickinson University Press, 1985.

Nevin, Donal (ed.), *James Larkin: Lion of the Fold*. Dublin: Gill and Macmillan, 1998.

Nic Shiubhlaigh, Máire, *The Splendid Years*. Dublin: James Duffy, 1955.

Nicholson, Hubert, 'O'Casey's Horn of Plenty', in Ronald Ayling (ed.), *Sean O'Casey: Modern Judgements*. London: Macmillan, 1969, pp. 207–20.

O'Brien, Paul, 'Sean O'Casey and the Abbey Theatre', in *Echoes Down the Corridor: Irish Theatre – Past, Present, and Future*, ed. Patrick Lonergan and Riana O'Dwyer. Dublin: Carysfort, 2007, pp. 69–80.

O'Casey, Eileen, *Sean*. London: Macmillan, 1972.

O'Casey, Sean, *Autobiographies*, 3 vols. London: Faber, 2011.

—, *Blasts and Benedictions*, ed. Ronald Ayling. London: Macmillan, 1967.

—, [Seán O Cathasaigh], *More Wren Songs*. Dublin: Fergus O'Connor, [1918?].

—, *Niall: A Lament*. London: Calder, 1991.

—, 'Preface', in Bonar Thompson, *Hyde Park Orator*. London: Jarrolds, 1934, pp. ix–xiii.

—, [Sean O Cathasaigh], *Songs of the Wren, by Sean O Cathasaigh, Author of 'The Grand Oul' Dame Brittannia [sic]: Humorous and Sentimental*. Dublin: Fergus O'Connor, [1918].

—, *The Complete Plays of Sean O'Casey*, 5 vols. London: Macmillan, 1984.

—, *The Flying Wasp*. London: Macmillan, 1937.

—, *The Green Crow*. London: Comet, 1987 [1957].

—, *The Harvest Festival: A Play in Three Acts*. Gerrards Cross: Colin Smythe, 1980.

—, *The Letters of Sean O'Casey*, ed. David Krause, 4 vols. London and Washington: Macmillan and Catholic University Press, 1975–92.

—, *The Silver Tassie: A Tragi-Comedy in Four Acts*. London: Macmillan, 1928.

—, [P O Cathasaigh], *The Story of the Irish Citizen Army*. Dublin: Maunsel, 1919.

—, [Sean O Cathasaigh], *The Story of Thomas Ashe*. Dublin: Fergus O'Connor, 1917.

—, *Three Dublin Plays*. London: Faber, 2000.

—, *Under a Coloured Cap: Articles Merry and Mournful with Comments and a Song*. London: Macmillan, 1963.

—, *Windfalls: Stories, Poems, and Plays*. London: Macmillan, 1934.

—, *Within the Gates*. London: Macmillan, 1933.

O'Connor, Garry, *Sean O'Casey: A Life*. London: Hodder and Stoughton, 1988.

O'Connor, Joseph, *Ghost Light*. London: Harvill Secker, 2010.

O'Connor, Patrick, 'Theatre', *The Furrow*, 16, 10 (October 1965), pp. 631–33.

O'Faoláin, Seán, 'The Strange Case of Sean O'Casey', *The Bell*, 6, 2 (1943), p. 118.

O'Riordan, John, *A Guide to O'Casey's Plays: From the Plough to the Stars*. London: Macmillan, 1984.

O'Toole, Fintan, *After the Ball*. Dublin: TASC at New Island, 2003.

—, *Ship of Fools: How Stupidity and Corruption Sank the Celtic Tiger*. London: Faber, 2009.

Owen, Wilfred, *Collected Poems of Wilfred Owen*, ed. Cecil Day Lewis. London: Chatto and Windus, 1963.

Pearse, Patrick, *Collected Works of Padraic H. Pearse: Political Writings and Speeches*. Dublin: Maunsel, 1922.

Pittock, Malcolm, *Ernst Toller*. Boston: Twayne, 1979.

Prince, Harold, *Grandchild of Kings*. London and Toronto: Samuel French, 1993.

Pugh, Martin, *'Hurrah for the Blackshirts!': Fascists and Fascism in Britain between the Wars*. London: Jonathan Cape, 2005.

Redman, Mark and Merit Mikk, *Country Profile on Rural Characteristics: Romania*. Frankfurt am Main: RUDI/Seventh Framework Programme for Research and Technological Development of the European Commission, 2008.

Ricks, Christopher, *Tennyson*, 2nd edn. Berkeley/Los Angeles: University of California Press, 1989.

Robinson, Lennox, *Ireland's Abbey Theatre: A History 1899–1951*. London: Sidgwick and Jackson, 1951.

Bibliography

Rose, William Ganson, *Cleveland: the Making of a City*. Kent: Kent State University Press, 1990.

Ross, Shane, *The Bankers*. Dublin: Penguin Ireland, 2009.

Ross, Shane and Nick Webb, *Wasters*. Dublin: Penguin Ireland, 2010.

Ryan, John, 'The Founder of Muintir na Tíre: John M. Canon Hayes 1887–1957', *Studies: An Irish Quarterly Review*, 46, 183 (1957), pp. 312–21.

Said, Edward, 'Yeats and Decolonization', in *Nationalism*, in Seamus Deane (ed.), *Colonialism and Literature*. Minneapolis: University of Minnesota Press, 1990, pp. 69–95.

Samuel, Raphael, Ewan MacColl and Stuart Cosgrove, *Theatres of the Left: 1880–1935: Workers' Theatre Movements in Britain and America*. London: Routledge and Kegan Paul, 1985.

Sbrockey, Karen, 'Something of a Hero: An Interview with Roddy Doyle', *TLR: The Literary Review*, 42, 4 (1999), pp. 537–52.

Schrank, Bernice, 'In the Aftermath of the Spanish Civil War: A Previously Unpublished Letter from Sean O'Casey to the Veterans of the Abraham Lincoln Brigade', *Canadian Journal of Irish Studies*, 25, 1/2 (1999), pp. 216–18.

—, 'Performing Political Opposition: Sean O'Casey's Late Plays and the Demise of Eamon de Valera', *BELLS: Barcelona English Language and Literature*, 11 (2000), pp. 199–206.

—, *Sean O'Casey: A Research and Production Sourcebook*. Westport: Greenwood, 1996.

Scrimgeour, James R., *Sean O'Casey*. London: George Prior, 1978.

Siegmeister, Elie, Edward Mabley and Sean O'Casey, *The Plough and the Stars: Opera in Three Acts*. New York: MCA, 1970.

Shakespeare, William, *Julius Caesar*, ed. T. S. Dorsch, in Richard Proudfoot, Ann Thompson and David Scott Kastan (eds) *The Arden Shakespeare Complete Works*, London: Thomson, 2001, pp. 333–60.

—, *Richard III*, ed. E. A. J. Honigmann, rev. edn. Harmondsworth, Penguin, 1995.

Shaw, George Bernard, *The Complete Plays of Bernard Shaw*. London: Paul Hamlyn, 1965.

—, *John Bull's Other Island*. Harmondsworth: Penguin, 1984.

Shelley, Percy Bysshe, *The Major Works*, ed. Zachary Leader and Michael O'Neill. Oxford: Oxford University Press, 2003.

Shields, Arthur, and J. M. Kerrigan, 'Great Days at the Abbey', in E. H. Mikhail (ed.), *The Abbey Theatre: Interviews and Recollections*, Houndmills, Macmillan, 1988, pp. 133–5.

Shyre, Paul, *Drums Under the Windows*. New York: Dramatists Play Service, 1962.

—, *I Knock at the Door*. New York: Dramatists Play Service, 1958.

—, *Pictures in the Hallway*. New York: Samuel French, 1956.

Singleton, Brian, 'The Revival Revised' in Shaun Richards (ed), *The Cambridge Companion to Irish Drama*. Cambridge: Cambridge University Press, 2004, pp. 258–70.

Simmons, James, *Sean O'Casey*. London and Basingstoke: Macmillan, 1983.

Smyth, Gerry, *Decolonisation and Criticism*. London: Pluto Press, 1998.

Songs of Ireland and Other Lands. New York: D.J. Sadlier, 1847.

Spoo, Robert, '"Nestor" and the Nightmare: The Presence of the Great War in *Ulysses*', *Twentieth Century Literature*, 32, 2 (1986), 137–54.

Stapelberg, Peter, *Sean O'Casey und das Deutschsprachige Theater (1948–1974)*. Frankfurt am Main: Peter Lang, 1979.

Styan, J. L., *Modern Drama in Theory and Practice: Expressionism and Epic Theatre*. Cambridge: Cambridge University Press, 1981.

Szalczer, Eszter, 'A Modernist Dramaturgy', in Michael Robinson (ed.), *The Cambridge Companion to August Strindberg*. Cambridge: Cambridge University Press, 2009, pp. 93–106.

Thompson, W., *The Sacrifice of the Mass Considered. A Discourse Delivered at Christ Church, Cork . . . March 17, 1830*. Cork: Bleakley, 1830.

Thorpe, D. R., *Supermac: The Life of Harold Macmillan*. London: Pimlico, 2011.

Tóibín, Colm, *Beauty in a Broken Place*. Dublin: Lilliput, 2004.

Tolan, Padraig, 'Sean O'Casey', *New Theatre Quarterly*, 8, 4 (1992), p. 396.

Toller, Ernst, *Masses and Man: A Fragment of the Social Revolution of the Twentieth Century*, trans. Vera Mendel. London: Nonesuch, 1923.

Utley, Frieda, *Lost Illusion*. London: Allen & Unwin, 1949.

Walsh, Caroline, *The Homes of Irish Writers*. Dublin: Anvil, 1982.

Walsh, Townsend, *The Career of Dion Boucicault*. New York: Dunlap, 1915.

Walter, Bronwen, *Outsiders Inside: Whiteness, Place and Irish Women*. London: Routledge, 1998.

Watson, George, *Irish Identity and the Literary Revival*. Washington: Catholic University of America Press, 1994 [1979].

Weigel, Alexander, *Das Deutsche theater: eine Geschichte in Bildern*. Berlin: Propyläen, 1999.

Welch, Dave, *Staying after School with Frank McCourt* <www.powells.com/blog/original-essays/staying-after-school-with-frank-mccourt-by-dave/>.

Welch, Robert, *The Abbey Theatre, 1899–1999: Form and Pressure*. Oxford: Oxford University Press, 1999.

White, J. R., *Misfit: An Autobiography*. London: Jonathan Cape, 1930.

Wilhelm, James J., *Ezra Pound in London and Paris, 1908–1925*. University Park: Pennsylvania State University Press, 1990.

Willett, John, *The New Sobriety: Art and Politics in the Weimar Period 1917–33*. London: Thames & Hudson, 1987.

Williams, Raymond, *Drama from Ibsen to Brecht*. London: Hogarth Press, 1993.

—, 'The Writer: Commitment and Alignment', in John Higgins (ed.), *The Raymond Williams Reader*. Oxford: Blackwell, 2001, pp. 208–18.

Wills, Clair, *Dublin 1916: The Siege of the GPO*. London: Profile, 2009.

Worth, Katharine, *The Irish Drama of Europe from Yeats to Beckett*. London: Athlone Press, 1978.

Yeates, Padraig, *Lockout: Dublin 1913*. Dublin: Gill and Macmillan, 2000.

Yeats, W. B., 'Introduction', in W. B. Yeats (ed.), *The Oxford Book of Modern Verse 1892–1935*. Oxford: Clarendon Press, 1936, pp. v–xlii.

—, *The Collected Works of W. B. Yeats: Volume I: The Poems*, ed. Richard J. Finneran, rev. edn. Houndmills: Macmillan, 1991.

—, *The Collected Works of W. B. Yeats: Volume II: The Plays*, ed. David R. Clark and Rosalind E. Clark. Houndmills: Palgrave, 2001.

Zadek, Peter, *My Way*. Cologne: Kiepenheuer and Witsch, 1998.

Newspaper Sources

'A Reigning Success', *Irish Times*, 9 July 1884, p. 2.

'Abbey "Deteriorating"', *Irish Times*, 4 July 1964, p. 24.

'Abbey Play Controversy', *Irish Times*, 5 June 1928, p. 7.

'Abbey Production of O'Casey Play: Revelations by a Director of the Theatre', *Irish Independent*, 29 August 1935, p. 5.

'Abbey Theatre', *Irish Times*, 14 September 1926, p. 3.

'Abbey Theatre Scene', *Irish Times*, 12 February 1926, p. 7.

'An Irishman's Diary', *Irish Times*, 17 March 1960, p. 6.

Anikst, A., 'A Most Extraordinary Spectacle', *Current Digest of the Russian Press*, 6 October 1965, pp. 9–13.

'Another Outbreak by Mr. O'Casey', *Irish Independent*, 20 September 1952, p. 4.

'At the Play', *Observer*, 10 January 1926, p. 11.

Atkinson, Brooks, 'A Coupl'a Irishmen', *New York Times*, 4 December 1927, p. X1.

—, 'Critic Recalls the Dramatist as 'a Darlin' Man', *New York Times*, 19 September 1964, p. 1.

—, 'The Play', *New York Times*, 23 October 1934, p. 23.

'Attitude to O'Casey Plays "Quite Absurd"', *Irish Times*, 29 January 1966, p. 7.

'Award of Hawthornden Prize', *Irish Times*, 24 March 1926, p. 7.

Ayling, Ronald, 'Sean O'Casey and the Abbey Theatre', *Manchester Guardian*, 5 August 1958, p. 4.

'Blonde No. 1 Makes a Hit', *Irish Times*, 28 July 1956, p. 3.

Boell, Heinrich, 'Wilde Poesie Der Flüche', *Der Spiegel*, 24 November 1969, p. 204.

'Boston Mayor Bans "Within the Gates"', *New York Times*, 16 January 1935, p. 20.

Brantley, Ben, 'A Mother Whose Life Song Is About Tenement Nightmares, Not Broadway Dreams', *New York Times*, 29 March 2008, http://theater.nytimes.com/2008/03/29/theater/reviews/29juno.html?ref=garry_hynes.

Brown, Ivor, 'The Week's Theatres', *Observer*, 11 February 1934, p. 15.

Child, Harold Hannyngton, 'Johnny Casside Grows Up', *Times Literary Supplement*, 7 March 1942, p. 118.

Clarke, Austin, 'Cock-a-Doodle Dandy', *Irish Times*, 6 November 1954, p. 6.

—, 'Mr. O'Casey in London', *Times Literary Supplement*, 1 August 1952, p. 502.

—, 'Och, Johnny, I Hardly Knew Ye!', *Irish Times*, 29 January 1949, p. 6.

—, 'Tales from Dublin', *Times Literary Supplement*, 6 September 1963, p. 674.

—, 'The Making of a Dramatist', *Times Literary Supplement*, 4 March 1939, p. 131.

'Clontarf v. Dublin University', *Irish Times*, 19 January 1914, p. 4.

Coker, Katherine, 'I Knock at Sean O'Casey's Door', *New York Times*, 3 December 1972, p. D17.

Cookman, Anthony Victor, 'Self-Expression', *Times Literary Supplement*, 5 November 1954, p. 699.

—, 'The Unfulfilled Nation', *Times Literary Supplement*, 17 November 1945, p. 548.

—, 'Vale Atque Ave', *Times Literary Supplement*, 19 February 1949, p. 115.

Corry, John, 'O'Casey Centenary Fans Flames of His Works', *New York Times*, 26 March 1980, p. C26.

'Crucifix Poster', *Manchester Guardian*, 5 March 1937, p. 11.

Daily Chronicle, 20 September 1927, cutting in NLI, Seán O'Casey Papers, MS 38,149/2.

Daily Sketch, 12 October 1929, cutting in NLI, Seán O'Casey Papers, MS 38,149/1.

'1986: Das Ende vom Anfang', *Berliner Morgenpost*, 19 June 2008, <www.morgenpost.de/ printarchiv/infoscan/article571586/1986-Das-Ende-vom-Anfang.html>.

Deane, Seamus, 'Fact and Fury', *Guardian*, 6 January 2001, p. B3.

—, Seamus, 'Roddy's Troubles', *Guardian*, 4 September 1999, p. B8.

'Dominican's Protest', *Standard: An Irish Organ of Catholic Opinion*, 16 August 1935, p. 3.

'Drama and the Reputation of the Dead', *Irish Times*, 2 November 2004, <www.irishtimes. com/newspaper/letters/2004/1102/1097847332631.html>.

Ervine, St John, 'At the Play', *Observer*, 16 May 1926, p. 4.

—, 'At the Play: Why do Good Plays Fail?', *Observer*, 1 March 1936, p. 15.

Fallon, Gabriel, 'Sean O'Casey', *Irish Times*, 18 March 1960, p. 9.

—, 'To Irish Press', 30 March 1955, reprinted in O'Casey, *The Letters of Sean O'Casey: Volume III, 1955–58*, ed. David Krause. Washington: Catholic University of America Press, 1989, p. 98.

Foley, Donal, 'O'Casey Play Withdrawn after Objections by Lord Chamberlain', *Irish Times*, 19 July 1963, p. 1.

'Football', *Irish Times*, 1 April 1913, p. 4.

'Football', *Irish Times*, 2 November 1912, p. 6.

'Football', *Irish Times*, 18 October 1913, p. 4.

'Football', *Irish Times*, 23 October 1911, p. 4.

'Football', *Irish Times*, 27 January 1914, p. 4.

'Fr. O'Flanagan on Spain', *Irish Times*, 12 November 1938, p. 15.

'Frank Apology Wanted', *Irish Independent*, 13 September 1935, p. 7.

John Freedman, 'Interview with Dodin', *Moscow Times*, 1 July 2000, available in English translation at <http://afronord.tripod.com/thr/dodin.html>.

Funke, Lewis, 'Theatre: Self-Portrait', *New York Times*, 17 September 1956, p. 23.

Gaffney, M. H., 'Readers' Views: "The Silver Tassie"', *Irish Press*, 12 September 1935, p. 6.

'Gaiety Theatre', *Irish Times*, 19 December 1893, p. 5.

'GBS Speaks Out of the Whirlwind', *The Listener*, 7 March 1934, reprinted in O'Casey, *Blasts and Benedictions*. London: Macmillan, 1967, pp. 198–9.

Gelb, Arthur, 'Campaigner in the Cause of Sean O'Casey', *New York Times*, 25 September 1960, p. X1.

Gilman, Richard, 'The Letters of Sean O'Casey', *New York Times*, 16 March 1975, p. BR1.

Gribachev, Nikolai, 'Literature and the Present', *Izvestia*, 2 April 1958, pp. 32–3.

Grimes, William, 'Frank McCourt, Whose Irish Childhood Illuminated His Prose, Is Dead at 78', *New York Times*, 19 July 2009, <www.nytimes.com/2009/07/20/ books/20mccourt.html>.

'Gunman' to Stay at the Abbey', *Irish Times*, 26 August 1964, p. 4.

Gussow, Mel, 'Theater: Shyre's Winning O'Casey', *New York Times*, 30 April 1971, p. 50.

'Hansa Theater Heiterer Oktober: Komödien, Slapstick, Evergreens', 29 July 2002, *Berliner Zeitung* <www.berliner-zeitung.de/archiv/chaos-putzt-mit-hansa-theater-heiterer-oktober–komoedien–slapstick–evergreens,10810590,10031630.html>.

Héliot, Armelle, 'O'Casey, populaire, politique, poétique', *Le Figaro*, 20 February 2009, p. 32.

Hetrick, Adam, 'Tony Winner Shyre's *I Knock at the Door & Pictures in the Hallway* Begin NY Run Nov 24', 24 November 2007, <www.playbill.com/news/article/112987-Tony-Winner-Shyres-I-Knock-At-the-Door-Pictures-in-the-Hallway-Begin-NY-Run-Nov-24>.

Hogan, Robert, 'O'Casey's Court', *Irish Times*, 23 February 1957, p. 6.

Holden, Stephen, 'Gentler 'Juno' but it Sings', *New York Times*, 6 November 1992, p. C6.

Hynes, Garry, '"The Plough" at the Abbey', *The Irish Times*, 23 May 1991, p. 11.

'Ireland's Roll of Honour', *Irish Times*, 28 August 1915, p. 7.

Irish Independent, 1 June 1915, p. 6.

Irish Independent, 8 January 1949, p. 4.

Irish Times, 12 November 2011, <www.irishtimes.com/newspaper/ireland/2011/1112/1224307460318.html>.

Irish Times, 17 November 1921, p. 5.

Irish Times, 28 July 1958, p. 1.

Irish Times, 30 March 1960, p. 8.

Isakov, Boris, 'About Depraved Tastes and a Sense of Responsibility', *Current Digest of the Russian Press*, 13 February 1957, pp. 9–11.

Jackson, T. A., *Sunday Worker*, 24 June 1928, p. 8.

Johnson, Paul, 'Genius of the Terrible Tongue', *Times Literary Supplement*, 6 May 1988, p. 495.

Johnston, Denis, 'Sean O'Casey: An Appreciation', *Daily Telegraph*, 11 March 1926, in Ronald Ayling (ed.), *Sean O'Casey, Modern Judgments*. London: Macmillan, 1969, pp. 82–5.

'"Julius Caesar" at the Gaiety', *Irish Times*, 6 March 1894, p. 6.

'Juno and the Paycock', *Irish Times*, 4 March 1924, p. 4.

Kenny, Enda, 'This is a Republic, Not the Vatican', *Irish Times*, 21 July 2011 <www.irishtimes.com/newspaper/opinion/2011/0721/1224301061733.html>.

Kerr, Walter, 'Where O'Casey's Career Went Wrong', *New York Times*, 2 February 1969, p. D1.

'"Kikeriki" von Sean O'Casey am Deutschen Theater Berlin, Regie Rolf Winkelgrund', *Neues Deutschland*, 2 December 1986, <www.berliner-schauspielschule.de/kikeriki.htm>.

Lemarchand, Jacques, *Le Figaro Litteraire*, 12 May 1962, reprinted in Nesta Jones, *File on O'Casey*. London: Methuen, 1986, p. 32.

Leonard, Hugh, 'Hugh Leonard's Log', *Sunday Independent*, 11 June 1989, cutting in the Abbey Theatre Archive, Box 52, *Purple Dust* 1989.

—, 'Not While I'm Eating', *Sunday Independent*, 19 May 1991, p. 3L.

Linehan, Fergus, 'Boylesday', *Irish Times*, 18 June 1962, p. 8.

Liverpool Post, 22 September 1927, in NLI, Seán O'Casey Papers, MS 38,149/2.

'London Letter', *Irish Times*, 28 June 1962, p. 7.

Mac Conghail, Fiach, 'I am bemused', *Irish Times*, 3 April 2008, <www.irishtimes.com/newspaper/features/2008/0403/1207113944836_pf.html>.

Magel, Eva-Maria, 'Männer in Schürzen: Sean O'Caseys "Das Ende vom Anfang" in Wiesbaden', *Frankfurter Allgemeine Zeitung*, 17 June 2002, p. 59.

Massiani, Martial, 'But nothing happened at new 'Lourdes', *Universe*, cutting in NLI, Seán O'Casey Papers, MS 38,149/2.

Miles, Alice, 'Shocked by Slumdog's Poverty Porn', *The Times*, 14 January 2009, <www. timesonline.co.uk/tol/comment/columnists/guest_contributors/article5511650.ece>.

'Month in Gaol for a Kiss', *Irish Press*, 15 January 1944, p. 1.

'Mr De Valera Criticises Midland Cities: Irishmen Said to be Living in "Appalling" Conditions', *Birmingham Post*, 29 August 1951, p. 1.

'Mr O'Casey's Latest', *Irish Independent*, 14 March 1939, p. 6.

'Mr O'Casey's Memoirs', *Irish Independent*, 12 November 1945, p. 4.

'Mr O'Casey's New Play', *Irish Times*, 21 April 1928, p. 6.

'Mr O'Casey's New Play', *Observer*, 3 June 1928, p. 19.

'Mr Sean O'Casey's New Play', *The Times*, 1 March 1955, p. 6.

Na Gopaleen, Myles, 'Cruiskeen Lawn', *Irish Times*, 19 February 1958, p. 6.

'New Play by Sean O'Casey', *Irish Times*, 24 April 1928, p. 4.

New York Times, 2 October 1957, p. 27.

'No Beckett Plays for Tostal', *Irish Times*, 17 February 1958, p. 1.

Norris, David, 'Iconic Marriage of Yeats and Pearse in Abbey GPO', *Irish Times*, 15 October 2009, <www.irishtimes.com/newspaper/opinion/2009/1015/1224256681742.html>.

O'Casey, Sean, 'A Miner's Dream of Home', *New Statesman*, 28 July 1934, p. 124.

—, 'Always the Plow and the Stars', *New York Times*, 25 January 1953, p. BR1.

—, 'Letters to the Editor: "The Bishop's Bonfire"', *Irish Times*, 23 March 1955, p. 5.

—, [An Gall Fada], 'Sound the Loud Trumpet', *The Peasant and Irish Ireland*, 25 May 1907, reprinted in Sean O'Casey, *Feathers from the Green Crow*, ed. Robert Hogan. London: Macmillan, 1963, pp. 2–6.

'O'Casey Agrees to Allow Abbey to Stage His Plays', *Irish Times*, 14 March 1964, p. 12.

'O'Casey and the Abbey', *Irish Times*, 25 April 1962, p. 9.

'O'Casey Bans Festival Production', *Irish Times*, 24 August 1961, p. 6.

'O'Casey, by Himself', *Irish Independent*, 30 October 1954, p. 6.

'O'Casey Cut in TV Film Condemned', *Irish Times*, 21 March 1960, p. 4.

'O'Casey: Geballte Faust', *Der Spiegel*, 12 July 1970, p. 209.

'O'Casey One-Act Play to be Televised', *Irish Times*, 25 June 1962, p. 1.

'O'Casey's New Play Rejected', *Irish Times*, 4 June 1928, p. 8.

O'Connor, T. P., 'Men, Women, and Memories', *The Sunday Times*, 4 April 1926, p. 9.

'Old Acquaintances: Kortner Scandal in Berlin', *AJR Information: Association of Jewish Refugees in Great Britain*, August 1953, p. 5.

Olden, G. A., 'O'Casey at Home', *Irish Times*, 1 October 1959, p. 6.

—, 'Radio Review', *Irish Times*, 28 October 1954, p. 6.

Orwell, George, 'The Green Flag', *Observer*, 28 October 1945, p. 3.

O'Toole, Fintan, 'Course of True Theatre Never Should Run Smooth', *Irish Times*, 8 October 2011 <www.irishtimes.com/newspaper/weekend/2011/1008/1224305440357.html>.

—, 'Finding a new stage for the Abbey is not a question of location', *Irish Times*, 24 October 2009, <www.irishtimes.com/newspaper/weekend/2009/1024/1224257356703.html>.

—, 'Time to Look beyond O'Casey's Successes', *Irish Times*, 1 November 1994, <www. irishtimes.com/newspaper/archive/1994/1101/Pg010.html#Ar01002>.

Bibliography

—, 'Wrestling for O'Casey's Legacy', *Irish Times*, 3 April 2008, <www.irishtimes.com/newspaper/features/2008/0403/1207113944832_pf.html>.

'Our London Correspondent', *Manchester Guardian*, 24 March 1926, p. 10.

Pearse, Patrick, 'Peace and the Gael', *The Spark*, December 1915, pp. 1–2.

—, 'The Coming Revolution', *An Claidheamh Soluis*, 8 November 1913, p. 6.

'Playwright and Critics', *Times Literary Supplement*, 15 February 1957, p. 99.

'Plight of the Younger Irish Writers: Lecture by Mr C. O'Leary', *Manchester Guardian*, 21 October 1924, p. 20.

'Ploughing the Star', *Manchester Guardian*, 4 June 1928, p. 8.

'Resignation of Abbey Director', *Irish Independent*, 4 September 1935, p. 9.

'Revolting Production', *Standard: An Irish Organ of Catholic Opinion*, 16 August 1935, pp. 1, 3.

Rich, Frank, 'Evoking the Youth of Sean O'Casey in Dublin', *New York Times*, 17 February 1992, p. C13.

'Scandal of Dublin Civic Conditions', *New York Times*, 15 March 1914, p. C4.

'Sean O'Casey', *Irish Times*, 21 September 1964, p. 7.

'Sean O'Casey and Yeats', *Irish Times*, 6 March 1962, p. 8.

'Sharing, Not Scaring is the Aim', *Irish Times*, 7 July 2000, <www.irishtimes.com/newspaper/features/2000/0705/00070500093.html>.

Shaw, George Bernard, 'Shaw Visits Russia', *Irish Worker*, 19 September 1931, pp. 1, 8.

Shepard, Richard F., 'Brooks Atkinson, 89, Dead; Times Drama Critic 31 Years', *New York Times*, 14 January 1984, p. 1.

'Shouters at Play Chided by O'Casey', *New York Times*, 7 October 1958, p. 40.

Simon, John, 'Pipsqueak's Progress, Playwright's Regress', *New York Magazine*, 9 March 1992, pp. 76–7.

'Slum Child Who Became World Famed Dramatist', *Irish Times*, 19 September 1964, p. 5.

Standard: An Irish Organ of Catholic Opinion, 16 August 1935, pp. 1, 8.

Ştefan, Adina, 'Bucureşti: Comedia "S-a sfârşit cum a început", la Teatrul Naţional', *Adevarul*, 29 May 2010 <www.adevarul.ro/locale/bucuresti/Bucuresti-_Comedia_-S-a_sfarsit_cum_a_inceput-la_Teatrul_National_0_270573079.html>.

'Stink Bombs in the Abbey', *Irish Times*, 4 May 1926, p. 7.

'Tenement Dust to Purple Dust', *Irish Times*, 14 December 1940, p. 5.

'The Best of the Irish', in *Newsweek*, 29 January 1940, reprinted in George Jean Nathan, *My Very Dear Sean: George Jean Nathan to Sean O'Casey: Letters and Articles*, ed. Robert G. Lowery and Patricia Angelin. Rutherford: Fairleigh Dickinson University Press, 1985, pp. 148–50.

'The Best Play', *Irish Times*, 31 July 1945, p. 3.

'"The Bishop's Bonfire" in Gaiety Theatre', *Irish Times*, 1 March 1955, p. 4.

'The Condemned Irishmen: Appeal for Reprieve', *Manchester Guardian*, 6 February 1940, p. 9.

'The Great Game', *Irish Times*, 28 June 1915, p. 5.

'The "Irish Church Missions": At Their Old Game', *The Nation*, 4 April 1885, p. 2.

The Nation, 11 April 1885, p. 8.

'The Parish and the World of O'Casey', *New York Times*, 5 February 1950, p. 178.

'The People of the Land', *Irish Times*, 23 November 1931, p. 5.

'The People of the Land', *Irish Times*, 31 March 1932, p. 4.

'The Plough and the Stars', *Irish Times*, 2 March 1926, p. 2.

'The Plough and the Stars', *Irish Times*, 10 May 1928, p. 8.

'The Plough and the Stars', *Irish Times*, 13 February 1926, p. 5.

'The Rejected Abbey Play: Mr St John Ervine on "The Silver Tassie"', *Irish Times*, 9 July 1928, p. 8.

'The Silver Tassie', *Irish Independent*, 14 September 1935, p. 10.

'The Silver Tassie', *Irish Press*, 14 August 1935, in NLI, Seán O'Casey Papers, MS 38,149/1.

'The Success of Sean O'Casey', *Irish Worker*, 26 September 1931, p. 2.

'Theatre: O'Casey Reading', *New York Times*, 19 March 1956, p. 27.

'This Dublin Play Sets World Record', *Dublin Evening Herald*, 29 July 1972, located in NLI, MS 34,905/2 Lantern Theatre Papers, fol.128.

'Tributes to Behan', *Irish Times*, 21 March 1964, p. 9.

'Trouble over O'Casey Play in Toronto', *Irish Times*, 7 October 1958, p. 8.

Troyan, Tatiana, 'Олег Дмитриев: «Человек в «обстоятельствах»', *Театрал*, 1 April 2008, <www.teatral-online.ru/news/1522/>.

'Turf-Cutting in County Sligo', *Irish Times*, 19 August 1915, p. 7.

Tynan, Kenneth, 'A Second Look at O'Casey and Osborne', *Observer*, 30 July 1961, p. 20.

Universe, 25 October 1929, clipping in NLI, Seán O'Casey Papers, MS 38,149/1.

'"Unseen" Play by O'Casey on Next Week', *Irish Times*, 2 June 1966, p. 6.

Weintraub, Stanley, 'GBS and the Despots', *Times Literary Supplement*, 27 July 2011, <www.the-tls.co.uk/tls/public/article707002.ece>.

'"Within the Gates" Ends Tour Tonight', *New York Times*, 19 January 1935, p. 8.

'"Within the Gates", Sean O'Casey's Provocative Play, Suggested for Capital', *Washington Post*, 27 June 1935, p. 16.

'Writers Join in Abbey Protest', *Irish Independent*, 10 November 1947, p. 2.

'Wrong Man Hanged', *The Sunday Times*, 6 July 1969, p. 1.

Unpublished and Archival Sources

Abbey Theatre Archives, *Shadow of a Gunman* programme, 1923, ATA IMPG, Vol. 19.

Abbey Theatre Archives, 'Plays Received' File, 10 April 1922–8 June 1932; 'Plays Received File', 5 January 1912–1 April 1922.

Fergusson and Mack, British Library, Lord Chamberlain's Collection, *Irish Aristocracy*, 53352.

Fletcher, Harry, NLI, Seán O'Casey Papers, MS 37,312, Harry Fletcher's letter of 24 February 1945.

Funge, Patrick, NLI, Lantern Theatre Papers, MS 40,206/22, unsigned letter from Patrick Funge to David Krause, 19 October 1965.

Greene, David, NLI, Eileen O'Casey Papers, MS 44,742/2, letter from Greene to Eileen O'Casey, 5 November 1975.

Liebrecht, Hans-Herman, NLI, Eileen O'Casey Papers, MS 44,709 /1, letters to Eileen from Hans-Herman Liebrecht.

Kelly, Francis J., NLI, Seán O'Casey Papers, MS 37,938, Francis J. Kelly letter of 16 May 1946.

Krause, David, NLI, Seán O'Casey Papers, MS 37,849/1 letter by David Krause of June 1954.

—, NLI, Lantern Theatre Papers, MS 40,206/22, letter by David Krause of 2 November 1965.

Jackson, Barry, NLI, Seán O'Casey Papers, MS 38,068, Jackson letter of 22 July 1926.

—, NLI, Seán O'Casey Papers, MS 38,068, Jackson undated letter.

Lowery, Robert, NLI, Eileen O'Casey Papers, MS 44,742/2, letters between Lowery and Eileen O'Casey.

—, NLI, MS 44,742/2, Eileen O'Casey Papers, Lowery's letter to Eileen, 9 May 1977.

Mac Anna, Tomás, NLI, Seán O'Casey Papers, MS 38,042, Mac Anna's letter to O'Casey on 28 January 1951.

O'Casey, Eileen, NLI, Eileen O'Casey Papers, MS 44,742/2, letters between Lowery and Eileen O'Casey.

—, NLI, Eileen O'Casey Papers, MS 44,742/3, Eileen's letter to Lowery, 16 February 1977.

—, NLI, Lantern Theatre Papers, MS 40,206/28, Eileen O'Casey letter to Patrick Funge of 5 July 1967.

O'Casey, Seán, Abbey Theatre Archives, *The Plough and the Stars* Promptbook, 1926/A/6.

—, NLI, Seán O'Casey Papers, MS 37,889/10, Sean O'Casey to Jane Rubin.

—, NLI, Seán O'Casey Papers, MS 38,042, O'Casey's 1951 letter to Mac Anna.

—, NLI, Seán O'Casey Papers, MS 38,045, copy of O'Casey's cable to the National Theatre, February 1935.

—, NLI, Seán O'Casey Papers, MS 38,047, letter to Patricia Turner.

—, NLI, Seán O'Casey Papers, MS 38,050, letter to Henning Risehbieter.

—, NLI, Seán O'Casey Papers, MS 38,079/2, letters from O'Casey to Shyre.

—, NLI, Seán O'Casey Papers, MS 38,149/2, scrapbook of wedding clippings.

—, NLI, *The Plough and the Stars* Typescript with MS Annotations, MS 29,407.

—, NYPL, Berg Collection, Seán O'Casey Papers, 'Articles: Ireland: 7 Typescripts: The Abbey Theatre'.

—, NYPL, Berg Collection, Seán O'Casey Papers, Holograph Notebooks, Vols 1–21.

—, NYPL, Berg Collection, Seán O'Casey Papers, *The Bishop's Bonfire* typescript, 70B5694.

—, NYPL, Berg Collection, Seán O'Casey Papers, + 70B6521, The National Broadcasting Company presents A Conversation with Sean O'Casey and Robert Emmett Ginna (1955).

—, Princeton University Library, 'The Cooing of Doves: A Converzatione in One Act'.

O'Donnell, Frank, British Library, *Anti-Christ: A Play in Seven Scenes*, MS, LC Add 66560A.

Ryan, Frank, NLI, Sean O'Casey Papers, MS 37,975, letter by Frank Ryan of 20 February 1926.

Sheehy Skeffington, Owen, NLI, Seán O'Casey Papers, MS 38,019, letter from Owen Sheehy Skeffington of 4 May 1942.

Shyre, NLI, Seán O'Casey Papers, MS 38,079/1, letters from Shyre to O'Casey.

—, NLI, Seán O'Casey Papers, MS 38,079/2, letters from Shyre to O'Casey.

—, NLI, Seán O'Casey Papers, MS 38,079/4, Shyre letters of 6 February 1956 and 13 August 1963.

—, NYPL for the Performing Arts, MWEZ + n.c. 26,166 #6, Paul Shyre I Knock at the Door Scrapbook.

—, NYPL for the Performing Arts, MWEZ + n.c. 25,398–25,400, Paul Shyre Scrapbook.

—, NYPL for the Performing Arts, MWEZ + n.c. 25,398, #8, Paul Shyre Scrapbook, programme for tribute show of 11 October 1964.

Sweeney, Cornelius J., NLI, Seán O'Casey Papers, MS 37,942, letter from Cornelius J. Sweeney of 4 April 1949.

Thompson, Mary Shine, Austin Clarke; A Literary Life-Chronology. Unpublished PhD thesis, University College Dublin, 1997, p. 292. Cited by Terence Brown, *The Life of W. B. Yeats: A Critical Biography*. Dublin: Gill and Macmillan, 1999, p. 287.

Yun, Hunam, Appropriations of Irish Drama by Modern Korean Nationalist Theatre: A Focus on the Influence of Sean O'Casey in a Colonial Context. Unpublished PhD thesis, University of Warwick, 2010.

Film, Television and Audio Sources

A Conversation with Sean O'Casey. Dir. Robert D. Graff. NBC. 22 January 1956.

Der Pott. Dir. Peter Zadek. Westdeutscher Rundfunk. 1971.

Die komplette Autobiographie in einer Kassette. Audio tape. Diogenes. 1973.

Juno and the Paycock. Dir. Paul Shyre. WNTA Newark. 1960.

Juno and the Paycock/The Shame of Mary Boyle. Dir. Alfred Hitchcock. British International Pictures. 1930.

Penzion pro svobodné pány. Dir. Jiří Krejčík. Barrandov Film Studios. 1967.

Pictures in the Hallway. LP. Riverside. 1957.

Sean O'Casey: Under a Coloured Cap. Dir. Shivaun O'Casey. RTÉ/BBC2. 4 January 2005/6 March 2005.

Sean O'Casey Reading From His Works. LP. Caedmon. 1953.

The Exile: Omnibus. Dir. Don Taylor. BBC1. 6 February 1968.

The Plough and the Stars. Dir. John Ford. RKO Radio Pictures. 1936.

Usporená libra. Dir. Ján Rohác/Vladimír Svitácek. Televizní Filmová Tvorba. 1963.

Young Cassidy. Dir. John Ford and Jack Cardiff. MGM. 1965.

Young Indiana Jones, Chapter 7: 'Love's Sweet Song'. Dir. Gilles MacKinnon and Carl Schultz. ABC. 11 March 1992.

INDEX

Index